DATE DUE

FEB 2 6 1999

D0961966

BRODART   Cat. No. 23-221

MITTERRAND

MITTERRAND

A Political Biography

WAYNE NORTHCUTT

Holmes & Meier
New York / London

Published in the United States of America 1992 by
Holmes & Meier Publishers, Inc.
30 Irving Place
New York, NY 10003

Book design by Adrienne Weiss

This book has been printed on acid-free paper.

Library of Congress Cataloging-in-Publication Data

Northcutt, Wayne.
   Mitterrand : a political biography / Wayne Northcutt.
      p.   cm.
   Includes bibliographical references and index.
   ISBN 0-8419-1295-5 (acid-free paper)
   1. Mitterrand, François, 1916– —Influence.   2. Presidents—
France—Biography.   3. Socialists—France—Biography.   4. Political
leadership—France—History—20th century.   5. France—Politics and
government—20th century.   I. Title.
DC423.N67   1992
944.083'8'092—dc20   91-29986
[B]   CIP

Manufactured in the United States of America

To my parents

Contents

Photographs appear following page 208.

Tables

Preface

History is filled with surprises. Contemporary French and European history is no exception. When François Mitterrand was elected in 1981 as the first Socialist president of the Fifth Republic, few in France or abroad knew what to expect. The previous president, Valéry Giscard d'Estaing (1974–81), had even warned that if Mitterrand and the Socialists came to power, "It will be Communist order or Socialist disorder."[1]

However, after the 1981 presidential elections and the subsequent legislative elections which produced a historic Socialist victory, Mitterrand and his Socialist party (*Parti Socialiste*—PS) were forced to shed much of their anticapitalist philosophy and rhetoric and launch a concerted effort to appeal to centrist voters in order to maintain public confidence. Although in 1981 the Socialist president represented *le peuple de gauche* (leftist voters), in time Mitterrand professed to represent "all of the French," suggesting, like Charles de Gaulle earlier, that he was the father of the nation. This transformation of Mitterrand's persona, image, and policies had far-reaching consequences. It aided, for instance, the electoral fortunes of the Socialist president by preparing the way for his reelection in 1988, an unprecedented event in the history of France. The changing image of French socialism, namely the transformation of Mitterrand's Socialist party into a social democratic party, also helped the PS to forestall disaster at the polls in the 1986 and 1988 legislative elections and maintain its position as the strongest political party in France. While the metamorphosis of Mitterrand and the Socialist party since 1981 weakened France's revolutionary political culture,[2] the changes also produced a republic that would be governed from the center.

Ironically, Mitterrand's presidency has helped to give new credibility to the institutions of the Gaullist Fifth Republic and to solve the long-standing problem of political legitimacy in France, which has plagued the nation since the Revolution of 1789. When General de Gaulle created the Fifth Republic in 1958, Mitterrand, a significant number of Socialists, and the Communists vehemently opposed the new republic. Mitterrand even called it the product of a coup d'état. However, with his election in 1981, Mitterrand made peace with the Fifth Republic and began to play the role of a "Prince-President," in Jacques Julliard's phrase,[3] providing the French with a new level of political legitimacy. On the one hand, he tried to project the image that he himself embodied the historic legitimacy of the nation. On the other hand, he often reminded French citizens that as president he symbolized popular sovereignty. Thus, the Mitterrand presidency has had a significant impact on de Gaulle's republic, but this same republic has also left its mark on the president.

During Mitterrand's second term, other historical surprises of enormous magnitude occurred: the collapse of the Berlin Wall, the overthrow of communist regimes in Eastern Europe, and the decline of Soviet power and influence. These fast-moving and sweeping changes, beginning late in 1989, forced Mitterrand to assume a major role in keeping the planned economic and monetary union of the European Economic Community on track, in seeking ways to anchor a reunited Germany securely to the Western camp, and in envisioning a new political future and security system for the Continent as the postwar era came to an abrupt end. While during much of Mitterrand's first term he focused on domestic economic and political concerns, the opening phase of his second mandate saw him take an overriding interest in the European evolution that the entire world is now watching. In many ways, Mitterrand II was "Mitterrand the European."

In spite of the length of his career and the historic significance of his presidency, Mitterrand is not fully understood in or outside of France. Abroad he is not only misunderstood, but often underrated, especially in the United States. There are only two biographies of his political life in English. One, Denis MacShane's *François Mitterrand: A Political Odyssey* (1982),[4] is a highly enthusiastic and uncritical account of Mitterrand's rise to the presidency. The other work is the translated version of a best-seller by the French political journalist Catherine Nay: *The Black and the Red: The Story of an Ambition* (1984).[5] Nay, however, is an unrestrained enemy of Mitterrand, viewing him as a man who believes that power is more important than identity, and is committed only to himself. There is a need for a political biography in English that goes beyond the polar biases of MacShane's and Nay's books. My interest in writing a political biography of the Socialist president actually began on boulevard St. Michel in Paris on May 21,

1981, as I observed Mitterrand and his entourage in a procession marching to the Pantheon, a famous memorial for France's greatest heroes, for an elaborate installation-day ceremony. In May of 1981 it was clear that Mitterrand's election victory marked a watershed in the political history of modern France that needed to be documented.

There is much to learn, too, from Mitterrand's more than four-decade-long political career. Following his stunning reelection victory over the Gaullist Jacques Chirac in the 1988 presidential elections, many in Europe called Mitterrand a political magician and the most accomplished political tactician in government. By studying his career, one can take the measure of Mitterrand the statesman as he confronted the numerous problems and opportunities that faced Europe during his presidency. This in turn sheds light on French perceptions of European and global issues, as well as on France's role on the international stage. It also illuminates the way in which another liberal democracy practices politics. By studying other nations, especially those with multiparty political systems such as France, we learn more about the strengths and the limitations of our own two-party system. Moreover, Mitterrand's life lends itself well to the pen of a biographer. He has had a fascinating life, filled with high drama, deep conflict, crushing setbacks, exhilarating victories, as well as ambiguities and contradictions. His life is a story worth telling if for no other reason than it represents an intriguing study in political perseverance.

This biography views Mitterrand as a political warrior who is driven by his determination to create a "vital center" in France. Convinced that General Charles de Gaulle's return to power in 1958 was nothing more than a coup d'état, Mitterrand became one of the most pragmatic politicians in modern French history as he attempted to weaken the hold of the Right on the political life of his nation, to restore what he viewed as democracy, and to enhance social justice. To fashion a strong Center in France he has used pragmatism and ideology, as well as his ability to play the role of a national unifier, what the French call a *rassembleur*. In his long march to the presidency in 1981, he was motivated more by his desire to chalk up political victories over his foes, namely the Gaullists on his right and the Communists on his left, than by a strong desire to bring socialism to France. Although some recent French accounts of his career have portrayed him simply as a politician and a complete tactician seeking to enhance his own personal power, his motives are much more complicated. He is a man who has been shaped largely by his religious upbringing, his experience as a member of the French Resistance, and his varied ministerial career under the postwar Fourth Republic. As a soldier of politics representing the Center-Left, he has inadvertently become a great political modernizer by facilitating the development of a more pluralistic and consensual nation. French exceptionalism vis-à-vis other Western industrialized nations has diminished considerably during the Mitterrand presidency. Internationally, Mitterrand has also played the role of a modernizer, especially with regard to recent European developments. For instance, he has been a driving force behind European integration and the creation of a single market by the end of 1992. His oppositional role to de Gaulle and his strong belief in Europe have helped to give France a new political identity.

Thomas Carlyle once said that "history is the biography of great men." This work is an attempt not so much to prove Carlyle's dictum as to quarrel somewhat with the practitioners of the *Annales* school of history in France who maintain that what counts is *la longue durée*, the vast sweep of history. Members of the *Annales* school argue that to a great extent individuals do not make history but submit to it. According to Fernand Braudel, one of the great practitioners of the *Annales* school, "The history of individual will is an illusion, a drop of water in the ocean."[6] While the works of Braudel and others of the *Annales* school are usually favorably received, their books often leave out not only the individual but politics as well. Without denying the great contribution of the *Annales* school to our understanding of history, Mitterrand's life clearly demonstrates that individuals can and do help to shape the contours of history and that politics is enormously important.

In writing this book I made a conscious decision to organize it chronologically rather than topically, because I wanted to avoid the reductionist tendencies that are sometimes inherent in the topical approach. The chronological organization allowed me to show the multiplicity of events and forces that a politician/statesman must confront at any given time. Furthermore, the chronological organization tends better to reflect the true nature of historical reality, for the unfolding of events is often not orderly and predictable, but unexpected and even chaotic.

Like most authors, I am indebted to many people for their assistance and encouragement. A special debt of thanks is owed to the Camargo Foundation in Cassis, France, which awarded me a fellowship in the fall of 1986 that facilitated the completion of an earlier draft of a portion of this manuscript in a beautiful and inspiring setting overlooking the Mediterranean. The director of the foundation, Michael Pretina, and his staff took great pains to ensure that all fellows had a stimulating environment in which to write. A number of my colleagues at the foundation offered valuable suggestions, especially Roger Little of Trinity College, Dublin, and Alec Stone of Middlebury College. A friend of the Camargo Foundation, René Viton, often listened to my ideas and provided numerous insights into postwar French politics.

Although it was not possible to interview Mitterrand himself, several French personalities close to the president granted me interviews for which I am most grateful. I am heavily indebted to Laurent Fabius, Mitterrand's second prime minister (1984–86), who agreed to a lengthy interview. Danièle Molho, a journalist in Paris, long-time acquaintance of Mitterrand, and recognized authority on the Socialist party, also accorded me a valuable interview. Jacques Julliard, a noted historian and political commentator in France, gave me the benefit of a lengthy conversation at the annual meeting of the Society for French Historical Studies at the University of Virginia. A much briefer conversation was held with Régis Debray, activist, writer, and adviser to Mitterrand, when he gave a series of lectures at the State University of New York at Buffalo. Mitterrand's first prime minister, Pierre Mauroy, was kind enough to send me important documentation.

A number of friends and acquaintances in France and in the United States must also be acknowledged for their assistance. A special French-American couple, Steve Ekovich and Francine Simon, often extended their hospitality to me when I visited France and provided the setting for lively discussions of French politics. Jean Lesieur, a Parisian journalist, took an interest in my work in the early stages and assisted me more than he realizes. Pierre Aubéry, formerly professor of French at the State University of New York at Buffalo and the former review editor for *Contemporary French Civilization*, has been a constant source of encouragement since our first meeting in the early 1980s. Thanks, too, are owed to Charles Morazé, one of the great historians of modern France, for his encouragement during the early years of my professional career. Since meeting Morazé in the late 1970s when I attended his seminar on social and economic history at the Ecole Pratique des Hautes Etudes in Paris, he has been an inspiration. Over the years, he has aided and inspired several generations of historians, French and American.

Fortunately, Mitterrand's election victories in 1981 and 1988 have sparked a tremendous level of scholarly interest in contemporary French politics. Consequently, I am indebted to the work of scholars, too numerous to mention, whose work has appeared in such journals as *Pouvoirs, Contemporary French Civilization, French Politics and Society, The Tocqueville Review, West European Politics,* and the *Proceedings of the Annual Meeting of the Western Society for French History.* It is often said that scholars build upon the contributions of others. This book is no exception. Over the years that this book was in preparation, I presented a number of papers and seminars on Mitterrand and his party and owe considerable thanks to numerous colleagues who commented on my work at such meetings as the Society for French Historical Studies, the Western Society for French History, the Middle Atlantic Historical Association of Catholic Colleges and Universities, the Southwestern Social Science Association, and the International Studies Association. These commentators include: Kim Munholland of the University of Minnesota, William Keylor of Boston University, Edward Berenson of the University of California, Los Angeles, and A. W. Deporte of New York University. I am also grateful to an anonymous reviewer whose suggestions strengthened this manuscript. An October 1987 conference on "A France of Pluralism and Consensus" organized by colleagues at Columbia University and New York University brought together French, American, and Canadian scholars and political observers that provided an extraordinary forum for ideas on Mitterrand's France. Like others in attendance, I am greatly indebted to the conference organizers: Robert Paxton, Mark Kesselman, Jean-Philippe Antoine, Martin Schain, and Nicholas Wahl. George Ross and James Hollifield organized a conference/workshop entitled "In Search of the New France" at Brandeis University for approximately one hundred scholars on May 13–15, 1988, which also provided numerous insights into contemporary French politics.

As is well known, the writing of books often requires financial as well as intellectual help. I must thank the Research Council at Niagara University for six consecutive summer research fellowships that facilitated frequent travel to France in order to complete the research for this political biography. The Academic Vice President at Niagara University, John Stranges, and the Department of History generously supported my conference travel over the years and this debt of gratitude, too, must be recognized. Other institutional debts must also be acknowledged, especially to the courteous staffs of the

Fondation Nationale des Sciences Politiques and the Centre National d'Art et de Culture Georges Pompidou in Paris.

I owe a large debt of thanks to Jeffra Flaitz, who also works on contemporary France, for her assistance, support, and encouragement. She served as a sounding board, editor, and critic. Her input enhanced the overall quality of this study from start to finish. Sheila Friedling, my editor at Holmes & Meier, also made many valuable suggestions that strengthened this manuscript. I am also indebted to Gavin Lewis for his skillful copyediting. Christopher Forth, a budding young scholar, assisted me with some details of the early research and helped proof the final typed copy of the manuscript.

In addition to these debts, I must acknowledge the following organizations for permission to reprint a number of the tables found in this volume: Editions Robert Laffont, *Libération*, *Le Point*, and the Economist Newspaper Limited. I am grateful for several photographs of Mitterrand supplied by the French Embassy Press and Information Service in Washington, D.C. I should also like to thank Julius W. Friend for his assistance in obtaining several of the rare photographs of Mitterrand.

With these numerous debts acknowledged, the reader should know that I take full responsibility for any errors of fact or interpretation.

INTRODUCTION

The Enigma, the Man, and History

Contrary to what people say, my strength is that I have a
simple mind. But all of the works on me present me as
someone who is very complicated. My complexity consists
of not losing my basic simplicity.
— François Mitterrand
(television documentary)

For over two years, in 1985 and 1986, a journalist and
a psychoanalyst filmed and conducted nineteen hours of interviews
with François Mitterrand in order to present the French public with a
portrait of their president. When their work aired on television on
January 21, 1987, many viewers were struck by Mitterrand's statement
that he possesses a "simple mind."[1] In reality, he is an enormously
complex man and political personality. He has been depicted in
France in a variety of ways: as a "mystery," a deeply contradictory
personality driven by ambition, a Machiavellian politician par excellence, a Gaullist of the Left, a character out of a nineteenth-century
novel, an imaginary monarch, a realistic liberal, a vacillating "baroque
Socialist" who is often out of touch with the times, a man of many
masks, or of many "religions," and most recently as a Faust-like figure
and a grand political manipulator without scruples when political
power is at stake.[2] For those on the far left he is often seen as a
bourgeois reformer; for those on the far right he is viewed as a crypto-

1

communist. According to Dorothy Pickles, an English authority on contemporary France, "no French political personality is more elusive."[3] To many of his admirers and critics in and outside France, Mitterrand is an enigma, a living sphinx. Curiously, the phonetic translation of his name in Chinese means: "a perfectly clear enigma."[4]

Part of the problem in understanding Mitterrand has been his many changes of political perspective over his long political career—he is the only active national politician in France today to have devoted his entire adult life to politics. When he launched his political career as a deputy from the Nièvre in central France in 1946, he joined a small center/center-right party, the Democratic and Socialist Union of the Resistance (*Union Démocratique et Socialiste de la Résistance*—UDSR). In time, the force of events, especially the reemergence of General Charles de Gaulle on the political stage, pushed Mitterrand slowly to the left. As a result of his first bid for the presidency in 1965, when he ran as the common candidate of the Left, Mitterrand discovered the political potential of a leftist union in France. Following the presidential election, Mitterrand began to commit himself to socialism, or to what might more accurately be termed socialism *à la française* since there have been numerous varieties of socialism in the contemporary world. In discussing his changing political views during his lifetime, Mitterrand wrote in *Ma part de vérité* (My part of the truth), "I was not born a leftist, much less a socialist."[5] Commenting on the Socialist party, an organization that he joined late in his career, he once stated, "Although the Socialist party grants a great importance to the theories of Marx, it is not a Marxist party."[6]

On his desk at the Elysée Palace at one time were three photos that suggested Mitterrand's desire to be viewed as a man of movement, a man identified with a long republican tradition in France. One photo was of Victor Hugo, symbolizing the romanticism of the Second Republic; another photo was of the early twentieth-century socialist Jean Jaurès, representing a humanistic socialism; and the third photo was of Georges Clemenceau, conveying a sense of the state.[7]

Mitterrand's pragmatism, as well as his extensive experience as a professional politician, has greatly aided his political survival and confused many observers attempting to analyze and comprehend him. Unlike a man of strict principle such as his old friend Pierre Mendès-France, who once told the French "to drink milk instead of wine," Mitterrand is a firm believer in the notion that politics is the art of the possible. This is one of the key factors that has made him a consummate politician. Mitterrand has succinctly summed up his commitment to political pragmatism in his book *Un Socialisme du possible* (Socialism of the possible): "The ideological debate is interesting, but does not lead to anything . . . ; the pragmatic debate can lead to everything. . . ."[8] In this regard, one is tempted to liken his way of thinking to that of a Mikhail Gorbachev in the Soviet Union or a Deng Xiaoping in China, men who have elevated pragmatism to an ideology. As with these men, his pragmatism has also earned him among some the unflattering reputation of an opportunist and what the French call a *Florentin*, a pejorative term for a Machiavellian. Moreover, his pragmatism has often been mistaken for inconsistency, a confusion that has only reinforced his enigmatic reputation.

Related to Mitterrand's pragmatism is his own peculiar brand of utopian socialism, which also contributes to the enigma surrounding him. Mitterrand's socialism, like that of Jaurès, comprises three key elements: pragmatism, social justice, and the rights of the individual. Mitterrand has often defined socialism as a "superior form of practicing freedom." When he was once chided for not appearing more ideological, he said, "What do you want me to be, a Lenin?"[9] In September 1982 he told a crowd in Figeac, "Socialism *à la française?* I do not make it my Bible."[10] Mitterrand's socialism, for the most part, is a variant of the social democracy that has been practiced in Western Europe for three-quarters of a century. However, one of the major differences between Mitterrand's social democracy, at least from the early 1970s to the mid-1980s, and that of his predecessors was his firm belief in nationalization as a key to social and economic transformation. While other contemporary social democrats have not stressed nationalization, Mitterrand gave it high priority during the 1970s and the early years of his presidency. This is one of the reasons that he has referred to his own socialism as "radical social democracy."

Mitterrand's numerous defeats over the course of his forty-five-year political career have also added to the enigma that surrounds him, because of his uncanny ability to survive them. In France he is sometimes referred to as "a man who is beaten, but never defeated," and as a politician who is often most imaginative and pugnacious when he has his back against the wall.[11] He also has an almost irrepressible will to triumph over his adversaries. This strong determination to duel with and to conquer his political foes was revealed, for example, after two scandals that almost ruined his political career in the 1950s. In 1955, he was falsely charged by members of the Right with divulging national defense secrets to the Communist party (*Parti Communiste Français*—PCF), and in 1959 he was the victim of new right-wing allegations, that he had arranged his own assassination in order to gain public sympathy and support.[12] Yet Mitterrand was able to survive these dangerous scandals and mount three presidential bids—in 1965, 1974, and 1981—before winning his first mandate. As president he was able to survive the infamous Greenpeace scandal in 1985 when his Socialist government was accused of sabotaging the vessel of an environmental group seeking to prevent French nuclear testing in the South Pacific.[13] During his career he has risen from the ashes of defeat and scandal like a phoenix, another aspect of his political life that has mystified many observers.

These political ups and downs as well as his fluctuations in popularity with the French electorate have contributed to the Mitterrand puzzle. For instance, in 1958 voters and supporters abandoned him to support a triumphant de Gaulle who returned to the political stage, forcing Mitterrand to remain in opposition for twenty-three years. After his stunning election victory in 1981, more than 71 percent of the electorate expressed confidence in their new president. Yet by the spring of 1984, following a turn to economic austerity and a maladroit attempt to reform private schools (most of them Catholic), Mitterrand's public confidence rating hovered around the 30 percent mark, the lowest rating of any president of the Fifth Republic.[14] Following Socialist losses in the March 1986 legislative elections, which forced him to share power with a right-wing cabinet, an arrangement known as "cohabitation," he was able to burnish his image and dramatically improve his political standing. By 1988, public confidence in Mitterrand had rebounded to such a degree that he handed his rival in the presidential elections, Gaullist Jacques Chirac, a crushing defeat. By the end of his first term, public-opinion polls revealed that he was the second most popular president of the Fifth Republic, trailing, of course, de Gaulle.[15] A friend and colleague of Mitterrand, Laurent Fabius, who served as Mitterrand's second prime minister (1984–86), has stated, "[There is an enigma] . . . because he has had a long political career with extraordinary high and low points. . . . Fundamentally, there is an enigma because he has been able to transform situations and make them more favorable to him. . . . For Mitterrand, where there's a will there's a way."[16]

The failure of many to understand the political, economic, social, and intellectual milieu from which Mitterrand emerged has also added to his enigmatic character. Within this context five key life experiences have greatly influenced Mitterrand the man and the politician: his bourgeois Catholic upbringing; his wartime experiences, especially his capture by the Nazis and his subsequent Resistance activities; his extensive ministerial experience under the Fourth Republic (1946–58) during which he served in eleven different governments; his relationship with French Communists and his anti-communism; and his relationship with and perception of de Gaulle and the Gaullists as well as the evolution of his own anti-Gaullism.

He is an eloquent humanist who could have been a journalist or a member of the French literati had he not decided to enter politics. He has written a dozen books—among them *Le Coup d'état permanent* (The permanent coup d'état), *Ma part de vérité*, *La Paille et le grain* (The wheat and the chaff), *Politique* (Politics), and *Ici et maintenant* (Here and now). These books, which are primarily political critiques, memoirs, or reflections, have kept his name before the public throughout his career. Mitterrand has used the power of the pen repeatedly to enhance his popularity as a politician; and as a writer he is keenly aware of the power of words and images, two crucial elements of survival for professional politicians.

Yet Mitterrand is more than an accomplished writer. He is also an intellectual in politics, one of the few true intellectuals occupying the presidency of any Western nation. He possesses the ability to deal with concepts and to present them in convincing ways. For example, his 1984 campaign to modernize France, which was also an effort by a president with record-low popularity ratings to rationalize high unemployment and economic mistakes during Year I of the Socialist experiment with power, revealed his ability to manipulate words and images to his own advantage.

Mitterrand is also a trained jurist who could well make an excellent constitutional lawyer. At various times during his career he has used his vast knowledge of the Constitution of the Fifth Republic to his own advantage. This was the case with his surprising proposed referendum of July 1984 on "public liberties" supposedly to enhance the decision-making powers of the electorate, his decision to retire controversial legislation on private schools in order to transcend a grave crisis over Socialist educational reform, and his novel attempt at cohabitation with the Right.

Mitterrand, the shrewd pragmatist and skilled politician, is also an idealist, another trait that complicates his political personality. During his lengthy career he has shown himself to be an intellectual humanist in the political arena who has the capacity sometimes for hard, cold realism, and at other times for lofty idealism. On occasion his idealism, sometimes bordering on naïveté, has threatened his career and his party; for example, his professed ignorance of economics, which he has called simply "a branch of the humanities,"[17] led Mitterrand to attempt to reflate the French economy in 1981 when other Western nations pursued austerity. Such economic idealism during Year I of his presidency created enormous problems for Mitterrand, his government, his party, and the nation.

When one of his long-time acquaintances, journalist Danièle Molho, was asked why Mitterrand was viewed as a mystery, an enigma in his own country, she stated, "He is complicated, not a mystery." According to Molho, also one of France's most noted authorities on Mitterrand and the Socialist party, he is complicated because his politics have been complicated. He is a man whose career has been characterized by considerable though gradual political movement, beginning his political career on the center/center-right and slowly moving to the left. Moreover, during his career his political popularity has risen to great heights and fallen to great depths. According to Molho, Mitterrand's style has additionally complicated his persona; he is a politician who sets plans in motion in an effort to anticipate the future, but he is also one who plays his cards close to his chest.[18] He does not usually announce his real intentions and confides only in a few close personal friends. The enigma that surrounds Mitterrand can be explained, but politically he is still enormously complicated.

Mitterrand the man is almost as interesting as Mitterrand the politician. The English scholar Dorothy Pickles described Mitterrand's personal qualities as follows.

> Among his personal qualities are persistence (if not obstinacy), patience and tactical skill; a sense of the continuity of French Republican history, and of French Socialist history, in which he sees himself as the heir of Jaurès and Léon Blum; a recurrent need for solitude and reflection in the French countryside and the companionship of books; a consuming interest in history and poetry, rather than in Marxism or economics. He is a writer, something of a stylist. All these characteristics do not really add up to a personality easy to classify. Nor do his attributes as a Socialist politician. He appears traditionalist rather than modern, indisputably of the left but not the

far left; uninterested in ideological subtleties. As a leader he attracts loyalty rather than hero-worship and his methods have been described as combining ruse, guile, prudence, and the flexibility of a trapezist with calculation, touchiness, modesty, reserve, distance, reflection and boldness, ambition and ambiguity . . . to which could be added, apparently, an incurable unpunctuality![19]

His personality and political life would also make excellent material for a psychohistorical study.

When one talks to his friends and acquaintances, they often say that he greatly values friendships and has many of them.[20] For instance, in the spring of 1984 Mitterrand took time away from his presidential duties to make weekly visits to the hospital to see Jean Chevrier, owner of the Hôtel du Vieux-Morvan in Château-Chinon where the president had served as mayor prior to 1981.[21] Furthermore, he has friendships that cut across generational lines, and many friends and close acquaintances who are journalists. While his sincerity need not be doubted, it is clear that Mitterrand is a man who sees the practical value of friendship.

Among his friends and acquaintances Mitterrand can appear immensely charming and sincere, while others who view him on television say that he seems aloof and distant. This contradictory aspect of his persona is a product of his rather shy and reserved nature. When Molho was asked to describe Mitterrand the man, she responded, "Mitterrand is distant, very reserved, very educated, and very courteous."[22] His reserved nature is one of the reasons why he dreads television appearances, even though he is a long-time politician who recognizes the value of projecting the proper image on the television screen. This aspect of his personality also helps to explain why he has given far fewer press conferences than his predecessors.[23] Furthermore, as many will attest, Mitterrand is a loyal friend, but one who demands loyalty in return. Partially because of this strong sense of loyalty and because he does not readily delegate power, he awarded a large number of friends and close associates influential positions in his government following the 1981 election, leading some of his critics to charge that he instituted a "Republic of friends," or a "Republic of fidels." Throughout his political career he has relied heavily upon the advice of his closest and oldest friends, such as the late Georges Dayan who served with him in the same infantry unit during World War II, François de Grossouvre or Georges Beauchamp. Nevertheless, because he is hesitant to confide even in intimate friends, let alone delegate authority to those who are not close to him, Mitterrand held a tight rein on his Socialist government between 1981 and 1986. As his press secretary Nathalie Duhamel revealed, Mitterrand's administrative style is such that "he reads everything [that appears on his desk] and decides alone."[24]

Mitterrand the man is marked by contradiction, especially between his upbringing and his contemporary political philosophy. He was raised in a provincial bourgeois Catholic family and was a practicing Catholic himself until the early 1960s. Today he professes to be an agnostic socialist.[25] The curious blend of religion and socialism in Mitterrand's background led the journalist Catherine Nay to portray Mitterrand the socialist as a product of his early Catholic upbringing.[26] Related to his contradictory nature is the fact that Mitterrand likes to appear modern and progressive but at the same time retains more traditional values. For instance, he has strongly advocated technological modernization for his country but simultaneously defended a humanistic *Weltanschauung*.

Throughout his political career, Mitterrand has demonstrated a strong will to power and a drive to overcome his adversaries. Former Prime Minister Fabius suggests that Mitterrand firmly believes that "the will of a man, a group of men, a party can change things."[27] A combination of sensitivity and a certain will to power, however, makes insults from adversaries difficult to forget. His desire to triumph over opponents, even symbolically, was clearly seen shortly after the 1981 presidential elections when Mitterrand decided to occupy de Gaulle's old office in the Elysée Palace, the official residence of the president of the republic, and to use the general's desk. Former President Valéry Giscard d'Estaing had refrained from occupying de Gaulle's quarters out of respect for the founder of the Fifth Republic and his intimidating legend. Mitterrand, however, had a statement to make and an old axe to grind. But when he was questioned on this decision, he simply stated, "I like to see the park [a view of the Elysée grounds can be seen from the office]"; then he added, "de Gaulle is not the only one in the history of France. This is the office of the head of state."[28]

Mitterrand is also patient and tenacious. Like any good fisherman from his native Charente, a fertile wine-producing region near Bordeaux, he knows that patience and time can be great allies. As Fabius observed, "[Mitterrand is a person who understands] the climate of opinion. Things are good at one time and bad at another;

things are not possible at one moment but possible at another."[29] He has a sense of time that is more traditional than that of many politicians today. One might even say that his sense of time is akin to that of people who live in small towns and villages where the rhythm of life is slower and more relaxed than that of the big city. Mitterrand is known for his lack of punctuality, having been late even for summit meetings with President Ronald Reagan at Tokyo in 1986 and at Venice in 1987.[30] Reportedly, Mitterrand never wears a watch.[31] Nevertheless, time has been a partner for Mitterrand; over the years he has slowly but surely weakened his opponents to his left and right. He is also fiercely tenacious, a character trait that has been well documented. When he was a prisoner of war, for instance, he made three escape attempts before finally succeeding. As a presidential candidate, he ran three times against de Gaulle and his heirs before winning his way to the Elysée.

In addition, Mitterrand has a deep attachment to the land, due principally to his upbringing in Charente. He prides himself even today on knowing the names of plants, trees, and insects; as he once wrote: "I am a child of my province and intend to remain that way. It shows in my writing as an accent might show in a person's speech. To give an example, I am proud to be able to call trees and stones and birds by their names. I would consider myself learned enough if I could identify all creatures and all things."[32] He takes great pleasure in escaping the burdens of the Elysée by retiring to his country home in Latche near Bordeaux where he likes to take strolls, often alone as his father used to do. (Interestingly enough, Mitterrand does not own a home or apartment in the Nièvre, his local political base for more than forty years.) His love of the land is also seen in his frequent references to it in his books and speeches. He has also intimated that he does not want to be buried in Paris, but in the countryside.[33] In essence, Mitterrand is a sophisticated man with strong provincial sensibilities. According to Jacques Julliard, a historian and well-known political commentator, Mitterrand is not only a man from the provinces, but is somewhat ill at ease in the Anglo-Saxon world.[34] His knowledge of English is rudimentary. His upbringing in Charente has significantly influenced the man who now occupies the Elysée. This, then, is a brief portrait of Mitterrand the man. The politician and his career, however, are our principal concerns.

In the political history of France, Mitterrand will have an important place because he has been a political modernizer, albeit an inadvertent one at times, who has transformed the French political landscape. As his second prime minister noted, before 1981 there were two major political forces in France, the Right and the Communists. Yet since French voters would very likely never vote the Communists into power, this meant that the political system was dominated by the Right. Mitterrand's skillful leadership of the Socialist party (*Parti Socialiste*—PS), founded in 1969, and his strategy of anchoring the Socialists on the left by means of an alliance with the Communist party, eventually broke the dominance of the Right, seriously weakened the Communists, and changed the political terrain of contemporary France.[35] Furthermore, under Mitterrand's tutelage, the Socialist party has been transformed. No longer do the Socialists represent a culture of opposition; today they are a culture of government. For many in France in the 1970s, it was unthinkable that Mitterrand's new party would come to power. Now, however, the Socialist party represents a viable alternative to the parties of the Right that dominated the Fifth Republic since its founding in 1958. In this regard, Mitterrand has played a major role in making the French Socialist party more closely resemble other social democratic parties in Western Europe.[36] The Socialist party that assumed power in 1981 was not the same party that went into the opposition after the March 1986 legislative elections returned a conservative majority, or after the 1988 legislative elections forced the party to enter into a minority government. By 1986, Mitterrand's party had lost its radical identity and rhetoric.

Mitterrand has also played a key role in detraumatizing what the French call *alternance*, alternating right-wing and left-wing governments, as well as cohabitation. Prior to 1981, many wondered if a left-wing government could come to power without civil or even military revolt. Mitterrand has helped to make alternating left-wing and right-wing governments more acceptable to the French, due, in part, to the bipartisan Gaullist-like foreign and defense policy adopted by the Socialists and their conversion to realism after a year of reckless spending in 1981. He has also introduced France to a new concept in its long political history, namely cohabitation. When de Gaulle founded the Fifth Republic in 1958, he envisioned that the president would always have a loyal majority in the National Assembly, as was the case from 1958 to 1986. However, the 1986 legislative elections gave France a National Assembly with a slim right-wing majority, despite the fact that Mitterrand still had two more years remaining to complete his seven-year presidential mandate. Ignoring the counsel of many of his advisers, Mitterrand decided to remain in office and to attempt to share power with a right-wing government.[37] Not only did this experiment with cohabitation show the elasticity of the Gaullist constitution of the Fifth Republic, as well as some of its defects, but Mitterrand was able to use the power-sharing arrangement to strengthen public confidence in his presidency and to solidify the position of the Socialist party. Furthermore, after the 1988 legislative elections, Mitterrand was compelled to lead a nation without a majority of either the Left or the Right in the National Assembly, a third experiment with *alternance*. As an opposition leader under the Fifth Republic and as president, he has contributed to breaking the monopoly of power once enjoyed by the French Right, and has contributed to the democratization of the political system.

Moreover, Mitterrand's Socialist government of 1981–86 represented a watershed in the political history of modern France. It was the longest period that the Left had ever been in power in France, and the only time since the Revolution of 1789 that the Left had occupied the executive and legislative branches of government. From the Liberation until 1981, the Left had held power a total of only six years. Mitterrand's first prime minister, Pierre Mauroy, totaled 1,153 days in office, marking the longest tenure of any Socialist prime minister. During Mauroy's term and that of his successor, the young Laurent Fabius, Mitterrand and his party learned how to govern a nation. Despite Mitterrand's strong record as a cabinet minister under the Fourth Republic, the period between 1981 and 1986 represented an apprenticeship in power and, eventually, in realism for the Socialist leader and his party.[38]

Mitterrand will find a prominent place in French political history because he has played a central role in developing a non-Communist Left—at the expense of the Communists—and has constructed a powerful Socialist party that now captures slightly less than 40 percent of the vote in legislative elections, giving it a hegemonic position on the Left. Although the Communist party was the major party of the Left under the Fourth Republic and during the early years of the Fifth Republic, claiming approximately a quarter of the electorate, Mitterrand has successfully marginalized the Communists and made the Socialists the first party of the French Left.[39] He has transformed the Socialist party into a mass-based "catch-all" party that appeals to a wide spectrum of voters, including centrists. In this regard, in 1981 he helped to introduce to France what he calls the "third path of socialism," differing from Russian communism or Scandinavian social democracy.[40] While his government attempted to extend the democratic liberties of its citizens in various areas, it also placed an emphasis on extending the public sector in France. However, after the Socialists encountered serious economic difficulties in 1982, Mitterrand began to stress technological competitiveness instead of nationalization as the way to ensure France's economic future.

The numerous reforms of the Socialist government will also ensure Mitterrand a significant place in French history. The Mitterrand government launched the most important period of social and economic reform in France since the Popular Front of 1936, a reform-minded coalition government of left-wing and center parties opposed to fascism. Among the notable reforms introduced during the first five years of his presidency are the following: a nationalization program that brought nine large industrial groups under state control; social reforms that aimed to aid those at the bottom of the socioeconomic scale; reforms in the area of health care; changes in the housing laws, especially the Quillot law which reformed the relationship between landlords and tenants, giving tenants extensive new rights; a decentralization program that defied French tradition by granting more decision-making authority to the provinces; numerous reforms dealing with justice and liberty; electoral reform involving a system of proportional representation that would have far-reaching consequences; reforms and initiatives in cultural areas; and the liberalization of the state-dominated field of communications.

While future historians will most assuredly view Mitterrand as a man who brought political change to France, and to a lesser degree economic and social change, a number of highly controversial issues will also draw the interest of scholars and ensure a lively debate among those writing on Mitterrand and his place in history. Such issues as the changing economic policies of the Socialist government, the battle over private-school reform, the long period of political polemics between the Left and the Right during 1982–86, the controversial Socialist press law aimed at curtailing press monopolies, the infamous Greenpeace affair, the Carrefour affair (a complicated embezzlement scheme), the Luchaire affair involving the sale of ammunition to Iran, the Péchiney affair revolving around an insider trading scandal, as well as Mitterrand's Gaullist foreign and defense policies will ensure controversy among future scholars.[41]

Mitterrand will also generate debate over the way in which he exercised political power. In 1981 many wondered what kind of leader he would make after being in opposition during the first twenty-three years of the Fifth Republic. Would he be a wheeler-dealer as he had been under the Fourth Republic? Would he be a man of high principle as suggested by his 1981 presidential campaign? Would he be a leader who would relinquish more power to the National Assembly, or would he maintain the presidential system that de Gaulle had inaugurated in 1958 and that he had criticized? Would he initiate Socialist foreign policy, or would he maintain a Gaullist foreign policy founded on a strong independent nuclear strike force? These were some of the questions that many pondered as Mitterrand assumed power.

Pierre Mendès-France, one of Mitterrand's early political tutors, once said that "to govern is to choose."[42] Mitterrand has sometimes been a vacillating leader, chiefly in the area where he is weakest, namely economic policy. Yet he also has on occasion made decisive strategic decisions, as in the Euromissile controversy (over the emplacement of U.S. medium-range missiles in Europe), the launching of an industrial modernization program, and the abandonment of his government's controversial efforts to exercise more control over private schools. He has also played a strong role in the direction of government and in the affairs of the Socialist party, and has at the same time played the role of a national arbitrator.[43] With the beginning of cohabitation in March 1986, he emphasized his role as arbitrator with considerable success. Regarding this newfound role as a national umpire, Mitterrand once said, "Others have written that the Left represents freedom, or equality, or progress, or happiness. I will say that it represents justice."[44] "Justice" is a theme that he has stressed throughout his presidency. As president, Mitterrand has also shown a penchant for grand political maneuvers, in keeping with his earlier political style. Despite the vacillation, the arbitration role, and the occasional political coups, he has not significantly relinquished his presidential authority. In fact, shortly after his 1981 election he said of the presidential system of the Fifth Republic, "The institutions were not created for me, but they suit me extremely well."[45]

With regard to France and the larger world, the Mitterrand presidency has seen both change and continuity. Mitterrand has, as journalist Serge July noted, through both his mistakes and his conscious choices opened France to the modern industrial and technological forces of the Western world.[46] In this regard, Mitterrand has been a good European, seeing a revitalized Europe as a way to restore

French greatness. He has been a major force in the movement toward the economic, monetary, and political integration of Europe and has played a key role regarding the German question and European security following the tumultuous changes in Eastern Europe beginning in 1989. He believes that an integrated Europe will aid France and the Common Market's competitiveness vis-à-vis the United States and Japan, and that Europeans should gain more control over their own security matters. However, his foreign policy has been decidedly Gaullist and for the most part has not broken significantly with tradition. Like de Gaulle, he has supported a strong nuclear strike force for France, rejected military integration into NATO, pursued something other than an exclusively pro-Israeli policy in the Middle East, resisted U.S. hegemony in global affairs, practiced a combination of containment of and cooperation with the Soviet Union, sought cooperation with West Germany but insisted on French military superiority, and maintained an active French presence in the Third World.[47] This continuity in external policy has allowed Mitterrand and his Socialist confreres to maintain national consensus in one area while attempting to bring about change at home, especially during 1981 and 1982 when the Socialist government enacted a large number of reforms.[48]

In studying the political career of Mitterrand, especially his presidency, one is struck by the irony that surrounds him. Regarding his role at home, although Mitterrand was elected in 1981 as a candidate of the Left, his presidency has transformed France into a centrist republic in which consensus politics is the norm. Moreover, while he will be remembered to some degree as a reformer, the lengthy series of social and economic reforms introduced by the Socialists were financed by a misguided neo-Keynesian reflationary economic policy that caused serious problems for Mitterrand after Year I. Another ironic aspect is that Mitterrand, a long-time enemy of de Gaulle, finally accepted the institutions of the Fifth Republic founded by the general. In 1958 Mitterrand vehemently opposed the abandonment of the Fourth Republic and later charged that de Gaulle's "new republic" was in reality a coup d'état. It is also ironic that Mitterrand managed cohabitation with more finesse and more success than he managed the 1981–86 period when the Socialists controlled the government and also dominated the National Assembly. One of the great ironies of his presidency is that in his second term he appointed his archrival in the

Socialist party, Michel Rocard, prime minister, a man who was more popular with the public than with the Socialists and who became the leading candidate to succeed Mitterrand. With regard to external policy, there are also ironies. For example, after the 1981 elections the Socialist president adopted a Gaullist foreign policy, especially with regard to the French nuclear strike force and his determined efforts to strengthen it, a close relationship with West Germany, and a concern about a Pax Americana.

The French make a careful distinction between a *politicien* (politician) and an *homme politique* (a man of politics), the former term usually being pejorative and the latter relatively positive. In this study, however, Mitterrand is viewed as a politician, but without the negative connotation that the term carries in France. Throughout his political career and his presidency, he has demonstrated his political dexterity, pragmatism, and survival instincts. He once stated, "In my life I have never accepted having no margin of maneuver. If I am cornered, I am going to get out of the corner."[49] In this regard, he has often used ambivalence as a tool to aid his ability to maneuver, developing in the process a formidable reputation for elusiveness. One of his recent critics charged that "he never does what he says. He never says what he does."[50] If politics is the art of the possible as well as the art of survival, normally the case in liberal democracies like France, then Mitterrand must be regarded as one of the greatest politicians of modern French history.

The Mitterrand presidency, however, has proven without a doubt that he is a poor economist. He himself has admitted to making a number of economic errors during the early years of his presidency. His firm belief that France could surmount the economic crisis of Western capitalism, namely the recession of the late 1970s and early 1980s, by simply reflating the French economy—even though other Western nations were pursuing an austerity policy—and his refusal to devalue the franc in the early days of his presidency revealed his poor understanding of the world's monetary system. Fortunately for France the economic realists in his earlier Socialist government, such as Minister of Finance Jacques Delors and Minister of Planning and Agriculture Michel Rocard, eventually prevailed.[51] Besides having realists within the Socialist party to steer him in the right direction when he made mistakes, especially with economic policy, he has been extremely lucky. For example, a steep fall in the value of the dollar as well as oil prices in the mid-1980s helped Mitterrand escape what could have been financial disaster.

History will also record that there have been four distinct periods, to date, of the Mitterrand presidency: reform (1981–82), austerity (1982–86), cohabitation (1986–88), and Rocardism and the European challenge (1988–). In each of these periods Mitterrand adjusted his political rhetoric to fit the situation at hand. His ability to change his rhetoric at the appropriate time—one of the consistent characteristics of his political career—coupled with significant policy shifts, has given a different face to each period of his presidency. For instance, Mitterrand I, the reform-minded and leftist-oriented president elected in 1981, was far different from Mitterrand II, the re-elected president of 1988 who had shed much of his leftist image, appeared as the father of the nation, and was willing and eager to govern France with a coalition government of Socialists and centrists. While the first term of his presidency saw him launch a vast reform effort inspired by a common program of the Socialists and Communists and devote enormous energy to the nation's economic crisis, the beginning of his second term saw him attempt to govern a more prosperous France and leave much of his nation's domestic policy to his right-wing Socialist prime minister, Michel Rocard. The outset of Mitterrand's second seven-year term as president saw him concentrate primarily on the integration of the European Economic Community, as well as on means to ensure French security in the aftermath of sweeping changes in Eastern Europe and the Soviet Union, and the possibility of a reunified Germany. While Mitterrand has been a highly pragmatic president, his actions have been guided by more than just political expediency. His ideal has been a France free of the domination of the far Right and the far Left, playing a leading role in a united Europe. Obviously, his pragmatism has helped him not only to survive politically, both as president and throughout his long political career, but also to realize his ideal. Mitterrand's pragmatism has helped him weaken the grip of the Right, notably the Gaullists, on the French republic and to marginalize the once-powerful Communists. The new centrist republic is more a product of Mitterrand's grand political design than most realize. His pragmatism, too, has helped him to extend social justice, although with some limitations. Pragmatism has been the key tool that has allowed him to change drastically the political landscape of France. In order better to understand Mitterrand's motivations, however, we must turn to his early years in

Jarnac, his university days in Paris, his wartime experiences, his ministerial role under the Fourth Republic, and his oppositional role under the first twenty-three years of the Fifth Republic. For he is not only a political leader who is the product of his times, but also one of those rare individuals who has shaped his era.

1

THE EARLY YEARS

Jarnac, Paris, and World War II

I lived my childhood in another century and had to make
an effort to jump into ours.

—François Mitterrand

François Maurice Adrien Marie Mitterrand was born
on October 26, 1916, in Jarnac in southwestern France, 271 miles
southwest of Paris, 67 miles east of Bordeaux, and 9 miles away from
Cognac. Jarnac, a small town in Charente of approximately 5,000
inhabitants, has, like its native son, an interesting history. It is located
on the banks of the Charente River in the heart of the Cognac vine-
yards; one of the prominent features of this small town is the presence
of a large Courvoisier distillery. Originally named Agernacus in Celtic
times, the town played a key role in the prosperity of Saintonge, one
of the ancient provinces of western France. During the Roman occupation it was a significant pottery center. In the Middle Ages the
town was a fortress; it was alternately captured and sacked by the
Arabs and the Vikings, and then subsequently during the Hundred
Years' War by the English and the French. Before the birth of François
Mitterrand, however, Jarnac was known to the outside world for two
events that occurred in the sixteenth century.

One event that marked the history of Jarnac involved a duel on July 10, 1547, before the court of Henry II at the Château de St. Germain. Here, Guy Chabot de St. Gelais, the seventh Baron of Jarnac, dueled with the Lord of Chataigneraie and defeated him by using an unorthodox but legal thrust of his sword. The Baron of Jarnac delivered a crippling blow behind the knee of his opponent; later, the Lord of Chataigneraie died of this injury. This famous thrust of the sword gave rise to the French expression *le coup de Jarnac* which is still used today in France. During Mitterrand's long political career, he too would thrust a number of *coups de Jarnac*—unorthodox but legal—against his opponents on the right and on the left in order to win key political duels.

The other event that has left its mark on Mitterrand's birthplace occurred in 1569 during the wars of religion. In this year, Catholic forces defeated a Protestant army led by Prince de Condé. The Catholicism that triumphed and eventually flourished in Jarnac would greatly influence the early life of the young Mitterrand. Besides these two events, the small town of Jarnac hosted several kings, including Francis I and Henry IV, and saw Voltaire spend some time there. Today, however, Jarnac is known as the birthplace of President Mitterrand.

The future president of France was born in the family residence located at 22 rue Abel-Guy near the center of town and close to the Charente River. He was the fifth of eight children of Yvonne and Joseph Mitterrand. (In the distant past, the word *mitterrand* meant a measurer of grains.) Even though his mother had a heart problem and was warned by a physician not to have a large family, the Mitterrands added a significant number to the population of Jarnac. Besides four sisters, Marie-Antoinette, Marie-Josèphe, Colette, and Geneviève, the president has three brothers. Robert, his eldest brother, graduated from the prestigious Ecole Polytechnique and has often traveled on behalf of President Mitterrand to transmit messages to foreign heads of state. Jacques, who graduated from the military training school at St. Cyr, became director of the aerospace company Aerospatiale after his brother was elected president. His youngest brother, Philippe, became a farmer and also mayor of St.-Séverin in Charente.[1]

Both parents had a great influence on the life of the future president. His mother, like his father, was a devout Catholic. She usually rose at six o'clock in the morning, went to Mass and, after breakfast, went out to aid the poor in the community. Yvonne Mitterrand was also an avid reader. Besides newspapers, she read the classics and the works of romantic writers. Late in the evening she often read, under the light of an oil lamp, the works of Balzac, Chateaubriand, Lamartine, and especially Barrès.[2] Yvonne Mitterrand died in 1936 of a heart attack at the age of forty-nine.

Joseph Mitterrand shared his wife's deep commitment to Catholicism and her love of the printed word. Perhaps even more than his mother, his father had the greatest influence on the young Mitterrand. He once said of his father, "He was one of the most intelligent people that I have ever met. He had a great mind."[3] His father was a pillar of the Society of Vincent de Paul,[4] a lay Catholic organization dedicated to helping the poor and the downtrodden that would significantly influence the thought and the actions of his fifth child. Joseph Mitterrand was also president of an association of private schools, or *écoles libres*, in Charente.[5] (Throughout France, such schools are primarily Catholic, and as president, Mitterrand would attempt to bring them under state control.) Joseph Mitterrand, like his wife, also liked to read and was proud of his small library.

By profession, Joseph Mitterrand was a railroad man. After graduating from high school he began working for the railroad. He worked his way up from baggage carrier on the *quai* to ticket collector, then to stationmaster in Angoulême, seventeen miles from Jarnac and the principal town in Charente. Since Angoulême was relatively close to Jarnac, he returned home on weekends and during vacations. Three years after the birth of his fifth son, Joseph Mitterrand retired from the railroad after inheriting a vinegar-making business from his wife's father; he later became president of the Union of Vinegar Makers of France.

Even today, when Mitterrand remembers his father, he says that he "was reserved, very reserved."[6] When Joseph Mitterrand did return to Jarnac to be with his family, he liked to take long and solitary walks, a pastime that his son would later adopt.

While the young Mitterrand was respectful and obedient toward his father, the future leader of France would, according to one French authority on Mitterrand, live out his revolt against paternal authority in his later relationship with General Charles de Gaulle.[7] When de Gaulle, something of a symbolic father figure for many in France during and after World War II, rejected Mitterrand the emerging political leader of the Left may have attempted to solve a long-suppressed Oedipus complex by mounting a persistent campaign against de Gaulle and his supporters. If so, by the end of his first term, Mitterrand had successfully overcome this complex and had even become at ease as a father figure himself. While it is extremely difficult to prove that Mitterrand's life has been shaped by an Oedipus complex, it is tempting to use Freudian insights to speculate about Mitterrand's private and public life.

Another influential figure in his early life was his maternal grandfather, Jules Lorrain, who would often read to and take long walks with his grandson. Later, Mitterrand would say that his grandfather—whom he often referred to as "papa"—was "my dearest and oldest friend." His grandfather was a generous and popular man who loved human contact, liked to travel, and had a good business mind. Besides opening a vinegar factory in Jarnac, he launched the National Federation of Vinegar Manufacturers and retained the title of honorary president until his death. Papa Jules also served on the city council of Jarnac. Although the Mitterrand family considered him a tolerant republican, he did advocate revenge against Germany and had a front-row seat at the funeral of Napoleon III.[8]

Robert Lorrain, son of Jules Lorrain, was another relative who played an important role in the formation of Mitterrand's persona. Robert was a deeply religious young man who was one of the founders of a Catholic social movement, the *Sillon*. Robert had met the regional writer François Mauriac at an early age and became one of his close friends. (Later, Mauriac would become one of Mitterrand's favorite writers.) Robert died of tuberculosis at the age of twenty, a tragedy that had the effect of strengthening the family's belief in the idea of social Catholicism.[9]

At the age of nine, Mitterrand's parents sent him to nearby Angoulême to attend the Catholic College of St. Paul, where he received rigorous instruction along with the other children from bourgeois families who attended this school. At the College of St. Paul students were required to attend a retreat each semester in a religious community in the Dordogne region under the direction of a Jesuit priest. His family and his education provided him with a solid religious training and a strong social conscience. As Mitterrand himself once wrote, "The Bible nourished my childhood."[10]

Like his parents and his uncle Robert, the young Mitterrand came to believe in an activist type of Catholicism. Regarding his own religious upbringing, he once proudly wrote, "I have been raised in a Catholic milieu, very devout and very open."[11] Following in the footsteps of his father, François Mitterrand also became active in the Society of Vincent de Paul. During his university years in Paris in the 1930s while he attended the Sorbonne and the Sciences Po, for instance, he participated regularly in the Society's activities and praised its work in an article for a student publication, the *Revue Montalembert*.[12] As a young student in Paris he spent numerous Saturday afternoons with poor and deprived families, sometimes even taking them a pair of worn shoes or a coal ticket. He even became president of his group of volunteers, much like his father who was president of the lay Vincent de Paul association in the department of Charente.[13] He would remain a practicing Catholic until the early 1960s. Even today, he still quotes from the Bible. In many ways, Mitterrand's socialism would have a strong basis in religion.

In addition to instilling a deep devotion to the Catholic faith through their example and charitable works, Mitterrand's parents also inculcated in him a love for books. As a child, Mitterrand was an avid reader. He often missed school, complaining that he was ill, in order to find time to satisfy his appetite for reading. During his early years, he liked to read Vigny, Pascal, Brunetière, and the Symbolists. At the College of St. Paul, he often preferred to spend his leisure time reading rather than playing soccer with his classmates. Often when he returned home to Jarnac, he would go to his room, known as the "bird room" because it was wallpapered with red and green paper that depicted birds, and read.[14] Today, of course, Mitterrand still possesses a great love for books and has written a number himself.

Mitterrand was not just a bookish boy, but was also quiet and rather timid. At school he trembled at the thought of taking oral exams and had difficulty passing the oral exam for his high school diploma. One of the dominant characteristics, however, of young Mitterrand was his strong will. His sister Geneviève, to whom he was the closest, describes him as "stubborn."[15] In the topsy-turvy world of French politics, his extreme obstinacy turned out to be a great advantage. Nevertheless, some of the low points in his political career were due, in part, to his obstinacy, especially his determination to duel with de Gaulle and his heirs.

Another aspect of Mitterrand's character that is a product of his childhood in Charente is his deep love for nature. The proximity of Jarnac to the countryside and his long walks with his father and his grandfather aided him in learning the names of most birds, insects, trees, and plants, names that he still remembers today.[16] Before and after the 1981 election, his writings and speeches have often been laced with references to nature. But after all, Mitterrand is from an area of France where there is a deep attachment to the land.

Mitterrand's early political education, like his religious upbringing, came from his family. Although Joseph Mitterrand was a devout Catholic, he was not a conservative, but a moderate republican or even an early Christian Democrat. Grandfather Jules had in his youth voted for the Radicals and supported the *Cartel des Gauches* in 1924; later in life, however, he became an intransigent monarchist. As a consequence, the bourgeoisie of Jarnac viewed him with distrust.[17]

Like so many French families, the Mitterrands introduced their children to the world of politics at the dinner table. Around a table that often seated at least twelve people, Mitterrand heard his father, uncle, and others discuss the political events of the day. According to one account, Joseph Mitterrand often spoke out at the dinner table against the "two-hundred families" that ruled France, according to the populist mythology of the day.[18] While political discussions occurred over dinner, Joseph Mitterrand had two rules that he insisted on at the table: "do not speak poorly of others," and "do not discuss money."[19] Perhaps owing partly to his father's influence, young Mitterrand developed a strong distaste for money and for the world of commerce. Commenting on his childhood, Mitterrand stated in a 1972 interview: "My father took a harsh view of bosses, capital, and money. I was deeply affected by his opinions. As a result, I have never felt I belonged to that milieu. I have always had a mistrust of it, though no doubt certain elements of my own character had something to do with that. . . . Despite my bourgeois existence, I have never had any link of any kind with the world of business."[20]

At home and away from home the political socialization of the young Mitterrand developed over meals. In the summers the Mitterrand family usually went to their vacation residence at Touvent for a few weeks. At the table there were often two priests, one from Pillac who was a royalist, and another from La Prade who was a republican. The young Mitterrand fancied the more progressive priest from La Prade.[21] Perhaps the first hint that the young Mitterrand was interested in politics and power came early in his youth when he told a family member, "I want to be king, or pope."[22] Although for Mitterrand it would take World War II to generate a genuine interest in politics, his family instilled in him a powerful social conscience that prepared their son for his future career as a socialist leader.

Another interesting facet of Mitterrand's early life is that his parents sent their children to England during vacation periods. Ostensibly the Mitterrands were interested in trying to transcend the dominant nationalism of the post–World War I years and wanted their children to travel abroad. Although François Mitterrand went to England on several occasions during his youth, he never developed an affinity for the Anglo-Saxon world. Even today, while Mitterrand claims that he understands English, he does not speak it.[23] The Mitterrands also received a number of strangers passing through Jarnac, especially wine agents conducting business in the area.[24] For a provincial bourgeois Catholic family, the Mitterrands were somewhat unusual in their openness and friendliness toward strangers.

Before traveling to Paris to attend the university, the young Mitterrand was much more interested in literature than in politics. This dimension of Mitterrand's personality has been verified by Claude Roy, one of Mitterrand's childhood acquaintances who often rode the train with him to and from nearby Angoulême. Ironically it was Roy the future novelist who observed, "I was a royalist at this time. I was interested in political problems. He [Mitterrand] preferred to discuss literature."[25] One of Mitterrand's early teachers also noted that he had some ability for writing, but needed to work harder in Latin and was quite mediocre in math and in physical education.[26] Where Mitterrand excelled as a student was in history, geography, French, Latin prosody, and religious instruction.

Thus, as a child Mitterrand was raised in a solid bourgeois Catholic family that was relatively open and progressive for the day, especially in a small provincial town like Jarnac. From his parents he learned about the plight of the poor and about the value of the printed word. At an early age, a shy and timid young Mitterrand developed a strong penchant for reading and later for writing. While he was not an exceptional student in his early years, he was fortunate to attend the College of St. Paul, for as he later said, the students were left free "to find their own truth."[27] In 1934, this bookish young bourgeois *Charentais* student, who was more interested in literature than politics, went to Paris to begin his studies at the university. The experience in Paris and the outbreak of World War II transformed this withdrawn young provincial into a political organizer and leader.

The mid-1930s was a turbulent time in Paris, the period when Mitterrand began his real political education. The worldwide depression and the rise of fascism in Italy, Germany, and Spain led to numerous clashes between the Right and the Left. The very year that Mitterrand arrived in Paris, serious royalist and fascist riots rocked the capital. The rising level of political demonstrations, the emergence of Léon Blum's Popular Front government of 1936, and Hitler's acts of aggression slowly began to transform Mitterrand into a more passionate and politically involved intellectual.

Mitterrand arrived in Paris at the age of seventeen and took up residence in a *foyer* (student center) at 104 rue Vaugirard, which was run by Marist priests and offered housing particularly to students from the provinces. One reason he stayed at this Catholic center was that his uncle Robert, whose social Catholicism had an important influence on the young Mitterrand and his family, had resided there earlier.[28] Here Mitterrand met and became friends with François Dalle, the future head of the L'Oréal cosmetic firm, and André Bettencourt and François Fontanet, both future ministers under de Gaulle. In the capital, Mitterrand simultaneously enrolled as a law student at the Sorbonne and as a political science student at the *Sciences Po;* four years later he would be awarded degrees in both disciplines.

When this seventeen-year-old arrived in Paris, his first love was literature and, to some degree, music, notably jazz. Writing in *Ma part de verité*, he said of this period, "The friends that I made there . . . were more in love with music and literature than politics. Thanks to them I was introduced to [the composers] Erik Satie, Honegger and Stravinsky before [the politicians] Doumergue and Daladier."[29] According to Mitterrand, he had little real exposure to politics in Jarnac or Angoulême, especially to the thought of Marx and Engels: "At the university, I was intimidated by my socialist comrades. My high school in Angoulême had not instructed me in Marxist disciplines. Marx and Engels were, I suppose, taboo . . .: I received my diploma without hearing their names pronounced. In high school I took pleasure in Latin prosody. Virgil was my happiness."[30] The young Mitterrand demonstrated his love for literature during this period by writing several articles for ephemeral student publications.

Like perhaps many students in Paris, Mitterrand attended several meetings of antifascist intellectuals where he heard the likes of André Malraux, André Chamson, and Julien Benda. Two of his intellectual heroes during these years were André Gide and Benda. In 1936, Gide, who had been infatuated with the Soviet Union in the 1920s, published a book titled *Retour de l'URSS* (Return from the

USSR) that criticized Stalinist Russia and the personality cult that surrounded its leader. Benda, on the other hand, had published a book in the late twenties, *La Trahison des clercs* (The Betrayal of the Intellectuals), that drew considerable attention because it criticized the politicization of intellectuals and their drift toward communism or fascism. For Benda, the first responsibility of an intellectual was to defend "reason."

Besides becoming acquainted with the ideas of Gide and Benda, Mitterrand also attended political rallies where he heard a variety of speakers, such as the Socialist Léon Blum, the Communist Maurice Thorez, a former Communist deputy, Jacques Doriot, who had gravitated toward fascism, and the archconservative Colonel La Roque.[31] Although he was not consumed by politics during his university years in Paris, with the rise of fascism and the growing polarization in politics in France and in Europe in general, he slowly began to take an interest in political developments. This slow but sure initiation into politics was tested when right-wing students protested against one of his professors, Gaston Jèze, who served as an adviser to the Ethiopian government when this small African country was invaded in the mid-1930s by Mussolini's forces. Mitterrand stood solidly behind Jèze and defended individual liberty. During this time, Mitterrand met and developed a long-standing friendship with Georges Beauchamp, who was then the secretary of a Socialist student group.

On the eve of World War II, Mitterrand, who described his general orientation as "antimilitarist," sensed that the world was on the brink of a catastrophe. He later wrote that he felt horrified by Franco and his gang of fascists in Spain.[32] When Hitler annexed Austria in 1938, Mitterrand published his first political tract. The *Revue Montalembert*, published by the students living in the Marist house in Paris, included an article by Mitterrand, titled "Up to Here and No Further," that criticized French and British weakness and timidity before an aggressive military machine. Mitterrand wrote: "Forgetting the axiom that the righteous must be stronger than the strong if they want to be involved in world affairs, the victorious countries from the Great War rested on their laurels and went to sleep in the cardboard castles of the postwar treaties. . . . What is chastity once violated? What is strength of will if it bends? What is liberty if given away?"[33] The outbreak of World War II provided the young Mitterrand with an interest in something other than literature and jazz. For the remainder of his life he would devote himself to politics.

While his political education began ever so slowly in Paris during his university years, Mitterrand's political consciousness greatly expanded during the war. World War II was a turning point in his life, a major life experience that left a permanent mark on him. Had it not been for the war, Mitterrand might well have become a literary figure, a journalist, or a practicing lawyer, but not likely a professional politician.

The war years quickly revealed Mitterrand's strong will, his obstinate character, and his organizing and leadership skills. When the war broke out he was already a sergeant in the infantry, having refused an earlier opportunity to go through officer training. At this time he was sent to the Verdun region in northeastern France where he was in charge of the munitions depot at Stenay. In early May 1940, Mitterrand was wounded by mortar fire near Verdun, captured, and imprisoned first in Stalag 9A near Cassel, and later in Stalag 11A near Weimar. For eighteen long months, he was a prisoner of the Nazis.

With chaos reigning among the forty thousand prisoners in Stalag 9A, Mitterrand and others began to restore a sense of order and discipline among the prisoners. Classes and even lectures were organized. Mitterrand himself studied Greek and began writing a book called *The Seven Hills of Paris*, which he never finished.[34]

In his book *Ma part de vérité*, he revealed how his experience in a Nazi prisoner-of-war camp helped him to discover a new "social contract." The Germans brought in pans of rutabaga soup and small round loaves of bread, leaving it to the prisoners to divide the food. At first the "law of the jungle" prevailed and the first to reach it took the spoils. But eventually Mitterrand and others worked out a system of dividing the food equally. Commenting on this experience, Mitterrand wrote:

> It was a rare and instructive sight. I was assisting at the birth of the Social Contract. I shall not be telling anyone anything new if I observe that the natural hierarchy of courage and uprightness, which had just emerged as more powerful than the knife, was only distantly related, in the world of the camps, to the old hierarchy, the old social and moral order. What a mockery! The old order had not withstood rutabaga soup.[35]

If some degree of equality could be created in a prisoner-of-war camp, certainly, he would later feel, the same could be done in de Gaulle's France.

During his captivity Mitterrand made three escape attempts, succeeding only on the third try. The first came in March 1941 when he and a priest—a rather ironic occurrence given Mitterrand's strong religious upbringing—climbed over an unattended fence and headed for the Swiss border, 360 miles to the south. After a twenty-two-day trek, they found themselves three miles from the Swiss frontier. Unfortunately, they risked walking near the village of Egesheim in open daylight and were caught and returned to the camp. Just six months later, Mitterrand and two others fled their prisoner-of-war camp and attempted to cross the German border into France. This time, he and his comrades tried posing as foreign workers as they traversed the German countryside. Crossing into occupied France, Mitterrand stumbled into a hotel in Metz, only to be betrayed by the receptionist. The German authorities took Mitterrand to a camp in Lorraine and, realizing that he would be a bothersome prisoner, planned to send him to Poland where an escape would be unlikely. Yet Mitterrand, hearing that a café close to the camp had helped fugitive prisoners, decided to make another attempt at freedom. This time when he fled the camp, German guards were in close pursuit. However, he made his way to the café and was sheltered there for several days before beginning his flight back to Jarnac and eventually unoccupied France. Aided by Communist railway workers who had organized escape routes for prisoners of war, Mitterrand appeared at his family home in Jarnac on Christmas Eve, 1941.

After escaping from his Nazi captors, he joined the Resistance and made a national reputation for himself. Since Jarnac was in occupied France, Mitterrand ran tremendous risks by staying there; consequently, he made his way to Vichy. In unoccupied France, with the aid of family friends, he found employment in a semiofficial organization to aid prisoners of war and at the same time became involved in the Resistance. Because of his work in the prisoner-of-war operation, in the autumn of 1943 he was awarded the *Francisque*, an award routinely given to civil servants under the Vichy regime. Throughout his political career, he would be reproached, especially by Communists and right-wing opponents, for receiving a decoration from the collaborationist Vichy regime. In his own defense, however, Mitterrand stated repeatedly that he was in London on a mission for the Resistance when the *Francisque* was awarded and that he never received it. Mitterrand also defended his work under Vichy by saying that the *Francisque* was a "marvelous cover" for an underground Resistance operative.[36] (After the war, it should be noted, Mitterrand received the *Grand croix de la Légion d'honneur,* the *Croix de guerre,* and the *Rosette de la Résistance* for his wartime and Resistance activities.)

Shortly after entering the Resistance, under the code name "Morland," he made it a full-time occupation. When the Germans occupied Vichy France, Mitterrand ended his work with the government and established an organization to support prisoners of war and deportees. Part of Mitterrand's Resistance activities included making false identity papers, which were smuggled into Nazi prison camps. While the Resistance movement in France lacked unity, three important centers emerged: Mitterrand's group, the Communists, and a group led by de Gaulle's nephew Michel Charette.

In November 1943 Mitterrand traveled to London in order to make contact with de Gaulle's Free French forces, a journey that proved to be a lesson in futility. Once in London, representatives of the Free French group wanted him to sign a loyalty oath to General de Gaulle. Mitterrand flatly refused this offer because he was instructed to merge his Resistance group with the one headed by Charette, who seemed to have little experience in the Resistance movement and who had rather strong right-wing proclivities. Following this refusal, Mitterrand's hosts left him stranded in London without money or a change of clothes.

In the same month the twenty-seven-year-old Mitterrand went to Algiers for his first meeting with de Gaulle himself, a rendezvous that quickly revealed the basic incompatibility of the two emerging French political leaders. After questioning Mitterrand about why he chose to fly to Algiers on an English airplane, a silly question from Mitterrand's point of view and one aspect of the meeting that irked the young man from Jarnac, the general asked him once again to merge his group with that of Charette. When Mitterrand hesitated, he drew a cold stare from de Gaulle.[37]

One important reason Mitterrand hesitated was that he never fully accepted the authority of de Gaulle and the Free French Forces. The emerging Socialist leader felt that the Resistance within France and de Gaulle's forces outside the country were not identical. In other words, de Gaulle was not necessarily a legitimate figure within the

French Resistance. Mitterrand wrote in *Ma part de vérité*, "He was far away. He talked a lot. He was the general. France seemed to me closer and larger than him."[38] He would also write that later works on de Gaulle by Gaullists would imitate Stalinist works by identifying "service to de Gaulle as service to France, while service to France that did not add to the general's glory was considered to be negligible if not actually suspect."[39] Thus the Resistance and its operation were major issues that first separated Mitterrand from de Gaulle and his supporters.

Besides the Gaullists, another group that Mitterrand had a first-hand opportunity to observe in the Resistance was the Communists. According to Mitterrand, it was during the Resistance that he became acquainted with French Communists: "From this period date friendships that the years have not diminished. Among the other benefits that I owe them [the Communists] is that they taught me not to shut my eyes if I did not want to be crushed by their formidable machine. It was difficult to maintain the right balance between watchfulness that allowed you to do nothing and overconfidence that allowed them to do everything. I still have that difficulty."[40] This perception of the Communists, like his perception of de Gaulle and his supporters, carried over to the Fourth and Fifth Republics and to his own presidency.

In addition to molding Mitterrand's views of his future political opponents on the right and on the left and giving him a national reputation, the Resistance provided him with an opportunity to meet his wife, Danielle Gouze. Danielle's sister, who worked for Mitterrand's Resistance group, introduced him to his future spouse, the daughter of a staunch Burgundy Socialist family of teachers actively involved in the Resistance movement. In the spring of 1944, the young couple became engaged; they were married at St.-Séverin in a religious ceremony on October 28, 1944. The Mitterrands had three sons, Jean-Christophe, Gilbert, and Pascal who died in infancy at the age of two months. Jean-Christophe became an expert in African affairs, an area where his father has considerable expertise, and would become in October 1986 Mitterrand's adviser for Africa. Gilbert won a seat as a Socialist deputy in the wake of his father's historic election victory in 1981. Although his wife has often stayed out of the public spotlight, Mitterrand is fond of saying, "You know, she is much more leftist than I."[41]

In the early spring of 1944 a merger finally occurred between the three major Resistance organizations aiding prisoners of war—the Morland group, the Charette group led by de Gaulle's nephew, and the Communists—with Mitterrand emerging as the leader of the unified organization. Consequently, at Liberation, de Gaulle selected Mitterrand as the temporary secretary general of the Organization for Prisoners of War, War Veterans, and Refugees (earlier Mitterrand had founded the national Movement for Prisoners of War). Until de Gaulle arrived in Paris, fifteen secretary generals were charged with the administration of France. According to some accounts, when the general did return to Paris, Mitterrand actually saved de Gaulle's life when the Free French leader appeared in a large open window and lost his balance before a cheering crowd below. Supposedly, Mitterrand caught de Gaulle from behind and helped him regain his balance before he tumbled from the high window.[42] Yet when de Gaulle created a more permanent government, the twenty-eight-year-old Mitterrand found himself without a job.

In 1945 and 1946, the young man from Jarnac dabbled in both journalism and politics. For a while he collaborated with a newspaper called *L'Homme libres* (The free man), a paper for prisoners of war and deportees. In this paper Mitterrand wrote scathing attacks on the leaders of the defunct Third Republic, especially editorials aimed against Edouard Daladier and Edouard Herriot. He also severely criticized politicians of the Third Republic who wanted to return to active political life. At this time Mitterrand found a job as president and managing editor of *Editions du Rond-Point* which, along with other periodicals, published a women's magazine entitled *Votre beauté* (Your beauty). For a short period he served as the vice president of the union for French periodical publications. At the end of the war, too, Mitterrand was one of the founding members of the Democratic and Socialist Union of the Resistance (*Union Démocratique et Socialiste de la Résistance*—UDSR), a small center/center-right political party that became an important "hinge party" in the Fourth Republic. The UDSR was, in essence, a political formation centered on non-Communist Resistance figures, a heterogeneous party in which Mitterrand would launch his more than four-decade-long political career.

At the war's end, the shy young provincial student who came to Paris in 1934 had been changed by the course of events. The rise of fascism, the war, and the Resistance demonstrated to Mitterrand the importance and the power of politics, an interest that would soon override his youthful passion for literature. As he himself said of this formative period in his life, it provided him with a "new education."[43] The momentous events of 1939–44 transformed him into a national figure who had close contact with Gaullists and Communists, but trusted neither. The war and the Resistance provided Mitterrand with a new orientation, perspective, and career.

2

THE FOURTH REPUBLIC

The Making of a Politician

1946–1958

> He knew everything and everybody and played parliament like an expert.
>
> —Pierre Mendès-France

With the formation of the Fourth Republic in 1946, Mitterrand launched his lengthy political career. In particular, he gained rich ministerial experience by working for an ever-changing procession of prime ministers. As a result of his numerous ministerial roles and his willingness to participate in various governments, Mitterrand developed a reputation in some quarters as a power-seeking opportunist. Governments of the Fourth Republic—often referred to as a "regime of parties"—were short-lived, due partly to a proportional representation voting system that gave many small parties representation in the National Assembly but minimized the possibility for durable parliamentary coalitions. While Mitterrand would later write that he was a socialist during this period, his political perspective was closer to that of a radical or a liberal democrat. In many ways, Mitterrand today is a child of the Fourth Republic.

The political regime that formally initiated the future president into politics was a tripartite government comprising three large parties: the socialist French Section of the Workers' International (*Section Française de l'Internationale Ouvrière*—SFIO), the Communist party, and the Christian Democrats (*Mouvement Républicain Populaire*—MRP). While de Gaulle presided over this tripartite government from the end of the war until the founding of the Fourth Republic in 1946, tripartitism reigned until the spring of 1947 when the Communists were forced to leave the government due to mounting Cold War tensions and rising unemployment. Yet this tripartite government did push through a notable list of reforms, especially a far-reaching nationalization plan. The government nationalized, among others, the electric, gas, and coal industries, the Bank of France as well as principal deposit banks, the Renault automobile firm, over thirty insurance companies, and a share of the aircraft industry. It also introduced France to state-led economic planning and initiated a reform of administrative structures. This, then, was the republic whose service the thirty-year-old Mitterrand entered as he began his political career.

During the 1946–58 period he acquired many of the characteristics that later made him an appealing presidential candidate: his wide-ranging experience as a political leader; his nondoctrinaire socialism; his history of standing up to the Communists; his progressive stances on major issues; his pro-European and pro-Atlantic views; his anti-Gaullism; and his understanding of the need for cross-cutting alliances in order to form a large electoral base. A discussion of these characteristics and the way in which he acquired them under the Fourth Republic will shed considerable light on Mitterrand's career and also help to explain why he ascended to the presidency in 1981.

In the postwar years Mitterrand gained wide-ranging political experience. After dabbling in journalism he decided to try his hand at politics. His first election campaign was for a seat in the National Assembly representing the Rally of the Republican Left (*Rassemblement des Gauches-Républicaines*—RGR), which grouped together the UDSR and the Radical party, from the fifth electoral district of the Seine in an election on June 2, 1946. His efforts failed. At the urging of an acquaintance, Henri Queuille, in 1946 he "parachuted" into the department of the Nièvre in Burgundy and ran for a National Assembly seat once again. Campaigning under the banner "Republican Action and Unity" in this conservative rural department, he launched a rather opportunistic campaign, criticizing tripartitism, nationalizations, and the bureaucracy of the existing government. The citizens of Nièvre responded favorably and gave Mitterrand 25 percent of the vote, placing him second behind the PCF candidate who had captured 33 percent in the November 10, 1946, elections. The department of the Nièvre sent Mitterrand and three other deputies to represent them in the National Assembly. In 1951 and 1956 he was reelected as a deputy from Nièvre, making him Nièvre's representative in the National Assembly during the entire twelve-year life of the Fourth Republic.[1]

Under the Fourth Republic, Mitterrand served in eleven out of twenty-four different governments, gaining invaluable political experience in the realm of domestic and international politics. Mitterrand's first ministerial appointment came in January 1947 when he was asked to serve in the cabinet of Socialist Paul Ramadier (January–October 1947), and then in the cabinet of centrist Robert Schuman (November 1947–July 1948) as minister of war veterans, making the thirty-year-old Mitterrand the youngest minister to serve in France in 100 years.[2] He next held the post of minister of information in the cabinet of the Radical André Marie (July–August 1948), and held a ministerial-level appointment in the short-lived government of Schuman (September 1948). Schuman had wanted Mitterrand to become his minister of the interior, but the emerging young political star declined, in part, because of the unstable political situation at the time. Mitterrand's next appointment was as secretary of state to the Presidency of the Council in the government of Radical Henri Queuille (September 1948–October 1949). He then held a post as minister of overseas territories in the cabinet of centrist René Pleven (July 1950–February 1951). Regarding this ministerial position and the problems that emerged in French zones of occupation in Africa at the time, Mitterrand later wrote, "It is in effect the major experience of my political life because it began my evolution."[3] From this point onward, he became more interested in French colonial problems and more sensitive to the plight of Third World nations. After holding this post, he was given an assignment as a minister of state in the cabinet of the radical Edgar Faure (January–February 1952). Mitterrand followed this appointment by serving as minister to the Council of Europe in the government of Joseph Laniel (July–September 1953). He next served as minister of the interior in the government of the Radical Pierre Mendès-France (June 1954–February 1955). His last ministerial appointment under the Fourth Republic was as minister of justice in the cabinet of the Socialist Guy Mollet (February 1956–May 1957). This highly varied and rich ministerial career was interrupted with the return of de Gaulle to the political stage and the founding of the Fifth

Republic in 1958. From 1958 to 1981 Mitterrand found himself in the political wilderness as an opposition figure under the new republic ushered in by the general.

Due to his ministerial record and his general competence as a French civil servant working on the national level, the young politician from Jarnac won admiration from many. For instance, when Mendès-France formed his government in 1954, the popular Radical relied heavily on Mitterrand for advice. Explaining the value of Mitterrand's counsel, Mendès-France stated: "No one knew better the deputies, their talents and weaknesses, their current performances and past record, their secret ambitions and confidential dealings. He knew everything and everybody and played parliament like an expert."[4] Mendès-France even told one interviewer in 1974 that Mitterrand was his teacher: "I was completely ignorant of the parliamentary world of the Assembly; there was a multitude of groups of which I did not know the leaders and, from the beginning, Mitterrand instructed me."[5]

Yet admiration for Mitterrand went beyond his friends and colleagues like Mendès-France. When Mollet's Socialist government fell in 1957, several major publications—notably *Le Monde* and *France Observateur*—mentioned Mitterrand as a possible successor.[6] Some of his political adversaries also saw him as a potential candidate for prime minister. Roger Duchet, for example, who was a hard-liner on Algeria, said that "Mitterrand as prime minister would have constructed a new-style cabinet. Under these conditions, would General de Gaulle have had the same chance to make his coup of May 13 [1958]?"[7]

Mitterrand was also successful in local and party politics. In 1947 he was elected municipal counselor of the Nièvre, a position that he retained until 1959. And in 1949 he was elected general counselor of the canton of Montsauche, where he was reelected in 1955 and 1966. Beginning in 1950 he assumed responsibility as the political director of the newspaper *Le Courrier de la Nièvre*. (From 1959 to 1981 he also served as mayor of Château-Chinon in western Burgundy.)

Mitterrand's political ascendancy within his political party, the UDSR, paralleled his rise on the national level. Joining the UDSR after the war because of his opposition to the SFIO, the PCF, and Christian Democrats, and because he "did not want to be smothered" by a large party, he joined this small center/center-right "hinge party" and quickly became one of its leaders.[8] In 1951 he assumed leadership of the UDSR's parliamentary group in the National Assembly. Then, in 1953 at the national congress of the UDSR at Nantes, he was elected president of the party, a position he used to make the UDSR more dynamic and progressive.

Consequently, by the end of the Fourth Republic, Mitterrand had become a seasoned political veteran with a national reputation who headed a small but influential party. His experience in government during the Fourth Republic prepared him for his role as an opposition leader under the Fifth Republic, a factor that cannot be overlooked in explaining his eventual rise to the highest office in 1981.

Another characteristic that helps to explain his later success is his nondoctrinaire socialist views. Mitterrand's socialism, a political philosophy that he arrived at late in his career, differs markedly from Soviet collectivism and Scandinavian social democracy. As mentioned earlier, he once said rather naïvely that "economics is only a branch of the humanities, that is to say a discipline whose approach and methods are not bound by the precision of the exact sciences."[9] The primary mission of socialism, according to Mitterrand, is "to organize society in order to liberate the individual."[10] As a latecomer to socialism, Mitterrand is closer to the practical humanism of Jaurès than the orthodox socialism of Jules Guesde, a rival of Jaurès at the beginning of the twentieth century. Under the Fourth Republic Mitterrand slowly developed his socialist views in the context of a France deeply divided by the Cold War and by the rhetoric of class struggle after the PCF left the tripartite government in 1947.

As previously mentioned, Mitterrand had received an education as a captive in a Nazi prisoner-of-war camp where he witnessed in a graphic way the grotesque horrors, the misery, and the exploitation of the weak and powerless.[11] This new consciousness was only slowly translated into a socialist perspective during the 1960s and 1970s. Nevertheless, Mitterrand claims that during his tenure in the National Assembly under the Fourth Republic he "voted for all of the Socialist economic and social laws."[12]

Mitterrand's first political party, the UDSR, was created in 1945 from several Resistance groups that were not absorbed by the PCF after the war; in 1946 it officially became a political party. Mitterrand joined the UDSR because for him there seemed to be no other choice: the Radicals were discredited because they had signed the Munich agreement of 1938, Mollet and the SFIO were taking a quasi-Marxist line after the war, the Christian Democrats were a large and somewhat divided party, and Mitterrand opposed the Gaullists and the PCF. He told delegates at the third national congress of his party in June of 1949: "The UDSR will grow and will take the place that it must have in the history of our country and which must be between the Marxists and the men of the Right . . . the non-Marxist left will make the French understand that the Republic is not lost."[13] Claude Manceron, a Socialist close to Mitterrand, has said that Mitterrand thought that the UDSR would give him a chance to define "a secular socialism . . . unconstrained by Christian and Marxist dogma."[14]

During the early years of the Fourth Republic, the UDSR was opposed to the tripartite government headed by de Gaulle. As a small party with never more than twenty deputies in the National Assembly, it was much more influential than its size because it was a hinge party between the Right and the Left.[15] For this reason, a noted authority on postwar France, Philip Williams, maintains that the UDSR was "the most important of all the small parties" under the Fourth Republic.[16]

Mitterrand played a major role in the UDSR, a party that attracted a diverse membership. Besides Mitterrand, the party included several Gaullists in the early years (René Capitant, André Malraux, Jacques Soustelle, and others), non-Marxist socialists (Pierre Bourdan), and liberals (Jean Marin, Jean Legaret, Edouard Bonnefous). As Mitterrand gained national political prominence in the late 1940s and early 1950s, he began to play a large role in party affairs and in defining the political orientation of the UDSR.

In the late 1940s he led an attack against the Gaullists and the Gaullist tendencies within the UDSR, succeeding in forcing the followers of de Gaulle out of the party.[17] His influence, as well as his thinking, was also seen in a speech that he gave in October 1951 at the national congress of the UDSR in Marseille, where he became head of the party's parliamentary group. This important speech to the delegates stressed that the mission of the party was to modernize France and to guard against totalitarianism of both the Right and the Left, a theme that he would repeat often in the future. For Mitterrand, fascism and communism represented two forms of the same revolution, a dangerous revolution threatening the world and the gains ushered in by the French Revolution of 1789. Continuing with the theme of the mission of the party, he told his colleagues that the UDSR was a socialist party but emphasized that it was not Marxist, and that liberty and equality would be its hallmark. As a socialist party, stated Mitterrand, the UDSR stood for the socialization of the means of production. He stressed, however, that "I am far from being doctrinaire! . . . because I think that in 1951 the best way to free man is to remain faithful to the Great Revolution of 89." He also told the congress that under no circumstance could the UDSR accept an alliance with the Gaullist Rally of the French People (*Rassemblement du Peuple Français*—RPF). The USDR, said the young leader, must support a strong Europe.[18] Two years after delivering this speech, Mitterrand was promoted to head the UDSR itself.

While Mitterrand has said that he voted Socialist during the 1946–58 period, his economic philosophy at the time was far from socialist. In terms of economic thought, he was a liberal pragmatist. For instance, in his first election campaign in the Nièvre in 1946, his platform opposed nationalizations. Yet when he began to oppose the Gaullists in the UDSR and move the party leftward, he emphasized the need to socialize the means of production. This position would, as he learned in time, allow him to separate himself from the Right and to attract Communist votes. With the exception of his 1946 election campaign in the Nièvre and the period following serious economic difficulties during his first term as president (1982–83), he has favored nationalization. Nevertheless, Mitterrand has remained faithful to the idea of a mixed economy. The individual played a central role in his economic and political philosophy. His belief that the best way to free man was by remaining true to the French Revolution of 1789, as he stressed at the 1951 congress of the UDSR at Marseille, reveals his commitment to liberal democratic principles; after all, the French Revolution that he so admired was a bourgeois revolution. His economic philosophy and his slowly emerging socialist consciousness were indeed rooted in humanistic and religious concerns, but also in political necessity.

His general political philosophy during the Fourth Republic was that of a liberal politician who believed in pluralistic and consensual politics. The multitude of small parties, including his own UDSR, and the changing procession of governments conditioned this young politician to favor a highly pluralistic political system. Under such a system, he learned the art that made him famous—political maneuvering. The electoral collaboration necessitated by the Fourth Republic's "regime of parties," and his growing openness to such collaboration, strengthened his sense of pluralism and his understanding of the need for consensus as a national leader, two aspects of his developing political mind-set that prepared him well for his presidency.

Under the Fourth Republic, Mitterrand emerged as a national political figure and a pragmatist par excellence. When he entered the UDSR in 1945–46 he was a moderate entering a small party that allowed him the opportunity to quickly emerge as one of its leaders. As he made his political ascent on the ministerial and party level, he began to articulate a non-Marxist variant of socialism, informed to a degree by his religious upbringing, that characterized his years in the opposition under the Fifth Republic. As the 1951 speech at the UDSR congress indicates, by the early 1950s Mitterrand was moving toward the socialist camp, but a camp that was nondoctrinaire and highly suspicious of the PCF.

Throughout his long political career, Mitterrand has consistently taken a strong stand vis-à-vis the Communist party. This particular characteristic contributed to his appeal as a presidential candidate in 1981. His first real contact with the Communists came during the Resistance in which members of the PCF played a large and significant role. During the Resistance, Mitterrand had the opportunity to work with Communists and to understand the political tactics of the PCF. His uneasiness with the PCF, which originated in the Resistance, would continue under the Fourth and Fifth Republics.

In fact, Mitterrand's very entry into the political life of the Fourth Republic was marked by a strong strain of anticommunism. When he ran for election in the Nièvre in November of 1946, his rhetoric was anticommunist as well as opposed to tripartitism and nationalization. During the early years of his political career, too, he did not hesitate to take a firm stand against the Communists. When he was appointed minister of war veterans in January of 1947—his first ministerial post—Mitterrand found his ministry barred by striking picketers. His predecessor had tried to terminate a ministerial car pool that the Communists had used to transport their members to party meetings. This action prompted the Communist trade union in the ministry to call a strike. Mitterrand did not hesitate to take action to solve his first "ministerial crisis." He ordered the dismissal of the strike leaders and announced "that they would be replaced by local ex–prisoners of war." Maurice Thorez, one of the key leaders of the PCF, who was participating in the tripartite government, even told

Mitterrand later, "I understand you. There are some things that one must do when one is in government and you have done well."[19]

One of the most important events that colored Mitterrand's view of the PCF was the Cold War. In May 1947, Socialist Prime Minister Paul Ramadier dismissed the Communist ministers and thereafter the PCF remained in a political ghetto during the Fourth Republic and for more than two decades of the Fifth Republic. The dismissal of the PCF from the tripartite government came not long after the announcement of the Truman Doctrine in March 1947 and the Marshall Plan in June of the same year, and these events demonstrated to many in France that hard new political lines were being drawn at home and around the world. At this time, too, the French economy was in a monumental slump: industrial production was running at 60 percent of the 1938 level and prices had jumped from an index of 100 in 1938 to 497 in 1945, and to 1,645 by 1948.[20] When the Cold War and the economic conditions in France led to the dismissal of the PCF, the largest of the political parties and commanding almost one-third of the vote, Mitterrand took a firm stand on the side of the established government and its Western allies. The Socialists under Mollet's leadership did a quick about-face and began a long-standing anticommunist campaign. General de Gaulle at this time launched his own political party, the Rally of the French People, which was vehemently anticommunist. Therefore, flanked on the left by the large PCF and on the right by de Gaulle, the post-tripartite government shifted its center of political gravity to the right and commenced a new invigorated anticommunism that Mitterrand shared.

Mitterrand's anticommunism surfaced in a pronounced way in his book *Présence française et abandon* (French presence and withdrawal). During the 1950s the French had numerous colonial problems, not only in Indochina but in Africa as well. In his book, Mitterrand argued that rising African nationalism in French Black Africa was a product of Communist propaganda:

> The Communist Party—knowing full well that the stage of economic evolution of black people offers them [the PCF] only a step toward the expansion of their doctrine—has placed itself neatly under the nationalist banner. Its cells have seized all pretexts, have put forward their slogans, and have hashed and rehashed their own propaganda. Its militants, in the ports and in the factories, have taught the modern methods of agitation and propaganda.[21]

Such an interpretation of French colonial problems was not uncommon in the bipolar postwar world.

But there was also a more pragmatic side to Mitterrand's communism. A few years earlier he had told a Communist journalist:

> I am not a maniacal anticommunist, even though such a position would be justified because the Communists are heaping mud on me. In my own constituency their smears about the Vichy decoration I was awarded [the *Francisque*] are unspeakably foul because they know that I fought alongside them in the Resistance. It is true that I want to defeat the Communists. But through the ballot box. I do not mean to use administrative methods against them. I will never send a Communist to prison. [22]

In 1954 he made a similar comment in the newspaper *Combat* about his intention to defeat the PCF at the polls. Mitterrand stated: "We are confusing the anticommunist struggle with anticommunist hazing. We do not consider that the millions of people who vote Communist are definitely lost to the nation. . . . It is in the realm of ideas and reality that we must combat communism." [23]

The official tone of Mitterrand's party, however, was considerably more anticommunist. Anticommunism was one of the party's essential ingredients and it was expressed in a 1952 party brochure that read: "The UDSR intends to lead the struggle against communism on all planes: to expose them [Communists] without falsehoods, to utilize the existing laws against them . . . to let the incompatibility of an electoral alliance with the Communist Party be known, and their exercise of administrative functions of authority or of security." [24] Obviously, this party brochure was a product of the Cold War in which political parties in France expressed both real and imaginary fears of the PCF.

Thus under the Fourth Republic Mitterrand developed a reputation for standing up to the Communists. In the National Assembly and in the press Mitterrand normally responded point by point to the PCF's attacks on the government. [25] Like many in France and elsewhere in the world, Mitterrand was impassioned by Cold War fever and engaged in his share of anticommunist rhetoric. Yet the breakdown of the tripartite government in 1947 and the onslaught of the Cold War encouraged him to begin to see the need for and the possibility of attracting Communist voters, but it would not be until de Gaulle upset the political balance in France in 1958 that Mitterrand dropped some of his anticommunist baggage and sought electoral cooperation with the PCF.

As a man of government under the Fourth Republic, Mitterrand took a number of progressive stances on domestic and international issues that aided his eventual rise as a leader of the Left. In the eleven governments in which he participated, he found himself taking a number of controversial positions: his call for a new African policy; his willingness to negotiate an end to the war in Vietnam; his resignation from the Laniel government because of its repressive policy in Tunisia and Morocco; and his decision to fire a reactionary Paris police chief, Jean Baylot. An examination of these stances reveals an interesting but seldom studied dimension of Mitterrand's background.

Mitterrand became deeply interested in Africa and its problems after making an extensive visit in 1949 to Senegal, Niger, Liberia, Dahomey, and French West Africa. Concerning this important period in his life, he wrote, "I had seen Africa in movement, but uncertain, hesitant, and suffering."[26] Then, in July 1950 he joined Pleven's cabinet as minister of overseas territories, which included responsibility for the area of Africa that he had just visited. He has said that this ministerial assignment was one of "the major experiences of my political life."[27]

At this time French overseas policy lacked coordination, in part because the foreign minister was responsible for Tunisia and Morocco, the minister of interior held responsibility for Algeria, and another minister was in charge of Indochina. Mitterrand, however, devoted considerable time and energy to the question of French colonization in Africa, and published two books under the Fourth Republic concerning colonial policy: *Aux frontières de l'Union française* (At the frontiers of the French Union), and *Présence française et abandon*. He also wrote regularly in the newsweekly *L'Express* on the subject. His views, of course, drew a barrage of right-wing criticism accusing him of wanting to sell off the empire.

As minister of overseas territories and as a member of the National Assembly, Mitterrand challenged the old conception of the French empire. Under the constitution of the Fourth Republic, the empire was referred to as the "French Union." The overseas territories of the French Union could elect deputies to the National Assembly but on a disproportionate basis—eighty-three deputies to represent 62 million people outside of France compared to 544 deputies for the 50 million citizens of metropolitan France. In his book on the French

Union, Mitterrand argued for a subtle incorporation of the French territories. He also criticized the lack of a clear policy for the French Union and called for a larger measure of autonomy to head off rising African nationalism. He made a similar argument in *Présence française et abandon*, which was widely read when it appeared in 1957.

Mitterrand believed that Africa played a special role in the future of France, especially in the control that it would give his country over the western Mediterranean. In fact, for Mitterrand, control over the western Mediterranean was one of the keys to a successful foreign policy. Speaking before the National Assembly in 1954, he declared, "The future, the security, the grandeur of France are found above all in our union with Africa and can only be assured by our control of the western basin of the Mediterranean."[28] Regarding the importance of Africa, he stated: "A strongly structured central power in Paris, autonomous states and territories federated in the bosom of an egalitarian and federated community, the fraternity of which will go from the plains of Flanders to the forest of the equator, such is the perspective that is up to us to define and to propose, for without Africa there will be no history of France in the twenty-first century."[29] France and Africa were inextricably linked in his view.

Consequently, North Africa had a special place in Mitterrand's vision of French policy. In early September 1953 he wrote in *L'Express* that a French presence in North Africa "is the most imperative of all national policy."[30] This perspective led Mitterrand to make a famous declaration before the National Assembly while he was minister of the interior in the Mendès-France government: "Algeria is French. . . ."[31] As minister of the interior and as minister of justice, Mitterrand had to deal directly with many of the problems stemming from the crisis over Algeria for which he proposed economic aid, social reform, and a form of federalism. On the general Algerian question it must be remembered that his position was shared by most leaders of the Left in France, including Mendès-France, Mollet, and key figures in the PCF. Although he favored keeping Algeria French, in early 1956 he criticized the illegal arrest of Claude Bourdet, the codirector of *France Observateur*, and Professor Henri Marron for opposing the Algerian war and the accompanying torture. Mitterrand warned the Council of Ministers that illegal arrests ran the risk of weakening liberal opinion in France on which the government depended.[32]

Africa forced politicians to take controversial stands, but so too did the war in Indochina. During the height of the long war in

Indochina, Mitterrand favored a negotiated settlement to the conflict. At a meeting of the Council of Ministers on July 22, 1953, when he was serving in the Laniel government as minister to the Council of Europe, he shocked his colleagues when he declared, "Why not negotiate directly with Ho Chi Minh and Mao Tse-tung?"[33] In *Aux frontières de l'Union française*, he raised the same question. But unlike others in government, Mendès-France, who wrote the preface for this 1953 publication, praised Mitterrand for taking such a courageous stance on the drama in Indochina.[34] In 1953 Mitterrand also told the National Assembly that the Vietnam War was a mistake and that it should be ended.[35] He favored a negotiated settlement in Indochina, but one directly between France and Vietnam; he did not favor internationalizing the conflict through multilateral discussions.

Why did he favor negotiations in Vietnam? One of the principal reasons was the fear that a protracted war in Asia might very well mean that France would lose the opportunity to solve the all-important African problem. He stated, "From here on, France, which is immobilized, attracted, and consumed by Asia, will miss her European rendezvous and mission in Africa."[36] Given the choice of Asia or Africa, Mitterrand wanted to solve the African question first because of the special geopolitical advantage that Africa held for France.

Mitterrand's position on the colonial question inspired a number of serious right-wing attacks. One right-wing deputy, Jean Legendre from Oise, insinuated in a speech before the National Assembly that the disastrous French defeat at Dien Bien Phu in 1954, which symbolized the defeat of France in Vietnam, was the product of high treason in Paris. Legendre pointed an accusing finger at Mitterrand by charging, "Why Dien Bien Phu? Why had the French army, superior in number and in material, been defeated in Indochina? It is because it has been betrayed in Paris."[37] In another attack, right-wing deputies, Gaullists and other hard-liners on Africa, wrote to the president of the republic, Vincent Auriol, and demanded that Mitterrand be forced to resign from the Council of Ministers because he "had surrendered Black Africa to international communism."[38] Though far from wanting to give independence to French colonies, Mitterrand's desire to liberalize his country's colonial policy inspired right-wing attacks and eventually heightened his image as a leader of the Left.

Another progressive stand taken by Mitterrand involved his resignation as a minister in the Laniel government because of its repressive policy in Tunisia and Morocco. In June 1953 Laniel formed a government in which Mitterrand served as minister for the Council of Europe. Without being informed, the young politician discovered in mid-August of 1953 that the government had overthrown the Moroccan sultan, Mohammed Ben Youssef. Three weeks later he learned that the government was putting in place a repressive policy in Tunisia. Maintaining that the full Council of Ministers had not been consulted on these matters, he resigned.[39]

As minister of interior in the Mendès-France government in 1954, Mitterrand also took a courageous stand. Two weeks after assuming this ministry, he fired the reactionary police chief of Paris, Jean Baylot. Baylot had used a large number of illegal wiretaps, had infiltrated the PCF with former Nazi collaborators, and had even enticed workers to riot by using forged leaflets. Earlier, in 1952, Baylot had arrested the general secretary of the PCF, Jacques Duclos. Besides firing this "institution" in Paris, Mitterrand clamped down on the number of illegal wiretaps. Among those that Baylot had harassed, especially the Left, his dismissal was celebrated.

The Baylot case was linked indirectly to the first major scandal that threatened Mitterrand's political career, the affair of the leaks. Two days before Baylot was fired, two police inspectors informed Christian Fouchet, minister for Tunisian and Moroccan affairs, that someone in government, supposedly Mitterrand, had given the politburo of the Communist party an account of a recent meeting of the Defense Council. Without telling Mitterrand of the incident, Prime Minister Mendès-France initiated an investigation that subsequently proved Mitterrand innocent because the minutes of the Defense Council meeting were leaked one month before he joined the council. Nevertheless, rumors abounded in the Paris press concerning the security leak, and Mitterrand was implicated. Eventually, two civil servants, a pacifist and an ultraleftist employed by the Defense Council, were charged with the crime. For Mitterrand the affair revealed the effort by rightists to discredit him and Mendès-France on account of the government's decision to conclude a peace treaty with the Vietminh, for appearing conciliatory on the question of independence for North African nations, and for dismantling police plans to disgrace the PCF. While Mitterrand survived the scandal, it weakened his relationship with Mendès-France. The aspiring young politician never forgave the prime minister for not informing him about the initial charges or the investigation into the affair. Mitterrand believed that had he been informed, he could have quickly defended himself. Moreover, Mitterrand would not forget this attempt by the Right to smear him.[40]

Many of the progressive stances taken by Mitterrand under the Fourth Republic centered on French colonial policy. As he noted at the end of the twelfth national congress of the UDSR, "The Fourth Republic disappeared because it had not been able to confront the revolutions of our century, because it had not solved the colonial problems."[41] His controversial stances pushed him into the national limelight; and after the French retreat from Indochina, and the independence of Tunisia, Morocco, and Algeria, Mitterrand appeared to be one of the few politicians with a vision of the future. Furthermore, indirectly and somewhat ironically, his colonial policy views helped to give impetus to the independence movement in French Africa. (Given his view on the African question, it should not surprise contemporary observers to see President Mitterrand attempt to maintain a strong French sphere of influence in Africa, as in Chad.) One of Mitterrand's most progressive stances was the position that he took in 1958 opposing the return of General de Gaulle, but this story must await discussion of his views on Europe and the Atlantic Alliance.

From the late 1940s onward, Mitterrand has supported the idea of European integration, of European political cooperation, and of the Atlantic Alliance, another aspect of his career that has made him an appealing presidential candidate. In 1948 he began his participation in the European movement, an attempt to integrate West European policies on important matters. As a member of government, he voted for the creation of the European Coal and Steel Community (1952) which greatly enhanced European industrial production, for the European Economic Community (Common Market, 1957), and for Euratom (1957). In the Mendès-France government, however, he did abstain in the preliminary vote on the question of creating a European Defense Community. This record reveals a politician who favored the construction of a strong Europe.[42]

Concerning the Atlantic Alliance, Mitterrand voted in favor of NATO and has been a long-time advocate of guarded friendship with the United States.[43] Since 1954 when the United States developed the hydrogen bomb and the Soviet Union became a major nuclear power, he has not wanted to allow exclusive control over NATO to fall into the hands of the Americans. After President Eisenhower announced in 1954 that the decision to use atomic weapons rested solely with the United States, Mitterrand criticized U.S. hegemony over NATO and said that control over the use of atomic weapons would be "one of the essential points" of a confrontation between the U.S. and its allies. He also declared that he would like to see "a new definition of the responsibilities and the task of the allies . . . in Asia, Africa, and in Europe."[44] Several weeks later he made a similar statement in *L'Express* regarding his fear that the United States might make a decision to use atomic weapons that would not be in the best interests of France. He found it "unbearable that the United States would be the only judge of the decision that will change the face of the world."[45] In the pages of *L'Express* he also warned against "unconsciously transforming the Atlantic Pact into an offensive arm."[46] Under the Fourth Republic, Mitterrand was a consistent defender of the idea of a strong Europe and a strong but democratic Atlantic Alliance. Between 1946 and 1958 he developed many of the views on NATO and Europe that he would eventually advocate under the Fifth Republic as an opposition leader and later as head of state.

One of Mitterrand's most pronounced characteristics has been his anti-Gaullism, an issue which, in time, added to his stature as a presidential candidate. To a large degree, his political career has revolved around his opposition to General de Gaulle and the authoritarianism that the general represented. Even before the formation of the Fourth Republic, Mitterrand felt antipathy toward de Gaulle, the man whom many in France regarded as their savior. As mentioned earlier, he and de Gaulle first met during the war years in Algiers. At that time, the general tried to convince Mitterrand to merge the Resistance forces with those of his own nephew, who would then play a leadership role in an enlarged and more unified Resistance. Mitterrand, of course, initially failed to comply with the general's request.

One of the main reasons Mitterrand refused to accept de Gaulle's legitimacy as a Resistance leader was that the general did not seem to be a bona fide part of the movement inside France. In 1975 Mitterrand wrote:

> The special figure of the head of Free France both seduced and chilled me. In my view, our resistance to the Nazis inside France, and our constant contact with torture and death was quite different from the resistance carried out from abroad, and I did not accord the latter the preeminence that it presumed for itself. I questioned whether the

word "resistance" was really applicable to the combat carried on from London or Algiers, simply another episode in a traditional war.[47]

This view was shared by many in the Resistance movement. From this time on, Mitterrand's anti-Gaullism mounted. At the 1949 national congress of the UDSR, in the course of his struggle against the Gaullists in the party, Mitterrand declared: "We think that you [Gaullists] are more dangerous than others that participate today in different parties of the majority. . . . We think that you are more dangerous because of your contempt for government."[48] During the same congress he denounced the "sectarianism" and the "fascism" of de Gaulle's newly formed political party, the RPF, and did not hesitate to draw a parallel with the German brand of fascism.[49] Responding to this attack, the Gaullists left the party. The purge of the Gaullist members symbolized a significant turning point in the history of the party and also in the political career of one of its most notable anti-Gaullists. From 1949 onward, the UDSR and its leadership were more open to seeking allies with parties on the Left.

Under the Fourth Republic, Mitterrand took a strong stand against totalitarianism, which for him also included Gaullism. What worried him was not just the political appeal of General de Gaulle, but the personal power that he commanded. Committed to the idea of parliamentary government, Mitterrand feared that de Gaulle's re-emergence on the political scene threatened liberal democracy.[50] Mitterrand expressed this fear not only in the late 1940s as he denounced the Gaullists in the UDSR, but also in 1958 on the eve of de Gaulle's return to power under the new Fifth Republic. When the Algerian war deeply divided France in the late 1950s, many notable politicians—including Mollet of the SFIO and the president of the Republic, René Coty—supported de Gaulle's return to power. On June 1, 1958, the general was installed as prime minister and given exceptional powers, among them the right to put a new constitution before the electorate in a referendum. Not everyone in France, however, rallied behind the general.

Perhaps even de Gaulle sensed in the last days of the Fourth Republic that he had a formidable opponent in Mitterrand. On May 31, 1958, when the general met with Mitterrand and other government officials after returning to Paris to assume leadership of the government, the young political star of the Fourth Republic was critical of de Gaulle and his usurpation of power. In response, de Gaulle declared, "You want my head, Monsieur Mitterrand."[51] If de Gaulle's coup taught Mitterrand one important lesson, it was that electoral alliances were necessary in the post-1958 period.

Other events, too, during the Fourth Republic forced Mitterrand to see the value of dropping a certain amount of ideological baggage and forming broad electoral alliances to secure a large base of political support, one of the keys to his success under the Fifth Republic. At the start of the Fourth Republic, given his hostility to tripartitism as well as to Gaullism and communism, he favored an alliance with the Radicals, a party founded in 1901 and based primarily on opposition to organized authority and situated between the Gaullists and the Socialists. Mitterrand consistently sought an alliance with the Radicals during the Fourth Republic. At various national congresses of the UDSR, in 1949 and 1956 for instance, he referred to the Radicals as "friends" and "allies" of his own party.[52] After the tripartite government broke down in 1947 and the Communists were forced into opposition, Mitterrand swung toward the SFIO and sought a regrouping of the Center-Left. This effort was especially pronounced in the 1950s as France confronted the Cold War and a PCF that supported the main adversary in this conflict. Mitterrand felt that such an alliance would help to stabilize the political system which was being divided by the extreme Left and the extreme Right. He expressed this desire to regroup the Center-Left at the 1951 national congress of the UDSR when he stated, "We are ready to [ally with] republicans . . . and with others like us who are socialists."[53] At the end of the 1951 congress, a motion was passed that called on "progressive republicans" to withhold their cooperation from any government unwilling to institute profound reforms conforming to a "democratic and constructive socialism" respectful of existing institutions.[54] Mitterrand repeated his call for regrouping the Center-Left in 1956 and also in 1957 at the last national congress of the UDSR during the Fourth Republic.[55] In short, what Mitterrand sought at this time was an SFIO-Radical-UDSR alliance against the far Left and the far Right, believing that such a coalition could provide France with a stable government and reform the nation.[56]

Mitterrand's understanding of the importance of alliances and his adeptness in creating them is clearly demonstrated in his successful effort at wooing the Democratic African Rally (*Rassemblement Démocratique Africain*—RDA) away from the PCF in the early 1950s. The

RDA was a progressive grouping of African deputies in the National Assembly that included Félix Houphouët-Boigny, Sékou Touré, Diori Hamni, Léon M'ba and Modibo Keita. Led by Houphouët-Boigny, a doctor from the Ivory Coast, the RDA supported national independence for the countries it represented and was allied to the PCF in the National Assembly. When Mitterrand served as minister of overseas territories from 1950 to 1951, he decided to invite the leader of the RDA to meet with him for a frank discussion of African affairs. Houphouët-Boigny was in hiding in the Ivory Coast at the time because of "radical" statements made by the RDA, and Mitterrand had to assure him safe passage to Paris. He advised this important African leader to enter into discussions with local French administrators and try to solve outstanding local problems. Mitterrand even removed some of the uncooperative African administrators in order to facilitate a dialogue with the RDA. This position, of course, was a reversal of previous French policy in Black Africa. During their meeting, Houphouët-Boigny signed a letter assuring Mitterrand of his commitment to "French authority." Thus Mitterrand won an important friend and ally for the UDSR in the National Assembly, much to the dismay of the Communist party and the right wing. This detente with the RDA aided Mitterrand in instituting his African policy and brought him and his small party a new and valuable partner in the National Assembly.[57]

Under the Mendès-France government, Mitterrand also came to understand the importance of political alliances. Although he thought highly of Mendès-France, the Radical Prime Minister's disdain for political allies on his left did not escape Mitterrand's attention. In 1955 Mendès-France's government fell, due, in part, to his unwillingness and inability to form broad-based alliances. The Socialists had even refused to support him fully, due, in part, to his progressive colonial policy in North Africa. Mendès-France's tactical myopia taught Mitterrand a lesson in political survival.[58]

Even before that, however, Mitterrand was one of the leaders of an electoral alliance formed in 1951 known as the Republican Front. This anticonservative coalition agreed to be conciliatory in Algeria but lacked a coherent program.[59] In the 1956 legislative election the Republican Front won 166 seats, the PCF 151 seats, and 200 seats were shared by independents, Gaullists and other conservatives, as well as Poujadists (a group committed to right-wing economic policies favoring the small businessman, shopkeeper, and farmer). By the late

1950s, with the Algerian crisis and the reemergence of de Gaulle threatening, the possibility increased for regrouping the Center-Left in France to prevent the demise of the Fourth Republic.

On June 29, 1957, Mitterrand gave an interview to *Paris-Presse* in which he commented on the need to broaden the electoral base of the Center-Left and on the importance of the Communist vote. "The regrouping of the small parties of the Left and Center-Left," he said, "is desirable . . . but a regrouping based on clearly announced principles: in particular . . . the position on communism, on the evolution of the French Union, on the Western Alliance, and on European construction."[60] When asked if he thought that there could be a left-wing majority without the Communists, he replied, "The Communist Party is on the left if one looks at the five million electors who vote for it. It is not on the left if one recalls its methods of action, its refusal of free discussion, its authoritarian sectarianism. Without communist voters there is no left majority, but instead center-left majorities or rather 'third force' majorities stretching from the Socialist Party to certain liberal conservatives."[61] This growing need to fashion a broad electoral alliance was made all the more apparent when de Gaulle overthrew the Fourth Republic and instituted the Fifth Republic, which gave its president enormous powers.

Charles de Gaulle's coup in 1958 was the most important factor in motivating Mitterrand later to make his "historic compromise" in which he accepted the reality of an electoral alliance with the powerful PCF. Of course, this did not happen overnight, but slowly over the years following de Gaulle's takeover in 1958. In time, Mitterrand saw the great political advantage of allying with the French Communist party. In his book *Le Coup d'état permanent*, which appeared shortly before the 1965 presidential elections where he ran as the common candidate of the Left, Mitterrand stated that the Right in France was dominant because it had succeeded in keeping the "citizens who vote Communist in an electoral ghetto" and had rendered it "impossible to rally the popular forces."[62] Several years earlier, the Communist leader Waldeck Rochet told the central committee of the PCF, "François Mitterrand cannot ignore that anticommunism aids fascism and that . . . in the face of peril . . . it is indispensable that all republicans and antifascists unite. . . ."[63] During the last days of the Fourth Republic as the threat of civil war over Algeria and the possibility of a coup by de Gaulle loomed heavily over France, Mitterrand came to understand the urgency of linking progressive forces. When he began his career in 1946 with the UDSR, he had been content to utilize the hinge position of his party to influence national policy. As the Gaullist movement grew in strength at the end of the Fourth Republic, however, he realized that only large electoral coalitions could save France from right-wing domination. This lesson would not be lost on Mitterrand as France entered the Fifth Republic.

3

THE GAULLIST FIFTH REPUBLIC

The Second Resistance

1958–1981

. . . For Mitterrand, where there is a will there is a way.
Fundamentally, [he believes] the will of a man, a group of
men, a party can change things.

—Laurent Fabius

When the Algerian crisis catapulted de Gaulle into
power in May 1958 under the guise of a new Fifth Republic, Mitterrand's ministerial career came to a sudden halt. For the next twenty-
three years, he found himself in the political wilderness with others
who opposed de Gaulle and his heirs. Mitterrand had never before
been a member of a major political party, but in 1971 he became
secretary general of a new Socialist party that would be transformed
into the dominant party of France under his leadership. Early in the
Fifth Republic, he came to realize that if the Left wanted to come into
political equilibrium with the Right—one of Mitterrand's primary
objectives following de Gaulle's takeover—the noncommunist Left had
to forge an alliance with the Communists. With time, Mitterrand
found himself calling for "republican authenticity" and then "socialist
authenticity" as he prepared his battle plans against de Gaulle and his
supporters. The reemergence of the general on the French political
stage motivated Mitterrand to lead a second resistance—this time

against the Gaullists and the Right in general. De Gaulle and the Fifth Republic provided Mitterrand with a destiny.[1]

After a twenty-three-year battle with the Right, and a more subtle duel with the Communists on his left, Mitterrand emerged victorious in May and June 1981 when he became the first Socialist president of France elected through universal suffrage, while his party won an absolute majority in the National Assembly. Ironically, de Gaulle's takeover helped to restore the Left in France by encouraging Socialist and Communist unity. However, the reemergence of the general on the political stage in 1958 and the rise of a dynamic Socialist party in the 1970s had negative repercussions for the PCF at the ballot box.[2] By 1981 Mitterrand had accomplished a historic political victory over the Right and a less heralded triumph over the PCF. Persistence, tenacity, and shrewd political maneuvering contributed to his long march back to political power.[3]

From the beginning of the Fifth Republic, Mitterrand opposed de Gaulle's May 1958 takeover as an illegitimate coup d'état. A majority of French men and women, swept away by a strong wave of nationalism brought on by the Algerian war, supported the general's return to power and the death certificate he subsequently wrote for the Fourth Republic. The events that contributed to de Gaulle's reemergence as national leader began on May 13, 1958, with a demonstration by French *colons* (settlers) in Algiers against the French government, which had earlier indicated its willingness to be more conciliatory toward the Arab and Berber majority on the issue of Algerian independence, but in reality had been slow to take any action to that effect. Receiving support and encouragement from Gaullist supporters, a crowd stormed government buildings. Later, French troops in Algeria joined the rebellion. General de Gaulle, living in "retirement" 140 miles to the east of Paris in the village of Colombey-les-Deux-Eglises, refrained from criticizing the revolt and let it be known that he was ready and willing to assume power. Despite the fact that France faced the prospect of civil war over the crisis in Algeria, de Gaulle was nonetheless eager to assume the position of prime minister when he was called upon. The general was granted exceptional powers and the "right" to draw up a new constitution for adoption through a national referendum.

The general's assumption of power prompted an immediate response by the young political star of the Fourth Republic. On May 28 Mitterrand participated with Mendès-France, PCF leaders, and others in a massive demonstration in Paris, two to three hundred thousand strong, for a mile and a half through eastern Paris, from the place de la Bastille to the place de la Nation. Following the demonstration, de Gaulle conferred with political leaders, including Mitterrand, but not with the PCF. At this meeting Mitterrand told the general flatly that he would withhold his support because he (de Gaulle) had failed to condemn the French military revolt in Algeria. Later, Mitterrand wrote, "The only way to be at peace with myself was to refuse de Gaulle's takeover."[4] Mitterrand also said that "everything made me shun that dictatorship visible to the naked eye, beneath its innocent-looking mask."[5]

Besides Mitterrand, Mendès-France, a faction of the SFIO, and the Communists opposed de Gaulle's regaining power. In the National Assembly, Mitterrand was openly defiant in the debate over de Gaulle's investiture, stating:

> Since General de Gaulle invites us to keep quiet or allow ourselves to be silenced, it is now the time to tell the nation that those of us who fight for freedom and the sovereignty of the people, even if their hearts are full of concern and anxiety, will not fail to despair. There is much to do and France continues to exist. At the end of the day, with faith and with will, freedom will emerge victorious in a nation reconciled with itself. That hope is enough; . . . I vote against the investiture of General de Gaulle.[6]

When the vote was tallied, 329 deputies voted for de Gaulle, while 224 opposed his return to power. Mitterrand would remain in the opposition for the next twenty-three years of his political career.

Shortly after de Gaulle's takeover, Mitterrand, along with Mendès-France and an SFIO splinter group, attempted to form a non-Communist left alliance known as the Union of Democratic Forces, dedicated to opposing de Gaulle's new constitution. However, unity among the non-Communist Left dissipated due to the exodus of its former leaders, such as Mollet and Defferre, who joined de Gaulle's government.

Nevertheless, in de Gaulle's September 1958 referendum Mitterrand campaigned actively in the Nièvre against the abolition of the Fourth Republic and of the proportional representation voting procedure that had ensured the presence of numerous small parties under that republic. In the Nièvre, four-fifths of Mitterrand's constituency voted in favor of de Gaulle, and the nation as a whole voted by a large margin to adopt the new constitution. A further humiliation came to Mitterrand in the November elections to the National Assembly in which he lost his seat to a Gaullist, Jean Faulquier. Mitterrand was not alone in suffering a major setback. The Gaullist machine reduced the SFIO from 160 seats to 40, and the PCF managed to win only 10 seats in the new Assembly.

The only option for a professional politician like Mitterrand was to attempt to rebuild his local political base. After practicing law for a short period of time in partnership with Irène Dayan, the wife of his close friend Georges Dayan, Mitterrand returned to his constituency in the Nièvre in March 1959 and successfully ran for mayor of a small town, Château-Chinon. A short time later he became president of an association of mayors in the Nièvre and president of the region's general council. He also was able to obtain a seat on a regional economic development commission that was primarily Gaullist in composition. All of this paid off for Mitterrand in April 1959 when his constituency in Burgundy elected him to the Senate. He would have to wait until 1962 before making a successful bid for a seat in the National Assembly, but for the time being, the Senate seat provided him with national visibility.

Another development that kept him in the public eye was the observatory affair, a sordid scandal that echoed the affair of the leaks earlier in the 1950s and almost destroyed his political career. While Mitterrand may have been courageous in opposing de Gaulle's investiture, it earned him increased derision and hatred from the Right, a Right that seemed to think of him as enemy number one of the newly created Gaullist regime.

In the autumn of 1959 Mitterrand learned of a threat to his life by Algerian extremists. The bearer of this news was an extreme right-wing deputy, Robert Pesquet, who was an acquaintance of one of the policemen who had tried to smear the young minister in 1954. Pesquet told Mitterrand that he could not take part in a conspiracy against his life. Shortly thereafter, Mitterrand reportedly received threatening phone calls. On the night of October 15–16 at approximately 12:45 A.M. when he was driving home from a dinner engagement at the Brasserie Lipp on the Boulevard St. Germain, Mitterrand sensed that he was being followed. He proceeded to drive quickly through the Latin Quarter of Paris to the observatory near the Luxembourg Palace, jumped out of the car and threw himself behind a protective wall. Seconds later, submachine gun fire riddled Mitterrand's Peugeot 403. When the police arrived, Mitterrand failed to report Pesquet's earlier warning.

This bizarre murder attempt initially won Mitterrand a great deal of public support and sympathy. But several days after the incident, Pesquet went to the police and told them that Mitterrand had plotted his own assassination in order to embarrass supporters of French Algeria. Pesquet even produced two letters which allegedly detailed the plot. Later, the extreme right-wing newspaper *Rivarol* published Pesquet's account of the incident. Once this information reached the Parisian press, Mitterrand found himself involved in the midst of a major political scandal. The Senate even voted by a margin of 175 to 27 to take away his immunity as a result of the affair. Mitterrand believed that Pesquet and other right-wing politicians— including the present-day leader of the extremist National Front (*Front National*—FN), Jean-Marie Le Pen—were involved in this plot to frame him. As part of his defense, Mitterrand pointed out that Pesquet had approached other politicians earlier with the same warning, and that Mendès-France had received a similar threat. Mitterrand also told the Senate of a 1957 incident in which a deputy approached him during his tenure as minister of justice to plead his innocence in a plot to kill the French commander in Algeria—that deputy, said Mitterrand, was now the prime minister of France, Michel Debré. Twenty years after the observatory affair, Pesquet accused Debré of instigating the plot against Mitterrand.[7] Some political observers have argued that Mitterrand simply lost his sang-froid and was imprudent when the plot began; others have wondered why a man with the political savvy and experience of Mitterrand, often characterized as Machiavellian himself, would be such an easy prey for Pesquet.[8] While the case against Mitterrand was never finally settled and simply faded away as French scandals sometimes do, it certainly wounded him.

Whether the affair was a product of Mitterrand's machinations as the Right claimed, or whether it was part of a right-wing smear campaign as the victim claims, the result was that it heightened Mitterrand's anti-Gaullism and reinforced his determination to play a leading opposition role under the Fifth Republic. As one of his French biographers stated, after the observatory affair Gaullism became "the absolute evil" for the young and ambitious Mitterrand.[9] His hatred of

Gaullism and the Right in general would in time encourage him to rise above his animosity to the Communists in order to build an electoral alliance capable of defeating de Gaulle and his supporters. Yet with strong suspicion lingering in the public mind after the affair, Mitterrand's political credibility with the electorate would not improve significantly until the 1965 presidential elections, in which he would become the common candidate of the Left against General de Gaulle.

Not only did the reemergence of de Gaulle and the observatory affair turn Mitterrand into the primary opponent of the new regime, but these events also began to heighten his class consciousness. After 1959, for instance, his writings reflected a new awareness—in his mind de Gaulle and the bourgeoisie were inexorably linked. In *Ma part de vérité*, he wrote:

> At Jarnac, at Nevers, in my Paris street, in my Stalag alleyway I had already met them [bourgeoisie]. In a way, I was one of them; because we had the same background, because we spoke the same words in the same way, because we had received the rudiments of the same culture, because we wore the same clothes, they treated me as an accomplice or a partner—until the day I realized we had nothing to say to one another, the day I could bear to hear them no longer.[10]

The Right, he thought, would go to any length to preserve their power and privilege. The observatory affair changed Mitterrand. According to one of his close friends, André Rousselet, "The Observatoire was a social break for him—he isolated himself, then reconstructed a character for himself."[11] In Mitterrand's estimation, General de Gaulle and right-wing efforts to smear him discredited a system that he had once supported. At the same time, they pushed Mitterrand to the left. Eventually, he would embrace socialism and even align himself with the Communists in order to defeat his opponents.

From 1959 until 1963 Mitterrand traveled, wrote, and continued to criticize de Gaulle. In early 1961 he journeyed to the People's Republic of China where he met Mao Zedong for the first time. Following this trip to the Far East he wrote a book titled *La Chine au défi* (China under challenge) and began stating publicly that France should establish diplomatic relations with China. While he was impressed with the way that Chinese leadership had organized the far-flung nation, he was critical of Mao's continued propaganda campaign throughout the nation and the cult of personality that had developed around the Chinese leader.

Although Mitterrand took a progressive stand on China, it appeared that de Gaulle was the progressive reformer on a major issue dividing France, the Algerian question. In 1961, the general presented the electorate with a referendum on Algerian independence. While both the SFIO and the PCF called for a "no" vote on the Algerian referendum, in part, to mount opposition to de Gaulle, the Left failed to unite. The initial referendum carried by a relatively large margin. In the final referendum in 1962, the Left backtracked and called for a "yes" vote, realizing that the general had won over public opinion.

Mitterrand at this time criticized the growing personality cult surrounding de Gaulle. When the general began his campaign to strengthen the presidency of the republic by having the chief executive elected by universal suffrage, Mitterrand spoke out against the reform. Nevertheless, in a November 1962 referendum on this issue, two-thirds of the electorate voted in favor of de Gaulle's proposal. Under the Fourth Republic parliament reigned supreme and the president's power was disproportionately weak. The new voting system for the presidency now enhanced de Gaulle's personal power, a development that concerned Mitterrand considerably. In *Ma part de vérité* he wrote:

> From 1962—that is, since the time it had been decided that the election of the president of the Republic would take place by universal suffrage—I knew I would be a candidate. When? How? I could not predict it—I was alone. I had neither support nor party, nor Church, nor counter-Church, nor newspaper, nor public support. I had no money, and could expect none of the traditional, if discrete, sources of finance that are all too well known . . . .[12]

Ironically, the 1962 decision to elect the president of the republic directly helped to polarize France between Left and Right, which in time worked to Mitterrand's advantage. Mitterrand began to build his power base for an attempt at the Elysée by first gaining control over the "club movement," and by later assuming the leadership of a new Socialist party that would sign a historic electoral accord with the Communists.

The 1962 legislative elections were held after the Algerian settlement and in the midst of an economic boom that was linked to France's entry into the European Economic Community in the late 1950s and a rise in the general level of prosperity in the Western world during the 1960s. Partially as a result of these economic factors, the

Gaullist party, the Union for the New Republic (*Union pour la Nouvelle République*—UNR), won an absolute majority of seats in the National Assembly. Mitterrand, who was assisted by Socialists and Communists standing down for him in the Nièvre, was reelected to the Assembly. The opposition improved its position slightly over their poor showing in the 1958 elections, placing sixty-six SFIO members, forty-nine PCF candidates, and thirty-nine Radicals in the new Assembly. General de Gaulle's abolition of the proportional representation voting system in favor of a majority system worked against small parties in the 1962 elections and strengthened the formation of left/right blocs. This eventually helped to produce a striking bipolarization of the French electoral system. As a result, Mitterrand identified with the left bloc and began to plan strategy to increase the power of the Left in France. After 1962 it was clear that he had finally arrived on the left.[13] Mitterrand clearly revealed his new-found militancy in his 1964 book, *Le Coup d'état permanent*. This work aimed to injure the Right, especially de Gaulle and Debré, and it sought to reinforce Mitterrand's image as a dedicated opponent of the Gaullist regime as well. Mitterrand's rhetoric in this most recent publication had grown dramatically more hostile. He wrote:

> I call the Gaullist regime a dictatorship because, when all is said and done, that is exactly what it is like; because it is moving ineluctably toward a continuous strengthening of state power; and because it no longer depends on him [de Gaulle] to change direction. I am quite willing to concede that this dictatorship was established despite de Gaulle. I am quite willing to call this dictatorship by a pleasant name: *podestà*. A king without a crown seems to me even more to be feared.[14]

Mitterrand's hard-hitting polemic, appearing as it did on the eve of the 1965 presidential election, began to lift the veil of silence that had fallen over the opening phase of de Gaulle's presidency.

Slowly, the Socialists began to gain new allies. In particular, two organizations emerged that played an important role in the politics of the nation. One of them was the political club movement, which first emerged in the late 1950s and early 1960s and drew its support from the Center and Center-Right. To begin with, the clubs addressed problems of political disillusionment at the end of the Fourth Republic and avoided identification with a political party, but after 1962, some began to identify with the Left. The chief organization that emerged from the club movement was the Convention of Republican Institutions (*Convention des Institutions Républicaines*—CIR). Created in 1964 by one of Mitterrand's friends, Charles Hernu, the CIR represented more than fifty clubs with a membership of left-wing sympathizers who, for one reason or another, could not identify themselves with either the Socialists or the Radicals. Shortly thereafter, Mitterrand became president of CIR and used the organization to promote his own political ambitions.[15] It functioned as his organizational base before he joined the Socialist party.

The other important organization that emerged in the 1960s within the non-Communist Left was the Center of Socialist Study and Research (Centre d'Etudes et de Recherches Socialistes—CERES). This organization was led by graduates of the highly regarded Ecole Nationale d'Administration, such as Jean-Pierre Chevènement, Didier Motchane, and Pierre Guidoni. CERES adopted a Marxist approach to solving French problems and attempted to change the SFIO from within, intending to reform what they considered to be the "social mediocrity" of the party, which was declining rapidly in the face of the Gaullist political machine.[16] Later, at various junctures in the 1970s and the 1980s, CERES became an important ally of Mitterrand within a rejuvenated Socialist party.

For Mitterrand, the key event of the 1960s was the presidential election of 1965, an election that greatly enhanced his political stature as a leftist candidate. Ironically, Mitterrand, who eventually became the common candidate of the Left in the 1965 elections, initially supported the candidacy of Gaston Defferre, the SFIO mayor of Marseille, and even worked for Defferre's campaign organization, Horizon '80. Defferre, however, dropped out of the race because he refused to work with the PCF, though he needed its support. On the other hand, the PCF hesitated to run a candidate in 1965 for fear of suffering a major setback at the hands of the Gaullists. With Defferre out of the race, several of Mitterrand's associates promoted him as a candidate. When Guy Mollet of the SFIO promised support and when it was realized that the PCF would not create obstacles for Mitterrand, his candidacy became a reality. On the left, only the United Socialist Party (*Parti Socialiste Unifié*—PSU) opposed his campaign initially, but shortly thereafter gave its support. Mitterrand publicly announced his candidacy on September 9, 1965, and spoke in rather vague terms to his supporters. He told them that he opposed the vast personal power of de Gaulle, that he would respect laws and freedoms, and that he was pro-European. He emphasized that he was running as an independent candidate of the Left, and that he would accept the support of leftist parties but would not be willing to strike political deals with them.

While Mitterrand stood to lose a great deal by running against a formidable figure like de Gaulle, he also had a chance to make considerable gains, especially as he looked toward the future. He knew that he did not have a chance of winning against the general, but he was astute enough to realize that his own candidacy could enhance his political stature in France by making him the primary opposition figure to the Gaullist regime.

To aid Mitterrand's bid for the presidency, the non-Communist Left formed the Federation of the Democratic and Socialist Left (*Fédération de la Gauche Démocratique et Socialiste*—FGDS). This loosely-knit organization attempted to strengthen cooperation of leftist parties. Mitterrand desperately needed electoral cooperation because polls at the beginning of his campaign showed he had a mere 11 percent of the vote. With the support of the FGDS and the promise of the PCF's support, Mitterrand became the common candidate of the Left. Electoral cooperation on the left in the 1965 elections would point the way to the future for the pragmatic and tenacious Mitterrand. Two years earlier, writing in the newspaper *Le Courrier de la Nièvre*, published in his home constituency, Mitterrand had discussed his desire to use the PCF in his duel against de Gaulle. "My attitude toward the Communist party is simple: anything that helps in the struggle against and victory over a regime tending to the dictatorship of a single man and the establishment of a single party is good. Four or five million electors—who belong to the people, who are workers— vote Communist. To neglect their help and votes would be either culpable or, quite simply, stupid."[17] He had practiced the art of pragmatic politics under the Fourth Republic; under the Fifth Republic he perfected his art.

While Mitterrand toured France and campaigned actively, de Gaulle underestimated his challenger and failed to take him seriously, at least until the second round of the contest. Indicative of Mitterrand's hard-hitting campaign was his declaration in his televised address just before the first round: "[The Gaullist regime] is that of a single man . . . [who] will designate an unknown successor who will appoint his friends, a faction that will be worse than a party, an anonymous collection of interests and intrigues. I am not the representative of a party. I am not the representative of a coalition of parties. I am the candidate of all the Left, the warm-hearted Left. . . . To believe in justice and to believe in happiness, that is the message of the Left."[18] One unforeseen and controversial dimension of Mitterrand's candidacy emerged during the elections. He publicly asked for the repeal of a 1920 law forbidding the sale or advertising of contraceptives. While this play for women's votes would aid Mitterrand in later campaigns, it cost him votes among practicing Catholics who gave de Gaulle almost 90 percent of their vote in the first round. Nevertheless, Mitterrand won a strong 31.7 percent in the first round compared to de Gaulle's 44.6 percent. Only a few years earlier the general had won 78 percent of the vote in the 1958 referendum on the creation of the Fifth Republic and 62 percent in the 1962 referendum for direct presidential elections. The first round of the 1965 contest suggested that de Gaulle had begun to lose his grip on power.

Consequently, the incumbent took the second round more seriously and bombarded the electorate with a massive propaganda campaign. Despite endorsements for his campaign from such figures as Jean Monnet, the highly regarded proponent of European union, as well as from many of the almost one million repatriated Algerians who were discontented with de Gaulle's handling of the Algerian question, Mitterrand lost the second round in a surprisingly close vote—55.2 percent to 44.8 percent. The Left had lost, but the election had shown that it was possible to organize a non-Communist Left that would receive electoral cooperation from the Communists. Mitterrand realized that the power of a united Left could make the Right shudder. He now had a strategy for the future. Given his relative success in the 1965 presidential elections as an opponent of the Gaullist regime, he became a shadow president.

Due in part to Communist insistence, the PCF and the FGDS signed an electoral accord in December 1966 that pledged their cooperation in the upcoming legislative elections. In this election, like the 1965 presidential election, Mitterrand and the Left attacked the authoritarianism of the Gaullist regime. When the final tally of the second round was counted, the FGDS increased its representation in the National Assembly by twenty-eight seats and the PCF gained thirty-two new deputies. Now, the Left had 193 seats compared to 244 for the Gaullists. It appeared as if Mitterrand's belief that the left and right blocs could be balanced was realistic. Despite some disagreements between Mitterrand and the PCF—notably over NATO and the Common Market—the emerging Socialist leader and the Communists found themselves united in their opposition to de Gaulle's authoritarianism and his efforts to provide France with a nuclear strike force. The future looked bright for Mitterrand and the Left.

The presidential election of 1965 was a high point in the rising political career of Mitterrand. But in the late 1960s his career took an unforeseen turn for the worse as a result of the 1968 student-worker revolt and his imprudent response to it. The massive uprising of May–June 1968, which grew out of a demand for university reform, an end to the war in Vietnam, large-scale reform in France, and a reversal of growing unemployment, almost toppled de Gaulle but also came near to ending Mitterrand's political career. De Gaulle's mistake was not taking the revolt seriously as hundreds of thousands of young people and their supporters, including a sizable segment of the working class, demonstrated in Paris and elsewhere in France, with nine million people on strike against the Gaullist regime by late May. This nationwide protest, coupled with a wave of factory occupations, seriously weakened the government. Mitterrand's mistake was acting too quickly in an obvious attempt to take political advantage of the situation. On May 28 he called a press conference and told reporters that the crisis in France was so extensive that the state no longer existed and that a provisional government should be formed immediately. Mitterrand suggested that Mendès-France—with whom he had not discussed the matter—serve as prime minister and stated that he himself would run for president. With France paralyzed by the student-worker revolt, de Gaulle addressed French citizens on television and promised a referendum on his government. After de Gaulle's address, Mitterrand declared, "The voice that we just heard came from the distant past. It is the voice of 18 Brumaire [Bonaparte's coup d'état of 1799] and the voice of the thirteenth of May. It is the one that represents the power of a minority that is insulated from the people; it is the voice of dictatorship."19

Despite Mitterrand's denunciation of the general and the seriousness of the domestic situation, de Gaulle was able to save his government. To do so, the general used a strong dose of anticommunism. He told the electorate in his televised address that the student-worker revolt was part of a Communist plot to bring him down, a clear distortion of the situation but one that saved his government, at least for the time being. In reality, the only political party that supported the students was the United Socialist party. The overwhelming vote for de Gaulle was a testimonial to Mitterrand's imprudence, haste, and tactical error, and made him appear as a grand opportunist. In the June elections the Left suffered a humiliating defeat, with the FGDS winning a mere 57 seats compared to its previous 118, and the Communists capturing only 33, compared to their former 73. As a leader of the opposition, Mitterrand appeared defeated.

By late 1968 and 1969 it seemed as if Mitterrand's hope for a united non-Communist Left with electoral support from the Communists was no more than a dream of the past. Although Mitterrand was interested in seeing a new socialist party emerge from the groups constituting the FGDS, infighting and criticism of Mitterrand's actions in 1968 made this practically impossible. In November 1968 Mitterrand resigned as head of the FGDS. Just three months earlier Soviet troops had rolled into Prague to crush Alexander Dubcek's effort to liberalize the Czechoslovak state. Consequently, Communism, whether in the Soviet Union or France, came under heavy attack. At the time, Gaston Defferre was still trying to construct a non-Communist "third force," which he unsuccessfully employed in the 1969 presidential elections.

In the 1969 contest, necessitated by de Gaulle's resignation following his loss of a referendum on the relatively minor question of restricting the power of the Senate, and the creation of twenty-one regional councils, the SFIO veteran Defferre and his party suffered a major blow. While the PCF suggested a united electoral effort with Mitterrand as a common candidate, the SFIO rejected the idea. The PCF, unwilling to accept Defferre, ran its own candidate, Jacques Duclos. The PSU, another leftist party in the race, advanced the candidacy of a young and rising political star, Michel Rocard. The results of the first round of the 1969 election proved disastrous for Defferre and the SFIO, with the Socialist candidate winning only 5 percent of the vote compared to almost 22 percent for Duclos. Thus, General de Gaulle's heir, Georges Pompidou, won the election with relative ease.

The experience in 1965 and 1969 clearly demonstrated what was necessary if the Left wanted to bring the two voting blocs in France into equilibrium. Electoral cooperation was the key to a successful Left; without it the Gaullists and the Right could expect to be the political masters of France indefinitely. This was exactly the conclusion reached by Mitterrand in *Ma part de vérité*.[20] Partly autobiographical, this book published in 1969 traced the author's political evolution under the Fourth and Fifth Republics and told readers that the choice for France was essentially between capitalism and socialism. It also stressed the importance of working with the PCF which still controlled some five million voters. While Mitterrand called for electoral cooperation with the PCF, he did not refrain from attacking what he saw as repressive Soviet communism. Nonetheless, learning from past history, Mitterrand believed that the future of the Left as well as his own political future lay with unity. With the SFIO humiliated in the 1969 elections and the Left fragmented, Mitterrand's appeal for unity seemed sound to many progressive forces in France.

The 1969 election debacle led to the birth of a new party in July of that year—the Socialist party. This new party realized, unlike the SFIO, that it had to ally itself with the PCF to prevent disaster at the polls. The PS was headed by Alain Savary, who contended that the Left must unify in order to generate policy and plan strategy against the Right and Center-Right. Although Mitterrand eventually joined the PS in 1971 and became its leader, he initially labeled the PS as a "hundred years old before it was born,"[21] because this new party apparently carried much of the baggage of the old SFIO.

For Mitterrand, the formation of the Socialist party signified an important historical juncture. Ironically, the man without a party became the first secretary of the PS in 1971, only days before he officially joined it, and eventually transformed it into the dominant party of France. Prior to this time Mitterrand had shied away from large parties and had built his reputation as a man representing small political parties or groupings. The force of Gaullism in France and his hatred of it convinced him that only a large political formation could lead to victory. This is why he joined the PS. Thus, at the 1971 PS Congress at Epinay on June 11–13, Mitterrand's CIR merged with the PS. In this enlarged party, Mitterrand won the votes of CIR members in addition to the support of Defferre, Mauroy, and the left-wing CERES group. Shortly after Mitterrand's election to the position of first secretary of the PS, the party adopted its *Changer la vie* program, a comprehensive outline for reform in France that called for creating economic democracy, providing citizens with more power, improving the quality of life, and launching a "new internationalism." This program prepared the way for an electoral agreement with the PCF. In 1972, Mitterrand also assumed the vice presidency of the Socialist International. With a party behind him now committed to leftist unity, Mitterrand, sometimes referred to as the "foreign prince" by some PS leaders,[22] quickly began to build a formidable political force.

Shortly after his entry into the PS at Epinay, Mitterrand traveled to another part of the world to visit a nation where a united Left had just come to power, Chile. There he met Salvador Allende who had become head of the first freely elected Marxist government in Latin America. When he returned to France, Mitterrand praised Allende's government and his nationalization plan. Later, when the Chilean leader was overthrown—as the French saw it, by the machinations of the CIA—Mitterrand wondered if he would become the Allende of France.[23] For the Left, the overthrow of the Allende government symbolized the evils of American imperialism.

In 1972, as the winds of détente blew across the East-West divide, the new PS and the PCF concluded negotiations for an electoral alliance between the two parties. Mitterrand and Georges Marchais, head of the PCF, signed a historic pact known as the Common Program. This accord called not only for electoral cooperation between the Socialists and the Communists, but also for nationalizations should the Left come to power. Under the terms of the Common Program, the PS and the PCF pledged to nationalize nine major industrial groups, including the defense, computer, chemical, electrical, pharmaceutical, and textile industries. Prior to signing the agreement with the Communists, Mitterrand had argued in another book, *Un socialisme du possible* (Socialism of the possible), that nationalizations were a key means by which to introduce socialism to France.[24] Later, he called the nationalization program his "economic strike force."[25] Under the terms of the 1972 accord, the PCF agreed to support the PS on the Common Market and the Atlantic Alliance, and both parties pledged to support the democratization of the Common Market and to work for the reduction of the two military blocs, NATO and the Warsaw Pact. The Movement of Left Radicals (*Mouvement des Radicaux de Gauche*—MRG), a small center-left party, also signed the Common Program.

Mitterrand's objectives in agreeing to the Common Program were threefold. First, he wanted to build a "flexible and modern" party, equal in strength to the PCF. Second, in any future pact with the PCF he wanted to make it the junior partner. Third, he wanted to see the Left become the majority in France.[26] Mitterrand astutely realized that the isolation of the PCF meant the isolation of the Socialists and the continued dominance of the Right. One way of enhancing the non-Communist Left in France was by aligning with the Communists, because an electoral alliance with the PCF would give Mitterrand access to the five million people who traditionally voted Communist. In a revealing statement made at the Socialist International meeting in Vienna just days after he signed the Common Program, Mitterrand told his socialist audience: "Our fundamental objective is to rebuild a great Socialist party on the terrain occupied by the Communist party . . . and to show that of the five million Communist voters, three million can vote Socialist. This is the reason for the accord [Common Program]."[27] What Mitterrand intended was to win back from the PCF the large number of voters lost by the old SFIO, which had passed out of existence with the founding of the PS.[28] Thus, his immediate tasks after signing the Common Program were to develop a Union of the Left and to capture votes for the Socialist party.[29] (Both the PS and PCF realized that the Common Program entailed cooperation and competition.) For Mitterrand, the Union of the Left could help him in his longstanding duel with the Right and, in time, weaken his opponent on the left, the PCF.

To publicize and to explain the Common Program to the electorate, Mitterrand published still another book, *La Rose au poing* (The rose in the fist). This volume explicitly outlined the program of the newly formed leftist union: launching nationalizations, increasing the minimum wage, reducing the work week, lowering the retirement age, providing equal pay for women, decentralizing power, and introducing a supreme court. Once again, Mitterrand used the power of his pen to popularize his political message.

The first election test for the new leftist union came in 1973. For the PS and for the Left in general, their new and dynamic image paid off handsomely. The PS, for instance, captured 21 percent of the vote, only one percentage point behind the PCF. These elections represented the first time since 1936 that the Socialists had won almost as many votes as the Communists. By 1976–77, the PS would become the first party of the French Left.

Building on the 1973 elections, Mitterrand and his colleagues convened a special Socialist congress in which the party welcomed new and important members. Michel Rocard and about 1,500 members from the PSU as well as thousands of members from Edmond Maire's French Confederation of Democracy and Labor (*Confédération Française Démocratique du Travail*—CFDT), France's second largest labor union, joined the ranks of the newly created Socialist party.

Rocard and the CFDT members brought to the PS a strong *autogestion* (self-management) wing that provided the new party with a second approach to socialism. *Autogestion* was a rather vague notion that many found appealing in post-1968 France because the concept emphasized decentralization and grass-roots democracy. Besides the antistatist dimension of *autogestion*, Rocard and his followers also advocated economic efficiency and modernizatoin. The effort to enlarge the PS attracted two men who would later become important advisers to Mitterrand—Jacques Delors and Edgard Pisani. While Delors had been an adviser to the Gaullist prime minister Jacques Chaban-Delmas, Pisani had been a Gaullist minister.[30] These new recruits to the Socialist party, however, foreshadowed the emergence of a broad-based party, a "catch-all party," which would be fraught with internal contradictions. As Mitterrand himself later said of the PS, "It cannot be both a big party and homogeneous. We must learn to bear contradictions. Unanimity is dangerous, and I fear nothing more than conformists. The party must organize its own contradictions."[31] Mitterrand, however, proved to be a great juggler who could play the various tendencies within the PS against one another and to his own advantage as well.

Within the PS, three major tendencies or factions emerged. One was represented by the Mitterrandists who, in many ways, were an extension of the Radical tradition. They wanted reform but not a complete break with capitalism. A second faction was led by Rocard and his supporters who sought social democracy with a strong measure of *autogestion*. The third tendency formed around Chevènement and the CERES group which stood for revolutionary socialism. From the founding of the PS until its Metz Congress in 1979, Mitterrand kept the radical CERES faction in a minority position to ensure that this group would not frighten away moderate voters. To accomplish this "centering," Mitterrand aligned himself with Rocard, sometimes referred to as Mitterrand's *"homme-gadget"* (literally a gadget-man, someone that Mitterrand uses to his own advantage).[32] Later, however, after the 1978 legislative elections when Rocard challenged him for the presidential nomination of the PS, Mitterrand aligned himself with the CERES faction and pushed the Rocardians into a minority position within the party. At this time, Mitterrand said of Rocard, "This character wants power. Well, he shall have war. . . . And I can tell you that it will be [waged] without pity."[33] Given the various tendencies within the PS and Mitterrand's juggling ability, it became a party capable of projecting various images to fit different political situations, a party for all seasons.

The political situation in 1974, despite some problems on the international scene for the PS, allowed the PS and the Union of the Left (an alliance between the PS, PCF, and relatively small Left Radicals, MRG, that included an agreement on electoral cooperation and the Common Program) to demonstrate their strength. In the 1974 presidential election, following the untimely death of President Pompidou (1969–74) due to a long and difficult bout with cancer, Mitterrand entered the political ring once again as the common candidate. This time his principal opponent was Valéry Giscard d'Estaing, a former finance minister under both de Gaulle and Pompidou. To prepare for the election campaign, Mitterrand organized his own team of experts that shunned Chevènement for the less radical Jacques Attali, a man who had a reputation as a brilliant young economist and writer. With Attali's help, Mitterrand received tutoring in economics to counter criticism that he lacked knowledge and experience in this area. Mitterrand, too, realized that in France one must beware of finance ministers because traditionally they have been popular presidential candidates.

While the Union of the Left organized around Mitterrand, an international issue created the potential for friction between the PS and the PCF. The issue was the revolution in Portugal. The PS sided with the Socialist faction in Portugal led by Mario Soares, while the Communists backed the pro-Soviet Alvaro Cunhal. Fortunately for Mitterrand, this issue did not greatly hamper leftist unity in France in the 1974 presidential contest.

The 1974 election campaign centered largely around the Common Program of the Left and Giscard's free-market approach to the economy. France at the time was ripe for a national debate on economic issues, especially because in the mid-1970s a number of studies, including an Organization for Economic Cooperation and Development (OECD) report published after the election, showed that of all Western nations, France had the largest gap between rich and poor. Furthermore, the first "oil shocks" were beginning to be felt in Europe and inflation was quickly rising. After the first round of voting in the 1974 election, Mitterrand was in a strong position to capture the Elysée since he had won more than 43 percent of the vote, compared to 33 percent for Giscard, and 15 percent for the Gaullist Chaban-Delmas.

Between the two rounds of voting, Mitterrand and Giscard agreed to a two-hour television debate, an exchange that gave the edge to the former finance minister. With twenty million viewers watching, Giscard, generally considered an excellent TV performer, outshone his challenger on various aspects of the economy and portrayed Mitterrand as a man of the past. When the Socialist leader blamed the rising inflation rate in France on Giscard and his supporters, Giscard adroitly placed the blame on the Arabs. Many French citizens thought this was the case. This debate demonstrated the importance of television in French politics and revealed that Mitterrand would have to improve his media image as well as his grasp of economic issues. In the second round of voting, Mitterrand captured 49.1 percent of the vote, while Giscard won 50.9 percent, the difference being only a few hundred thousand votes. Despite this second defeat in a presidential contest and the emergence of a younger generation of Socialist leaders—Rocard, Chevènement, and others—Mitterrand remained the primary opposition figure in France. He met Giscard again in a televised debate in the midst of the 1981 presidential contest in which he worked closely with a public relations specialist to enhance his image on the all-powerful TV screen. Mitterrand had learned his lesson.

Despite the 1974 loss to Giscard, public opinion polls showed in the mid-1970s that Mitterrand's party was the most popular in France, and that the PS had become the first party of the Left. The strength of the Socialist party was clearly seen in its increasing membership rolls and its ability to attract voters. From 1971 to 1978, the number of members in the PS more than doubled, from approximately 80,000 to over 180,000.[34] In 1981, PS membership rolls showed more than 200,000 adherents.[35] Election results revealed similar trends. The March 1976 cantonal elections proved to be the strongest Socialist showing since 1936, with the PS receiving a stunning 30.8 percent of the vote, compared to 17.3 percent for the PCF.[36] The March 1977 municipal elections brought another victory to the PS and to the Left in general. In these elections the Left won an unprecedented 54 percent of the vote and captured an additional thirty-two cities and towns with populations of more than 30,000 inhabitants. After the elections the Left controlled three-quarters of the large cities of France.

In spite of the alliance between the Socialists and Communists, the relations between them remained highly competitive. With the emergence of a dominant Socialist party in France and the winds of Eurocommunism blowing through Italy and Spain,[37] PCF leader Marchais attempted to promote a new image. At the twenty-second PCF congress in February 1976, the Communists dropped the notion of the "dictatorship of the proletariat" from their rhetoric. The following year the PCF leadership, without debate from within the party, announced that it now favored a nuclear strike force for France. Not to be outdone by the PCF and with an eye toward the electorate, the Socialist party followed the Communist lead and also decided in 1978 to support a French nuclear strike force. Both parties had dramatically reversed themselves on the issue of nuclear weapons. Then the PCF began to put direct pressure on the PS. In 1977, prior to the 1978 legislative elections—elections that the Left was expected to win— Marchais and his comrades provoked a rupture in the Common Program by demanding that the agreement be revised. The PCF insisted that the number of industries targeted for nationalization be increased. According to many observers, including intellectuals close to the PCF such as Louis Althusser and Jean Elleinstein, Marchais' objective was to prevent further gains at the polls by the Socialists.[38] Mitterrand's response to the Communists' new demands was blunt, "Yes to the Common Program, no to a Communist program!"[39] With a visible split now on the left, the Union of the Left failed to win the 1978 legislative elections as expected. However, this rupture with the PCF helped the Socialists because it bought the PS candidate many centrist votes.[40] The PS gained nine new seats for a total of 110 in the National Assembly, while the number of votes received by the PCF represented the worst showing for the Communists since 1945.[41]

The rise of Mitterrand's Socialist party in the 1970s can be attributed to a number of key factors. One of the most important reasons for the success of the Socialists was the astute political leadership of Mitterrand himself, an agile politician who skillfully guided a heterogeneous party comprised of three major factions. A reformed Socialist party also aided the Socialists at the polls. The PS's opening to the Left in 1972, when it signed the Common Program with the PCF, strengthened the appeal of the Socialists with left-wing voters. The Common Program also helped the PS because it depicted the Socialists as reformers who had a well-publicized plan to ameliorate many of the deep-seated problems facing the republic. Also contributing to the rise of the PS were significant changes in the economic and social structure of contemporary France. During the postwar years,

France became more industrialized, more urban, and more secularized, changes that created a large base for the Socialists in the 1970s and early 1980s. Persistent economic problems—namely unemployment, inflation, and great social inequalities—festered in France during the 1970s and paved the way for the emergence of the PS. Finally, the ability of Mitterrand and the PS to remain firm with the Communists, especially during the 1977–81 period, convinced many French voters that the Socialists would not be captives of the PCF if the PS came to power.[42]

While the Socialist party increased its popular support and became the first party of the French Left, some within the PS were concerned that Mitterrand, a two-time loser in presidential contests, would not be the best candidate to represent the party in the 1981 elections. Much to his displeasure, Mitterrand was confronted in the late 1970s with a major challenge within the Socialist party. In 1978 Rocard activated his own campaign for the presidency, gaining the support of Mauroy and a number of other Socialists. Responding to this challenge, Mitterrand loyalists said that Rocard's candidacy was desired by Giscard in order to divide the Socialists and facilitate another right-wing victory at the polls. At the 1979 Metz Congress of the PS, as mentioned earlier, Mitterrand utilized an adroit political maneuver to win additional support within the party to counter Rocard's challenge. Elevating Chevènement and the left-wing CERES faction to a majority position, Mitterrand forced the Rocardians into a minority role.[43] This political maneuver provided him with sufficient support to maintain his leadership of the party and also provided the PS with a new left-wing profile during a period when the Socialists and the PCF were feuding. This would help to attract Communist votes in the upcoming presidential elections as well.

Many of the reasons mentioned above also shed light on Mitterrand's victory in 1981 after three tries at the presidency; but a number of short-term economic, political, institutional, and personality factors also played a part in the Socialist leader's long march to the Elysée. First and foremost was a serious deterioration of the economy under Giscard and the emergence of new economic problems that proved extremely difficult to solve. Pushed along by the oil shocks of the 1970s, inflation in France rose from 3.4 percent in 1974 to 13 percent on the eve of the 1981 elections. During the same period, unemployment tripled, hitting 7.4 percent in 1981, with almost two million people out of work—60 percent of them women.[44] Giscard had attempted to solve the twin problems of inflation and unemployment by backing the so-called Barre plan that had been pursued since 1976 by Prime Minister Raymond Barre. What Barre wanted to do was to maintain the external balance of payments and to foster a healthy rate of growth. He cut state support to many industries, hoping that French business would become more efficient and competitive. Barre hoped, too, that as a result of the removal of price controls, business would make more profits and increase its levels of investment. In order to minimize some of the short-run problems of his long-term strategy, Barre sought to increase wages, social security benefits, and unemployment compensation. Giscard's prime minister felt that this quasi-supply-side approach to the economy would minimize the possibility of social upheaval, and at the same time provide French business with time to modernize.[45] For many, Barre's plan was a dismal failure because the economy failed adequately to respond to his measures.

Mitterrand, on the other hand, promised voters a different approach to the economic crisis. Besides the Common Program, he also offered voters a specific set of remedies and proposals that were outlined in a PS manifesto adopted in January 1981, the famous "110 Propositions for France" which became the platform of the Socialist party. For a liberal democracy like France, with its great gaps between the rich and the poor and numerous social inequalities, the 110 Propositions constituted a radical program for change. In addition to calling for the nationalization of key industries, the PS also promised that it would decentralize state power, reduce the presidential mandate from seven to five years, increase the minimum wage, reduce the work week to thirty-five hours, support equal opportunity and pay for women, create more than 200,000 public-sector jobs, increase state allocations to research so that 2.5 percent of the GNP would be devoted to research efforts, bring private schools into a unified public education system, create a decentralized and pluralistic radio and television network, and even give the vote to immigrants in local elections after five years of residency in France. On foreign policy issues the 110 Propositions called for the removal of Soviet troops from Afghanistan, supported the rights of Polish workers, condemned U.S. support of dictatorships in Latin America, advocated a North-South dialogue to promote a new world economic order, and favored the development of an independent nuclear deterrent policy for France.[46] In reality, the 110 Propositions represented a slightly toned-down version of the CERES position within the PS. The document envisioned a transition to socialism via a "Third Way" that was different from Eastern Europe and Scandinavian social democracy.

To further amplify their program for the future, Mitterrand and the PS published a book on the eve of the 1981 elections titled *Projet socialiste pour la France des années 80* (The Socialist project: For France in the 1980s). Written under the direction of Chevènement and the CERES group, this volume, too, reflected the leftist bent of its authors. The 380-page document stated, "In [our] daily life, we clearly see . . . that the substance of France is more menaced by capitalism than by the USSR."[47] This campaign document also asserted that one of the party's major tasks was "to break with the international capitalist order."[48]

There was indeed a strong desire among the electorate for economic change. Results of a poll released after the elections revealed that reducing the work week to thirty-five hours, as the PS had suggested, was favored by 51 percent of the respondents; increasing the number of civil servants by 210,000 per year by 45 percent; setting the retirement age for men at sixty years of age was supported by 88 percent; increasing paid vacations to five weeks was favored by 76 percent; nationalizing major industries was advocated by 43 percent; imposing a wealth tax was called for by 72 percent; raising the minimum wage was favored by 81 percent; and decreasing wage differentials was supported by 72 percent.[49] Mitterrand's program for reform, as outlined in the 110 Propositions and the *Projet socialiste* found support among a relatively large sector of the electorate. While some voters simply wanted to change various aspects of the economy, such as unemployment and inflation, others desired structural changes, such as nationalizations and a hefty wealth tax.[50] Nevertheless, the strong desire for reform worked to Mitterrand's advantage in the 1981 elections.

Significant political considerations also undermined Giscard's leadership and aided Mitterrand's drive for the presidency. As president, Giscard always maintained an aristocratic style, despite his occasional dinners with average citizens, his invitation to immigrant workers to join the president for breakfast, or his declaration that he was the "citizen candidate" in the 1981 elections. As an orator, the incumbent president was eloquent, but was not a man of the people. While Giscard's rhetoric asked that the French help him build an "advanced liberal society," he often gave the impression that he was a monarch or an imperial president. Reportedly, at official dinners he insisted on being served first from a gold platter. Some press speculation about his extramarital affairs also surfaced prior to 1981 and did little to bolster Giscard's public image. As one noted political authority on France stated, "Giscard discredited himself in many ways before 1981."[51] Moreover, television, which played an increasing role in French elections, allowed the public to make judgments based on the images created by Giscard and his Socialist opponent. (Mitterrand had improved his television performances by hiring public relations consultants and receiving tutoring on economic and financial questions.) While Giscard was an excellent debater on or off television, his public image appeared tarnished prior to the 1981 elections.

In addition to having image problems, Giscard also faced criticism for his political decisions. For instance, he further centralized power, especially in the university system where he helped to destroy the limited autonomy won by the academy in 1968. He also centralized the courts, setting up a new emergency tribunal known as the State Security Court that had ad hoc power to deal with terrorism and general security matters. He also supported laws that gave the French police wide-ranging power as well.[52] In many ways, the incumbent seemed out of step with his times.

Another political problem for Giscard was that he lost the support of two significant voting groups in France, the young and women. After his 1974 election, he had enfranchised the eighteen- to twenty-one-year-olds, adding almost six million new voters to the rolls. Yet these new voters directly experienced the impact of rising unemployment and inflation—as did women—and consequently in 1981 twice as many young voters marked their ballots for Mitterrand as for the incumbent.[53] Women, too, swung to the left in 1981 due in large measure to their economic plight under Giscard and to the supportive image that Mitterrand projected as a presidential candidate. The 1981 elections marked the first time since women were given the right to vote in 1944 that a majority of the female electorate voted for a leftist candidate.[54] The youth vote and the vote of women ensured a victory for Mitterrand and an end to the incumbent's tenure as president.

As if these problems were not enough, Giscard made some serious political blunders on the eve of the 1981 presidential campaign. On September 17, 1980 the well-known satirical newspaper *Le Canard Enchaîné* charged that Giscard had taken diamonds as a personal gift from the tyrant Emperor Bokassa of the Central African Republic.[55] Then, on October 3 a right-wing group exploded a bomb at a synagogue on the rue Copernic that resulted in four deaths and numerous injuries. Instead of denouncing this action, the president remained silent for a long period,[56] giving the impression that he was soft on right-wing terrorists as well as anti-Semitic.

One of the most important political considerations that explains the defeat of Giscard in 1981 centers around the split between the incumbent and the ambitious Jacques Chirac, a determined Gaullist who had served as Giscard's first prime minister (1974–76) and who won a hard-fought election battle against Giscard's candidate in 1977 for mayor of Paris (he was reelected in 1983 and 1989). The antagonisms between the two men were more personal than ideological. After the first round of the 1981 election, Chirac did not formally instruct his supporters to back Giscard in the final round; Chirac simply told his loyalists that he himself would vote for the incumbent. In the final round, 16 percent of Gaullist voters transferred their votes to Mitterrand, while 11 percent of Chirac's voters abstained.[57] Later, Giscard charged that Chirac's failure to endorse him amounted to "premeditated treason."[58]

Mitterrand had his own problems with Communist leader Georges Marchais and the PCF, but was able to overcome them. Despite the fact that between 1977 and 1981 the PCF had increased its attacks on Mitterrand and the Socialists in an effort to minimize PS gains with the electorate, the Communists were eventually forced to support the PS after the first round. Marchais's name was among the ten candidates, including three women, on the ballot. However, the poor performance of the PCF in the first round, where it gained only 15.54 percent of the vote, left the Communists with only one viable option—support Mitterrand in the final round. All the while, Giscard had counted on a split between the PS and the PCF to assist his own bid for a second term. Thus, while the electoral strength of Chirac's Gaullist party hurt Giscard, the electoral weakness of the PCF actually helped Mitterrand.

Another political consideration that played a role in the election was Mitterrand's style. Generally he was viewed as a man of culture, intelligence, and deep-seated humanism. Mitterrand's image—although he was considered Machiavellian by his opponents, especially on the Right—was far removed from Giscard's aristocratic persona. For decades the Socialist leader kept his name and his pragmatic and nondoctrinaire vision of politics alive in the National Assembly, in his three presidential campaigns, and in his books. In 1980, just in time for the presidential campaign of 1981, Mitterrand published yet another book, *Ici et maintenant* (Here and now), a frank discussion of his views on a number of subjects, including the "Giscard state," relations with the Communists, and NATO. He criticized Giscard for his monarchist tendencies, including his tight control over the broadcasting media. Concerning the PCF, Mitterrand defended the electoral alliance with the Communists and insisted that they could be forced to change. On the subject of NATO, he charged that it was a "phony alliance" because the United States used it as a front to exploit Europe, especially economically. It represented a phony alliance, too, because it demanded only that the United States consult its partners in the case of aggression, nothing more. A Soviet attack on Western Europe, claimed Mitterrand, would not automatically trigger a U.S. response.[59] In this particular instance, his bold language and his ability to publicize his views eloquently through his writing helped to shape Mitterrand's image as a leader. Thus, his humanism, his extensive political experience, his tenacity, and his skillful leadership of the PS all contributed to making him a successful candidate in 1981.

Institutional considerations also aided Mitterrand's election bid. The president of France is elected for a seven-year renewable term. Since Giscard had already served one term, a second term would mean that he might be head of state for a total of fourteen years; de Gaulle himself had served only eleven years. Mitterrand charged that fourteen years was too long for any person to be president and advocated changing the Constitution to shorten the president's tenure to five years.[60] (As president, Mitterrand to date has not reduced the presidential mandate.) Another institutional problem concerned the vast power in domestic and foreign affairs accorded to the president under the constitution of the Fifth Republic. Giscard, of course, had often used these powers to his own advantage, while Mitterrand had opposed the power granted to the president as early as 1958. A third institutional consideration that had great significance in the 1981 election was the question of *alternance*, the change from a right-wing to a left-wing government or vice versa. For twenty-three years the Right had dominated the French political system; many voters sensed that a change was needed.[61] During the campaign, Giscard presented himself as the only candidate who could bring change to France without harmful consequences. Mitterrand, however, combined an image of both reform and stability to counter the charges of Giscard and others that the Socialists and their Communist allies would bring chaos to France. These institutional considerations weighed heavy on the minds of voters in the spring of 1981.[62]

In addition, there were a number of personal and psychological factors that contributed to Mitterrand's successful campaign. One was his ability to project the image of an international statesman, but one feared by the Soviet Union. Prior to the campaign, Mitterrand traveled to China for a two-week visit which helped to underscore his capacity for statesmanship. Mitterrand was also aided inadvertently by the Soviet Union. When the Soviets invaded Afghanistan in December 1979, Mitterrand denounced their actions; when the Polish government clamped down on the Solidarity movement at Soviet insistence at the end of 1980, Mitterrand was again critical, despite the facts that the PS was aligned with the PCF and that the French Communists supported Soviet involvement in both Afghanistan and Poland. Mitterrand's Socialist party also played a leading role in encouraging the Socialist International to condemn the repression in Poland. During the French presidential campaign itself, the Soviet newspaper *Pravda* published an editorial praising Giscard for a positive foreign policy and suggested that Mitterrand's policy toward the Soviet Union would be negative.[63] For many in France, the *Pravda* editorial, widely reported in the French press, suggested that Mitterrand would take a firm stand against the Soviet Union, something that many in France favored anyway with a "new Cold War" beginning to cast its long shadow across East and West. Therefore, before the election, Mitterrand appeared more vigilant toward the Soviet Union than Giscard.

Another factor that influenced the election was the campaign strategy used by the Socialists. Mitterrand's public relations advisers decided that in order to defeat Giscard the technocrat, the Socialist candidate must appear as a man who was reasonable and open on all problems. In the campaign itself, Mitterrand presented himself as the candidate who would represent all of France. In this regard, he attempted to appeal to ecologists by using slogans like "nature is important to us all," or to the female electorate with "justice for women."[64] Following the advice of Jacques Séguéla and other public relations experts, the Socialists plastered France with a poster depicting Mitterrand's face with a caption above his head reading "La Force

Tranquille" (The calm force). The Socialists then utilized a highly effective poster showing Mitterrand before a village with its church bell tower, sky, and background awash with the blue, white, and red of the republic. This poster, of course, attempted to associate Mitterrand with an image of an eternal France, suggesting a candidate with strong ties to the land who favored continuity, not disruption of tradition.[65] An earlier campaign poster portrayed Mitterrand with the slogan, "Socialism, An Idea Which Is Making Its Way."[66] This association with steady but sure change and with *la France profonde* appealed to many voters.

The campaign also saw the Socialists round up celebrity support for their candidate. For instance, Françoise Sagan, Willy Brandt, Léopold Senghor, and others like them publicly voiced their support for Mitterrand. Between the first and the second round of voting, more than fifty television and motion picture directors and actors signed a statement supporting the Socialist candidate, stating that the nation under Giscard had witnessed "a veritable cultural and social decline." Some of the better-known signatories included Henri Costa-Gavras, Michel Piccoli, and François Truffaut.[67]

A last, but significant, factor in the campaign was Mitterrand's appearance in a televised debate with Giscard that was viewed by thirty million people. The debate was broadcast after the first round of the presidential contest in which Mitterrand had won 25.84 percent of the vote, compared to Giscard's 28.31 percent, Chirac's 17.99 percent, and Marchais's 15.34 percent. With the memory of his unspectacular performance in the 1974 debate with Giscard still fresh in his mind, Mitterrand sought coaching from Séguéla and was able to improve his image over his 1974 effort. When Giscard tried to expose his opponent's weakness in economics and finance by asking him the exchange rate of the West German mark, Mitterrand scornfully refused to answer, saying that he was not on television to "take an exam." Later in the debate, Mitterrand gave the exact exchange rate. Unlike his 1974 television duel with Giscard, Mitterrand's performance consituted a media victory.[68]

Before traveling to his constituency in the Nièvre to wait for the results of the final round of the presidential race, Mitterrand gave his last televised campaign address in which he proposed five objectives for France: to solve the unemployment problem, to promote economic growth, to construct a more just and open society, to restore French strength and independence, and to advance world peace.

When voters went to the polls on Sunday May 10, they clearly revealed that the roots of the Socialist party had spread throughout France, even to the traditionally conservative west and east. In the early evening of the election night, as he waited in Château-Chinon for the election returns, Mitterrand learned that he had been elected president of the French Republic and exclaimed, "What a moment in history!" His wife, Danielle, who was equally ecstatic, declared, "It's not true!"[69] In a brief election address later that evening from Château-Chinon, the president-elect declared that his victory represented "the forces of youth, the forces of labor, the forces of creation, [and] the forces of renewal which are united in a general national movement for jobs, peace, and freedom. . . ."[70] The long march to power was now over. But what lay ahead for the new Socialist president would be more difficult than he perhaps ever imagined.

4

DREAMS, ILLUSIONS, AND REFORMS

From the Pantheon to Versailles

May 1981–June 1982

I was carried away with victory; we were intoxicated.
—François Mitterrand

Mitterrand's first prime minister, Pierre Mauroy, once stated that "to govern is to foresee."[1] If Mauroy's axiom is applied to Year I of the Mitterrand presidency, the Socialist leader and his confreres did not govern in Year I—the allusion to the revolutionary calendar of 1792 seems appropriate to the hopeful beginnings of Socialist rule—but simply drifted. Mitterrand's election in 1981, followed one month later by the election of a new National Assembly where his party won an absolute majority of seats, gave him false hope and confidence. After learning of the extent of the victory of the Socialist party on election night, the new president told a confidant, "This is too much; this is much too much."[2] When Jacques Delors, minister of the economy and finance, learned of the Socialists' margin of victory in the National Assembly elections, his reaction was similar: "Our success is too large."[3] What especially worried Delors was that such a large victory might tempt Mitterrand and members of his new government to entertain illusions concerning reforms possible in the context of 1981 and the following years. While the Common Program of 1972 had been drawn up in an era of economic prosperity and international détente, the Left came to power in a milieu that was far different. Now the Western world faced recession and the onslaught of a new Cold War. *L'Année politique, économique et sociale en France*, a yearly review of major developments affecting France, labeled 1981 and 1982 as "the world in danger."[4] What was possible in 1972 would not necessarily be so in 1981. In fact, the economic situation in 1981 was far worse than that in the mid-1970s after the first oil shock hit the Western world. After a year in the Elysée, or the Château as the Socialists sometimes call the presidential palace, Mitterrand slowly learned this lesson and attempted to rectify his government's faulty economic theories. Nevertheless, many of the initial Socialist reforms were based on misconceived notions about the economy. Paradoxically, Year I was the year when the Socialist president governed the least but accomplished the most, at least in terms of the long series of reforms enacted.

Mitterrand's first thirteen months of power began and ended with two highly symbolic occasions: a festivity at the Pantheon, the resting-place of the greatest heroes of republican France, on the day of his inauguration, which marked the beginning of a year of Socialist dreams and illusions; and a summit meeting of the Western industrialized nations at Versailles, the palace of the Sun King, which suggested France's past glory and world power, where Mitterrand encountered the chilling reality of international politics and finance. Between the Pantheon where Mitterrand launched his symbolic *fête révolutionnaire* (revolutionary celebration) and Versailles where he unsuccessfully appealed to international leaders for worldwide change, the new president of France engaged his government in dreams, illusions, and reforms.

The Pantheon ceremony came on May 21, 1981, at the end of a busy day of inaugural ceremonies and receptions. The day began with a brief tête-à-tête at the Elysée between the president-elect and the outgoing Giscard. There followed an official inauguration ceremony at the palace attended by five hundred invited guests, including Mendès-France and other close associates, religious leaders, and a number of special guests, among them such international literary figures as William Styron, Elie Wiesel, Arthur Miller, Carlos Fuentes, and Gabriel García Marquez. In his first official address as president, Mitterrand called for a "just and united France." He added that he would "advance [his program] without ever tiring of the road of pluralism."[5]

These inauguration day activities were followed by a visit to the Arc de Triomphe where he laid a wreath, and a luncheon with friends and representatives from Socialist parties abroad and local officials from Latché and Jarnac, and then by a reception at the Hôtel de Ville hosted by the Gaullist Chirac.

Mitterrand concluded the public ceremonies by leading an early evening procession in the Latin Quarter that ended at the Pantheon.[6] As was the case on his election-night victory earlier in May, the procession included hundreds of people carrying red roses, the symbol of the PS, and shouting, "We have won." When the new president and his entourage—including the Portuguese Socialist leader Mario Soares and the widow of the slain Chilean leader Salvador Allende—reached the Pantheon, Mitterrand proceeded to enter the resting place of France's great heroes alone, while the Orchestre de Paris played Beethoven's "Ode to Joy." Viewed only by five strategically placed television cameras inside the building, Mitterrand paid homage to three French heroes by laying a red rose on each of their tombs: the Socialist leader Jean Jaurès, his spiritual mentor; the Resistance fighter Jean Moulin, symbolizing his own fight against fascism and his entry into politics; and the government official Victor Schoelcher who ended slavery in 1848 in the colonies, denoting the new president's commitment to the Third World. These three French figures were politically useful to Mitterrand because Jaurès symbolized a humanitarian and nondogmatic socialism, Moulin the struggle against fascism and oppression, and Schoelcher a commitment to activism on the world scene. When Mitterrand emerged from the Pantheon carrying a red rose in his hand, the internationally known tenor Placido Domingo, accompanied by the chorus of the Orchestre de Paris, sang the Marseillaise. Devised by Minister of Culture Jack Lang, this elaborate ceremony was designed to link Mitterrand's new Socialist government in the public mind with the nation's glorious past in order to give it added legitimacy. (While Lang played a key role in planning the ceremony at the Pantheon, during Mitterrand's presidency the popular and creative minister of culture would emphasize promoting popular culture, in contrast to the high culture normally associated with Giscard and the Right.)

Following the installation of the new president, the Socialist leader appointed a forty-two-member government headed by the Socialist mayor of Lille, Pierre Mauroy. The prime minister, a warm and amiable man who represented the grass-roots socialism of the industrial north, was on good terms with the Mitterrandists, a close friend of Rocard, tolerated by CERES, and more or less acceptable to the PCF. Consequently, Mauroy seemed the best suited to lead the left-wing government. Commenting on his appointment, Mauroy said, "I assume my responsibilities as prime minister with lucid optimism."[7] The prime minister's first government comprised mainly Socialists representing the various tendencies within the party. In the formation of this government and others during the 1981–86 period, Mitterrand revealed his keen ability as a juggler and political strategist. While Chevènement headed the Ministry of Research and Technology, Rocard, the new president's nemesis, assumed the innocuous Ministry of Planning. To maximize left-wing unity prior to the legislative elections, Mitterrand chose the Marxist-oriented Pierre Joxe to head the Ministry of Industry. The new Socialist government also included six women, a relatively large number for a Western liberal democracy at the time. Mitterrand appointed the Socialist feminist Yvette Roudy to a new Ministry of Women's Rights and placed Edith Cresson in charge of the Ministry of Agriculture, an appointment that startled many in France because the position had previously always been held by men. (In May 1991 Mitterrand would appoint Cresson as prime minister, the first woman prime minister in the history of France.)

At the outset of his government, Mitterrand carefully cultivated the image of a leader who would be a strong Atlanticist. When the West German Social Democratic Chancellor Helmut Schmidt traveled to Paris in late May to meet the new French president, the first Western leader to do so, Mitterrand stated publicly that he supported Schmidt's view that new American NATO missiles should be installed in West Germany to balance the Soviet's SS-20 missiles, assuming that negotiations begin immediately to limit the total number of missiles in Europe. Several weeks later, Mitterrand traveled to Bonn and told reporters from the German magazine *Stern:* "The Soviet SS-20 missiles and Backfire bombers destroy the nuclear balance in Europe. I cannot accept that, and rearmament is necessary if the balance is to be restored. Then, from that position, negotiations can be started."[8] While Schmidt was on friendly terms with Giscard and had shunned Mitterrand in earlier years, the two men found that they had common interests. Schmidt needed help with the new NATO missiles scheduled to be deployed in late 1983, and Mitterrand needed support in the Common Market given Britain's reluctance to reform the organization. One long-term objective of the Mitterrand government was to seek an increase in French farm prices from the EEC because the net income of French farmers had fallen by 2.5 percent a year since 1973. Given this economic reality and the fact that only one-third of French farmers had voted for Mitterrand, it seemed that great economic and political gains could be made by seeking EEC increases for French farmers. Since British Prime Minister Margaret Thatcher resolutely opposed such reform, Mitterrand needed the support of Schmidt. While both men needed one another, one thing worried Schmidt about Mitterrand: the reflationary economic policies of the new Socialist government and Mitterrand's resolve to get the EEC to back reflation and to articulate a social policy that emphasized alleviating unemployment rather than fighting inflation.[9] Nevertheless, Mitterrand and Schmidt met several times in 1981 and early in 1982 to tighten a fragile Franco-German partnership. Despite Mitterrand's efforts, the EEC never adopted a reflationary approach for its member states.

Not only did Mitterrand begin a series of meetings with Schmidt after taking office, but the new French president also let it be known shortly after assuming power that he would visit Israel, something no other French president or prime minister had done. The Socialists had supported the Camp David Accords and under Mitterrand's direction were seeking more leverage in the Middle East with a more evenhanded approach to Israel, compared to de Gaulle's pro-Arab position, a turn in policy that some Arab states would come to resent. At the same time that Mitterrand, who had long been interested in Jewish history, announced his intention to visit Israel, he sent his brother Jacques, head of the Aerospatiale aviation group, to Saudi Arabia with a friendly message to King Khalid whose country supplied more than 50 percent of France's oil supplies. Mitterrand's initial actions as president suggested that he would try to cultivate leftist unity at home, promote an Atlanticist foreign policy abroad, and reorient French policy in the Middle East.

Before the first round of the approaching legislative elections, the PS and the PCF negotiated an electoral accord that was published on June 4. This agreement, negotiated by Lionel Jospin, the new head of the PS, pledged that the Socialists and the Communists would support the strongest leftist candidates in the second round of the elections and that the two parties would work together to constitute "a coherent and durable majority." The accord also listed several areas where the two parties were in general agreement: nationalizations, increasing SMIC (the minimum wage), lowering unemployment, reducing the work week to thirty-five hours, increasing family allowances, and raising allowances to the elderly. The agreement noted as well that several important differences existed between the PS and the PCF that needed to be resolved in the future, notably differing views on Afghanistan and Poland.[10] The PS, also, reached an electoral accord with the Left Radicals and the Unified Socialist party.

The new Socialist government under the leadership of Mitterrand and the first Mauroy cabinet contributed to the Socialist victory in the legislative elections. On installation day at the Elysée Palace on May 21, the Socialist president announced what he termed his three affiliations: the Popular Front, the Resistance/Liberation, and a "new alliance between socialism and liberty." He also let it be known that his perceptions of state power would be far different from Giscard's. On June 3, for instance, he said that the National Assembly would be asked to abolish one of Giscard's controversial creations, the State Security Court which had special powers and handled security cases.[11] Then, after the first round of voting in the legislative elections on June 14, Mitterrand announced that he would not "intervene" between the two rounds, meaning that he would not use the vast powers at his disposal to influence the electorate in the second round.[12]

While the president may not have directly intervened in the elections, the actions of the first Mauroy government certainly boosted the PS at the polls. On June 3 Mitterrand and his Council of Ministers adopted a set of measures that appealed to many in France. These important measures included raising the minimum wage by 10 percent beginning June 1 (from 15.20 francs to 16.72 francs per hour); increasing allowances to the aged by 20 percent beginning in July (from 1,416 francs to 1,700 francs per month): increasing allowances to the handicapped by 20 percent beginning July 1; and raising allowances for family lodgings by 50 percent (25 percent July 1 followed by 25 percent on December 1, 1981). These social measures cost approximately eight to nine billion francs and were to be paid for by increased taxes on the incomes of the wealthiest taxpayers and the profits of certain large companies.[13] Furthermore, on June 10 the new government announced the creation of 54,290 new jobs in the public sector to alleviate the unemployment problem. Then, on June 11 the government announced that it was preparing a tax on the wealthy that would be ready for the legislature in the fall.[14]

Besides these significant measures, the Socialist government took additional action to keep its campaign promises. In addition to abolishing the infamous State Security Court, the Socialists ended capital punishment. They also announced that construction at certain nuclear power stations would be stopped or frozen, and that a controversial military camp in the south would not be enlarged. The government, too, tried to reassure financiers and savers by enforcing exchange controls to prevent further flights of capital from France.

Shortly before the first round of the legislative elections, Mauroy announced that decentralization and regionalization would be the two great projects of the Mitterrand presidency. Through decentralization the Mauroy government intended to return power to elected departmental, regional, and local officials. Since the time of Napoleon, power had radiated from Paris to the departments and the decisions made in Paris had been carried out by prefects, provincial officials responsible to the central government in the capital. Following Mauroy's statement, the minister of interior and decentralization, Gaston Defferre, began a campaign to implement the government's decentralization scheme. Closely linked to this plan was the corollary idea of regionalization, providing the various regions of France with more power and a stronger sense of identity. These two major projects suggested that the new government was responding to attacks on the centralization of power that had been made in the recent past, especially during the student-worker revolt of 1968. The new government gave the impression that it would conform to the wishes of the electorate and bring a spirit of reform to France. But had the electorate given the Socialists a full mandate to reform the nation? Few in government seemed concerned about this question, even though it was clear—or should have been clear—that the 1981 vote was not a blank check. Moreover, few on the left were asking how an expensive agenda of reforms would be financed. Instead, Mitterrand and his prime minister seemed more concerned about giving the impression that the Socialists had a plan to relieve the economic crisis, especially unemployment, and to end the failure of France to adjust to postwar transformations.

Perhaps, to some extent, the initial euphoria and the dreams of reform of Mitterrand and the Socialists were justified. Not only had Mitterrand become the first freely elected Socialist president, but in

June 1981 in the second round of the legislative elections, his party won a victory of truly historic proportions. In these elections the PS captured 269 seats in the 490-member Assembly, while the PCF won 44 seats (down from 86 in the old Assembly). The election results meant, of course, that the new Socialist president had an absolute majority in the National Assembly and that the PCF would be a junior partner in any future government that included them. With Mitterrand's seven-year presidential term and with the Socialists in the National Assembly elected to five-year terms, the Socialist party found itself in full control of the executive and legislative branches of government. Following the legislative elections, *L'Unité*, the Socialist party's official newspaper, ran an article titled "The Summer of Democracy" and said that the legislative elections showed a profound desire for change in France.[15] Claude Estier, editor of *L'Unité*, hailed the elections in an editorial as opening "a new era."[16] Mitterrand had thus accomplished his long-term objectives: the Left had been brought into balance with the Right, the Communists now lagged behind the Socialists in the vote tally, and the Left was now in power. History had been made.

The unprecedented success of the PS in the Assembly elections encouraged Mitterrand and his colleagues to reach an agreement with the Communists, an accord that removed some of the obstacles between the two parties and prepared the way for PCF participation in the second Mauroy government. On the night of June 23 the PS and the PCF revealed an agreement that was published on the following day. In this accord, the Socialists and the Communists declared their intention to cooperate and to work for peace and disarament. In this regard, they agreed to work for the reduction of arms in Europe, including removal of Soviet SS-20 missiles and preventing the installation of U.S. Pershing-2 and cruise missiles on European soil. Both the PS and the PCF stated that they respected human rights as well as the sovereignty of nations. The document said that the people of Afghanistan had a right to choose their own government and asked for the removal of Soviet troops. The two parties also agreed that Poland should be allowed to determine its own course in a democratic manner. On the Camp David Accords, the parties reaffirmed Israel's right to exist and to be secure, as should others in the Middle East, including the Palestinians. The PS and PCF also expressed their solidarity with nations of the Third World, who "like El Salvador and

Nicaragua, struggle for their emancipation, their development, and their democratic and social liberation."[17] This document resolved, for the time being, the foreign policy disputes—especially Afghanistan and Poland—that had deeply divided the PS and the PCF. The poor performance of the PCF in the legislative elections left few alternatives for the Communists but to cooperate, at least on paper, with the Socialists. When Mauroy announced the formation of his second government on June 23, four Communist ministers—Charles Fiterman (transportation), Anicet Le Pors (public and administrative affairs), Jack Ralite (health), and Marcel Rigout (professional training)—were included, marking the first time since 1947 that Communists had participated in a government.

Why did Mitterrand agree to include Communist ministers in his government? Perhaps the most plausible reason for appointing PCF members to the new Socialist government was that he wanted to ensure social peace in France. Faced with a serious economic crisis stemming from high unemployment and inflation, the Socialist president realized that the PCF could use its leverage with the pro-Communist unions of the General Confederation of Labor (*Confédération Générale du Travail*—CGT), France's largest labor movement, to set off a wave of strikes if it remained in opposition. Moreover, in three of the four ministerial areas assigned to the PCF, the pro-Communist CGT had a strong influence. Mitterrand knew that this would certainly act as a brake on Communist-inspired strike activity. Mitterrand also knew from the past history of the tripartite government, in which the Communists participated between 1944 and 1947, that the PCF helped to contain not just union militancy but wage demands as well. He was also aware that the short-lived Popular Front government of 1936 had not included the PCF. Consequently, by bringing the Communists into his government, Mitterrand hoped to keep strike activity to a minimum and buy time for his government, thereby allowing it to freely implement its program. Furthermore, he believed for a long time that the PCF could be forced to change its ways if it was brought into an alliance with the Socialists. Shortly after the formation of the second Mauroy government, Mitterrand agreed to an interview with *Le Monde* in which he discussed Communist participation in government. In this interview, Mitterrand stated, "I have always said that I would form a government that would be an expression of the parliamentary majority." The president went on to say that during "all of our time of quarreling and quarreling with the communists, it is known that I have not ceded anything, and that I do not have the intention of beginning now."[18]

Of course, Mitterrand's gamble did entail some costs. On the international scene it meant that many Western governments, especially the United States, would proceed cautiously with the new French government. One of France's noted authorities on international relations, Alfred Grosser, maintains that while there was *alternance* (a true rotation of government) in 1981, there were few alternatives in the realm of foreign policy for the new Mitterrand government. This was the case, says Grosser, because Mitterrand had appointed Communist ministers and ran the risk of appearing a captive of the PCF and Moscow unless he took a strong stand on the side of the Atlantic Alliance and exercised a special vigilance toward the Soviet Union.[19] To do otherwise would alienate Western nations and mean the immediate loss of center voters who had assumed that Mitterrand would be firm with the PCF and Moscow. At home this meant that the Socialist president, as ironic as it might seem, had to pursue a Gaullist foreign policy in order to maintain a national consensus in one area while he attempted to make reforms on the domestic front. In brief, including the Communists in government gave Mitterrand a period of social peace and allowed the government to launch its reform program, in time weakened the electoral power of the PCF, and limited Socialist initiatives in foreign policy.

Besides the four Communist ministers, the second Mauroy government included a number of key Socialist ministers. Mitterrand and Mauroy assigned Rocard once again to the Ministry of Planning. The CERES leader, Chevènement, was retained at the Ministry of Research and Technology, an appointment that won Mitterrand support from the left wing of his party and from PCF supporters as well. At the important Ministry of Industry, Mitterrand replaced Joxe with the more moderate Pierre Dreyfus, a change that eased some of the anxieties within the business community. The president continued the new Ministry of Women's Rights to keep earlier campaign promises to French feminists and to repay women for giving him and his party a majority of their votes in the 1981 election.[20] Roudy, a Mitterrand loyalist, remained in charge of this new ministry and was given a relatively large budget to advance the cause of women throughout France. Cresson, another Mitterandist, remained at the Ministry of

Agriculture. Other notable appointments from the Mitterrandist faction of the party included Jacques Delors (whose economic ideas were close to those of Rocard) at the Ministry of the Economy and Finance, Laurent Fabius at the Ministry of Economics and Finance in charge of the Budget, Defferre at the Ministry of Interior and Decentralization, Claude Cheysson at the Ministry of External Relations, Charles Hernu at the Ministry of Defense, and Jack Lang at the Ministry of Culture. Mitterrand and Mauroy made these governmental assignments with great care in order to balance the factions within the PS.

The sociopolitical composition of the new National Assembly revealed a significant dimension of Mitterrand's France. The new Assembly was a "government of teachers." Not only did a majority of PS deputies, 59 percent, come from the teaching profession, but 34 percent of the entire Assembly had at some point been teachers. Of the PS deputies, twenty-five were university professors, ninety were secondary-school teachers, and thirteen were primary-school teachers. The new PS deputies also included among their ranks fifty-eight representatives from upper-level management, sixteen doctors, sixteen lawyers, three shopkeepers, two workers, and one farmer.[21]

Despite the "republic of teachers" that emerged in 1981, *énarques*, or graduates of the Ecole Nationale d'Administration (ENA), the most prestigious business school in France, held key positions in the Mitterrand government. While the number of *énarques* in the Assembly dropped from thirty-three to twenty-three, PS *énarques* rose from eight to thirteen in 1981. Furthermore, of the 360 private staff members of the Mauroy government, 152 were *énarques* or "X's" (the name of another *grande école*, the Ecole Polytechnique). One also discovered that of the 150 prominent posts on the Mauroy staff, 50 were headed by *énarques*.[22]

Another interesting facet of the National Assembly elections was that Paris played a disproportionate role in the political life of the new Socialist government. In the 1981 elections, for example, 3.5 percent of the voters were in Paris, but fifty-five of the 491 deputies, or 11.2 percent, were born in Paris. In the government formed by Mauroy after the elections, five of the fourteen full ministers were born in Paris. The president of the National Assembly, the Socialist Louis Mermaz, was also born in Paris as well as the leader of the Socialist deputies, Joxe. A Parisian elite also dominated the leadership of the Socialist party with 42 percent of the fifteen-member national secretariat of the PS, and 36 percent of the party's executive bureau, born in the capital.[23] As in the past, the weight of Paris was considerable in the new political life of the republic.

Mitterrand attempted to assemble a government and a personal staff that was decidedly loyal to him. For instance, besides placing PS members in all of the important positions, he chose his friends and supporters for key posts: Mermaz became president of the National Assembly, Joxe was chairman of the Socialist parliamentary group, and Jospin remained as head of the PS. These and other appointments gave the new president a strong hold on the legislative branch of government and on the PS itself.[24] In some quarters, Mitterrand earned a reputation as a president who placed loyalty before competence.

For his own staff, the new president assembled a group of personal friends, close political allies, and politically sympathetic technocrats. The Elysée staff comprises about 550 people with only about 200 of these part of Mitterrand's political staff; the remaining 350 Elysée employees are part of the domestic staff or hold secretarial or clerical positions. Among his political staff he appointed a number of friends, such as André Rousselet, a former director of a large taxi company; Régis Debray, a 1960s activist/intellectual known for his involvement in Latin American affairs; François de Grossouvre; and Claude Manceron, a historian. The president also chose close political allies for his personal staff: Jacques Attali, an ENA and Ecole Polytechnique graduate and author of a number of books on subjects ranging from economics to music; Paul Guimard, a journalist and author; and Jacques Ribs, a lawyer. A number of politically sympathetic technocrats were also brought in to fill positions on Mitterrand's personal staff including Jacques Fournier from the Council of State, Hubert Védrine from the Foreign Office, and François-Xavier Stasse from the Planning Commission. For his secretary general at the Elysée, Mitterrand chose a close friend, Pierre Bérégovoy, who was also a member of the executive committee of the PS, thereby strengthening the president's links with his power base.[25]

Mitterrand's staff soon discovered that as president, he continued his practice as head of the PS, of listening to several and often conflicting advisers at the same time before making a decision. On economic policy Mitterrand relied on advice from his staff—notably Jacques Attali and Alain Boubil—from successful businessmen and friends on the left like Jean Riboud, Gilbert Trigano, and François

Dalle, from ministers like Pierre Dreyfus, and even from journalists like Jean-Jacques Servan-Schreiber.[26] Among his own personal staff, Mitterrand insisted that one-page memos be forwarded to him through Bérégovoy.

Mitterrand's style of management proved to be rather individualistic. He seldom held a joint working session with the Elysée team and opted instead for a more individual and fragmented approach to management. During the Socialist government, 1981–86, he often announced presidential decisions at the weekly Council of Ministers meetings, meaning that once a decision was made, the entire government was committed to it. On occasion, he also announced policy without consulting or informing his ministers. This occurred, for example, in 1982 when he revealed that he would exempt works of art from the wealth tax, partially to make the tax more palatable, and in 1983 when he announced that the tax burden would be reduced by 1 percent. In many disputes within the Socialist government, Mitterrand was the ultimate arbiter. Although he was a long-time critic of Gaullist presidential power, he did not relinquish his authority to make decisions affecting various aspects of his government. It was he who decided between 1981 and 1986, for instance, not to devalue the franc in May 1981, that the government should assume 100 percent and not 51 percent of the industries targeted for nationalization, that there should be a thirty-nine-hour work week without a loss in pay,[27] and that Jospin and not Fabius should lead the 1986 legislative campaign. Thus, the decision-making process in the Socialist government was often hierarchical, with Mitterrand making the major strategic decisions, even though at times he equivocated in the face of decisions that carried tremendous consequences for his government. This indecision became quite evident later in economic and financial policy, a domain where the president had little expertise.

The first major decision to confront the Mitterrand government was what to do about a run on the franc that seriously threatened the financial stability of France. Between the first and second round of the presidential election alone 7 billion francs left the country.[28] During the three-day period following Mitterrand's election, $3 billion was sent across the frontier, with almost $1 billion a day leaving France on the eve of the inauguration of the new president. In the presidential motorcade on the day of his installation, Mauroy informed Mitterrand that $1.5 billion had left France that very day. The problem was the result not simply of Mitterrand's election and the expectations of a nervous wealthy elite, but of the refusal of Giscard's prime minister, Raymond Barre, to impose exchange controls.[29] Consequently, the franc made a dramatic fall immediately after Mitterrand's election, plummeting by 7 percent against the dollar compared to preelection rates. To stop this financial hemorrhage, the Mitterrand government imposed exchange controls on May 22. The president also decided to prop up the franc by spending $5 billion in the foreign exchange market.

Perhaps it is here that Mitterrand made one of his most serious economic mistakes. Instead of devaluing what many financial experts considered to be an overvalued franc, he made a strategic decision to defend the currency at all costs. On his first day as president of the republic, Mitterrand told Mauroy, "You do not devalue the money of a country when that country has just placed confidence in you."[30] Nevertheless, with the foreign trade deficit doubling during the first year in power and with inflation negating wage increases, in the eighteen months ahead Mitterrand had to devalue the franc three times to begin to restore confidence in the French economy. Mitterrand could have learned a lesson from the Léon Blum government of 1936, which had failed to devalue early and paid a heavy price for its delay. He could have learned another lesson from the Popular Front experience, namely its attempt to reflate the economy, which produced serious inflation and contributed to the fall of Blum's government. But the newly elected Socialist president proceeded to commit the same errors that Blum's Popular Front had made earlier.

The second major concern confronting Mitterrand during Year I of his presidency was the distressing level of unemployment in France, a concern that led Mitterrand and his Socialist confreres to make a number of serious errors. Part of the reason for this was that Mitterrand, like many of his supporters in and out of government, was a prisoner of leftist myths regarding the economy. As one astute political observer in France said later, Mitterrand went on to become a "prisoner of the economic crisis,"[31] greatly exacerbated by the actions of the Socialist government during Year I. What Mitterrand attempted to do was to reflate the French economy with increased government spending and hope, as the Organization for Economic Cooperation and Development had predicted, that the Western world would begin to pull out of its recession late in 1981. The new president and his advisers, too, believed that the U.S. government would soon begin to reflate its economy. If this scenario occurred, France—with a reflationary policy already in place—would be able to ride the crest of a wave of Western prosperity. Unfortunately for both Mitterrand and France, the OECD predictions, expectations for the U.S., and leftist economic strategy all proved to be wrong.

To solve the unemployment problem, the major economic concern of the Socialists in 1981, Mitterrand counted on reflationary measures to boost a sagging economy. Using an old-fashioned Keynesian approach, the president believed that increased consumer spending would lead to greater industrial productivity and more jobs. The measures taken by Prime Minister Mauroy between the two rounds of the legislative elections—the 10 percent increase in the minimum wage, the 20–25 percent hikes in family allowances, pensions, aid to the handicapped, and other social measures—were intended to heighten consumer spending among the neediest in France. The Socialist government also hoped that the creation of tens of thousands of public-service jobs promised in the Common Program would also contribute to consumer spending and the reduction of unemployment as well. Mitterrand thought, too, that the nationalization program, whereby the government would take over nine large industrial groups plus most of the major private banks and holding institutions, would produce a command that would enhance the state's ability to direct the economic levers of the world's fifth most powerful industrial nation. More precisely, Mitterrand and the Socialists, along with their Communist allies, assumed that nationalizations would help make French industry more dynamic, with state-owned industries becoming the motor of the economy; moreover, these industries would allow the state to control credit and to affirm the Left's commitment to economic equality.[32] After the nationalizations, the French state would control 16 percent of employment with nine hundred thousand workers shifted from the private to the public sector, 28 percent of added value, and 36 percent of investment.[33] The nationalization program meant that approximately 32 percent of the economy would be under state control, compared to 18 percent before 1981.[34] The Socialist party's weekly newspaper referred to nationalization as "a master word: the industrial strategy of the party."[35] What Mitterrand attempted at the outset of his presidency was what might be called Socialist supply-side economics, a state-led approach to reflate the economy, while governments elsewhere in the Western world pursued an austerity policy in an effort to reduce inflation.

Although Mitterrand's reflationary measures did not stabilize the rise in unemployment during 1981 and there was a 1–2 percent increase in economic growth, the increases in consumer spending led to a drastic increase in the sale of imported consumer goods, especially from France's major trading partner, Germany, and boosted the spiral of inflation. Later, the inflation rate for 1982 was projected to be as high as 18 percent, while other Western nations anticipated and actually experienced a fall in inflation. In time, the reflationary approach also produced massive new unemployment. Nevertheless, the budget for 1982, prepared by the young Fabius who would later issue austerity budgets as prime minister (1984–86), was expansionist. With hefty increases in social spending, the 1982 budget included a $17 billion deficit for 1982, 50 percent higher than that of 1981. While Mitterrand encouraged the government to make reforms, implement the 110 Propositions, and at the same time defend his reforms against critics in and outside of France, he failed to realize that his economic policies created exactly the opposite effect from what was desired— more unemployment and an ailing economy.

Following the opening session of the newly constituted National Assembly on July 2, the pace of reform was rapid during the first thirteen months of the Socialist government. Mitterrand's government, for instance, proceeded to suppress the State Security Court, liberalized restrictions on private radio stations, "regularized" the situation of clandestine immigrants, adopted an expansionist budget for 1982, agreed upon part of a decentralization law, ended the death penalty, passed a nationalization law, reduced the work week to thirty-nine hours, added a fifth week of paid vacation, lowered the retirement age to sixty, and adopted the Auroux laws giving workers a greater voice at the workplace. One factor that made the quick pace of reform possible was that Mitterrand had a long grace period due to the momentous legislative victory in June, the inclusion of the PCF in government, and the cooperation of the unions, especially the CGT and the CFDT.

When the new legislative session opened, deputies began to consider the first part of the law on decentralization, presented by the minister of interior and decentralization. This plan called for reducing the traditional power of the Paris-appointed prefects who had exercised broad authority in the provinces ever since the days of Napoleon. Defferre's plan called for handing over much of the power of the prefects to twenty-two directly elected regional assemblies. Under Defferre's plan the prefects would be retitled commissioners of the republic, and would only advise and facilitate contact between regional councils and Parisian authorities. From the government's point of view, this plan demonstrated the Left's commitment to popular sovereignty and at the same time eased pressure from independent-minded provinces like Brittany and Corsica. Yet passage of the full text of the complex and detailed bill was delayed until 1982 while the government prepared new legislation for the September *rentrée*, including legislation on new freedoms for local radio stations, nationalizations, the 1982 budget, a wealth tax, the status and employment of foreigners, retirement, duration of the work week, an audiovisual statute, administrative reform, and social security. The work agenda for the new Assembly between September and December 1981 proved to be heavy indeed and many items had to be scheduled for 1982.

With the *rentrée*, September and October were important months for the Mitterrand government. On September 18 the deputies in the National Assembly voted to end capital punishment. With the approval of 369 deputies, including sixteen members of the Gaullist Rally for the Republic (*Rassemblement pour la République—* RPR) and twenty-one members of the centrist Union for French Democracy (*Union pour la Démocratie Française—*UDF), the Assembly agreed to retire the guillotine to the museum. For Mitterrand, September and October were extremely important months because he held his first press conference, made a decision to devalue the franc, and made his first visit to the provinces.

On September 18 in the *salle des fêtes* of the Elysée Palace in the presence of all the ministers of state as well as other government officials, Mitterrand held the longest press conference in French history—two hours and thirty-one minutes. The image that the president projected at this meeting surprised many. Mitterrand appeared solemn and gave a Gaullist tone to the conference. In reporting the press conference, *Le Monde's* headline read, "De Gaulle? Non, Mitterrand." Throughout his discourse he underscored his authority as president and appeared convinced that he had a historic mission to accomplish. Like de Gaulle, he stressed the need for France to maintain its autonomy in foreign affairs, implying that the new government would continue the general's defense policy. He also spoke on the subject of domestic independence and told his audience that the government's nationalization program ensured such independence; the nationalized industries, he said, would be "the instruments for the next century."

Mitterrand also prepared his audience for future change by insisting that his government would pursue just social, economic, and fiscal reforms and would combat what he called "the wall of money" that had prevented reform in the past. The president also asked the French to mobilize themselves against unemployment and inflation. Yet Mitterrand did have something to say to private employers. He told them that as a result of the nationalizations, the economy would simply be a "little more mixed" than before and that a large majority of production would still remain in private hands. Mitterrand even told the business community that the government would exempt industrial profits from the wealth tax if employers spent the saved amount on investments to create jobs. The president's Gaullist-like image at this first press conference and his strong emphasis on future reforms served him well as a politician seeking some links with the past and at the same time trying to legitimize the reforms that the Socialist government intended to carry out. All in all, his initial meeting with the press attempted to ensure that the state of grace would continue.[36]

Also attempting to maintain support for his government as economic indicators revealed the pitiful state of the economy, Mitterrand traveled to Gascony and Aquitaine where he gave a speech at Figeac that surprised many. In this small town in the southwestern part of France, after the press office at the Elysée announced that the president would be making an important speech there, Mitterrand declared, "What I have called socialism is not my Bible." He tried to give the impression that he was not simply a Socialist president but the president of the entire nation. "It is my duty to express the wishes of the entire nation," he said. "How firmly I hold to that pluralism! And how I want France to remain profoundly diverse and different, without being divided." In this speech Mitterrand also indicated that his government would be more sympathetic to the demands of French business.[37] From this time forward, the word "socialism" all but disappeared from the president's public discourse.

A few days after the Figeac speech, the Council of Ministers, with Mitterrand presiding, adopted a nationalization plan. The government divided the targeted companies into four groups. First, the Dassault aircraft company, maker of the Mirage fighter-bomber, and the arms production division of Matra, a large diversified electronics firm, were scheduled to fall under state control. The Socialist government agreed that the production and sale of weapons should not be controlled by private industry. The second group included two large steel producers, Usinor and Sacilor, which were already heavily indebted to the state. The third group included five large industrial concerns—CGE (electrical equipment), Péchiney-Ugine-Kuhlmann (an important chemical company), Rhone-Poulenc (a textile-chemical firm), Saint-Gobain (a diversified industrial group), and Thomson (a huge electronics company). The fourth group comprised Honeywell Bull (a French–U.S. computer company), ITT's French interests, and Roussel-Uclaf (a chemical and pharmaceutical firm). In addition to these industries, the government planned to nationalize a number of banks and holding institutions to maximize the state's control over credit and investment.

The nationalization plan divided the government. The nationalized industries were theoretically to be used as "motors" for reindustrialization, research, and development, but this motor would be controlled by state technocrats. What provoked disagreement in government circles was not the "motor" role of the nationalized sector, but the extent of the takeover within each industrial group. Finance Minister Delors and Minister of Planning Rocard, for instance, argued that the government only needed to take over 51 percent of the targeted industries to gain control; this would save the government billions of francs that could be spent elsewhere. Other ministers, such as Chevènement, argued that the government had a mandate to fully nationalize the targeted industries and that problems would emerge within the ranks of the industries if they were not completely nationalized. The nationalization plan set off the first real debate between two Socialist factions that the president would have to listen to: the "minimalists" like Delors, Rocard, Minister of Foreign Trade Michel Jobert, and Minister of Industry Pierre Dreyfus, and the "maximalists" comprising some Mitterrandists, Chevènement and his supporters, and the four Communist ministers. Mitterrand himself arbitrated this debate and decided that the targeted industries would be nationalized 100 percent. After a passionate session in the National Assembly where numerous amendments were offered, the deputies approved Mitterrand's version of the nationalization plan. The president's desire to nationalize 100 percent of the nine industrial groups was based mainly on his attempt to keep the pledge made in the Common Program and ensure left-wing unity within his government, especially from the Communist side. With this decision, which would cost at least 44 billion francs, the maximalists won a key battle with their adversaries, but they eventually lost the war over control of French economic policy.

In late September the government approved a spending program that reflected the maximalist position. Drawn up by Fabius, who was in charge of the budget, and negotiated with the Elysée staff, the new budget included a 23 percent increase in public spending, now set at 135 billion francs. The projected deficit for the 1982 budget was expected to be about $16.7 billion, a postwar record for a French government. The government hoped partially to offset the deficit with a new wealth tax under consideration and the abolition of special tax privileges. Although Delors initially refused to countersign the 1982 budget as minister of the economy, the expansionist budget of Fabius was adopted, a budget that reflected many of the dreams and illusions of the Socialists at the outset of their experiment with power.

With pressure still heavy on the franc, Mitterrand decided it was now time to devalue. While he flatly rejected devaluation immediately after taking office because of the political damage that might be incurred, in early October he had little choice. On October 4, after Delors had consulted with the Germans, the government announced that the members of the European Monetary System (EMS) had agreed that the franc would be devalued 3 percent while the mark would be raised in value by 5.5 percent. This meant that the franc fell in value 8.5 percent vis-à-vis France's major trading partner. The day after the devaluation, Delors announced a price freeze on basic products and said he would discuss with the unions the necessity to moderate pay increases. The 14 percent inflation and a higher rate projected for 1982 worried the minister of the economy. The devaluation and Delors's October 5 actions were too little and too late.

On October 12 and 13 Mitterrand visited an area in eastern France hard hit by unemployment, Lorraine. Between May 1979 and May 1981 this region alone had lost 30,000 jobs in the steel industry. Mitterrand hoped that this official visit would allow him to explain the government's economic and social policy as outlined in his September press conference and to stymie any opposition effort to capture a foothold in this area. In the May 10 presidential elections 51.6 percent of the voters in Lorraine had voted for Mitterrand, but only one of the four departments in Lorraine had given Mitterrand a majority of votes. In the June legislative elections the Left had captured thirteen of twenty-five seats in this region. In terms of political calculus, Mitterrand knew that Lorraine was a key area of concern for the Socialist government.

During his visit to Lorraine the president was accompanied by several members of his government: Delors, Defferre, Bérégovoy, André Henry (minister of leisure), and Jean Auroux (minister of labor). The president and his entourage visited all four departments in Lorraine where they talked with mayors, heads of companies, union leaders, and workers. Among other themes, Mitterrand told the citizens of Lorraine that a powerful popular movement was galvanizing national unity around his government and that the nationalization program would permit the "structural reforms necessary to reverse the decline in Lorraine."[38] He also said that he hoped Lorraine would become a symbol of "hope" and not a "symbol of political setback."[39] This tour was followed in the coming months by a solo trip by Prime Minister Mauroy to various areas of France to explain further the government's economic and social policies. Like Mitterrand, Mauroy wanted to sensitize French citizens to the difficult problems of unemployment, the "priority of priorities" for the new government, at least during its first year.[40]

The dreams and illusions of the new Socialist government were clearly revealed in the October 14 meeting of the Council of Ministers where this body adopted what it termed an "Intermediate Plan" for 1982–83. According to this plan, the government's first objective was to stabilize unemployment and then to reduce it by creating 400,000 to 500,000 new jobs a year beginning in 1983. It also said that the government wanted to create conditions for economic growth (3 percent projected for 1982–83) and investment, to improve productive capacity, restore social solidarity, and establish an effective dialogue with various social groups.[41] Like other leftist governments in the past, such as Blum's Popular Front in 1936 or Harold Wilson's government in Britain after 1964, Mitterrand and the Socialists forgot how quickly inflation erodes confidence in a newly elected progressive government.

These campaigns in the provinces by the president and his prime minister were followed by the Socialist congress at Valence between October 23 and 25, a meeting dominated by radical rhetoric echoing 1789. After the 1981 victory, Mitterrand's strength within the PS jumped from about 47 percent of the party's membership to approximately 51.5 percent, while Rocard's support fell from 21 percent to 15 percent. Fearing a further reduction of his strength in the euphoria of 1981, Rocard did not present a countermotion at the Valence congress, despite Jospin's effort to encourage Rocard to draw up a set of counteraims for the party. The motion presented at Valence called on the government to work toward "a complete break with capitalism."[42] With debate in the government brewing over a new wealth tax and with some bankers, notably at Paribas (Banque de Paris et des Pays-Bas), resisting a government takeover, some PS members sensed a clash with the "wall of money" that Mitterrand had referred to earlier. One PS delegate at Valence, Paul Quilès, even resorted to quoting Robespierre by declaring, "It is not only necessary to say that heads are going to fall, but it is necessary to say which ones."[43] Another delegate said now that the banks had been nationalized, it was "necessary to nationalize the bankers."[44] The prime minister himself, referring specifically to the resistance of some banks, stated, "The government will not yield to any intimidation."[45]

In essence, the Valence congress was a victory celebration for the PS, especially for the more radical representatives. In a message to the delegates, Mitterrand attempted to moderate the rhetoric by telling his confreres, "We have a long period ahead of us [and] it is necessary to know how to manage it."[46] One right-wing Parisian newspaper dubbed the Valence meeting *"La terreur tranquille"* (the calm terror).[47] Valence may have been a victory celebration for the Socialists, but the extreme rhetoric contributed to mobilizing right-wing opinion.

In November, Mitterrand's economic dreams and illusions began to confront a harsh reality, not from the right wing, but from his own finance minister. In a TV broadcast on November 29 Delors called for a "pause in the reforms." Just as startling to Mitterrand and others in government, Delors stated: "The responsibility of the Socialist government is to create a climate more favorable to business." Delors also said that he did not believe that there was a "conspiracy" on the part of big business to subvert Socialist reforms.[48] Delors's pronouncement attracted considerable attention in the French and international press and got the attention of Prime Minister Mauroy, who proceeded to discount it, because Delors's statements contradicted official government policy. Traveling in the provinces at the time, Mauroy told the press that the government would continue its reforms "without accelerating or slowing down."[49] Mauroy also asked Delors to retract his statements, but the minister of finance refused. While Delors initiated the beginnings of a major debate within the PS, in the press this debate was soon eclipsed by events in Poland where on December 12 and 13 martial law was declared.[50] In a few months, however, Mitterrand began to listen closely to his finance minister. The coming year would be a "year of transition"[51] for Mitterrand and for the French as the euphoria of Year I became only a memory.

Thus, 1981 drew to a close for the Socialist president. In a New Year's Eve televised address, he summed up the past six months in power and looked ahead to the future. According to Mitterrand, "1981 has been a year of change that France and her people had wanted. . . ." He also stressed that the actions of his government had corresponded to his campaign promises: nationalizations, more individual liberty as well as more liberty for local and regional governments, social reforms, public liberties, and greater security. Concerning the future, Mitterrand mentioned what seemed to him to be the objectives of government reform in the months ahead—five weeks of paid vacation, lowering the age of retirement to sixty, and professional training for sixteen- to eighteen-year-olds. However, future reform, he said, depended on mastering the economic situation, namely unemployment and inflation.[52] Nevertheless, his government still viewed unemployment as its major priority during the first six months of 1982, after which time Socialist priorities radically changed.

On foreign affairs, Mitterrand took a Gaullist tone in his New Year's Eve message, as he had in his first press conference. He noted the declaration of martial law in Poland and asked European governments to be conscious of the perils that might follow. He also said he hoped that Europe could one day leave the Yalta system, the division between East and West that followed the Yalta Conference at the end of World War II. With Poland as well as Latin America on his mind, Mitterrand closed his New Year's Eve address by stating: "Happy New Year to all those people who suffer and who need freedom at home and abroad. Happy New Year to the nations that need to affirm their sovereignty."[53]

The Mitterrand government continued its long series of reforms in January 1982. In the middle of the month the Council of Ministers approved plans to reduce the work week to thirty-nine hours and to add a fifth week of paid vacation. Originally, Mitterrand and the Socialists wanted to reduce the work week to thirty-five hours, but the economic crisis, not to mention the protest of the business community, made the thirty-five-hour week extremely problematic. When the thirty-nine-hour week was decided upon, there was a heated debate within the government between the maximalists and the minimalists concerning whether to give workers forty hours of pay for thirty-nine hours of work. Mitterrand himself ended the debate by insisting that workers be paid for forty hours.[54] He realized that if workers were paid for only thirty-nine hours, purchasing power would decline, government popularity would fall, and the Socialists' reflationary policy would be hampered. Furthermore, left-wing unity would be threatened, a real concern at the time because the Socialists and Communists had differing views on the situation in Poland. With promises to reduce the work week further in the future, Mitterrand's government took an important symbolic step in reducing the length of the sacrosanct forty-hour week. Mitterrand's prime minister, too, gave many hope that 1982 would continue to be a year of reform when he announced later in January that he desired to see the pace of change accelerated so that essential reforms could be made before the beginning of 1983.

Despite the reforms, it was in January 1982 that the Mitterrand government encountered its first significant setback. On January 16, the conservative-dominated Constitutional Council, originally conceived by the drafters of the 1958 Constitution to be an oversight committee on executive supremacy and once labeled "de Gaulle's errand boy" by Mitterrand,[55] declared that the nationalization law did not conform to the Constitution, primarily because the compensation was inadequate. This ruling, according to PS party head Jospin, was the "first time in the history of the Fifth Republic that the Constitutional Council [had] blocked the promulgation of a law . . . at the heart of a program enacted by the president of the republic and a legitimately elected National Assembly."[56] While PS and PCF leaders denounced the decision, Mitterrand himself remained silent. If his government had to pay additional compensation for nationalized industries, at least it would buy what one legal scholar called a "certificate of authenticity."[57]

The announcement of the decision by the Constitutional Council stimulated cries of victory by the Right. With Mitterrand's overwhelming election victory in 1981, some members of the opposition viewed the council as their only remaining weapon. The startling decision suggested to many that the Socialist honeymoon was ending. From 1981 onward the case load of the Constitutional Council increased as the Right attempted to use this body to block legislation, a ploy that the Socialists themselves would use after their defeat in the 1986 legislative elections. During the 1960–May 1974 period, for example, the Constitutional Council handled only nine cases, while from June 1974 to May 1981, Giscard's presidency, the case load was sixty-seven. However, during 1981–86 when the Socialists were in power, the Constitutional Council deliberated on ninety-nine cases. Since Article 61(2) of the Constitution says that laws can be referred to the council by either the president, the prime minister, the president of the National Assembly or the Senate, or (since 1974) by sixty deputies or senators, it is relatively easy for opposition parties to use the Constitutional Council in an effort to block laws that they oppose. Thus during Giscard's term, sixty of the sixty-seven referrals to the council came from the opposition; and of the sixty-five referrals to the council during the period from June 1981 to December 1984, all came from right-wing deputies or senators. Furthermore, the decisions of the council were not necessarily advantageous for the Socialists. During the first three-and-a-half years of Mitterrand's government, twenty-one referrals (43.8 percent) were completely or partially ruled against by the council, compared to eleven referrals (23.4 percent) that received the same fate during Giscard's seven-year term. Political division had activated a potentially powerful judicial body that added a new dimension to French politics.[58] Some in France warned that the Constitutional Council was leading the nation to a "government of judges."

Mitterrand's government responded to this challenge by quickly drafting a new nationalization bill that was promulgated the following month. Under the new law the government increased its compensation to the nationalized industries by $8 billion, almost a 30 percent increase over what the government had planned to spend for the targeted industries. While the increased compensation precipitated a tax hike, it did meet the demands of the Constitutional Council and legitimized one of the principal reforms of the Mitterrand government. The decision of the council, too, marked the beginning of an experiment with "cohabitation" with the right wing that would formally begin four years later.

If January 16 was a setback for the Mitterrand government, so was the following day. On January 17, the Socialists lost four legislative by-elections in the first round of voting. These elections were necessary because in June 1981 results in four seats had been disputed. The outcome of the rescheduled elections added insult to injury following the ruling of the Constitutional Council. The election victory by the opposition was followed two months later by further gains in two rounds of cantonal elections where the opposition won the presidency of sixty-four general councils, compared to thirty-six for the left-wing majority. The growing unemployment, reaching 2 million at the beginning of 1982, the rising inflation rate, and the increased tax load to pay for the social reform began to have an effect on the electorate. Public opinion polls, nevertheless, still showed strong support for Mitterrand and his prime minister.

In late January it was not domestic politics but gas that caused problems for the Socialists. At that time the Mitterrand government signed a contract with the Soviet Union for the delivery of natural gas via a new Euro-pipeline; Mitterrand would also sign an agreement with Algeria, paying an inflated price in order to ensure the friendship of this important ally.[59] The agreement with the Soviet Union, however, caused friction with the Reagan administration and embarrassed the French prime minister. Reagan, who opposed the pipeline from the beginning because he thought it would make European nations dependent upon the Soviets, attempted a number of legal and political maneuvers to sabotage European-Soviet cooperation. The American president let it be known that he opposed France's contract with the Soviet Union, even though there were clear indications that Mitterrand was more concerned about Soviet armament than he was about preserving détente.[60] Mitterrand, of course, defended his government's decision to purchase gas from the Soviet Union. Mauroy, who opposed the arrangement, had to defend it in the National Assembly.[61]

Art also caused problems for Mitterrand. In early March 1982, Mitterrand, like his predecessors, announced a series of "great projects" that he wanted for France. These were another means by which he could build popular support for his presidency and at the same time leave his mark on the cultural life of contemporary France. On March 9, after consulting with the mayor of Paris, Mitterrand revealed eight projects for the capital: La Villette, a park in northeastern Paris that would include a science and industry museum as well as a center for music; Le Zenith, a rock concert hall; the reconstruction of the Théatre de l'Est Parisien; the expansion of La Défense, France's largest commercial center, which is located in western Paris at pont de Neuilly, in order to house two ministries and an international communications center; the transfer of the Ministry of Finance from the rue de Rivoli to make room for an expansion of the Louvre; the creation of an Institute of the Arab World at the quai Fossés-St.-Bernard on the Left Bank; the construction of a people's opera at the place de la Bastille; and a new entrance for the Louvre. While the president obviously attempted to appeal to a large variety of groups in announcing his great projects, from the young aficionados of rock to patrons of art, his plan for the Louvre engendered a great degree of debate and criticism. Mitterrand's selection of Ieoh Ming Pei, a Chinese-American architect, to carry out this project, coupled with Pei's glass pyramid design for the entrance to France's most illustrious art museum, generated intense criticism. Later, after the 1986 legislative elections, the right-wing Finance Minister Balladur would refuse to give up his office in central Paris and permit the planned expansion of the Louvre. Art and culture, as many in France knew, were riddled with politics.[62]

In March the feisty Defferre began to cause Mitterrand some concern, when Defferre was ordered to pay a one-franc fine in a slander suit filed by the Gaullist mayor of Paris, Jacques Chirac. Earlier, Defferre had accused Chirac and other Gaullist leaders, namely Charles Pasqua and Bernard Pons, of having protected Marcel Francisci, a Paris gambling-club boss who was murdered in January. Francisci had been a Gaullist councillor in his native Corsica. Besides this embarrassment for the man who was supposed to represent the law in France, Minister of Interior Defferre also had problems with the Parisian police. When Defferre ordered the transfer of the head of the Paris criminal brigade to Marseille, police authorities revolted. Not only did the criminal brigade chief refuse to go to Marseille, but his superior resigned in protest and 450 inspectors denounced what they viewed as Defferre's effort to undermine the authority of the Paris police force. Defferre had also become embodied in a controversy involving the mysterious death of René Lucet, a civil servant appointed by the Giscard government to untangle bureaucratic problems at the social security center in Marseille. The opposition charged that Lucet died because the Socialists had failed to prevent local union attacks on him. In March a newspaper leaked news of a death threat against Defferre and several other ministers by the infamous international terrorist Carlos. At this time, too, Defferre differed with the Socialist minister of justice, Robert Badinter, on how to carry out identification checks. While Defferre preferred to maintain existing

TABLE 1

Level of Taxes, Social Charges and Obligatory
Payments
(percentage of GDP)

1980	42.5
1981	42.8
1982	43.8
1983	44.6
1984	45.4
1985	45.5
1986	44.4

SOURCE: Compiled from data found in Dominique
Frémy, *Quid des Présidents de la République . . . et des
candidats* (Paris: Robert Laffont, 1987), p. 584.

identity checks, Badinter and later Prime Minister Mauroy disagreed
with the view of the minister of interior on the question of freedom of
movement in France.[63]

With pressure mounting from the business community for tax
relief (see table 1), a trade deficit running at about 6 billion francs or $1
billion per month (see table 2), the setback handed the government by
the Constitutional Council and by voters in the January by-elections,

TABLE 2

Balance of Payments
(billions of francs)

1980	−17.7
1981	−25.8
1982	−79.3
1983	−33.8
1984	−3.6
1985	−1.4
1986	+25.8

SOURCE: Compiled from data found in Frémy, *Quid
des Présidents*, p. 583.

and controversy swirling around the minister of interior, Mitterrand had to make concessions. In an effort to prepare French citizens, especially Socialist supporters, for future government backtracking, *L'Unité* published an editorial titled "The Time for Reflection" and admitted that Mitterrand's government had made some mistakes since coming to power ten months before. *L'Unité* tried to rationalize Socialist errors by telling its readers, "There are no perfect governments, and . . . [our government], having less experience with power than the Right, cannot be exempt from errors."[64]

On April 16, Mauroy announced that the government would reduce business taxes and social security contributions. Since coming to power, the Mitterrand government had imposed roughly $10 billion in new taxes and social costs that squeezed business profits and had a negative effect on industrial investment. Besides a heavier tax burden, business was also confronted with high interest rates imposed by the Socialists to defend the franc, not to mention the general threat to the economy posed by high inflation (see table 3). Given the economic situation in France and recession in the Western world, a record 21,000 bankruptcies and closures occurred in 1981, and the business community predicted more bankruptcies unless the government relieved the burden on industry. In this regard, Yvon Gattaz, president of the National Employers Association (*Confédération Nationale des Patrons Français*—CNPF), met jointly with Mitterrand and Delors and then Mauroy and urged a $3–4 billion relief package for business. After the mid-April meeting between Gattaz and Mauroy, one of the prime minister's aides told the press that the government was anxious "to restore . . . cooperation with and the confidence of the business community."[65] In addition, Mitterrand soon revealed a plan to cap the 1983 budget deficit at 3 percent of the gross domestic product (see table 4). Mitterrand's partners in government, the PCF, quickly branded this plan to reduce business taxes and charges as a "gift to employers."[66]

Trying to rally the country behind his policies, Mitterrand made his second official trip to the provinces. On May 3 and 4 he visited another area hard-hit by unemployment, Limousin, in the center of France, with a population of approximately 730,000. In various towns he said that the fight against unemployment was the chief priority of his government. The president focused on three other themes as well during his visit: solidarity, security, and national unity. Regarding solidarity, he declared that "it was time to put an end to this

TABLE 3

Annual Inflation
(percentage)

1980	13.7
1981	13.9
1982	9.7
1983	9.3
1984	6.7
1985	4.7
1986	2.2
1987	3.1

SOURCE: Compiled from data found in Frémy, *Quid des Présidents*, p. 584; also French Embassy, *News From France*, February 1, 1988, p. 4.

regime of injustice where the rich become richer and the poor become poorer."[67] On the question of security, Mitterrand stressed that "the struggle against all forms of terrorism will be led in a determined fashion. . . ." Terrorism was a subject on the minds of many in France, because a bomb had exploded in late March on a Paris-Toulouse train killing five people, and a car-bomb exploded in April on rue Marbeuf in Paris in front of a building housing pro-Iraqi

TABLE 4

The Budget Deficit
(billions of francs)

1980	− 30.3
1981	− 80.9
1982	− 98.9
1983	− 126.8
1984	− 146.0
1985	− 140.2
1986	− 145.3

SOURCE: Compiled from data found in Frémy, *Quid des Présidents*, p. 583.

Lebanese. Concerning another subject, Mitterrand told his audience that as president his major interest was "national unity." He also stressed his authority as president of the republic by declaring, "I will complete my term as it is fixed by the Constitution."[68] This statement revealed Mitterrand's awareness of the growing opposition to his presidency and government, as well as his anticipation of the problems that lay ahead.

This call for national unity by Mitterrand drew a quick response from Chirac. The ambitious and contentious mayor of Paris stated on May 10 that the majority should respect French business because the Socialists were not owners of French institutions. He added, "This is the only way that national unity can be preserved. . . ." Later at a republican dinner rally, the Gaullist mayor charged that Mitterrand's government was creating a "leviathan state."[69]

The worsening state of the economy and the political sparks beginning to fly encouraged Delors to try and send another message to Mitterrand and his government. On May 20, Delors again called for a "pause" in the reforms and said it was now time to "put the accent on effort."[70] On May 21 at a Socialist gathering at Epinay-sur-Seine," the prime minister stated that "the company is first of all and above all a place of work,"[71] hinting a change of attitude toward business. Then, in late May, following a 1.2 percent increase in inflation in April, Mauroy declared that "a change of tempo is necessary."[72] With the further deterioration of the French economy, Mitterrand considered another devaluation of the franc. However, with the upcoming June summit at Versailles with the leaders of the industrialized Western world, he realized that the second evaluation should occur after the Versailles meeting so as not to weaken any leverage that he might have in encouraging Western leaders to drive their economies with more vigor. At the same time, Mitterrand was concerned about the domestic political repercussions of abandoning reflation. He told members of his government: "It is necessary to quickly make the essential reforms: nationalizations, decentralization, and extended rights for workers. It is necessary to give satisfaction to those who voted for the Left's program. The French who have voted against the austerity of M. Barre will not accept a return to constraints. . . ."[73] Nevertheless, the economic situation left Mitterrand with little choice regarding devaluation, other than the timing of the announcement. Mitterrand now realized that if France and the Western world were to get out of the economic crisis, it would take considerable joint effort. In a speech before the International Labor Organization in Geneva on June 2, he rejected the philosophy of each for himself, "the shortsighted view of certain directors of the world economy" (an oblique reference to the Reagan administration).[74] At Versailles he wanted to gain more cooperation from his Western partners and support for a grandiose plan for the future.

Versailles was not Mitterrand's first meeting with Western leaders since becoming president. In Ottawa in July 1981, Mitterrand had already attended a summit of the leading industrialized nations where he had made an unsuccessful effort to encourage the United States to lower its interest rate and control the fluctuation of the dollar. Mitterrand knew that high interest rates in the United States drew investment capital from France and Europe and that the rapidly rising dollar had dire consequences for a country like France, where approximately 40 percent of all imports are dollar-denominated. Versailles gave Mitterrand a second opportunity.

The Versailles summit in early June was organized by Mitterrand's special adviser, Jacques Attali, at the cost of 25 million francs, a costly affair to reflect the power and glory of a once-formidable world power. With Attali's assistance, Mitterrand devised a speech that focused on modernization, a theme that the Socialist government would return to in future years. Mitterrand's speech called for cooperation in technological development, in biotechnology to reduce famine, sickness, and overpopulation; in electronics to increase production and creative capacities and to aid economies; and in new energy technology pointing the way to the next century. Mitterrand also called on Western leaders for further assistance to underdeveloped nations.[75] He also hoped to achieve some agreement on such issues as rising interest rates, the consequences of technological unemployment, and North-South relations. Yet the Germans remained indifferent to Mitterrand's call and the United States likewise refused to budge.

On the important question of monetary policy, the final statement of the summit simply said that the seven nations promised "to work for a constructive and orderly evolution of the monetary system."[76] Mitterrand now understood that his Western partners would not reflate their economies. Unfortunately, the meeting at Versailles was overshadowed to some extent by serious international developments: an Israeli offensive into Lebanon and the Falklands war between Britain and Argentina.[77] While the courtly ceremonies at Versailles did not produce the Western economic cooperation that Mitterrand desired, the summit did have a lasting effect—it further revealed to the Socialist president the limits of reform. The dreams and the illusions of Year I were now over. From 1982 onward, Mitterrand and his government began a painful apprenticeship in realism.

5

AUSTERITY

From the Plain to the Mountain

June 1982–December 1983

The economic battle will be for Mitterrand what Algeria was for de Gaulle.

—Jacques Attali

While Mitterrand and the Socialists dreamed many dreams during 1981, in 1982–83 the president and his party returned to reality. This realism was manifested in two successive austerity plans—one unveiled in June 1982 and the other an intensified plan announced shortly after the municipal elections of March 1983—that abruptly ended dreams of implanting socialism in one country with a reflationary policy while the remainder of the Western capitalist world pursued austerity measures. Mitterrand's decision to change economic gears eventually resulted in a steep decline in popularity for both the president and his prime minister and created friction between the Socialists and their Communist partners. This era, too, was marked by a crisis in East-West relations over the NATO plan to deploy approximately 600 Pershing II and cruise missiles in Europe late in 1983. Mitterrand, in an effort to draw attention away from the domestic crisis in France, campaigned vigorously for deployment of the new

NATO weapons. Socialist mistakes with the economy in Year I and new international realities forced Mitterrand and his party to become more realistic and at the same time revealed his strong attachment to the Atlantic Alliance.

During Year I of Mitterrand's experiment with power, his government launched a number of reforms but aggravated the economic crisis in France with a reflationary economic policy. For the most part, these reforms were based on Mitterrand's conviction that reflation would spur French economic growth and that the West would soon leave the depths of recession, both mistaken beliefs. He was firmly convinced, at least until the middle of 1982, that heightened consumption and supply would reinvigorate the economy. Increases in wages and in social security benefits, according to socialist theory, would provide a short-run stimulus. Supply, so the theory went, would be boosted by nationalizations which would provide the government with a direct method of investing; the government would also invest in areas such as construction and encourage private investment.

However, this Keynesian socialist economic theory encountered major difficulties that discredited Mitterrand's solutions. Unemployment did not decrease as expected. Although reflation tended to stabilize unemployment, the number of jobless topped two million by the beginning of 1982, despite the president's pledge to keep it below this figure. A huge budget deficit emerged, with social benefits and aid to industry alone jumping a whopping 50 percent in the 1982 budget. Private investment failed to respond to Socialist initiatives, with a 12 percent decline in volume in 1981. The social security deficit deepened: in 1981 health expenditures rose 18 percent and in 1982 amounted to one-fourth of all social welfare costs. An enormous trade deficit appeared, above all with Germany where the deficit grew by 35 percent in 1981 and by 81 percent during the first quarter of 1982. Moreover, since two-fifths of French imports are paid in dollars, financing the deficit meant that the Mitterrand government had to strain its monetary reserves, which in turn helped to weaken the franc. Inflation increased from 13 percent to 14 percent during the first year of the Socialist experiment, and some predicted that inflation might possibly hit 18 percent by the end of 1982. This happened at a time when elsewhere in the Western world inflation was dropping due to austerity policies. In Germany, for instance, between March 1981 and March 1982 inflation was a mere 5.2 percent, while in the United

States it was 6.8 percent.[1] These harsh economic realities obliged Mitterrand to leave the world of Socialist illusion and enter a new world of Socialist realism.

On June 9 after the setback at the Versailles summit, Mitterrand held his second press conference and attempted ever so carefully to prepare the electorate for what he termed the "second phase." In a forty-minute address, he told his audience that national solidarity was needed to combat unemployment, that priority should now be given to investment and innovation, that the budget increase must be limited to 3 percent of GDP, and that the prime minister would discuss future economic policy with union representatives. The president proceeded to list five conditions that had to be met if the second phase was to be successful: conquering the domestic market, assuring a technological future for France, extending social justice, encouraging savings, and balancing regional development.[2] In this way, Mitterrand introduced the public to his newfound economic realism—what would be called *rigueur* (austerity). In an effort to maintain leftist unity in this new phase of government, Mitterrand employed great rhetorical skill and told his audience, "We are following the same policy [and] we are keeping the same objectives."[3] While journalists and others waited for Mitterrand to announce the beginning of austerity, he never used the word and instead left it to others within his government to announce exactly what he and his advisers had in mind for the "second phase."

On June 11 in a meeting of the Council of Ministers Mitterrand approved an austerity program, which Delors called a "little electroshock for the French."[4] The nation learned of the new policy on June 12 and 13. This was a dress rehearsal for a much more rigorous austerity program that would be imposed nine months later following the municipal elections, the first national referendum on the Mitterrand government. On June 12 the government announced a second devaluation, which Mitterrand had envisioned even before the Versailles summit but had withheld until the postsummit period so as not to decrease his leverage with international leaders. The second devaluation, coordinated like the first with members of the European Monetary System, saw the German mark increased by 4.25 percent while the franc was devalued by 5.75 percent. Accompanying this devaluation, which some said was insufficient,[5] the Mitterrand government attempted to reduce inflation below the 10 percent level by also imposing a four-month wage (SMIC—minimum wage—exempted) and price freeze. In reality, the wage and price freeze should have been imposed for a longer period, but the Socialists worried that this might weaken them politically before the March 1983 municipal elections. Justifying controls on the economy, Mitterrand told the Council of Ministers that the government must attack the structural causes of inflation in order to protect the purchasing power of the masses, especially that of the workers.[6] Consequently, the government promised to hold the budget deficit to 3 percent of GDP as the president had mentioned in his press conference; the government also announced that it wanted to deindex wages.

Somewhat grudgingly the PCF supported these austerity measures but stressed, as did the PS, that any austerity policy must not forget the imperative of social justice. PCF leader Marchais, however, in a June 22 statement from Ajaccio told journalists that the wage ceiling was "unjust" and "not at all necessary economically."[7] The Communists found themselves in the position of using revolutionary rhetoric while at the same time supporting a government pursuing an austerity program that reduced purchasing power by 1.25 percent during the four-month wage and price freeze.[8] Mitterrand realized that the PCF's double stance on austerity would in time undermine Communist electoral strength. It was now clear to the Left as well as to the Right that Mitterrand had shifted economic gears. Instead of trying to create new jobs, the task of the government was to make French industry more competitive by increasing research and investment and by forging a new relationship between the state and business.[9] Inflation replaced unemployment as the top priority for the Socialists.

Following the devaluation and the introduction of austerity measures earlier in June, Mitterrand publicly criticized the Reagan administration's economic policy. High interest rates in the United States were driving up the value of the dollar, draining investment capital, and increasing the cost of French imports, especially oil. By the end of June the dollar stood at 6.92 francs and was rising; it did not reach its peak until the summer of 1986 (see table 5).

Mitterrand worried about the impact of the new turn in economic policy on leftist unity as well as on the unions, not to mention the change it would cause in the psychological climate of the electorate. He had to also concern himself with PCF involvement in the emerging controversy over the deployment of the Euromissiles. On June 20 the PCF and the CGT organized what they called "a march for peace" which attracted 200,000 people.[10] In the coming months

TABLE 5

The French Franc and the Exchange Market

		Dollar	Mark	Pound	Yen
March	1980	4.53	2.35	9.72	.0170
April	1981	5.41	2.38	11.43	.0248
May	1982	6.09	2.60	11.00	.0256
June	1983	7.66	3.04	12.17	.0331
May	1984	8.20	3.08	11.53	.0359
June	1985	9.36	3.05	11.97	.0377
June	1986	6.97	3.19	10.74	.0400
March	1987	6.13	3.33	9.64	.0400

SOURCE: Frémy, *Quid des Présidents*, p. 584.

Mitterrand would use the Euromissile debate further to marginalize the Communists and to strengthen his consensus on foreign policy so as to offset voter disenchantment with the economic situation and Socialist economic policy in general.

The new austerity policy precipitated several key cabinet changes. Nicole Questiaux, minister of social affairs and national solidarity, refused to be what she called a "minister of accounts" and left the government, to be replaced by Mitterrand's trusted friend and adviser Pierre Bérégovoy. Mitterrand wanted Bérégovoy for the vacant post because he was a good negotiator, had rapport with the various factions within the PS, and was on good terms with the unions. His job was to find 3 to 4 billion francs for 1982 and for 1983; these amounts were necessary, in part, because health costs were escalating at about 20 percent per year.[11] Chevènement, a young "Jacobin" Socialist who favored a paternalistic state and a protectionist policy, was reassigned to the Ministry of Industry.

With the switch to austerity, Mitterrand placed Prime Minister Mauroy in an awkward position. Mauroy had presided over a reform-minded and free-spending government during Year I, but was now in the difficult situation of heading an austerity government. While Mitterrand kept Mauroy as prime minister because his standing was still relatively high in public opinion polls and because Mauroy's presence suggested continuity even though austerity was an abrupt switching of gears, Mauroy's presence suggested to voters that the economy was out of control under the Socialist government. Some close to the president recommended that Mauroy be replaced once austerity was under way. One such recommendation came from Mitterrand's public-relations expert Séguéla, who told the president in June, "Your prime minister is a minister of dreams; he cannot be one of austerity. You must replace Pierre Mauroy. . . ."[12] Mitterrand decided, however, to try to project an image of continuity by keeping Mauroy and seeking to preserve left-wing unity. Politically, the Socialists made a serious mistake by retaining Mauroy after the government initiated an austerity program.

Some Socialists hoped that a new issue would take attention away from the government's economic problems. On June 30, Defferre presented a plan to the Council of Ministers for the administrative reform of Paris, designed to weaken the power and the visibility of the Gaullist mayor, Jacques Chirac. Defferre's plan called for the creation of twenty mayors, one for each of the arrondissements or districts of the capital, instead of a single mayor. This plan, as might be expected, unleashed a strong reaction from Chirac and his supporters. At a July 1 press conference the mayor condemned the project, one that he attributed to Mitterrand himself.[13] Chirac also had the capital plastered with posters calling for demonstrations of support so as to "save Paris." The "battle for Paris," as the press dubbed the affair, had begun.[14]

Lulled into a false sense of confidence by the great victory of 1981 and the euphoria that followed, the Mitterrand government made a mistake in trying to unseat the mayor of Paris, a mistake that brought renewed life to a relatively dormant Right. For many Parisians this effort to weaken Chirac seemed excessive and vengeful. Nevertheless, Defferre and other government officials argued that by giving each arrondissement of Paris a mayor they would make the capital an urban community and not simply a city. The Socialists also maintained that each mayor would have separate budgetary powers to deal with issues and problems in his or her district. On the other hand, Chirac claimed that the Socialist plan would turn Paris into twenty feuding arrondissements and that separate administrative costs would greatly add to the existing economic crisis. Many in France wondered if the government would also try to break up other large cities like Marseille or Lyon, or if the reform was simply limited to Paris. During the summer of 1982 the major newspapers, such as *Le Monde* and *Le*

Figaro, were filled with charges and countercharges by the opposing sides in the struggle. In the midst of the debate between the government and Chirac, public opinion polls showed that two out of three Parisians opposed the reform of the capital.[15] When Defferre proposed negotiations to Chirac, the Gaullist mayor remained resolute, declaring, "One does not negotiate with the absurd. I do not see what type of negotiations could be opened."[16] Besides winning Parisian public opinion to his cause, Chirac also received support from former president Giscard. Furthermore, in the fall of 1982, Giscard made his first television appearance since the 1981 elections and launched a barrage of criticisms against the government. The mayor of Paris also found support from the new director of *Le Monde*, André Lauren, who publicly came out against the Socialist plan for the capital.[17] Confronting strong opposition from public opinion and a Right that was showing new life, Mitterrand's government retracted the planned reform after a summer of acrimonious debate.[18] Several months later, in the scheduled mayoral election in Paris, the PS ran Paul Quilès in a futile effort to dethrone the feisty and powerful Chirac.

The growing problem of terrorism, both Corsican and Middle Eastern, also held the attention of the Mitterrand government in the summer of 1982. When the Corsican National Liberation Front demanded independence from France, the government responded by denouncing terrorist acts and by promising more autonomy for Corsica under its proposed decentralization plan. In addition to Corsican terrorism, the government had to concern itself with terrorism sponsored by groups in the Middle East that seemed to be responding to French policy in the region. Mitterrand had decided early in his presidency to improve France's less-than-cordial relationship with Israel, a state of affairs that dated back to de Gaulle and his efforts to end his nation's exclusively pro-Israeli policy. Early in March 1982, Mitterrand became the first French and European head of state to visit Israel. This prompted the Israeli president, Itzhak Navon, to call Mitterrand a "true friend." When the French chief of state addressed the Knesset, he declared that both Israel and its neighbors had a right to live in peace. His general policy position on the Arab-Israeli conflict was that the Palestinians had a right to an independent state and that Israel had a right to expect Arab recognition as well as security guarantees. The French president's rapprochement with Israel was short-lived, however, due to the Israeli invasion of Lebanon in June, which sparked considerable criticism in France. Mitterrand's unprecedented visit to

Israel surprised and angered segments of the Arab world and was probably one factor leading to the increase of terrorist attacks against France. Besides Corsican and international terrorism, the French government would also be faced with a home-grown variety of terrorism by a group calling itself "Direct Action," an anarchist band that carried out a number of assassinations and bombings in Paris and elsewhere in France.

The terrorist attacks that drew the greatest attention in the summer of 1982, however, occurred in the heart of Paris. Early in the afternoon of August 9, several armed men opened fire on the Jewish restaurant "Jo Goldenberg" on the rue des Rosiers in the Marais near the Pompidou Cultural Center, leaving six dead and injuring a number of others. While Mitterrand took the initiative to visit the scene of the attack shortly after it happened and while Defferre referred to it as an "odious crime" and accused the Palestinian Abu Nidal of responsibility for the attack, the Israeli embassy in Paris made reference to the "climate of opinion" in France that fostered such attacks. The incident also sparked a march on the Champs-Elysées against anti-Semitism. Shortly after the terrorist attack, Israeli government officials made statements that implicated the French press and even Mitterrand. For example, Israeli Prime Minister Menachem Begin noted that the crime in Paris was the result of distorted views in the French press of the war in Lebanon and Israeli involvement in the war.[19]

Mitterrand took the opportunity to respond to terrorism on French soil and to the dangerous situation in the Middle East. On August 17 he gave a television address in which he condemned the rue des Rosiers incident, promised a government effort to fight terrorism, and reiterated French foreign policy in the Middle East. He said he intended to create a Public Security Ministry to be headed by his close ally Joseph Franceschi, formerly in charge of the matters involving retired persons. Concerning the Middle East, Mitterrand restated three principles that he said guided French policy in the troubled area: (1) the right of Israel to live in peace with secure borders, (2) the right of Palestinians to have a homeland and to create institutions of their choice, and (3) the right of the Lebanese to regain their unity and independence. Mitterrand also said that his government recognized the Palestinian Liberation Organization, referring to the PLO as a "combat organization."[20] Begin quickly responded to Mitterrand's address by saying that he was astonished that the French president would declare that the PLO had won the "right to fight." Yet Israeli opposition leader Shimon Peres defended Mitterrand by declaring, "I admire his address a lot. It is necessary to solve the Palestinian problem in a peaceful way, in a compromise acceptable to all."[21] This, of course, would not be the last time that French policy and perceptions of that policy in the Middle East contributed to international discord and acts of terrorism in France. Worse was yet to come.

The terrorist attack on the rue des Rosiers as well as an earlier attack on the rue Marbeuf in April prompted the head of the CIA-like Agency for External Security (*Direction Générale de la Sécurité Extérieure*—DGSE), Pierre Marion, to propose to Mitterrand that ten internationally known terrorists be "eliminated." Two of those on Marion's hit list were well-known in France: Abu Nidal, who was the suspected instigator of the rue des Rosiers incident, and the infamous "Carlos," who had terrified many for years with his daring bombing attacks. According to Marion, "I proposed to François Mitterrand the physical elimination of them [terrorists] by my agency. The president refused."[22] The French public learned of Marion's proposal and the president's response only in early September 1986 when *Le Nouvel Observateur* published an interview with the former DGSE chief as France experienced one of the worst waves of terrorism in its history.[23]

After millions of vacationers returned from their summer holidays at the end of August, Mitterrand made a personal effort to rally public opinion to his government's economic policy. On September 5 at the invitation of the Press Club of Europe, Mitterrand said that "we are executing a policy that is the [only] one possible in the current international environment." He also promised that the wage and price ceilings would be effective, adding: "When the French know the results of the wage and price ceilings, they will support the policy of the government."[24]

In early September the government found itself in the midst of a veritable economic crisis, much of which it had brought upon itself by the misguided reflationary policies of 1981. Not only was the dollar rising in value against the franc, but so were other European currencies and the Japanese yen. With the prospect of growing inflation—exacerbated by the reflation policy—with a huge trade deficit, and with monetary reserves dwindling, the government had to borrow money from foreign lenders in order to bolster a sinking franc. On September 15 Minister of Finance Delors contracted a $4 billion loan from a consortium of international bankers. Since this loan was quickly spent in an effort to maintain the franc, three months later the government arranged a $2 billion loan from Saudi Arabia. France under Mitterrand was becoming one of the largest debtor nations in the world.[25]

In this situation, Mitterrand had to make a special effort to win support for his government's policies. In late September he made an official visit to the Midi-Pyrénées region of southwest France to generate support for the new austerity policy. When he met the Communist mayor of Tarbes on September 2, Mitterrand reaffirmed his commitment to the program on which he was elected. At Figeac he engaged in some cheerleading exercises by telling his audience, "We are not spectators in a world drama passing us by. We are actors in a France determined to become once again one of the strong nations of the world." He also said that there were two keys to success: "to resist sterile and dangerous provocation and to conquer the path to the future." In this regard, Mitterrand appealed to French citizens to rediscover "the great spirit of noble moments in their history." As mentioned earlier, he also suggested at Figeac that the government would begin to forge a new relationship with the business community. At Castres, the birthplace of Jean Jaurès, the president recalled the earlier socialist's nondoctrinaire socialism once again and suggested that the election of 1981 marked the reclaiming of that tradition. When challenged by his greeters, the president had ready answers at hand for many. For instance, when he met the opposition mayor of Toulouse, Pierre Baudis, who said that he would like to see more consultation between the state and the towns, Mitterrand replied: "We are inaugurating between the state and the local areas a contractual era" (a reference to the government's decentralization plan).[26] Summing up this presidential tour of the southwest, *L'Unité* said that Mitterrand was attempting to initiate a "language of dialogue and reason." *L'Unité* warned the Right that attempts to destabilize the government "might boomerang."[27]

In the midst of this campaign to win support for the austerity policy, Mitterrand lost an old and important friend. On October 18, Pierre Mendès-France died at his Paris home at the age of seventy-five. Mitterrand said of his old friend and colleague, "France has just lost one of its great sons." He added that Mendès-France had "left a faith, a method, and an example. His faith was the republic, his method the truth, and his example the untiring fight for peace and progress."[28] Earlier at his own installation ceremony, Mitterrand had leaned over to

Mendès-France and told his old friend, "It is because of you that I am here."[29] According to one French political observer, Serge July, Mendès-France's political record left a moral lesson for future politicians, that they must "respect the real." The deceased leader had believed that economic difficulties required international solutions, not one-country solutions such as the one Mitterrand had initiated when he launched his reflationary policy while the rest of the Western world pursued austerity. For July, also, the death of Mendès-France psychologically liberated Mitterrand and made it possible for him to reconcile within himself the inheritance of both Mendès-France and de Gaulle.[30] Although such an assumption is impossible to prove, the death of Mendès-France at this particular time probably reinforced the realism that Mitterrand was now applying to his government's policy, especially its economic policy.

In November Mitterrand employed some of Mendès-France's realism when he spoke to a group representing French industry. He stated that the next three years, 1983–85, would entail a period of "great effort," but at the same time he promised to stabilize social charges to French companies. Mitterrand asked his audience to confront the economic crisis with "the spirit of resistance and of conquest."[31]

As the government attempted to build support for its new policy, it also had one eye on the 1983 municipal elections, the first national referendum on the Socialist government. In October the Council of Ministers fixed the date of the elections for March 1983 and announced that a new voting system would be partially implemented in the upcoming elections; towns and villages of less than 3,500 inhabitants would continue to have a single-member voting system, while towns and cities over 3,500 would use a modified proportional system. Mitterrand's 110 Propositions had promised to reinstate proportional representation throughout France, a system that would work to the disadvantage of some of the larger parties, such as the Gaullist RPR, but would aid smaller parties and enhance the political representation of the Socialists at the expense of the right-wing opposition. (The Socialists did not put a full-fledged proportional representation system into effect until 1986.) While the new law on the 1983 municipal elections was promulgated in November 1982, due to pressure from feminists the government tried to give additional representation to women by requiring that all party lists include a quota of at least 25 percent women. Mitterrand's minister of women's rights, Yvette

Roudy, called this quota system "positive discrimination" to aid women. While all political parties agreed to this quota system, the Constitutional Council ruled that it was illegal.[32] Despite this legal setback, many parties would adhere to the quota.[33]

The approaching elections, coupled with the gravity of the economic situation, also influenced the government to grant concessions to business. It agreed to delay any further reductions in the work week, froze employers' contributions to social security until July 1983, and reduced the *taxe professionnelle* (business tax) by 10 percent. From 1982 onward, the new slogan for Mitterrand and the Socialists became discipline, austerity, and national effort.[34]

With the economic crisis beginning to be felt in France, late in 1982 Mitterrand began a series of international visits to promote his image as a leading statesman. Travels abroad offered an obvious advantage to the president; they helped to take his mind off of the gravity of the economic situation in France and also diverted public attention from it. Like many leaders who confront problems at home, Mitterrand made many trips to the airport from the end of 1982 through 1983.

From November 24 to 26 he visited Egypt for talks with Hosni Mubarak. Mitterrand used this opportunity to develop Franco-Egyptian diplomatic and economic relations. Coinciding with this visit to the Middle East, *Le Monde* published on November 26 an interview with the president in which he gave his views on requirements for peace in the troubled area. As he had stated earlier, Mitterrand said that the Arab states must recognize Israel's right to live within secure frontiers and the Palestinians must have a sovereign homeland. He also used this interview to stress that the new leadership of the Soviet Union under Yuri Andropov must withdraw from Afghanistan. Moreover, he used this interview to stress that France had to mobilize all the means necessary to surmount the economic crisis. He promised that obligatory social and fiscal charges would be stabilized and then reduced.[35]

Mitterrand followed up his visit to Egypt with a trip to India from November 27 to 30. There he praised New Delhi's attachment to democracy, its desire to do away with the two military blocs, and its emphasis on development.[36] With these official visits and others in the future, Mitterrand seemed to be following an old Chinese proverb as he directed the foreign affairs of France: "The more friends the better." During 1983 he averaged more than one trip abroad per month, including the Williamsburg summit of the seven leading industrialized nations of the Western world.

Mitterrand ended 1982 with the traditional New Year's greeting to the nation, a greeting in which, unlike 1981, he stressed the importance of business to the French economy. Prior to this address, the minister of finance had stated in an interview in the newsweekly *L'Express* that "there can be no expensive reforms in 1983 and 1984."[37] Mitterrand followed Delors's theme in the New Year's address and expressed his confidence that in the future France would be able to escape from what he termed a "universal crisis." Government policy, said the president, would now focus on professional training for the young between eighteen and twenty-five years of age, on family assistance, on national solidarity, and especially on business. He told the nation that France "must produce more and produce better." He added that the government would moderate taxes and charges on business; for France must "invest, invest, and know how to sell in order to be competitive."[38]

The government's austerity policy and the new recognition of the importance of business prompted the Socialists to promote the extension of certain "liberties" instead of costly social and economic reforms. Nevertheless, in the future the new emphasis on liberties would create dangerous problems for the Mitterrand government. Furthermore, in 1983 the Socialists and their allies in government found themselves in the minority with the voters.

Mitterrand intended to expand upon his New Year's greeting with an address on January 1 from his country home in Latché, near Soustons, but could not do so because a portable transmission antenna was not in place on time.[39] Somewhat embarrassed, Mitterrand finally gave his address on January 2 and expanded on various aspects of his December 31 remarks. He once again promised professional training for eighteen- to twenty-five-year-olds, additional assistance to families with two or three children, an expansion of social justice, a close examination of unemployment, and freedom of conscience in private schools (a remark to soothe both sides of a school reform controversy that was brewing). The president also came out against protectionism, saying that he saw hopeful signs, namely a belief that France would experience economic growth in the months ahead. He also said that there would be more consultation in the future between industrialized nations, and that the dollar as well as interest rates would soon fall.[40] These reassuring remarks, despite the austerity policy of the Socialists, were designed, in part, to comfort an electorate that would soon go to the polls and vote in municipal elections. Mitterrand knew that austerity, after a year of euphoria and free spending, inevitably meant a loss of popularity for the Socialist government.

By the beginning of 1983 Mitterrand and his socialist confreres recorded a significant drop in public support. For instance, in June 1981 74 percent of the public expressed confidence in Mitterrand, compared to 71 percent for Mauroy. After the introduction of austerity in June of 1982, the popularity of both leaders began a precipitous fall. In June 1982, 63 percent of the public expressed confidence in Mitterrand, while 55 percent had confidence in Mauroy. By January 1983 the president's and the prime minister's confidence ratings dropped to 48 percent and 40 percent respectively.[41] This significant fall in popularity occurred even though Mitterrand's four-month-long wage and price freeze produced positive results. At the turn of the year statistics revealed that during the period when the wage and price controls were in effect, inflation dropped by 0.4 to 0.5 percent per month, and the average inflation rate for 1982 was down to 9.7 percent. In December of 1982 unemployment had even fallen by 0.5 percent.[42] With the upcoming municipal elections approaching and Socialist popularity low, it was imperative to pump up public opinion.

On January 20, 1983 Mitterrand went to West Germany where he gave a speech before the German Bundestag to celebrate the twentieth anniversary of a Franco-German friendship treaty. In this speech Mitterrand shocked his old German Social Democrat friend Willy Brandt by stating that Soviet conventional and nuclear superiority left Europe with no choice but to deploy the newly-assigned NATO missiles at the end of the year as scheduled. With pacifist demonstrations on the rise throughout Germany and in Western Europe in general, but not in France since NATO missiles were not to be deployed in the "hexagon," Mitterrand gave his support to the conservative government of Helmut Kohl at a moment when the German chancellor needed it. Earlier Mitterrand had also announced that he supported the development of a French neutron bomb. Throughout 1983 he hammered hard at the need to deploy the almost 600 Pershing II and cruise missiles. In Belgium, for instance, he declared, "The pacifists are in the West, [while] the missiles are in the East."[43] For Mitterrand, this stance demonstrated his committed support for the Atlantic Alliance, embarrassed the PCF and forced them into a compromising position, and helped to divert public attention in France from the economic crisis and the government's austerity measures. Coupled with his numerous travels abroad in 1983, eighteen in number, Mitterrand made deployment of the NATO missiles a major issue. France and Europe, he said, must counter the Soviet threat—maintaining détente was not necessarily the main issue for him.[44]

Besides stressing the threat from the East, Mitterrand took action at home to demonstrate that he had acquired a better understanding of the requirements of business. At the Council of Ministers meeting on February 2, the president said that France's industrial policy must guard against "a fussy bureaucracy" and that the autonomy of the public sector must be respected by his government. His comments on the necessary autonomy for the public sector were precipitated primarily by a meeting on January 11 with six leaders of nationalized firms who had protested what they considered the rigid control of the minister of industry over their enterprises. When Chevènement took over control of the ministry in the summer of 1982, he had wanted to create what the French call national *filières*, a horizontal integration of industry, so that France would not be dependent on other nations. Chevènement also wanted to invest heavily in certain industries, especially computers and electronics, to give France a competitive edge in the international market. What Chevènement desired was an industrial sector, similar to the Japanese model, that featured heavy subsidies for research and development in key areas favored by the state which for Chevènement meant the minister of industry himself. Consequently, Mitterrand's announcement at the February 2 Council of Ministers meeting represented a setback for Chevènement and a victory for the leaders of certain nationalized sectors.[45] Chevènement wanted to resign after this presidential rebuke, but Mitterrand convinced him to remain in his post until at least after the March municipal elections. Published reports on Mitterrand's decision in the Council of Ministers suggested to the electorate on the eve of national elections that the Socialists were loosening their grip on the economy.

The prime minister, on the other hand, provided voters with strong suggestions that France was on its way to recovery. In a TV interview on February 16, Mauroy made positive statements that he repeated several times before the elections. The prime minister insisted that "the government's policy is fixed for 1983" and "we do not have further austerity plans in our pockets." He also told his audience that "the larger problems are behind us."[46] Mauroy made these exaggerated statements knowing the difficulties that lay ahead. The truth of the matter was that Mitterrand did envision another phase of austerity but had decided for political reasons to wait until after the municipal election to announce it. As time would show, Mauroy's heady rhetoric did not calm French concerns about the economic crisis.

On the eve of the March legislative elections, Mitterrand tried to gain the support of the foreign intelligentsia in order to legitimize his government. When Mitterrand was first elected he expected an outpouring of support from French intellectuals, which never materialized, to the alarm of the Socialists. The hesitancy of French intellectuals was due in part to the fact that Mitterrand had come to power with the assistance of an electoral alliance with the Communists and had even appointed several of them to his government; this came at a time when many Western intellectuals were becoming more critical of Marxism and the Soviet Union due to backwardness and repression in the East. Consequently, in February the Ministry of Culture sponsored an international meeting of 400 writers, artists, and cinema notables from five continents to try to counter the "silence of the intellectuals" in France in regard to the Socialist government. Mitterrand, the moving force behind the conference, tried to link the work of the intellectual to development by choosing the theme "Creation and Development" for his star-studded affair. Some of those in attendance included scholars Tom Bishop, Ezra Suleiman, and Norman Birnbaum; movie directors and actors such as Francis Ford Coppola, Sidney Lumet, and Sean Penn; writers such as Susan Sontag, Norman Mailer, and William Styron; and economists like Wassily Leontief and John Kenneth Galbraith. Mitterrand himself addressed the conference, affirming the important alliance between the intellectual and the artist at this time, similar to the one that had existed during the Renaissance and during the Enlightenment. The task of the writer-intellectual today, he said, is to invent "a civilization of work which is not separated from the intellect, but which reunifies man. . . . to invest in culture is to invest in the future."[47] Mitterrand wanted to remind his international guests as well as the French electorate that his government, unlike other Western governments, had doubled the budget for culture, despite widespread cutbacks elsewhere with the onset of austerity. According to some critics, Mitterrand's international conference of intellectuals was an effort to buy foreign legitimacy for a government that France's intellectuals had failed to legitimize. It was obvious to many that France's prominent intellectuals, such as Michel Foucault, Claude Lévi-Strauss, François Furet, Emmanuel Le Roy-Ladurie, Castoriadis, and Raymond Aron, were not in attendance.[48]

Only two intellectuals had climbed aboard the Mitterrand bandwagon in 1981, Debray and Attali. Several months after the 1983 conference of foreign intellectuals, government spokesperson Max Gallo renewed a call for French intellectuals to support the Socialist government. However, a number of French intellectuals responded to Gallo by arguing in the pages of *Le Monde* that the role of the intellectual was to criticize the state, not be seduced by it. The February conference of imported intellectuals and the later call for the support of intellectuals in France demonstrated the growing crisis of confidence in Mitterrand's government.[49]

This falling confidence surfaced openly in the March 1983 municipal elections. These elections, held on March 6 and 13, drew a heavy voter turnout of more than 78 percent. After the first round of voting the Left engaged in a strong mobilization drive to minimize the losses. When the second round was over, the Left had lost thirty-one towns of more than 30,000 inhabitants, including Paris and Lyon, with the PS losing fifteen cities and the Communists sixteen. Among the eleven largest towns over 200,000 in population, the Left lost all but three: Marseille and Rennes (PS) and Le Havre (PCF). Although the Left had won a majority in the large cities in the elections of 1977, 1978, and 1981, it won only 44.24 percent of the vote in 1983, compared to 53.6 percent for the Right. In March 1983, too, some Socialists, like Defferre, were barely reelected. (Later, in the Senate elections of September 1983, voters gave the opposition another twelve seats to add to the majority that they already possessed.)[50]

The municipal elections also revealed an alarming development. Jean-Marie Le Pen's extremist National Front (*Front National—* FN) with its racist and anti-immigrant rhetoric made significant gains, especially in Paris. In the twentieth arrondissement of the capital the National Front won 16 percent of the vote. In the upcoming European Parliament election the FN would make spectacular gains. Le Pen, as political analysis showed, pulled votes from the traditional Right, and also from the Communist party. The working class was not only hard hit by unemployment, but many workers felt that the PCF had a contradictory policy on immigrants. On the one hand, it criticized excessive immigrant populations in urban areas and at the same time used immigrant workers as shock troops in certain strike situations.[51] The FN offered disenchanted and often unemployed workers the most radical solution to France's dilemma over immigration policy: to send foreign workers, especially Arabs and black Africans, home.

There were many reasons that voters marked their ballots for the opposition in the 1983 municipal elections. One important reason was that the economy seemed to be out of control under the Socialist government. The abrupt switch to austerity in June 1982, for which the electorate was ill-prepared, alarmed many in France. In addition, centrist voters who had supported Mitterrand in 1981 opposed the inclusion of four Communist ministers in government. It appeared as if the PCF had "infiltrated" certain administrative posts and exercised a significant influence on the Socialists. Furthermore, numerous opposition voters were concerned about what they perceived to be the growing power of leftist unions in workplaces and public institutions, such as universities. Those opposing the Left were also hostile to Socialist policies that affected certain cherished institutions, like the plan for private schools, the Socialist statute on the press, or reforms in certain sectors of the health-care services. Again, the problem of security haunted many voters. Not only was international terrorism beginning to strike the republic, but secessionist terrorism had brought violence to Corsica, Brittany, and the Basque region, and France was beginning to witness racist terrorism by extreme right-wing groups aimed at Arab immigrants. Mitterrand's reform-minded minister of justice, Robert Badinter, appeared lax to some French citizens worried about security problems. Finally, the Socialist government had not adopted a clear immigration policy, trying to legalize the position of some immigrants and repatriating others. Consequently, the presence of more than 4 million immigrants in France—approximately 7 percent of the population and not excessive by European standards—was an issue that the extreme Right, namely Le Pen's National Front, exploited before and after the March 1983 elections as France experienced rising unemployment and increasing terrorist violence.[52]

While the municipal elections proved embarrassing to the Socialists, the week that followed was one of the most difficult for Mitterrand. On March 14, immediately following the second round of the municipal elections, Mitterrand met with Prime Minister Mauroy and told him that the elections were not the setback that he expected. According to one well-informed source, Mitterrand envisioned losing thirty-five to forty cities of over 30,000 inhabitants in 1983.[53] The final results undoubtedly gave new life to Prime Minister Mauroy who was convinced that he would be replaced after the municipal elections. While Mitterrand did not ask Mauroy for his resignation on March 14, he did, according to several journalists in France, tell Mauroy to be more rigorous with austerity and indicate that France should leave the European Monetary System (EMS), an arrangement of Western European nations designed to stabilize their currencies and prevent disruptive currency fluctuations. Mauroy, reportedly, was caught by surprise and pleaded for time. The prime minister quickly called a meeting with his own advisers and then informed the president that a new prime minister would have to take France out of the EMS. Not only did Mauroy's response shock the president, but Mitterrand had already announced a press conference for March 23 where he intended to inform the public about the new economic direction for France. In ten days' time Mitterrand, with the aid of his advisers, had to draw up a new economic battle plan. Confusion reigned at the Château.[54]

The Elysée and the government were divided over leaving the EMS. Some of Mitterrand's advisers—the industrialist Riboud, Minister of Social Affairs Bérégovoy, and CERES leader Chevènement—believed that leaving the EMS and the "snake" (the coordinated system of EMS currencies that keeps them closely aligned with each other) would allow the franc to float and help to restart growth. Others at the Elysée, such as Attali and Bianco, warned Mitterrand that the franc would fall by 20–30 percent if France abandoned the EMS. Delors even bombarded the Elysée with notes warning against dropping out of the system. At this point, the young Fabius reportedly intervened and suggested to Mitterrand that he reverse himself. Fabius reportedly stated later, "From this date on, I played an important role in economic policy."[55] However, Fabius himself claims that he had no knowledge of Mitterrand's directive to Mauroy to pull out of the EMS. Fabius does admit that there was a lively debate among members of the government over this vital issue.[56] Regardless of the exact scenario, Mitterrand decided to remain in the EMS. He instructed Delors to begin negotiations with the Germans for another devaluation of the franc. On March 21 the government announced its third devaluation in eighteen months; this time the devaluation was 8 percent against the German mark. In the midst of this drama, Mitterrand asked Mauroy to form his third government.

On March 22, Mauroy announced the composition of the new

government, one of "combat," which saw the number of ministers reduced from thirty-four to fifteen. While Delors and Bérégovoy had their ministries strengthened, Chevènement and Jobert resigned. Fabius became chief of the Ministry of Industry and Research. In the third Mauroy government, Chevènement was offered the Ministry of Urbanism and Lodging, a post that he refused. The CERES leader told Mitterrand that he wanted the Ministry of Industry or nothing.[57] With Chevènement no longer in the government, Mitterrand placed Edith Cresson at the Ministry of Foreign Commerce and Tourism and elevated Rocard to the difficult Ministry of Agriculture. By promoting Rocard, Mitterrand was able to balance the departure of Chevènement and at the same time provide Rocard, a rival of the president, with a post riddled with potential conflict due to discontent among French farmers. Once again, Mitterrand had "juggled" the tendencies within the PS to his own advantage. With this third government, six new ministerial appointments were made. The composition of the new government, especially with the elevation of Fabius and Rocard and the ouster of the Marxist-oriented Chevènement, meant that a significant *recentrage*, or movement to the center, occurred. The president himself dropped the word "socialism" from his vocabulary after the setback in the 1983 elections and the formation of the third Mauroy government. The new buzzwords for Mitterrand now became "industrial dynamism," "competitive technology," and "modernization." Mitterrand was looking ahead to the 1986 legislative elections.

As mentioned earlier, Mauroy had thought that he would lose his job at the Matignon (the prime minister's residence) after the 1983 municipal elections. Yet two events saved him. One, of course, was that the municipal elections were not as disastrous as the Left had anticipated. The second factor that aided Mauroy was that while Mitterrand preferred Delors as prime minister in the post-1983 election period, Delors wanted full power over economic and financial policy. The president was not willing to relinquish such power. Justifying the continuation of his prime minister, Mitterrand told reporters, "Mauroy is the hero of the Left." Mitterrand also cited a *BVA-Paris Match* poll showing 40 percent of the electorate satisfied with Mauroy, while 68 percent of those on the Left had confidence in him.[58] Thus Mauroy had the dubious distinction of being Mitterrand's prime minister during a period of reform and during a period of austerity.

With the formation of the new government Mitterrand made a national address and on March 23, without revealing the details of the

next austerity program, asked the French "to double [their] energy and
. . . tenacity for national reform." In this address, aired on all three
television channels, the president defended the government's policy as
necessary in order to change France and as just for the greatest
number. Mitterrand called on the French to mobilize themselves on
three fronts: the need to reduce unemployment, inflation, and the
foreign commercial debt. He announced six objectives for the new
Mauroy government: training the young, reducing inflation, balancing
the foreign trade deficit, supporting innovative exporting companies,
stabilizing the financing of the social security system and controlling
the budget, and encouraging savings.[59] In justifying Socialist austerity, the exact details of which the French would learn about two
days after Mitterrand's televised address, the president tried to link the
reforms of 1981 and the austerity of 1982 and 1983 by referring to
what he perceived to be "the continuity in policy." He argued that
"austerity is a necessary parenthesis."[60] Such an attempt by Mitterrand to project continuity in his policy instead of a *virage*, or U-turn,
was a rhetorical effort by the president to preserve left-wing unity.

Besides the devaluation announced earlier, the second phase of
austerity, which became known on March 25 and was instituted by
governmental decree in order to avoid damaging debate on the issue,
was aimed at stabilizing the foreign trade gap, reducing the deficit, and
lowering inflation. With the third devaluation of the franc, foreign
goods soared in price. To further reduce demand, especially for foreign goods which had a certain "snob appeal" according to the minister of finance,[61] the government announced that it would remove 65
billion francs from circulation. The new austerity plan also limited the
amount of money that French citizens could take abroad to a mere two
thousand francs. This was done, in part, to make citizens more aware
of the real financial situation in France. The March austerity plan also
included a 1 percent surtax and a 10 percent obligatory loan from the
taxable incomes of the 8 million wealthiest households in order to
generate revenue and reduce consumption. An additional means of
raising revenue included higher cigarette and alcohol taxes. The government announced that its contribution to the 60 billion franc deficit
of public funds would be cut and that the state budget would be frozen
at 20 billion francs. The new priorities for the Socialist government
became the private firm and industrial investment. In this regard, the
austerity package promised no new taxes on business in order to
encourage investment, and the Socialists agreed to lower the social

costs of businesses. The Mitterrand government also lifted certain layoff restrictions to aid the business community.[62]

Overall, the 1982 and 1983 austerity controls did have a positive effect on the economy if one overlooks the rising unemployment and the growing interest on the external debt. By the end of 1983 the trade deficit had been reduced by more than one-half, down to 42 billion francs. The balance of payments deficit had also been cut by more than one-half, 33 billion francs at the end of 1983. The inflation rate, though it did not fall to 8 percent in 1983 as Delors had hoped, was reduced to 9.3 percent.[63] Nevertheless, while France was just beginning to impose strict austerity measures, the economies of the United States, West Germany, and Japan began to experience economic growth. What worried many in France was the continued growth of unemployment (see table 6).

Increasingly, the president relied upon the international argument to explain the economic crisis in France, one shunned by Mitterrand and the Socialists before their ascent to power. More and more, Mitterrand and his ministers told the electorate that France was caught in a worldwide economic crisis.[64] Nonetheless, discontent with Socialist economic policies produced growing demonstrations, such as the violent one in Brittany in late April of 1983, and a steep decline in Mitterrand's popularity as well as that of his prime minister.

In an effort to offset the rising criticism, on April 25 and 26

TABLE 6

Growth of Unemployment

	Number	Percentage of work force
1981 (March)	1,657,200	7.3
1982 (March)	1,964,500	8.0
1983 (March)	2,017,100	8.1
1984 (March)	2,217,000	8.7
1985 (March)	2,419,800	10.1
1986 (April)	2,247,000	—
1987 (February)	2,698,700	11

SOURCE: Frémy, *Quid des Présidents*, p. 584.

Mitterrand made another official visit to the provinces to defend his government's policy. This time the president went to Mauroy's home base, Pas-de-Calais in the north of France. This trip to the industrial north occurred in the midst of social conflict in Paris and in the provinces. For example, a strike was under way by medical students, doctors and interns at university hospitals protesting proposed reforms in health services. Farmers, too, were protesting what they considered to be insufficient government price supports. During the visit to the north, an area hard hit by the austerity policy, Mitterrand attempted to reassert the authority of the state, his authority. At Dunkirk on April 25 he declared, "National unity cannot continue without the authority of the state, which I intend to make respected. . . ."[65] During his visit, he also spoke on the government's rationale for the austerity program: "Everything that I do and which seems so difficult for you is not done just to transcend the world [economic] crisis—it is done essentially to safeguard and to prepare France for the future. . . . Our objective is not austerity but reform, and austerity is necessary for reform."[66] At Lens, Mitterrand discussed the coal industry, which was anticipating large cutbacks. He declared rather bluntly, "Let us be clear, the state cannot at the same time carry the enormous deficit of the coal industry . . . and participate in an industrial renaissance. . . ."[67] While Mitterrand and Mauroy failed adequately to prepare public opinion for the onset of austerity, now that the municipal elections were behind them the president and his prime minister invested more time explaining austerity to counter the falling popularity of the government and begin to prepare for future elections.

In May, Mitterrand turned his attention to the international scene where he launched a new appeal and at the same time saw an old appeal fade from his priorities. At a May meeting of the Organization for Economic Cooperation and Development, he called for a "new Bretton Woods agreement" so as to stabilize their fluctuating currencies, as had occurred after World War II. Although Mitterrand's allies paid lip service to the idea, no substantial reform followed the president's appeal. At the OECD meeting Mitterrand also proposed a program for Third World development[68] and would later address the United Nations to stress the urgency for developed nations to cut back on military expenses and aid Third World countries.[69] He had employed this same theme at the Cancún conference of Western nations shortly after his election victory, and emphasized the need to improve North-South relations and the belief that East-West relations had too long dominated international affairs. Although Mitterrand began his presidency with a strong Third World thrust, this concern, which dates back to his ministerial roles under the Fourth Republic, diminished as a priority after he realized the gravity of the economic situation in France. After 1983 his attention focused on France and its relations with the industrialized West.

Also in May, Mitterrand met in Paris with Chancellor Kohl in preparation for an upcoming summit in Williamsburg, Virginia. On the same day that the French president and the German chancellor began their discussions, the European Economic Community announced a 4 billion ECU (European Currency Unit) loan to France, equivalent to slightly less than 27 billion francs, a loan that Delors negotiated with the promise to Germany that France would be diligent with its austerity plans. During the discussions with Kohl, the French president threw a verbal barb at President Reagan by declaring, "It is not normal that the American budgetary deficit must be paid by us" (a reference, in part, to high interest rates in the United States attracting European investment capital). Kohl quickly replied, "It is necessary to talk about one's friends with one's friends. We can do that at Williamsburg."[70] Mitterrand, of course, was hoping to gain Kohl's support for a joint request for a change in U.S. monetary and fiscal policy.

Before traveling to the summit, Mitterrand invited Marchais, Jospin, Chirac, Giscard, and others to the Elysée to prepare for Williamsburg and to consolidate support at home for France's position abroad. This meeting with majority and opposition leaders made it seem as if the president wanted to forge a bipartisan foreign policy for France, a feat relatively easy to accomplish since there was already a bipartisan consensus on Mitterrand's Gaullist-like foreign and defense policy, though the Communists would shortly break this consensus. France's experience in 1870, 1914, and 1940, where German armies threatened the sovereignty of the nation, had paved the way for de Gaulle's conception of foreign and defense policy.

At the Williamsburg meeting on May 28–30 Western leaders agreed on measures to aid economic recovery: reducing inflation, lowering interest rates, cutting budget deficits, avoiding protectionism, and renegotiating the General Agreement on Tariffs and Trade (GATT). When Mitterrand, as he had earlier at the OECD meeting, called for a new Bretton Woods conference[71] to consider the stabilization of fluctuating exchange rates, a large problem for the ailing French economy, Western leaders simply agreed to "study" the possibility of holding such an international monetary conference. Reagan, Thatcher, and others preferred only a loose coordination of Western economies. The summit representatives did sign a security agreement that expressed their willingness to support "a military force sufficient to deter any attack" and stated that they favored the deployment of the Pershing II and cruise missiles on European soil if negotiations with the Soviets in Geneva did not progress.[72]

While Mitterrand gained little at the Virginia summit, he soon discovered that he had lost some political support at home for what had transpired at Williamsburg. Mitterrand's partners, the PCF, interpreted the Williamsburg security agreement as one aimed at the Soviet Union and openly criticized the president's actions. The Communists wanted an "omnidirectional defense policy" and not one aimed against the Soviets.[73] In the months ahead, the Euromissile debate and Mitterrand's second austerity program, which Marchais said constituted "a contradiction with the objectives defined by the president of the republic in 1981,"[74] caused a growing rift between Mitterrand and the Communists.

The second austerity plan stimulated criticism not only from the PCF, but from within the ranks of the Socialist party as well. Some Mitterrandists and a large faction of the CERES group criticized the new economic policy at a PS meeting on May 28 at Pré-Saint-Gervais. Chevènement, for instance, even charged that austerity was not a "parenthesis," but a "U-turn."[75] This strong statement by the CERES leader directly contradicted Mitterrand's explanation of the government's economic policy.

The rising criticism stimulated by the new level of austerity provoked Mitterrand to make a televised broadcast on June 8, the third time in five months that the president felt compelled to explain his policies. Questioned by the head of the political staff of the television station, Mitterrand stressed that he was responsible for the new economic policy and that "no other policy will free the French from the necessary effort" to put the economy and the finances of the nation on firm footing. The president insisted that austerity would be carried out consistent with social and economic justice. When *Le Monde* reported the president's appearance, it ran a headline reading, "M. Mitterrand Wants to Clarify His Austerity Policy in Order to Prevent an Extension of Discontent."[76] In time, the major unions as well as the PCF gave their tacit approval to the new austerity program but insisted that the burden must be shared by all.[77] Mitterrand also used this television appearance to condemn a June 3 police demonstration in Paris, after which the minister of interior suspended several members of the force. The president labeled such a demonstration a "seditious event."[78]

Before continuing his effort to explain the austerity policy of his government, Mitterrand made an official visit to Corsica on June 13 and 14 to win support for unity with France. In the midst of rising violence on the island as a result of a heightened independence drive, he told the Corsicans that they would have autonomy in union with France and that Paris would respect cultural differences. When he arrived in Ajaccio he said that he "believed . . . in the right of Corsica to be different and to have its own cultural differences." Mitterrand, too, stressed the decentralization plan of his government, trying to suggest that the Socialists were sensitive to Corsican problems and had taken action to respond to them.[79]

Mitterrand continued his campaign to explain the new austerity policy in an early morning radio program later in the month. Trying to strike a tone of realism, the president said that he had never doubted that the "first three years [referring to his government] would be the most difficult." Mitterrand also tried to place some of the blame for France's economic difficulties on previous governments when he declared, "One does not solve in two years the problems that have existed for ten years." While Mitterrand said that he expected the level of taxes and social contributions to rise to 45 percent in 1984, he was optimistic that inflation would fall to 8 percent by the end of the year and to 5 percent in 1984. Responding to a challenge by Chirac, the president rejected a demand by the mayor of Paris that a referendum be called on economic policy, and added that he did not foresee any situation where the National Assembly would have to be dissolved and new elections called.[80] Chirac's appeal reflected the intensification of the political battle between the Right and the Left in France. In this regard, Prime Minister Mauroy charged in an article in *Le Monde* that the Right was putting democracy in peril with its provocations.[81] Both the president and the prime minister, however, tried to soothe public opinion and defend the new economic policies.

Besides trying to calm the public with regard to the austerity plan and to quell violence in Corsica, Mitterrand and the PS were somewhat embarrassed to learn in June that their Communist partners had been found guilty of electoral fraud in the 1983 elections, primarily in the Parisian suburbs. This ruling against the Communists meant that new elections would have to occur over a period of months in districts where fraud had been found. This unexpected political development further eroded public confidence in the PCF as a partner in government and also tarnished the image of the Union of the Left, including that of the Socialists.[82]

With discontent rising in France and Mitterrand determined to defend the new austerity program, he held a breakfast meeting with several journalists—not an uncommon occurrence—and made a number of confessions that made it seem as if he alone was responsible for the previous economic mistakes. Ostensibly this was an attempt by the president to reduce public discontent with the government and seek general support for austerity. According to the television journalist Philippe Bauchard, who was present, Mitterrand remarked: "I have not changed. I will be loyal to the image that the French had of me in 1981. Austerity does not please me, but it was I who imposed it on Mauroy and Delors in the spring of last year. I am the one that took all of the risks, for we should have devalued a little sooner in 1982." (Mitterrand added that only Jobert suggested that he devalue in 1981.)[83] Continuing with his views on the economy, Mitterrand told the journalists that he "believed a little too much, as did Jean-Pierre Chevènement, Jacques Delors, and Jacques Attali, that 1960s style growth could come back without effort."[84] Concerning the euphoria on the left, especially in the government after his election, Mitterrand said, "We dreamed . . . in 1981."[85] He also confessed that he and his government underestimated the role of lobbies and the media.[86] Reportedly, he also revealed some of his views on his American counterpart, calling Reagan "more dangerous, more unpredictable than he had believed. He personifies a strong Right. . . . Reagan does not govern," he added. "It is the military-industrial complex that governs the United States. I will not let him change me."[87] Raising the specter of an external threat, whether it be the Soviet Union or the United States, has traditionally aided French politicians at home, a fact that Mitterrand knows only too well. Despite the swipes at Reagan, Mitterrand's real purpose was to win media support for austerity and give the impression that he as head of state had made a conscious decision to forfeit the reflationary policy and was now embarked on the path of economic realism. The truth of the matter was that Mitterrand stumbled into the austerity program, or perhaps more accurately, was forced to accept austerity by Delors's warnings and by economic reality itself.

To some degree, the seriousness of the economic crisis at home was deflected by the president's external policy. The months of July and August found Mitterrand devoting considerable attention to foreign affairs. In July he tried to counter challenges from Marchais concerning France's position on the Euromissiles, while in August he involved France in a dangerous conflict in Chad. From July 11 to 13 Marchais visited Moscow where he criticized the French position on the Euromissiles. Mitterrand responded to Marchais and others in a Bastille Day television address, declaring that "all that concerns national independence and the integrity of the nation is decided neither in Moscow, nor Washington, nor in Geneva, but in Paris and by me!"[88] With this strong statement the president attempted to remind his critics that he had a privileged domain, what the French call a *domaine réservé*, and that it was he who would protect the national interest of France in the East-West conflict over the Euromissiles. To many, Mitterrand's statement had a definite Gaullist ring, but so too did the Socialist president's foreign policy in general.

Developments in Chad quickly turned French attention from Europe to Africa. On August 1 the French government announced that it was sending arms, notably anti-aircraft weapons, to Chad to aid the government of Hissene Habré who had requested assistance to protect his country from Libyan aggression. On August 10 Paris officials announced the beginning of Operation Manta which involved sending 3,000 French soldiers to assist the government of Chad. While the intervention may have momentarily diverted French opinion from the economic crisis, it also caused concern. Mitterrand, in an effort to ease anxieties at home, stressed that the Habré government had requested French assistance but that France's role would only be defensive, "I have said no . . . to a preventive war. I have said no to general war. And I have said no . . . to direct participation of France in a civil war."[89] Mitterrand continued by saying that "the desire for war and domination was Libya's, not France's."[90] Intervention in Chad would become France's largest military operation since the Algerian war. While this and other global issues focused French attention on the international situation, Mitterrand still had to make a concerted effort to stem the growing tide of disenchantment with his government's economic policies.

On September 15 Mitterrand continued his campaign to explain the austerity policy, a campaign now couched in the language of a realist. He was interviewed on television by several French personalities, including author François de Closets whose widely read book *Toujours plus* (Always more) commented on the attitude of greed that pervaded certain groups—notably trade unions and the privileged—as well as selfishness in France. Stressing again that his policy was the only one possible at the time, Mitterrand observed that the previous ten-year period had seen a retardation of French industry, and little attention had been paid to social justice. He told his viewers that the deficit required that taxes and social contributions be increased from 44.7 percent of the GDP to 45.6 percent in 1984, but such high tax levels are becoming "unbearable." The economic crisis, a world crisis according to Mitterrand, demanded such increases. He surprised the business community somewhat when he labeled the business tax as "horribly unjust, antieconomic because it works against a reduction in inflation and unemployment, and limits exports." Since it generated 50 billion francs in revenue for the government, the tax could not be reduced at the present time. The president did make a vague promise to "reform" the business tax in the future. Concerning his overall austerity policy, Mitterrand posed a rhetorical question, "Will it make me unpopular? Well, I would prefer that to not fulfilling my obligation." In this television appearance, like his other public appearances since his September 27, 1982 speech at Figeac where he proposed lifting the economic and financial burden on industry and business, Mitterrand employed the language of realism to reconquer public opinion.[91]

The turn to austerity and the realistic rhetoric of the president may have been applauded in some business and financial circles, but it brought dissent from the left wing of the Socialist party. At the Bourg-en-Bresse congress of the PS, October 28–30, the Socialists debated economic policy. CERES, of course, remained critical of Mitterrand's abandonment of reflation and presented a motion by Chevènement that won approximately 18 percent of the delegates' votes. Rocard, on the other hand, presented a motion that differed only slightly from the majority's and captured only 5 percent of the vote. Party chief Jospin's motion, representing the position of the government, won 77 percent of the delegates' votes.[92] Mitterrand knew that CERES opposed his policy, but Chevènement was no longer a member of government; since Rocard was now at the Ministry of Agriculture, the Rocardian dissidents would offer little resistance within the PS, especially since Rocard himself had demanded realism since the elections of 1981.

Nevertheless, the Bourg-en-Bresse congress was extremely important for Mitterrand because he wanted to drum up as much support as possible for his government's policies. One growing concern at this time was the rising disenchantment expressed in various public opinion polls. According to *Le Monde*, in October of 1983 only 32 percent of the electorate now had confidence in their president, a startling 42 percent drop in his popularity since the 1981 elections.[93] Another poll conducted at about the same time showed that the prime minister had even less support, with approximately 30 percent of the public expressing confidence in Mauroy. For Mauroy, this represented a 41 percent drop in popularity since his nomination.[94] Mitterrand reportedly told one of his advisers shortly before the Bourg-en-Bresse congress, "I have believed that the government would improve in public opinion polls. . . . I cannot wait much longer."[95]

Since there could be no expensive reforms in 1983 and 1984 as a result of the serious economic crisis, Mitterrand encouraged his government to tackle issues concerning civil liberties as a way of legitimizing the government and mobilizing the Left. Issues such as a new press law and a school reform bill were substituted for economic reform. Yet these new issues and the Socialists' position on them would in time create crises for Mitterrand and his government.

While Mitterrand was concerned about legitimizing his government and winning back public confidence, he also had to worry about the PCF and its actions. Dissatisfied with austerity and the U-turn in policy, not to mention the president's pro-Atlanticist and anti-Soviet views, the PCF decided to pursue a double tactic—to remain in government but at the same time heighten criticism of Mitterrand's policies. If possible, Mitterrand preferred keeping the Communists in government until the 1986 legislative elections.[96] In this regard, at the end of 1983 the PS and the PCF held a summit in Paris to "verify" respect for the accord on government that the two parties had agreed to earlier. From 1983 through the summer of 1984 a very uneasy truce existed between Mitterrand's PS and the PCF. Continuing to try to mobilize opinion to support his economic policy, Mitterrand traveled to the Poitou-Charentes region, his birthplace, in early November. Stressing many of the same themes on which he had focused since Figeac, he called on the French to "rediscover the dynamism of 1981."[97] Shortly after this official visit to the southwest of France,

Mitterrand returned to the issue of foreign policy and reasserted a certain Gaullist image in order to win public confidence.

On November 16 the head of state appeared on television with four journalists and responded to questions on foreign policy. While Mitterrand knew that he had a national consensus on foreign policy— due primarily to his Gaullist approach to external affairs—and while it was clear that his domestic rating was dangerously low, a televised discussion on French relations with the world, especially nuclear strategy, might aid his government's standing with the public. Mitterrand, in an exaggerated statement, stressed that the Euromissiles controversy was "the most serious since the Cuban missile crisis and the blockade of Berlin." He added that France was not an adversary of the Soviet Union, but that the buildup of Soviet missiles was a threat to the security of Europe. He pointed out that under the Constitution he and he alone was responsible for national independence and the integrity of French territory and he was commander in chief of the military forces. Then, Mitterrand proceeded to make a statement that could have been uttered by de Gaulle or a modern-day Louis XIV, "The key to nuclear deterrence is the chief of state, myself. . . ."[98] The president, of course, sought to remind French citizens of his authority and his determination to safeguard the nation's independence. When the Gaullist mayor of Paris heard the president's bold statement on nuclear decision making, he declared, "We are back to the days of Louis XIV's [notion that] I am the state."[99] Marchais's response was similar; he said that "the question of peace and war was too important to leave to one man."[100]

Mitterrand also stressed in his televised address the strong historical ties between France and the Middle East, as well as Africa, in order to justify the French presence there. Lebanon was on the minds of many at the time because of the late October terrorist attack in the war-torn country that had killed fifty-eight French soldiers. In a risky move, the president himself had flown to Lebanon to honor the dead soldiers. Concerning U.S. policy, especially in Latin America, Mitterrand stated, "I have condemned the intervention of the United States of America in Grenada, as I have deplored their general policy in Latin America."[101] This Gaullist performance by the president came just one month after he made an official visit to Belgium and declared, as mentioned earlier, "The pacifists are in the West, the missiles in the East."[102] In 1983, as indicated by a variety of pronouncements, including the mid-November televised discussion of

French foreign policy, Mitterrand launched a personal crusade for the deployment of new NATO missiles. Crusades, as he knew, often divert attention from more mundane matters such as economic policy.

During the period from 1981 to 1986 Mitterrand utilized various strategies to win public support for his Socialist government. From 1981 to 1983 he relied on a two-pronged approach. On the one hand, he dropped his utopian economic thinking and adopted a more realistic approach to the French crisis. On the other hand, he used foreign policy, as many world leaders often do, to create the image—real or imaginary—of a hostile power, or hostile powers, threatening the security of a France that he was charged to defend. Beginning in late 1983 and early 1984, Mitterrand discovered another way to bolster confidence in his government, by actively supporting, through the European Economic Community, the emergence of a strong and united Europe. As his rival within the PS, Rocard, stated, "Europe is a necessity of civilization."[103] Mitterrand tried to convince the electorate that the future of France was closely tied to Europe. When the ten leaders of the Common Market met in Athens during the first week of December 1983, there was little agreement or accord on any substantial matter. Yet beginning on January 1, Mitterrand was scheduled to preside over the organization. Concerning this important assignment and the general economic crisis in Europe, he said that he would make "good usage of the crisis."[104] His presidency of the European Community provided him with an opportunity to dream once again.

As 1983 drew to a close, Mitterrand began perhaps the most dangerous period of his presidency. Protest began to mount. The first waves of protest came from the Left, with rumbling from the major unions. On December 14, for instance, Edmond Maire of the CFDT denounced what he termed the incoherence and inflexibility of the government's industrial policy. The coming year brought protest not only by the Left, including the Communists, but by the Right as well.

Despite the rising discontent in France and the government's precipitous drop in popularity, the Socialists made some notable reforms between June 1982 and December 1983. These reforms included the Quilliot Law (June 10, 1982), which gave additional rights to renters in housing matters; an audiovisual law (July 8, 1982) that ended the state monopoly of audiovisual programming and creating a High Authority to guarantee the independence of public television channels; the first of several Auroux laws that gave workers additional rights on the job; a law abolishing oppressive "security and freedom" measures (May 3, 1983); laws aimed at reforming higher education to make the academy more responsive to the needs of the state (June 10 and December 21, 1983); and a law involving hospital reform (December 21, 1983). These reforms as well as the others adopted since the 1981 elections represented an effort by the Mitterrand government to follow through on the campaign promises contained in the 110 Propositions. But despite the reforms, the red rose was wilting badly at the end of 1983.

As the year drew to a close, Mitterrand presented his traditional New Year's Eve address on television and told the nation that for 1984 he would "promise nothing other than to continue the effort at national reform." While 1981 had been labeled by the Socialists and others "the year of change," 1982 "the second phase of change," and 1983 "austerity," Mitterrand said that 1984 would also be characterized by austerity. According to the president, "We have before us two major obstacles: the first is called inflation . . . [and] the second is the age of a part of our industrial structure. . . ." From the end of 1982 onward Mitterrand told the French that they must "produce more" and "produce better," a theme that was also reiterated in his New Year's Eve address and restated many times in the coming year as he emphasized the need to modernize industry. Concerning the tax burden, Mitterrand said that there would be a slight drop in both taxes and charges in 1985, but not in 1984.[105]

Mitterrand also mentioned foreign affairs in his New Year's Eve address. He expressed his sympathy with the families of the French soldiers killed in Lebanon.[106] Justifying the French presence in both Lebanon and in Chad, he stressed the nation's obligations to aid the cause of peace in the Middle East and in Africa. Earlier in December the Mitterrand government had used the French navy to rescue Palestinian leader Yasser Arafat from Palestinian extremists and Syrian forces who had trapped him in Tunisia.[107] With regard to the Euromissile debate, he insisted that his position was to ensure a balance of forces in Europe to better ensure peace. European affairs, independent of the East-West conflict, also received attention in this address. "Finally," said Mitterrand, "1984 will be the year of Europe, for better or for worse." Of course, he mentioned to the nation that he would take his turn presiding over the EEC on January 1. He reminded French citizens, too, that Europe was the world's largest trading bloc; nevertheless, Europe "lacked a political will, a consciousness of what it wants and what it can be. France, which is European, does not want to miss this chance."[108]

The industrial modernization of France and greater European cooperation and development would, as Mitterrand suggested in his New Year's Eve address, become two important themes for the Socialist government in 1984. The first theme was intended to suggest that France could escape the economic crisis if the nation pursued the modernization of certain industrial sectors; in part, the Socialists would also use this theme to justify growing levels of unemployment. The second theme suggested that Europe—under French leadership—could transcend the Yalta system that had existed since the end of World War II. Quite unexpectedly, a few years later France and her neighbors would have an opportunity to create a new Europe.

6

RETREAT AND MODERNIZE

1984

It is difficult to be president of the republic.

—François Mitterrand

If 1981 was the year when the French Left "dreamed a lot," as Mitterrand himself has stated, 1984 was one of delayed nightmares. That year saw a dramatic escalation in the magnitude of protests, especially by large segments of the working class as well as by hundreds of thousands of supporters of private schools. When Mitterrand yielded to the private-school demonstrators while holding fast to austerity, this led to the resignation in July of Prime Minister Mauroy; and when the president appointed a thirty-seven-year-old technocrat, Laurent Fabius, to fill Mauroy's post and continue austerity, the Communists withdrew from the government, formally ending the Union of the Left that had brought Mitterrand to power in 1981. Although Laurent Fabius has stated that 1983 was the most difficult year for the Socialists in power because of the abrupt shift to austerity,[1] 1984 was certainly the most dangerous year.

To escape some of the problems at home, the president intensified his travels abroad, making thirty-two trips to other nations and logging seventy days outside of France. By comparison, in 1981 he made only six trips abroad, and eighteen in 1982 and 1983; in 1985 and 1986, after his most dangerous year in office was over, he reduced his travel schedule significantly, with less than ten foreign visits in both years. Nevertheless, Mitterrand has traveled more outside France than any other president,[2] making not only scheduled voyages planned well in advance, but impromptu visits to observe a situation and to demonstrate France's presence in the world.[3] For 1984 foreign travel seemed to offer the therapy that the president needed and allowed him to use foreign policy issues to stabilize the popularity of his government.

The multiple crises of 1984, however, allowed Mitterrand to display his genius for maneuvering and counterattack. The president's response to the above-mentioned challenges saved him from the humiliation of dissolving the National Assembly and calling for early elections, and possibly from resigning his presidency. He retreated on the most dangerous issue, school reform, and made a reinvigorated effort to convince the nation that industrial modernization and greater French competitiveness, which would mean higher levels of unemployment, would eventually cure the deep-seated economic ills of France. Consequently, the new prime minister, Laurent Fabius, with a youthful cabinet minus the Communists, continued austerity while emphasizing modernization of the industrial base and making France more competitive in the international market. With this change in political discourse, words like "socialism" and "break with capitalism" were scarcely uttered by Socialist leaders. Both the president and the new prime minister projected an image of industrial dynamism and economic growth by constantly repeating the word "modernization" in their public statements. In many respects, the president and the new prime minister governed France by manipulating images of a modernized nation, images that appealed to the Left and the Right. This attempt to govern by images,[4] which followed a recentering of the government that forced the PCF to withdraw its support, eventually reversed Mitterrand's and the Socialists' slide in public opinion polls. Ironically, while 1984 was the most dangerous year for Mitterrand, in many ways it was also one of his best.

In January 1984 and the months that followed, the Mitterrand government, acting on the theme highlighted in his New Year's Eve address, began an operation of radical industrial surgery in the steel, coal, shipbuilding, and automobile industries. On January 6 the minister of finance refused a 6.2 billion franc request for additional funding from Usinor, the state-owned steel firm. Both Usinor and Sacilor, another nationalized steel firm, were told to balance their budgets by 1988, which meant cutting approximately 35,000 to 40,000 jobs and reducing production by 30 percent. The government had little choice but to trim the labor force in steel because of the industry's $1.2 billion projected deficit for 1984 in the steel industry, a deficit that was 60 percent higher than in 1983.[5] In the coal industry the story was similar. In 1984 the nationalized coal industry anticipated a deficit of $100 million. By 1988 the government, which had initially predicted an increase in coal production, estimated that 25,000 miners would lose their jobs and that production would fall by 30 percent. In shipbuilding and in the automobile industry the Socialists also ordered job cuts. The auto industry, once the "motor" of the French economy, found itself in serious financial difficulty in 1984, with layoffs at Peugeot and Citroën. The state-owned Renault automobile firm faced not only layoffs, but a declining share of the domestic market, and a long-term debt. Renault's top executive, Bernard Hanon, estimated that his firm had to lay off 7,000 workers early in 1984 and then make more substantial cuts later to enhance efficiency. During 1983 Renault's share of the French market had dropped from 39 percent to 32.3 percent due, in part, to foreign competition. This problem was compounded by a $3 billion long-term debt due to a capital investment program.[6] Earlier, Mitterrand had seen the nationalized industries as a magic springboard to a productive economy, but he now realized that his government could no longer continue to subsidize the massive deficits of the state-controlled firms and avoid serious economic and political problems in the future.

Mitterrand's industrial surgery entailed limiting government subsidies to the nationalized industries and encouraging them to balance their books through severe job-cutting measures if necessary. It also entailed a refusal by the government to come to the aid of private companies, such as the heavy-engineering group Creusot-Loire after an earlier bailout package. This type of industrial operation meant that France would lose between 200,000 and 300,000 jobs in the public sector during 1984, while the total "industrial restructuring" program would cost approximately 500,000 jobs.[7] In 1984 France experienced the strongest surge of unemployment of all European countries, while in West Germany, Belgium, and Great Britain unemployment levels actually dropped. Furthermore, industrial production grew by 6 percent in the United States in 1984, compared to 2 percent in France.[8] Although the increasing levels of unemployment in France necessitated by this surgery were high indeed, several significant factors influenced Mitterrand to reverse his thinking and actively promote an industrial modernization policy.

Mitterrand's modernization campaign, as *Le Monde*'s political editor Jean-Marie Colombani suggested, sprang from three imperatives: the lack of any coherent program, historical necessity, and the president's startlingly low popularity level with the electorate. His austerity plan for many in France seemed like a contradictory measure for a Socialist and an arbitrary ad hoc way of reining in an economy that was out of control. Mitterrand's modernization theme, however, suggested that the Elysée had a coordinated and well-thought-out economic and industrial program. Except for the growing levels of unemployment that modernization entailed, the Left and the Right had difficulty criticizing the proposed program. Historical necessity, too, motivated Mitterrand to launch a modernization program. France had an antiquated industrial base in many sectors and was losing its competitiveness in the international market. The lack of competitiveness, the flood of foreign imports, and the serious balance-of-payments problem convinced him that the solution to his nation's economic ills was not necessarily the nationalized industries, but efficient modernized industries in both the public and private sectors. A personal imperative also encouraged Mitterrand to adopt a modernization plan. His popularity was dangerously low, reaching in 1984 the lowest level of any president of the Fifth Republic. Mitterrand hoped that modernization would in time enhance French competitiveness, especially in technology, and that the modernization policy would mobilize voters to lend more support to their president and the Socialist government.[9] Yet a nation's industrial base is not modernized in a short period of time. Therefore, Mitterrand, Fabius and others had to create the image of a modernizing France in their political rhetoric.

When Mitterrand launched his modernization operation, it became clear to several patients—who were not fully under Mitterrand's anesthesia—that Socialist surgery would be costly. This realization, plus the declining membership of labor organizations, and the fact that the CGT and the CFDT did poorly in the social security board elections in October 1983, encouraged labor to speak out against Mitterrand's policy. In late January, the head of the CGT, Henri Krasucki, openly opposed the government because of the thousands of job cuts and the attempt by the Socialists to hold down wage increases. According to Krasucki, "It is our obligation to warn workers and to sound the alarm."[10] Unwittingly, labor organizations and their representatives aided Mitterrand in his desire to create the image of a recentered government.

In connection with his efforts to convince France that industrial and technological modernization had to be the primary goal of his government, Mitterrand also launched an appeal for a European effort in space, a program where he linked the destiny of France with that of Europe. On February 7, in his position as head of the European Economic Community, the French president delivered an address at the Hague before both houses of the Dutch Parliament and called on Europeans to orbit their own defense space station.[11] This appeal represented Mitterrand's effort to relaunch the European Community and to respond to President Reagan's Strategic Defense Initiative (SDI, better known as "Star Wars"). Mitterrand had consistently stressed that he did not want a separate European defense community, but a more self-reliant alliance within an alliance. His vision of a European effort in space represented a symbolic step in that direction. But it was also an attempt to utilize foreign and defense policy to relaunch the EEC and at the same time draw attention away from the serious economic crisis at home.

Another way that Mitterrand attempted to relaunch the EEC was by trying to revitalize in early 1984 the Western European Union (WEU), a dormant defense organization originally created without U.S. participation after World War II to function as a political framework for German rearmament and European military cooperation. At this time the Mitterrand government agreed to create a 47,000-man Rapid Action Force (FAR) that could quickly come to the aid of Germany in case of attack. Mitterrand knew that the economic health of his nation was tied closely to that of Europe, especially Germany, which, he feared, was sliding toward neutrality. As Pierre Lellouche, director of the European Security Program at the Institute of International Relations in Paris, stated, "The French have to find a way to relaunch the EC [European Community], and one option is to relaunch it in the strategic area."[12] Thus, Mitterrand gave French voters the impression that he desired to safeguard not only France, but Europe as well from another American challenge and from unification tendencies in Germany that threatened the continent's security, as well as from a buildup of Soviet and Eastern Bloc conventional forces.

In the midst of the government's campaign to restructure French industry and to relaunch a strong Europe, Mitterrand gave a televised address on February 12 to reassure the French about the future and to call for national unity. Telling his audience that France had to modernize its industry, an idea supported by a majority of voters according to a poll taken at the time,[13] the president stressed that "it is hard." Restructuring would have its cost, notably unemployment, but the current crisis was due in large measure to France's "failure to adapt to international competition." Calling for unity with his Communist partners in government, the president stated, "The majority must, side by side, confront the problems of France."[14]

In this same televised address Mitterrand also stressed France's strong presence on the world stage, including Chad and the Middle East. He also devoted air time to Europe and his efforts to revitalize the community. After reminding his viewers that in the past the EEC had had some setbacks and had often pursued contradictory goals, he promised, "I will do all I can to safeguard the community. . . ."[15] Modernize, maintain a strong French presence in the world, and strengthen Europe, this was the message that the French president delivered to a nation experiencing growing unemployment and protest. Mitterrand's words would not deter the mounting swell of national demonstrations that would sweep France in 1984. A tidal wave of protest was coming.

The first sign of this tidal wave was a nationwide strike by truckers protesting fuel taxes, limits on drivers' hours, and the government's preference for rail traffic. This strike began two days after Mitterrand's televised address and coincided with a demonstration in Paris by civil servants protesting a drop in real wages. During the third week of February, a strike of French and Italian customs officials at Mont Blanc touched off a truckers' strike that quickly spread from the Alpine region to the entire nation, with truckers blocking autoroutes and major roads. At this time, Mitterrand, who had sometimes worried about being a French Allende,[16] feared that such a strike might seriously damage his government and possibly even bring it down. However, time and negotiations, especially between the Communist minister of transportation, Charles Fiterman, and labor organizations, eased this threatening crisis.

Yet this protest was quickly followed by what became the largest demonstration in France in postwar history, with the exception of the 1968 student-worker revolt. What followed the truckers' strike was the beginning of a nationwide demonstration against the Socialist government's plan to exercise more control over France's ten thousand private schools (mainly religious schools and known as the *écoles libres*). In the 110 Propositions of the PS in 1981, the Socialists promised under Article 90 that "a unified lay public service will be instituted for national education."[17] Despite this campaign pledge, a 1982 poll revealed that only 31 percent of the electorate that voted for the Left in 1981 desired the takeover of Catholic schools, while 55 percent favored leaving the educational system as it was.[18] Nevertheless, Education Minister Savary launched negotiations in 1982 with the Church and education leaders to reform private education. At this point, private schools could receive government funding if they adhered to a state syllabus, but the schools retained control over hiring practices. In delicate negotiations, Savary and representatives of the private schools tried to work out details on the extent of state control in private schools. The right-wing opposition, seizing upon a potentially explosive issue, charged that the Socialist government was threatening the *école libre*, academic freedom, and the rights of parents and students to choose their school. Moreover, private parent-teachers associations began to mobilize public opinion against the Socialist reform measure. On January 22, 1984, 60,000 demonstrated in Bordeaux, while on January 29, 120,000 protested in Lyon, and on February 18, 290,000 in Rennes, followed by a demonstration on February 25 of 250,000 in Lille. Then, on March 4, 500,000 marched in the streets of Versailles protesting the Socialist plan for private schools. Suddenly a new slogan spread throughout France, "The Private School Will Survive."[19] This slogan resonated well with the French public since opinion polls now showed that 79 percent of the population favored the private schools.[20] Several months after the demonstrations in the provinces, a million-strong protest rally occurred in Paris that made Mitterrand and his government tremble.

With serious protest erupting among civil servants, farmers, truckers, supporters of private schools, and others affected by the economic policies of the Socialist government, Mitterrand had to decide on a modernization plan. Coupled with this rising protest, Mitterrand faced a 9.9 percent unemployment level that was destined to rise even higher, and a 9 percent inflation rate that was double that of West Germany. Within the government division was mounting between Prime Minister Mauroy and Industry Minister Fabius, who had earlier argued for industrial restructuring and who told a Council of Ministers meeting on March 19 that only an international upturn could save the French steel industry and that the nation must follow the international trend with respect to this problem-riddled industry. While Mauroy—who once said, "I am from the north . . . and have a factory in my head"[21]—wanted to limit unemployment, Fabius was more willing to see a higher level of joblessness. Mauroy, of course, knew that higher unemployment undermined his government. Fabius, on the other hand, realized that if France was to escape the economic crisis, industry and technology had to be modernized. Before making any decision on an industrial modernization policy for France, Mitterrand traveled to the United States in late March. Among other sites, he visited Silicon Valley in northern California, the heartland of American technological development. Impressed with Silicon Valley, the president returned home where his popularity was dangerously low—approximately 30 percent—and announced an industrial modernization plan for the nation.

On March 29 the Council of Ministers, under Mitterrand's guidance, adopted a modernization plan that included large job cuts in the steel industry. The government plan called for reducing capacity in the steel industry from 25 million tons a year to 18 million tons by 1987, meaning that 30,000 jobs would eventually be lost; one out of three steel workers would lose his job. Under this plan the Mitterrand government accepted 20,000 job losses for 1984. One of the hardest-hit areas, of course, was Lorraine where 15,700 steel jobs would be lost in 1984, followed by another 15,000 in 1985.[22] Communist party chief Marchais quickly responded to this government decision on April 2 by saying that the Socialist austerity policy coupled with the new industrial restructuring was "tragic," "negative," and "dramatic."[23] Since the introduction of austerity the PCF had criticized the Socialists for managing a crisis of capitalism. For the leadership of the PCF, the economic crisis in France demanded a return to protectionism, more controls on the exchange market, leaving the European Monetary System and the European Economic Community, and preventing French investment abroad, notably in the United States.[24] Despite their hostile critique and condemnation of Socialist economic policy, the Communists did not at this time withdraw from the government.

Workers in the depressed area of Lorraine also responded to Mitterrand's decision. They sacked Socialist party offices and even burned portraits of Mitterrand. On the morning of April 4, protesters shut down the Metz area for a day with steelworkers blocking roads, train workers walking off their jobs, and shopkeepers closing their businesses. Unions in Lorraine also called for a march on Paris on April 13, a demonstration that saw thirty-five thousand steel workers, accompanied by Communist leader Marchais, demonstrate in the capital. To add to the humiliation, four Socialist deputies from Lorraine resigned from the party whip and one Socialist even resigned from the party's national management committee.[25] Concerning the policy of the government in Lorraine, *L'Unité* told Socialist party members that "the decisions of the government on the steel industry in Lorraine have been difficult to take. They are courageous. But it is now necessary to quickly succeed in the reindustrialization of Lorraine."[26] *L'Unité* maintained that France was "between modernization and unemployment."[27]

In an effort to counter hostile reaction to the government's industrial policy, on April 4—the same day as the general strike in Lorraine—Mitterrand gave his first press conference in twenty-two months and continued his crusade to modernize industry, stimulate new technology, and make cutbacks in state-owned industries, such as steel, coal, and shipbuilding. Pursuing a theme that he had used earlier, he said that his goal was to make France internationally competitive. He told the nation that France was simply following the international trend in the steel industry, noting that the European Economic Community had decided that by 1986 state support for the steel industry would be ended. He said that France lost 10 billion francs a year to the steel industry and asked, "Can we continue to support deficit-ridden industries in such proportions . . . or must we provide credits to the technologies of the future?"[28] (Sacilor and Usinor, the two state-owned steel companies, lost $1.3 billion in 1983, amounting to 66 percent of the total losses of nationalized industry in France.[29]) Although Mitterrand's decision was clear, he did try to soothe tempers in the hard-hit area of Lorraine by announcing the establishment of a committee to examine the problems of the region, and stated that he had instructed Industry Minister Fabius to encourage new industry for the area.

Responding to Marchais's criticisms of Socialist industrial policy, Mitterrand took a hard line. The president declared, "In the interest of the majority and each of us that participate in government, the time has come to put things in order." At the end of his press conference, Mitterrand announced that he would make his first official visit to the Soviet Union in the near future.[30] With rising protest, a Communist party that was participating in government while its leadership was attacking Socialist economic and industrial policy, and the European Parliament elections due in June, Mitterrand needed "to settle things" with his governing partners in an effort to achieve some degree of government unity. On April 19 Mauroy was able to win a general vote of confidence in the National Assembly by a margin of 329 to 156, with the PCF supporting the government. While this was an important vote for Mitterrand, the motion put before the Assembly was one that called for a general vote of confidence and not a more specific one on Socialist economic and industrial policy. For the moment, the Communists remained in government.

Mitterrand continued his crusade to convince the public that modernization was the only choice open to France. On May 10, celebrating the third anniversary of his election, a published interview with the president appeared in the left-leaning newspaper *Libération*. Mitterrand chose this newspaper, in part, as a way of speaking directly to the Left and as a way to mobilize voters behind Socialist policy. The president told his interviewer, *Libération's* editor Serge July, that his government was following the same program that the Socialists proposed in 1981. Mitterrand, who wanted voters to believe that there was continuity in Socialist policy since 1981, stated that "the austerity policy is only a parenthesis" and "not an end but only a means. . . ." In an effort to maintain leftist unity he also stressed that the government sought "to modernize France with social justice."

In this important interview, appearing in the midst of a storm of protest, Mitterrand posited his view of the French economy. After insisting that the Left stood for a more equitable society as well as economic efficiency, he declared that he desired "a society with a mixed economy, a state closer to the people, and a market more accepting of entrepreneurs and more sensitive to the aspirations of workers." Not forgetting voters on the left, the president asserted his attachment to socialism by declaring, "I am very proud to be the second Socialist president of the French republic, and the first elected by the people." With rhetorical skill that aimed to reconcile the implicit contradictions, Mitterrand attempted to project the images of a Socialist and a Liberal so as simultaneously to appease both the Left and the Right.

In this interview Mitterrand also warned his Communist partners that their actions could further weaken public support for the

PCF. He pointed out that while the PCF had supported the government on the vote of confidence, it continued its hostile campaign against the Socialists and their policies. This, according to the president, could "ruin their credit with public opinion."[31] With the European Parliament elections just five weeks away, this interview in *Libération* was one way that Mitterrand attempted to mobilize voters and to prevent disaster at the polls.

On June 17 the electorate in France and throughout the European Community went to the polls to cast their ballots in the elections to the European Parliament. In this election French voters gave the Right 60 percent of their votes, marking the worst showing for the Left since 1969 (see table 7). According to Jérôme Jaffré, director of the polling agency SOFRES, if the legislative elections were held in early 1985, the Left could expect the Right to win 60 percent of the vote there as well.[32] The June 1984 election revealed significant political trends. First, the election saw a large drop in Socialist support. The PS list of candidates was headed by party leader Jospin who ran against thirteen other groups. Under the banner "Socialists for Europe," Jospin and the PS won only 20.76 percent of the vote—a loss of roughly 6 million votes since 1981 and the first time since 1973 that the PS had received less than 21 percent.[33] The Socialists probably prevented even greater losses by choosing Jospin to head their list rather than a member of government, such as Prime Minister Mauroy who had experienced a drastic decline in popularity since the introduction of austerity.

A second trend noticeable in these elections was the continued decline of the Communist party. Headed by the dogmatic Marchais,

TABLE 7

Evolution of the Vote for the Left

Legislative Elections 1978	European Elections 1984	Legislative Elections 1986
49%	39%	44%

SOURCE: Compiled from data found in Jérôme Jaffré, "Les élections législatives du 16 mars 1986: La défaite de la gauche et les progrès du PS," *Pouvoirs*, no. 38 (1986): 148.

the PCF list obtained a mere 11.28 percent of the vote, representing the worst showing for the Communists since 1928.[34] In only five departments—Seine St. Denis, Allier, Haute-Vienne, Corrèze, and Gard—did the PCF win more than 20 percent of the vote.[35] In one-third of all departments, the Communists garnered less than 8 percent. These elections also revealed that the PCF had lost the once-solid "red belt" surrounding Paris. After the European elections *Libération* questioned whether the PCF still constituted a national political force.[36] To a large degree, the leadership of the PCF had failed to realize that society had changed, that its working-class clientele had shrunk considerably, and that Communist rhetoric had to be based on this new social reality if the party was to remain viable.

The third significant trend was the strong showing by the extreme right-wing National Front headed by Jean-Marie Le Pen, a former paratrooper who was first elected to the Assembly in 1956 as a Poujadist. The FN, founded in 1972, won 11.06 percent of the vote in the European elections, roughly the same percentage as the once-powerful PCF. In 1981 the National Front had garnered only 0.35 percent of the vote.[37] The rising unemployment rate and the postwar pattern of immigration in France contributed to a xenophobic reaction that the National Front capitalized on. Some in France, for instance, blamed the unemployment problem on the 4 million immigrants residing in France. Prior to World War II the immigrant population was made up principally of Belgians, Italians, Poles, and Spaniards, all representing European Catholic countries. After the war, however, the flow of immigrants comprised mainly Portuguese, North Africans, and black Africans. For this group, assimilation has been much more difficult because of their diverse cultural backgrounds. Many in France knew that the immigration issue was one of the more difficult problems to resolve.[38] However, Le Pen's ultraconservative and simplistic stands on French immigration policy and national sovereignty during a period of economic decline attracted a relatively large number of voters. Industrial and urban areas, especially with large immigrant populations, showed strong support for the FN in 1984. In the Ile-de-France, for example, Le Pen's party captured more than 14 percent of the vote in six out of seven departments. In Paris the FN won more than 15 percent; in the large industrial area around Lyon, Le Pen captured in excess of 17 percent.[39] One postelection poll that appeared in *Le Nouvel Observateur* revealed that while most voters were concerned about the construction of a strong Europe and unemployment, voters who marked their ballots for Le Pen and the FN worried most about insecurity and immigration.[40]

Le Pen also received support from a relatively large number of votes from Chirac supporters. According to one poll, 25 percent of those who backed Chirac in 1981 voted for Le Pen in 1984,[41] a phenomenon that worried the Gaullist mayor. Many of Chirac's partisans rejected the joint RPR and UDF list because it was headed by a Jewish woman and Nazi concentration camp survivor, Simone Veil, who had actively participated in the 1970s campaign to legalize abortion. The racism and anti-Semitism of Le Pen's party obviously appealed to a sizable segment of Chirac's traditional voters. The rise of the National Front was an embarrassment for the opposition as well as for the Left.[42]

The list that triumphed in the 1984 European Parliament elections was the joint RPR-UDF list headed, as mentioned above, by Veil, a minister of health under Giscard and a former president of the European Parliament (1979–82). While the RPR-UDF list won an impressive 42.8 percent of the vote,[43] the combined vote for the Right totaled approximately 60 percent.

Despite the high abstention rate in the European Parliament elections, 43.4 percent, the outcome clearly revealed that Mitterrand had lost his domestic consensus. At the same time public opinion polls showed a strong wave of pessimism among the electorate. In June 1984, for instance, a *Figaro-Magazine/SOFRES* poll revealed that 69 percent of the population was pessimistic about the future.[44] The political and psychological climate in France meant that Mitterrand and his prime minister were in danger. Mauroy's days were numbered.

Hoping that another spectacular voyage abroad and the opportunity to play the role of an international statesman would enhance his government's popularity, on June 20 Mitterrand traveled to Moscow for talks with the Soviet leader Konstantin Chernenko. For the first three years of his presidency he had not been willing to visit the Soviet Union, partly because of the need not to appear too friendly toward the East since he had appointed four Communist ministers, and partly because of the new Cold War that followed the Soviet invasion of Afghanistan in late December 1979, and the 1980 election of Ronald Reagan. Now, however, Mitterrand believed that the time was right for a visit to the Soviet Union since the West had weathered the storm against the deployment of the Euromissiles, partially because of his own crusade for deployment. The president hoped that this visit would help to initiate an East-West dialogue on such issues as disarmament, would make France appear less dependent on the United States, and would aid France in cutting the trade deficit with the Soviet Union, $1 billion in 1982 and $0.5 billion in 1983.[45] Moreover, Mitterrand thought that this voyage would end the extremely chilly relations with Moscow, caused partially by the expulsion of forty-seven Russian diplomats a year earlier on spy charges. Needing to demonstrate his leadership role in the wake of a crumbling domestic consensus at home, Mitterrand believed that this official visit to the East could strengthen the popularity of the Socialist government among the electorate. While discussing a variety of issues with the Soviets, Mitterrand raised questions about the detention of the human-rights activist Andrei Sakharov and stated his opposition to the policies of the U.S.S.R. in Poland and in Afghanistan. Yet his international diplomacy was overshadowed by an antigovernment demonstration of historic proportions upon his return to the Elysée.

On June 24 more than a million people demonstrated in Paris against the government's planned reform for private schools, marking the largest single demonstration in French history since the Liberation. Just three weeks earlier the government had adopted a law on the reform of the *école libre* that made concessions to militants within the PS and that angered supporters of private schools. The newly adopted law, one that Mitterrand and Mauroy did not oppose, upset a delicate compromise that had been worked out between the government and private school partisans. Cardinal Lustiger, the archbishop of Paris, referred to the revised law as "treachery."[46] What followed had far-reaching repercussions on Mitterrand's political strategy.

Roughly 2 million children—17 percent of the total—attended private schools, and since 1959 these schools had received state support to cover teachers' salaries and general operating expenses. The only requirement for this funding was that private schools teach from a state-approved syllabus. The new law, the Savary law, adopted in May by the Socialists envisioned giving the state control over the selection of both directors and teachers in private institutions. As mentioned earlier, given the prohibition within the government against launching expensive social reforms, the Socialists had begun to pursue "freedom issues" such as the *école libre* reform, but this proved to be an expensive piece of legislation in terms of the anti-government sentiment engendered. The massive June 24 protest motivated Finance Minister Delors to say, "The is June 1936 completely reversed. The theme of liberties has become a theme of the Right. . . ."[47] The historic magnitude of the demonstration, plus the fact that the Right was now charging that Mitterrand was suppressing individual freedoms, spurred him to take action in the upcoming weeks to reverse the most dangerous situation of his term of office.

In order to respond to the serious domestic challenges confronting his government, in early July Mitterrand traveled to the provinces to reassert his authority and to explain government policy once again. Between July 5 and 6 the president toured Auvergne in the center of France where he defended the plan to reform private schools. In a strong statement on July 5 at Aurillac, Mitterrand responded to the growing opposition. The embattled president declared, "I will assume my responsibilities without being intimidated by invectives or obstructions." At Clermont-Ferrand he attempted to give support to Mauroy by saying that he, as president, "would remain loyal to his engagements." Mitterrand also stated that he would be "the president of all the French."[48] Despite the strong rhetoric, the critical situation forced Mitterrand to retreat on the private school issue and to recenter his government. The mounting protest and the government's low ratings in public opinion polls—Mauroy's public confidence level had hit a low of 25 percent—convinced the pragmatic Mitterrand that retreat was the only option open to him. Yet he would not follow the path of retreat suggested to him by former President Giscard, whom Mitterrand consulted in Auvergne (Giscard's home base) during this difficult period. Giscard strongly recommended that he dissolve the National Assembly, a demand that many on the right had also made. A poll taken after the June European Parliament elections showed that 35 percent favored dissolving the National Assembly, while 47 percent opposed such action.[49] Mitterrand's response to the crisis, one of the most crucial taken during his first term, eventually reversed the political fortunes of his presidency and his party.

On July 12 at 8 P.M. Mitterrand went before television cameras and revealed his new strategy, one that he had decided upon alone[50] and one that some political observers in France quickly labeled the president's *coup de Jarnac*. He gave a brief six-minute address to the nation in which he announced that he was recalling the contested private school law. He also said that he wanted to revise the Constitution to provide greater opportunity for referendums on what he termed "public liberties" in order "to open a vast space of freedom." This statement, of course, left open the possibility of a future referendum on private schools. Mitterrand realized, however, that a constitutional revision would need the approval of the Socialist-dominated National Assembly and the conservative Senate, but that the Senate would probably reject such a change, making the president appear as a guardian and promoter of public rights. (On July 5 the Senate had adopted a motion calling for a referendum on private schools, a motion that the National Assembly rejected.) At the conclusion of his speech the president told the nation, "above all, it is necessary to win the battle for the modernization of France and for employment. . . . But nothing will be possible or durable if there are expensive diversions."[51] Thus, in one six-minute speech Mitterrand defused the nationwide protest against his government. Worried about the outcome of the June European Parliament elections and the antigovernment sentiment generated by the Savary law, he drew upon his vast political experience and his ability to maneuver to turn the tables on the opposition.

Mitterrand's "minirevolution"[52] of July 12 had other important repercussions. On July 16 the president received a letter of resignation from his minister of education. Savary had not been fully consulted prior to Mitterrand's speech withdrawing the private school law and felt that he could not continue in his post. Prime Minister Mauroy, who consulted with his own friends and advisers after the July 14 Bastille Day parade and garden party at the Elysée, officially resigned on July 17. Mauroy was concerned that the president had not supported the minister of education. Furthermore, the prime minister was not in full agreement with the austerity program and the president's new emphasis on the virtues of a "mixed economy." When Mauroy came to the Elysée Palace for the last time as prime minister, the president told his old colleague from Lille as he departed the Château, "I just lived the most difficult moment of my term in office."[53] Later Mitterrand said of his first prime minister, "Under your aegis a considerable reform effort, without precedent since the Liberation, has been accomplished in all domains."[54]

Now the question became, who would replace Mauroy? The president considered two possibilities: Bérégovoy and Fabius. Realizing that the new prime minister had to be someone who could create the image of a modern and dynamic government, Mitterrand chose a youthful thirty-seven-year-old protégé, Laurent Fabius. Fabius was the son of a wealthy antiques dealer and a graduate of France's most prestigious schools, including the Ecole Normale Supérieure, an elite school known for its academic excellence, and the Ecole Nationale d'Administration. Fabius's age—eighteen years younger than Mauroy—pragmatism, and direct manner would be positive factors in a newly constituted Socialist government that had to position itself for the 1986 legislative elections. As Fabius stated, the role of his government would be "to give the Left a new chance . . . and to prepare for the elections [1986 legislative elections]."[55] Fabius, as Mitterrand knew, would give a new image to the Matignon. Many assumed that Fabius would be the new dauphin.

The new prime minister appeared dramatically different from Mauroy. For example, while Mauroy was a romantic idealist, Fabius was a realist; while Mauroy was a Socialist from the past, Fabius was a modern technocrat; and while Mauroy was a less-than-organized cheerleader for his own brand of working-class socialism, Fabius was an efficient leader with an imaginative entrepreneurial mind. The young prime minister was also the most patrician of all the Socialist leaders. But with the revival of liberalism as the national religion,[56] Fabius was well suited for a France that seemed disillusioned with socialism. For some, he symbolized the victory of social democracy over Mauroy's more Marxist brand of socialism,[57] a view that would be later reinforced at the Socialist congress in Toulouse. The appointment of Fabius provided a clear contrast to Mauroy, exactly what Mitterrand desired and desperately needed.

Another important repercussion of Mitterrand's mini-revolution was that it forced the Communists to leave the government, reinforcing the recentering that was taking place in Paris. When Marchais returned from a vacation in Romania to meet with the new prime minister, Fabius asked the Communist boss if his party was willing to accept the austerity policy followed since 1983. The PCF, in a terse statement read to reporters on July 19 at 9:30 A.M. at party headquarters at place du Colonel Fabien, announced that it could no longer support austerity and would not support the new Fabius government. According to Jacques Julliard, an astute political commentator, the leadership of the PCF wanted to be expelled from the government, while Mitterrand preferred to see the Communists leave of their own accord. Each preferred this solution so that they could blame the other for the breakdown of the Union of the Left.[58]

To compensate for the loss of the PCF, Fabius's government included several left-leaning Socialist ministers who appealed to the left wing of the PS and even to some PCF voters. Joxe, head of the PS parliamentary group since 1981 and one of the principal advisers to Mauroy, took over at the Ministry of Interior. Chevènement, the *enfant terrible* of the PS, took charge at the troubled Ministry of Education. Other key figures in the new Fabius government included Michel Delebarre at the Ministry of Labor who had to deal with an unemployment level of 2.5 million; and Bérégovoy who replaced Delors at the Ministry of Finance and attempted to reduce taxes and balance the budget for 1985. (Delors became head of the European Commission in Brussels.) Another important personality in the Fabius government was Roland Dumas, who replaced Claude Cheysson at the Ministry of External Relations. Dumas, a former deputy from Limousin, was a noted lawyer who had represented a number of famous artists, film stars, directors, and opera singers and was the executor of Picasso's will; he was also a close and trusted friend of the president. Dumas's influence within the Château became so pronounced after this appointment that the newsweekly *Le Nouvel Observateur* called him "the vice-president."[59] The new government not only included Mitterrand's friends, but also put an emphasis on youth to match the new image of modernization that Mitterrand desired to create. Joxe, for instance, was forty-nine years old, Delebarre was thirty-eight, Bérégovoy was fifty-seven, and Chevènement was forty-four. The youngest and the most influential member of the new cabinet was the prime minister himself.

Mitterrand's coup of July represented a watershed in the history of the Socialist government. June had been the low point for the Socialists and had convinced Mitterrand that action had to be taken to reverse the situation. The June 17 European Parliament elections revealed the Left with only 40 percent of the vote, to the Right's 60 percent. This election, followed by the huge antigovernment demonstration in Paris, showed that disenchantment with the Socialists was critically high. While Mauroy's popularity had fallen to 25 percent, the president's popularity was only slightly above the 30 percent mark. Yet Mitterrand's speech withdrawing the private school law and calling for a referendum on public liberties, the resignation of Mauroy, and the refusal of the Communists to participate in the new Fabius government eventually improved the psychological climate and aided the president and the Socialists at the polls. An editorial in *L'Unité* stated that the president's referendum on referendums and the appointment of Fabius represented "a shuffling of the cards."[60]

Following his July coup the long-awaited increase in Mitterrand's popularity slowly came about. His approval rating climbed above the 50 percent mark by the autumn of 1985—the first time since 1982 that a majority of voters had given their president a positive rating. In a February 1986 poll, 44 percent of those questioned said that the Socialists had done a good job fighting inflation, the highest rating registered on this question since the polling organization developed its survey in inflation in 1976. Moreover, following Mitterrand's July coup the intensity of hostility toward the Mitterrand government and the Socialists began to fade. By March of 1986, for example, 33 percent of Gaullist RPR supporters and the 40 percent of centrist UDF supporters acknowledged that the Socialists had made the best of a difficult period.[61]

On July 24 Mitterrand's new prime minister, a man often referred to at this time as "Mitterrand's double," presented a general policy declaration to the National Assembly. In this speech Fabius stressed that his objective was to "modernize the country and to reunite the French." Mitterrand's young protégé, echoing Mendès-France, also told the Assembly and the nation that he wanted to promise one thing to the French, "I shall tell you the truth."[62] This statement was an oblique reference to the lack of candor during Mauroy's tenure as prime minister; it also reflected the newfound realism of the Socialists. Although Fabius obtained a general vote of confidence on his policy declaration, the PCF abstained from voting. To aid the new image of a Socialist government that stressed youth, modernity, and national unity, Fabius initiated monthly televised "fireside chats" with the nation on a television broadcast called "Let's Talk France."

Mitterrand's decision to tap Fabius as head of a new government provoked an interesting reaction among the electorate. During the last half of 1984 political observers discussed what they called the "Fabius effect."[63] Mitterrand and others assumed that a new prime minister would bolster confidence in the government and the presidency. During the last six months of 1984 Fabius's popularity rose, but the president's remained relatively low. Fabius's youthful and modern image won him supporters, but Mitterrand had to wait almost a year before witnessing a significant surge in his popularity.

For the young prime minister the problems of government were different from what Mauroy experienced. The economy, while not completely healthy, had definitely improved. Inflation was now running at 6.7 percent per year and the foreign trade deficit had fallen to

25 billion francs in 1984, with the balance of payments reaching a healthy equilibrium. Fabius, too, took control of the government with the dangerous *école libre* issue behind him. However, he would have to contend with a hostile PCF that was no longer in government, and with rising opposition over the government's press reforms.[64] Fabius himself contends that his most difficult problem as prime minister was the potentially explosive issue revolving around the independence movement in the distant overseas territory of New Caledonia.[65]

While the recentered government under Fabius was much more difficult for the opposition to attack than Mauroy's cabinet and while public confidence in Mitterrand and the Socialists would eventually rise after the *coup de Jarnac*, in the autumn of 1984 public opinion polls showed a negative attitude toward politicians in general. A poll published in *Le Monde* revealed that 62 percent of the respondents said that their politicians did not consider the large issues that concerned France; 82 percent said that politicians did not tell the truth; and 55 percent said that politicians made too much money.[66] Fabius's new emphasis on truth and directness was exactly what the French public wanted to hear.

On September 12 the prime minister unveiled the new budget for 1985. This budget cut direct taxes by 5 percent (45 billion francs), while continuing to hold the state's deficit at a maximum of 3 percent of the GDP. Also, this new budget envisioned a 2 percent growth rate for France. While budgets are keyed to economic issues and realities, they are often geared to the electorate. The budget for 1985 suggested that the French economy was now on the upswing. With the 1986 legislative elections nearing, it was imperative that the Socialists loosen their control over the economy. In this regard, Mauroy once told reporters that the austerity policy was intended to produce an upturn in the economy before the 1986 elections.[67]

With the budget now in place, the Mitterrand government continued to "modernize" nationalized industries by authorizing further layoffs and by cutting back on subsidies to state-owned firms. The government also encouraged joint ventures between nationalized industries and foreign companies, especially American high-tech firms. Also, the Mitterrand government continued its earlier policy of aiding small private businesses with tax cuts and partnerships with state firms.[68]

The general economic situation in France, however, showed that while Mitterrand had made gains to reduce inflation, unemployment was still rising. In the early fall of 1984, inflation was down to 7.4 percent, but unemployment statistics between October 1982 and October 1984 showed that 330,000 had lost their jobs, meaning that 20,000 to 30,000 people per month found themselves out of work. To ease unemployment, especially among the hard-hit younger section of the population, the Council of Ministers adopted in September a French-style public works program (*travail d'utilité collective*—TUC) that permitted sixteen- to twenty-one-year-olds to work for a year at 1,200 francs a month. This proved to be a successful program that relieved some of the unemployment pressure. Another concern at this time was the growing strength of the dollar, which was at 5.20 francs in May 1981, but had risen to 9.4 francs by May 1984. Although the general economic situation was not rosy, the economic picture looked a little brighter than in the past.[69]

Now a passionate traveler, in late August Mitterrand made a "secret" visit to King Hassan of Morocco as part of French realpolitik in Africa. Yet in North Africa this visit produced some unexpected consequences. Mitterrand's presence in Morocco at this time was taken as French approval of a "union" between Morocco and Libya that went into effect on September 1. Furthermore, Mitterrand's visit angered Algerian leaders because of the competition between Morocco and Algeria in North Africa. Later, Mitterrand met with Algerian president Chadli Bendjedid to reassure him of French friendship.[70]

Shortly after his Moroccan voyage backfired, Mitterrand made another error in statesmanship, believing that Colonel Qaddafi could be trusted. On September 17 both Paris and Tripoli officials announced the "total evacuation . . . from Chad" of French and Libyan forces. As it turned out, there would be considerable difficulty in getting Qaddafi to honor the agreement. But during the *rentrée*, the French not only received the encouraging news about the planned tax cuts for the coming year, but also heard that all French troops were being evacuated from Chad.

In a further effort to demonstrate his statesmanship and his government's commitment to a strong Paris-Bonn axis within the EEC, Mitterrand invited Chancellor Kohl to attend a ceremony on September 22 at Verdun where more than 1.5 million men had lost their lives in almost a year of fighting in World War I. In a moving ceremony, Mitterrand took Kohl's hand to symbolize the friendship and the rapprochement between their nations. Widely published photographs of the incident conjured up images of two nations united in friendship. Mitterrand had wisely arranged this meeting with Kohl to make up for the chancellor's absence (he was not invited) at a ceremony earlier in June that included Western leaders celebrating the anniversary of the D-Day landings.

Still trying to ease antigovernment sentiment, on October 11–13 Mitterrand traveled to Aquitaine to try to rally the provinces. This visit came at the end of a September campaign in the Socialist weekly *L'Unité* that attacked the Communist party for its harsh criticisms of the government.[71] When the Gaullist mayor of Périgueux asked the president if national unity was possible with the current government, Mitterrand—now stressing his role as an arbiter—stated very diplomatically that when the nation is divided, the president's role is to intervene and calm passions. Throughout his tour of Aquitaine, Mitterrand called for national unity. At Mont-de-Marson he declared that he desired "to make France a great united nation with a rich future." According to the president, this was his "responsibility," his "obligation," and also his "conviction."[72]

Mitterrand began his tour of Aquitaine just as he and his government learned that the Constitutional Council had used its judicial power once again to set back one of the key reforms in the area of public liberties. On October 11 the council invalidated certain aspects of a press law adopted on September 12 that aimed to limit private monopolies of the press,[73] especially the monopoly of the right-wing Hersant group which controlled *Le Figaro* and eighteen other national and provincial newspapers. The Right hailed the decision of the Constitutional Council as an important victory.

The next month, November, Mitterrand experienced an embarrassing foreign policy setback at the hands of the unpredictable Colonel Qaddafi. In September, as mentioned above, Paris and Tripoli had announced the beginning of a "total evacuation" of Chad, except for a small strip of territory in the north that Libya had annexed. Seeking to remind Qaddafi of the withdrawal agreement, Mitterrand met the Libyan leader on November 15 on the island of Crete. One week later the French minister of external relations announced that all Libyan troops had evacuated Chad. However, U.S. reconnaissance photographs showed that Qaddafi had not honored the withdrawal agreement, and that three thousand well-equipped Libyan troops were still in Chad. After some delays, Qaddafi finally removed his troops from the contested areas of Chad, at least for the time being. Qaddafi's deception did not enhance Mitterrand's role as an international statesman.

This incident had further repercussions later in the year at a planned Franco-African summit at Bujumbura in Burundi. President Mobutu of Zaire, annoyed with the French decision to leave Chad before Libyan troops were fully evacuated, had sent a contingent of his own troops to help defend Chad from Libyan aggression. Only at the last minute did Mobutu agree to attend the Franco-African summit. Mitterrand stated at the summit that France had no formal defense agreement with Chad, trying to give the impression that France might intervene again or stay out of Chad depending on Libyan actions. Nevertheless, Mobutu and other African leaders worried about France's willingness to protect and to assist its friends in Africa.[74]

Another significant foreign policy issue that surfaced during this period was the Territorial Assembly elections in the overseas territory of New Caledonia, an election riddled with tensions between the Kanak Socialist National Liberation Front (*Front de libération nationale Kanak socialiste*—FLNKS) and the Rally for New Caledonia in the Republic (*Rassemblement pour la Nouvelle Calédonie dans la République*—RPCR), which opposed independence. The population of this overseas territory is composed of Melanesians (41 percent of the total population), who supported independence; settlers of European origin (38 percent), who favored close ties with France; and Polynesians (13 percent), who also desired a close relationship with France. While the National Liberation Front boycotted the November 18 elections, the RPCR received 70.9 percent of the vote and thirty-four of the forty-two seats in the Assembly, while 49.9 percent of the voters abstained.[75] Following the election, supporters of an independent New Caledonia blocked roads and intensified commando operations. Shortly thereafter, the forces of the independence movement took control of three-quarters of New Caledonia. Given the mounting tensions, two weeks after the elections Mitterrand appointed Edgar Pisani, a former minister in de Gaulle's government, as Paris's representative to New Caledonia, charged with the responsibility of proposing measures to accelerate self-determination.

Mitterrand's position on New Caledonia encouraged Giscard and six former Gaullist prime ministers to publish a declaration criticizing the Socialist government for jeopardizing "the fundamental rule of the republic and the interest of France." Fabius responded to this challenge from the Right by saying that the declaration was "irresponsible" and only added "oil to the fire" that was raging in the South Pacific.[76] Later, after completing his term as prime minister, Fabius said, "For me the greatest problem had been New Caledonia because it was very far from metropolitan France and it is difficult to settle problems that are so far removed."[77] This South Pacific island community had the potential to become a new Algeria, and both Mitterrand and his youthful prime minister worried that the Right would exploit the issue.[78]

Consequently, by the end of the year the Mitterrand government faced multiple foreign policy headaches. Algeria was annoyed by Mitterrand's visit to rival Morocco, the president had been deceived by Qaddafi, Mobutu was fuming because of the hasty French retreat from Chad, and New Caledonia threatened to explode as a major foreign policy and domestic issue. And all these problems arrived just when the economy began to show some improvement.

Before trying to ease French concerns over foreign policy with a major address on the subject, Mitterrand traveled to the depressed area of Alsace on November 22–23 where he appealed once again for national unity. This official tour of the region was precipitated by several specific factors. One was the growing level of unemployment. Just one week prior to the president's tour of Alsace, government statistics showed that unemployment had jumped 16 percent between October 1983 and October 1984, with the number out of work now at 2.5 million.[79] The other factor that encouraged the president to travel to Alsace was that a planned European research laboratory had been switched from Strasbourg to Grenoble. When Mitterrand arrived in Alsace, opposition figures boycotted his visit. At Mulhouse on November 23 he said that his role as president was not to arbitrate between competing regions, departments, or communes. He stressed that the decision concerning the site of the research laboratory was an international decision and not one solely confined to his government. Trying to temper criticism, he announced the creation of an interministerial mission to seek ways to modernize the industry and technology of Alsace. At Mulhouse, Mitterrand reiterated that as president he represented the entire nation. Once again echoing Louis XIV he declared, "The president of the republic personifies the nation, the state, the republic, the entire country."[80] At Mutzig he also reminded the population of Alsace of his political convictions, declaring, "I am a Socialist. . . . I believe that you knew this when I was elected."[81]

Just one week earlier, Mitterrand had published an interview in the review *L'Expansion* in a similar effort to mobilize the Left in the wake of the recent recentering of the government. "The government of Laurent Fabius," stated the president in the interview, "is inspired with the same principles as that of Pierre Mauroy. . . . My socialism is finding a true political, economic, and social democracy." Yet Mitterrand attempted to moderate the effect of these statements by adding, "You will not find any utterance of mine that is hostile to just profit. . . ."[82]

Despite Mitterrand's reassurances to labor and to business in the pages of *L'Expansion* and in Alsace, an antigovernment demonstration in Strasbourg drew eighty thousand protestors who marched behind their elected officials. According to some political analysts, however, the journey to Alsace was more successful for the president than it appeared on the surface.[83] Slowly Mitterrand's popularity began to rebound.

Before his planned broadcast on foreign policy, Mitterrand had a rendezvous with Africa. On December 8 an accord was signed at Lomé in Togo between the EEC and sixty-six nations of Africa, pledging cooperation between the two continents. To a degree, the Lomé Convention represented a small success for the North-South policy that the Socialists had advocated earlier. On December 11 and 12 Mitterrand was in Bujumbura for a traditional Franco-African summit.[84] Little did he know at this time that this summit, or at least the French francs appropriated for the meeting, would be the subject of a developing scandal, the Carrefour affair. At the summit, Chad and Libya were two important topics, as they were when Mitterrand addressed a television audience at home a few days later.

Mitterrand appeared before the television cameras on December 16 for an interview with journalists on foreign policy. In this broadcast the president, who appeared imperious throughout the exchange as he sat in a Louis XIV chair with a French flag in the background, asked the nation to judge his foreign policy "from a distance." Concerning Chad, Mitterrand maintained that his aim was to stop the Libyan invasion and to ensure the protection and security of black Africa. When questioned about the rationale for his meeting with Qaddafi in Crete, Mitterrand justified this rendezvous by saying that it was part of a strategy to maintain "constant pressure" on Colonel Qaddafi "by the means that I decide. . . ." On the question of New Caledonia, the president indicated that France would not bend to force, but that the people of the distant island must themselves decide what form of autonomy or independence they desired. With regard to the Middle East, Mitterrand affirmed the permanence of a French policy in the area. He noted that recent meetings with Syrian president Hafez al-Assad and Israeli prime minister Shimon Peres had been "contradictory but complementary." "France," he said, "is the only country that can . . . talk both with Israel and with the Arab countries." On Europe, the president stressed that many hitherto outstanding problems had been settled during his presidency of the European Community and that progress had been made in reinforcing the political union of Europe. Concerning one of his favorite themes, he told the nation that he would continue to strive to improve North-South relations, which he still considered one of the urgent tasks of the era. And concerning the arms race, Mitterrand supported an equilibrium of forces in the world, but he spoke out against the militarization of space, a clear reference to Reagan's Star Wars program. French relations with the Soviet Union, he said, must be active, friendly, and built on mutual respect, "but not to the detriment of our own security." During this major televised address on foreign policy, Mitterrand announced his intention to address the nation soon on internal affairs.[85]

With both domestic and foreign policy issues weighing heavy on the minds of many in France and with the 1986 legislative campaign beginning to draw considerable attention, the opposition in France began to discuss "cohabitation," power-sharing with a Socialist president if the Right won the upcoming election as expected. During the autumn of 1984 former Prime Minister Barre said that power-sharing with Mitterrand would be "treason to the principle of the Fifth Republic" since de Gaulle had not envisioned the president representing one party while the majority in the National Assembly represented another. However, former president Giscard, who had recently won a seat in the Assembly from Puy-de-Dôme, and the Gaullist Chirac stated publicly that a refusal to cohabit with Mitterrand could bring on a "crisis of the regime."[86] While the issue of cohabitation surfaced in late 1984, in the future power-sharing would be of great historical significance for France and its political system.

At the end of 1984 Mitterrand was in retreat. Disenchantment and popular pressure had forced him to withdraw the Savary law for private schools—one of the Socialists' major objectives—change its earlier position vis-à-vis the business community, and give up the proposed press law due to the decision of the Constitutional Council. The reform-minded Mitterrand government was also in retreat, if not defeated, with the fall of the Mauroy cabinet in July and the formation of a recentered government that did not include the Communists. The level of confidence in the Socialist government, coupled with the tremendous level of popular pressure against the government that peaked during the spring and early summer, forced Mitterrand to exercise a *coup de Jarnac* to save himself and his government from calamity. But while in retreat on several fronts, Mitterrand continued to advocate, as would his new prime minister, the need to modernize French industry, a political as well as an economic strategy that in time helped to salvage the popularity of Mitterrand and the Socialists.

Closing this year of retreat, on January 31 Mitterrand presented his annual New Year's Eve message and appealed once again for national unity. He expressed the hope "that the French could unify themselves on the important problems" and stressed the need for the nation to be tolerant as it faced some difficult problems in the days ahead—"unemployment, security, [and] New Caledonia." As if to suggest that he was the father of the nation, he repeated his own father's consistent advice to family members "to be tolerant among yourselves. . . . with the spirit of tolerance, you will see that we can settle our problems in the best interests of everyone." Concluding his address, Mitterrand echoed his prime minister's declaration: "My mission is to tell the truth. This mission I will fulfill." France, he said, had in the course of its history successfully faced many crises. "That of today is not the worst. But it requires the same virtues: unity, courage, and effort."[87] In his New Year's Eve address one year earlier, he had promised that he "would follow without weakness the attempt to reform the nation." Yet, by the end of 1984, the political climate in France, as *Le Monde* noted in its analysis of the end of the year message, had deteriorated so badly because of the economic situation and mounting opposition to his government's policies that he could now only make an appeal for national unity. The year 1984 had been a nightmare for Mitterrand.

7

PREPARING FOR THE
1986 LEGISLATIVE ELECTIONS

1985–March 1986

The only thing certain between 1986 and 1988 is that I
will be president of the republic. What is uncertain are the
other things. As for me, I will be here.
—François Mitterrand

During the fourteen-and-a-half-month period be-
tween January 1, 1985, and March 16, 1986, the day the nation went
to the polls to elect a new National Assembly, Mitterrand and his
socialist confreres took a number of steps to improve the standing of
their party in the 1986 elections and in the postelection period, when
the president would have to share power with right-wing opponents,
an unprecedented event in the political history of the Fifth Republic.
Toward the end of 1985 and during the months immediately preceding
the legislative elections, Mitterrand's popularity rebounded sharply as
a result of his active campaigning, which mobilized leftist voters, and
an upturn in the economy, with the inflation rate falling to 4.7 percent
in 1985 and unemployment dropping slightly before election time. Yet
with these positive economic trends aiding Mitterrand and the Socialists, he and his government faced in 1985 a French Watergate, the
"Greenpeace affair," which gravely threatened both the prime minister
and the president.

177

For the nation as a whole, the period up to March 1986 was one of increasing anxiety. Not only were French citizens concerned about the general state of the economy, the increasing cost of living, the threat of even more unemployment, and increasing incidence of crime, but they worried also about an escalation of terrorist bombings. Beginning in 1985 France experienced a marked increase in terrorist attacks by groups such as the radical Direct Action, opposing Mitterrand's domestic and foreign policies. Terrorist attacks sponsored by foreign governments, especially Iran and Libya which considered France to be an enemy of Islam, also became increasingly frequent. This increase in terrorist activity accelerated even more after the 1986 legislative elections. In 1985 alone the capital saw one assassination and a minimum of eight bombings that left fifty-three people injured. These attacks were aimed at government and public officials as well as government offices and public places.[1] Besides the increasing violence at home, metropolitan France also watched on their television screens a rising tide of violence in the distant territories of New Caledonia and Guadeloupe. Furthermore, in faraway Beirut, four French citizens, including two diplomats, were taken hostage to protest what was perceived to be Mitterrand's tilt toward Israel in the war-torn Middle East. Symbolic of this atmosphere of anxiety and fear that pervaded France during this 1986 period was the bombing that occurred in the chic shopping mall *Point Show* on the Champs-Elysées shortly after the 1986 election when Mitterrand's new prime minister, the Gaullist Chirac, was announcing the composition of his government. This terrorist attack, which killed two people and injured twenty-eight others, was linked to the situation in Lebanon where a total of eight French citizens were being held hostage. This attack revealed that both left- and right-wing governments in Paris were susceptible to terrorism. Some in France, especially the Socialists, had deluded themselves into thinking that Mitterrand's Third World emphasis would "neutralize" French territory in regard to international terrorism.[2] But this was not to be the case.

Related to the growing anxiety over terrorism and the exceedingly high level of unemployment, France witnessed an increase in xenophobia and racism, reflected, in part, by the growing strength of Le Pen's National Front. This xenophobia and racism encouraged young people to form an organization known as *SOS-Racisme* (SOS-Racism). Headed by Harlem Désir, SOS-Racism held a rally at the place de la Concorde in June 1985 that attracted three hundred thousand people. Désir, who was born in the suburbs of Paris and whose father was from Martinique and whose mother was from Alsace, began to plan future national and Europe-wide events to alert citizens about the dangers of racism. While Le Pen made immigration an election issue, SOS-Racism attempted to make an issue of racism.[3] Within this context of growing domestic and international agitation and violence, Mitterrand faced an uphill battle to safeguard his position and that of his party.

At the outset of 1985 Prime Minister Fabius, whose popularity in the polls was rising while the president's own rating remained low, told the nation that the Socialist government had made economic progress. On January 10 Fabius announced that while the economy had improved, the new government would "not change its economic direction for electoral reasons."[4] To a large degree, Fabius was correct about the economic situation; in 1984 inflation was 6.8 percent compared to 9.6 percent in 1983—the lowest rate in twelve years—and in 1984 the foreign trade deficit had been cut in half. The nagging problem, of course, was unemployment. In 1984 unemployment had increased by 13.3 percent.

Shortly after the prime minister's positive announcement on the economy, Mitterrand, in keeping with the modernization program or at least the rhetoric of modernization, approved a state-sponsored project to purchase up to 250,000 personal computers to facilitate a national program to upgrade computer literacy in French schools and workplaces. At this time the government was also supporting the introduction of a home computer system known as Minitel that increased the services available in France. Fabius also announced a plan called "Computers for Everyone" and said that the government planned to install microcomputers in all French universities and secondary and grammar schools by the end of 1985. The new prime minister then traveled to the provinces in a well-publicized campaign to see computer programs in action in the schools.[5]

Another government effort to tackle the problem of unemployment and to suggest to the public that the Socialists were preparing France for the future was Mitterrand's appointment of Gilbert Trigano, the founder of the Club Méditerranée resort chain, as France's special delegate for training. Trigano's task was to aid unemployed workers from the so-called "smokestack" industries, such as steel, to make a transition to service jobs, especially data-processing-related positions. As part of his training program, Trigano established several computer centers in depressed inner-city areas to train the unemployed.[6] Mitterrand, once labeled a man of the past, was now creating a forward-looking public image by becoming France's chief advocate for high-tech industries.

Besides economic concerns, Mitterrand had other problems during the opening months of 1985. One was the new challenge posed by the press magnate Robert Hersant. On January 10, defying a 1984 Socialist law limiting newspaper holdings, Hersant purchased his second newspaper in Lyon, *Le Progrès*. Hersant, who owned a large number of newspapers and controlled the circulation of 38 percent of national and 19 percent of provincial dailies, not to mention his radio stations, was counting on a new right-wing government being elected in 1986 that would rescind restrictive Socialist press laws. Mitterrand, however, had a plan to break the Right's monopoly of the press and telecommunication.

In early January Mitterrand announced that he favored authorizing the creation of private television channels. Until this date France's three television channels—*TF 1*, *Antenne 2*, and *FR 3*—were run by the state (there was also a new subscriber network called *Canal Plus*). Earlier in 1984 the Mitterrand government had legalized private commercial radio stations, and a move to end the state's broadcasting monopoly in television was a logical second step. Mitterrand envisioned creating approximately eighty private local stations throughout France, with some in operation by the summer of 1985. This television gambit by Mitterrand was an effort to strengthen his image as a leader of a government attached to liberty and modernization, but also to prepare for the post-1986 election period where the telecommunications system would probably be controlled by a right-wing majority if action was not taken to break the state's monopoly of the electronic media. To some it seemed like a contradiction, but the Socialist president was now calling for "privatization." Countering the president, Hersant soon announced his plans to set up his own television network.[7]

In addition to Hersant's challenge, Mitterrand also faced growing problems of law and order in New Caledonia. On January 7, Pisani, special delegate of the Mitterrand government to the troubled overseas territory, proposed a referendum for New Caledonia on whether the island should maintain its territorial status or be given independence in "association with France." This proposal also stipulated that if voters chose the association-independence alternative

France would continue to defend the island and to control its police force. Then, on January 11 a French teenager was killed in New Caledonia, reportedly by a pro-independence gunman. This incident immediately incited violent demonstrations by French settlers in the island's capital, Nouméa. These demonstrations led to the death on January 12 of Eloi Machoro, one of the principal leaders of the independence movement, who was reportedly killed by a police marksman. The violence that escalated on this tiny island of 145,000 people motivated authorities to impose a state of emergency on January 12.[8]

On January 16 Mitterrand addressed the nation in a televised interview in which he discussed positive facets of the economy, possible cohabitation with the Right, private television, and a presidential visit to New Caledonia. Regarding the upcoming legislative elections and cohabitation with the Right after March 1986, Mitterrand said that he would not resign as president if the Right won. He told his audience that although he would not be actively involved in the 1986 campaign, he would speak from time to time to define the direction of it. He noted, too, that he supported a new electoral system for the coming elections, proportional representation. Yet, the attention-grabbing statement of this presidential interview did not concern these matters; it was Mitterrand's announcement that he would leave the next day for New Caledonia.[9] This visit was rather dangerous for a president to undertake, given the level of violence there. But in view of his rating in the polls—only 36 percent of those surveyed in a mid-January SOFRES poll had confidence in their president—he needed a spectacular headline-making voyage to win support at home. As one English newsweekly reported, it was "a long way to go for a short walk in the sun."[10]

Mitterrand arrived in New Caledonia on January 19 for a twelve-hour visit "to say what I believe to be right and to support the efforts of the high commissioner, M. Pisani." While Mitterrand listened to both sides in this conflict during his visit to the South Pacific, he fully supported Pisani's plan. In many respects this had been his own solution to difficult overseas questions in the past. For example, in the 1950s when he was minister of overseas territories he had favored a form of independence-association with France's colonies in Africa. Moreover, in his earlier book, *Présence française et abandon* (French presence and withdrawal), Mitterrand argued that independence-association arrangements with colonies were the best way to maintain a French presence in the world in the face of growing independence movements. It is no wonder that Mitterrand declared at the end of his stay in New Caledonia: "I have understood you."[11]

After his return from the South Pacific, Mitterrand took further action with respect to New Caledonia. On January 23 the National Assembly was called out of recess to extend the state of emergency imposed by Pisani on January 12. The president announced that France would strengthen its military presence on the French military base on the island, letting the opposition at home as well as the French settlers in the South Pacific know that he was intent on maintaining the nation's strategic position there.

Mitterrand followed his visit to New Caledonia by keeping another promise he made in his January 16 televised interview. He appointed a new director for Renault, Georges Besse in place of Bernard Hanon. As Mitterrand stressed in his televised appearance, action had to be taken at Renault, a state-owned company that had lost 675 million francs in 1981, 1.2 billion in 1982, 1.5 billion in 1983, and approximately 12.5 billion in 1984. The new director of Renault had headed the Péchiney group and had been applauded in Socialist circles for taking this company out of the red. Besse's new challenge at Renault was to trim the 100,000-man force by roughly 20 percent and transform the ailing company into one that could compete with foreign firms.[12] While Renault workers worried about their jobs, the Mitterrand government eased the concerns of some auto industry consumers by announcing on January 29 that it was lifting gasoline price controls.

With the 1986 legislative elections just a year away and with his popularity and that of his party still exceedingly low, Mitterrand launched his first mass rally since the 1981 presidential election in an attempt to recapture the Left's vote. On February 1 he delivered a one-hour-and-forty-minute speech at the sports arena in Rennes before 10,000 Socialist supporters. Appearing before a vast red, white, and blue curtain on which appeared the words "liberty, equality, fraternity," Mitterrand gave what amounted to an address on the state of France. Focusing on two major themes, national unity and terrorism, he presented himself as an active president trying to prepare France for the future. Concerning the economic situation, he stressed that there had been significant improvements, reminding his audience that the 6.7 percent inflation rate was the lowest since 1971, that the 19 billion franc foreign trade deficit (down from 62 billion francs in 1980 and 93.3 billion francs in 1982) was the lowest since 1975, and that the balance-of-payments problem had improved considerably. But he added, "it is necessary to do better" and make the struggle against unemployment an "absolute priority." With unemployment in France at 2.4 million, compared to 1.7 million when Mitterrand took office, he said that "in most cases, today's unemployment is the result of the failure to modernize in the past." Economic growth, said the president, was tied to the nation's ability to modernize, to invest and to train its citizens. Reducing inflation, too, would also ensure economic growth. With reduced inflation "all the rest will follow from this. With less inflation, or no inflation, our industries can become more competitive, economic growth will be sound, jobs will cease to be lost and employment will appear on the horizon."

At the Rennes rally the president also discussed the subject of terrorism. This topic was on the minds of many at the time due to the January 25 assassination in Paris by Direct Action of André Audran, the director of international affairs at the defense ministry. Mitterrand stated that his government would cooperate with its European partners in an effort to minimize international terrorism. Under his government, said the president, France "will refuse any direct or indirect protection for active, real, murderous terrorism." He indicated also that he planned a tougher approach with terrorists, saying, "I will be among those who reject any compromise."

Throughout his speech, Mitterrand appealed for unity, thanking those who had remained loyal to the government and urging others to engage in what he termed "dialogue." At one point he stated, "People always think that French political life amounts to diatribes, polemics and disputes. No! There are some areas where the French people are capable of rallying together in an effort for peace, however hard it may be, just as they did during the war."[13] He told the huge crowd at the rally that it was necessary now, as in the war years, "to resist demagoguery and [the urge to] surrender."[14] According to some political analysts, this speech had a double objective: to relaunch a call for national unity, but also to affirm Socialist identity.[15]

Mitterrand followed the rally in Rennes by traveling to the provinces once again. This time he went to Picardy, the region between Paris and Pas-de-Calais, on February 7 and 8. During his tour, Mitterrand—confronting CGT protestors and for the first time a large number of PCF demonstrators—reasserted that he did not intend to change the government's economic policy. He also repeated a theme that he used earlier at Rennes: "Unemployment today is due to the failure to modernize in the past." He told his greeters in Picardy, friendly and hostile, "My obligation is to speak clear, and to oppose all demagogues." He also promised to "stabilize" unemployment in 1985.[16]

In another effort to prepare for the 1986 legislative elections, Prime Minister Fabius announced on February 19 that elections for the regional councils would take place in 1986 and that the government intended to carry through on one of its campaign promises and institute proportional representation. The Socialists knew that the decline of the Left at the ballot box was the product of two main factors. On the one hand, many of the Left's traditional voters were now abstaining. On the other hand, many moderate voters who had supported Mitterrand in 1981 had now abandoned the Socialists. This group of swing voters proved difficult to regain. Therefore, to offset this decline in voting strength, Mitterrand and his government decided to change the election law and adopt what the president called "a certain dose of proportional representation."[17]

This issue provoked debate and friction within the ranks of the Socialists. Rocard charged that the party's plan would be a step backward to the Fourth Republic where proportional representation had produced a "regime of parties." Mitterrand and other leaders, however, supported the introduction of proportional representation for two principal reasons. First, it would bring a measure of electoral equality to departments in France. In the past, some officials were elected in small departments with relatively few votes compared to officials in larger departments. Second, proportional representation was a way of minimizing a major victory of the opposition in the coming legislative elections, even though it would mean that the extreme right-wing FN would gain representation in the National Assembly. Yet, creating a sort of political "Frankenstein" on the extreme right would weaken the RPR and the UDF and create a divisive issue for any future right-wing majority. While proportional representation would be officially accepted by the government six months later, Rocard weighed his political options and in the coming months surprised Mitterrand and others with his response to the introduction of the new voting system.

During this preelection period Mitterrand continued to keep his vision of a strong Europe before the electorate and continued his frequent travels. In late February, for instance, the president announced that he would in the months ahead begin an initiative to transform European institutions. What Mitterrand desired was an EEC where decisions could be taken by majority vote among the members, instead of requiring a unanimous vote as was then the case. Such a reform would make it easier, hopefully, for the Common Market to resolve outstanding issues. Then, on March 13 Mitterrand resumed his global travels by flying to Moscow to attend the funeral of the Soviet leader Chernenko, where the French leader had an opportunity to meet the new Russian chief, Mikhail Gorbachev.

Shortly after returning from the Soviet Union, Mitterrand had an occasion to assess the voting power of the opposition. In the March 10 and 17 cantonal elections the Left won 248 cantons in the second round of voting while the Right won 381, with the extreme Right capturing 1; the results of this election meant that the Right had gained control of 69 of 95 departments. Then, on March 22 and 25, the opposition won 71 of the 100 presidencies of general councils throughout France, a total gain of 7 presidencies for the opposition while the Left lost a total of 10.[18] It was clear to Mitterrand that a "dose of proportional representation" for the 1986 elections was needed to save the Socialists approximately thirty seats in the National Assembly and heighten the chances that the PS could maintain a minimum of 30 percent of the vote. The president deemed the 30 percent figure necessary if he was to lead an "effective cohabitation" with the Right after the March 1986 elections.

Before the government acted to introduce proportional representation, rude international events reminded the French once again of the dangerous situation in the Middle East and France's involvement in this explosive area. On March 22 two French diplomats, Marcel Carton and Marcel Fontaine, were abducted in Beirut. Several weeks later two more French citizens were kidnapped in the Lebanese capital, a journalist, Jean-Paul Kauffmann, and a scientific researcher, Michel Seurat. For France, however, terrorist violence was only beginning. Mitterrand would have little success in freeing French hostages or in preventing terrorist violence from spilling over into the streets of Paris in the near future.

In late March and early April the primary concern for Mitterrand and the PS leadership was legislation to introduce the new proportional representation voting system. On March 28 the executive office of the PS voted on an informal motion to support party chief Jospin's wish to reinstate the old system of voting. This motion was put forward to test the waters of the PS leadership and to minimize infighting. The vote was thirty-three to three in favor of Jospin's proposal. Shortly thereafter, the government announced on April 3 that the 1986 legislative elections would be held with proportional representation in place and that there would only be one round of voting instead of the two rounds that had characterized the winner-take-all system. This decision by the government provoked Minister of Agriculture Rocard to resign in the early hours of the morning on April 4. Rocard opposed the new voting system because it meant that the Socialist party hierarchy would select the candidates on various lists in the 1986 elections and would thereby be less than democratic, even though proportional representation might aid the fortunes of the party. But other reasons motivated Rocard as well. A man with strong presidential aspirations, Rocard had to establish his own identity apart from Fabius who had overtaken him in the popularity polls. While his resignation surprised Mitterrand, Rocard's announcement in the coming months that he would be a presidential candidate in 1988, an election that was three years away, also caught the president and PS members off guard. As one political journalist in Paris said, proportional representation was to Rocard what cohabitation was to Barre, the most popular opposition figure at the time.[19]

The Socialist party newspaper *L'Unité* attempted to defend the new voting system by reminding its readers that it "conforms to the position taken by the party since 1972." The Socialist weekly also reminded party members that proportional representation was one of the 110 Propositions comprising Mitterrand's election platform and "constitutes, therefore, an election promise upon which the president was elected."[20] With a PS congress planned for the fall and with less than a year before the 1986 elections, Rocard's stinging resignation, followed by his announcement that he would run for the presidency, did not enhance the image of the Socialists as a party of unity.[21]

As the Socialists projected an image of disarray, the opposition created an image of unity. On April 10, less than a week after Rocard's resignation, the Gaullist RPR and the UDF signed an accord "to govern together and only together" in 1986. This agreement was designed to display the preelection collaboration of the opposition and to inform the electorate that neither party would ally itself with the extreme Right. Barre, on the other hand, seemed to be the Rocard of the Right during this period of RPR-UDF cooperation. Several days after Chirac's and Giscard's parties signed this accord to govern together, Barre stated that he would "not vote in a cohabitation government."[22] Nevertheless, the opposition still appeared in less disarray than the Left.

In an effort to minimize a divisive public issue before the 1986 elections, Mitterrand and his Council of Ministers held an extraordinary session devoted to the subject of New Caledonia. They decided that a vote on association-independence for the French overseas territory would be organized not before but after the 1986 elections and by December 31, 1987, at the latest. This session of the Council of Ministers also decided to submit to Parliament plans, known as the Fabius-Pisani law, for a transition regime in New Caledonia that recognized four regions of the island, each with a council elected through universal suffrage and proportional representation and whose members would participate in a semiautonomous Territorial Congress. Under this plan the boundaries were designed to guarantee that the indigenous population would control two of the four regions and to ensure that the white-dominated area would have fewer councillors per voters than the other regions. The Council of Ministers also took action to strengthen the French military presence on the island. This plan, the Socialists hoped, would mollify criticism of the Pisani plan by the FLNKS independence movement as well as by settlers desiring close ties with France. Opposition leaders, however, claimed that the Socialists wanted to create a separatist majority in New Caledonia, labeled the plan "a sort of apartheid policy," and said the arrangement was unconstitutional because the plan violated the right to "equal suffrage."[23] The decision to postpone the elections in the overseas territory until after the 1986 legislative elections in France, elections that the opposition was expected to win, meant that the Right would be forced to deal with the dangerous issue of New Caledonia.

Mitterrand, who had been relatively slow throughout his career to recognize the power of the media, relied on a novel hundred-minute televised interview and variety show on April 28 to win the support of the French electorate. This program, viewed by 20 million people, was organized by Yves Mourousi, a television anchorman and impresario specializing in *son et lumière* productions. While Mourousi designed this program to popularize the French president, Mitterrand used the opportunity to discuss the coming elections. He reiterated that he would not resign if the opposition won the 1986 legislative elections and that he would "not remain inert" after the elections. At one point in this interview–variety show, Mitterrand told Mourousi that he was not happy to be characterized as a pedantic frog in a recent television puppet program; yet the president recalled that in many legends frogs have turned into handsome princes.[24]

This unusual television appearance by the president was followed by a bold show of Gallic independence between May 1 and 4 at the Bonn summit of the seven leading industrialized nations of the Western world where Mitterrand attempted to bolster public confidence at home in his government. At Bonn, Mitterrand gave a "double no" to President Reagan on two important issues: free trade and the Star Wars program. The French president was alone in refusing to begin talks to eliminate barriers to free trade, arguing that he wanted to protect the common agricultural policy of the European Economic Community. In reality, reducing tariff barriers was not a topic that Mitterrand desired to discuss before the March 1986 elections because of the domestic repercussions of such an explosive issue. Mitterrand also refused to participate in Reagan's Strategic Defense Initiative, stating that he wanted to prevent a "brain drain" to the United States.[25] His firm opposition to Reagan's proposals was reminiscent of de Gaulle's earlier effort in the 1960s to preserve French autonomy in a bipolar world. Mitterrand's Gaullist-like performance at Bonn won him praise from the French press, from right-wing newspapers like *Le Figaro* to the left-leaning *Libération*. *Le Figaro* told its readers, "What will be remembered about the summit is above all the double no." *Libération* stated, "The summit of the seven dwarfs is really the fable of the giant [U.S.] and the six dwarfs. . . . François Mitterrand has every reason to be pleased with himself."[26] Mitterrand's stand at Bonn also contributed to a healthy five-point jump in his popularity in France—after the summit his popularity rose from 37 percent to 42 percent, marking the first time since June 1984 that the president had been above the 40 percent mark.[27]

Demonstrating to the French that the hexagon had its own independent nuclear deterrent to protect national independence, Mitterrand followed the Bonn summit by helping to launch France's sixth nuclear submarine, *L'Inflexible*, at Brest on May 25.[28] This first of a new generation of nuclear submarines was armed with sixteen missiles, each carrying six warheads and capable of striking targets more than 4,000 kilometers away. Mitterrand, who became a Gaullist convert on questions of national defense during his presidency, had approved plans to refit the other submarines in the fleet with the new multiple-warhead missile and had sanctioned plans to construct a seventh nuclear submarine that would be in service in the early 1990s. Mitterrand's stand at Bonn and his presence at the launching ceremonies at Brest reinforced the image of a strong France defended by a growing nuclear strike force. While this image was not one that he and his party had projected in the 1970s when the Socialists had been critical of de Gaulle's *force de frappe* and other aspects of the general's policies,[29] politicians in France, as elsewhere, depended on public amnesia to blur their contradictions on policies and issues. In the future, during cohabitation with the Right, the Socialist president proved to be more Gaullist than the Gaullist Chirac on questions of national defense.

The summer of 1985, like many of the summers of Mitterrand's presidency, was filled with significant developments, many posing serious problems. Besides Rocard's announcement that he would enter the race for the presidency in 1988, on June 14 Prime Minister Fabius commenced a "war of the dauphins" when he suggested in a speech in Marseille that he would lead the PS campaign in the coming legislative elections. While Mitterrand could afford to deal with Rocard at a later date, a battle between Fabius and party chief Jospin threatened to disrupt party unity on the eve of the legislative campaign. Jospin, incensed by Fabius's remarks, requested the executive office of the Socialist party on June 19 to discuss the issue of campaign responsibilities at the July 6 meeting of the executive committee. The open split between the two young Socialist leaders, which the Parisian press covered in great detail, pitted the prime minister, who ostensibly preferred to enter the legislative campaign with a "Republican Front" that would be composed of allies on the left and center, against the general secretary, who favored maintaining Socialist identity by keeping the party anchored to the left in order to attract Communist voters.[30] Even though Fabius stated in his monthly television program "Let's Talk France" that "there is neither a quarrel nor a fundamental difference between myself and Jospin," the public debate between two potential heirs embarrassed the president who consistently stressed the importance of national and party unity in his preelection speeches. On June 22 while he was in Athens attending an EEC summit, Mitterrand attempted to dodge the issue of the Fabius-Jospin quarrel by telling reporters that the affair was not for him to decide. At a private dinner party, however, the president reportedly remarked that "Fabius was still a little green."[31] Several days later he would take a public stand on the debate among the Socialists.

In the midst of this conflict, Mitterrand made a two-day official visit on June 24–25 to Languedoc-Roussillon in the south of France. Accompanied by three ministers—Georgina Dufoix (social affairs and government spokesperson), Pierre Joxe (interior and decentralization), and Henri Nallet (Rocard's replacement as minister of agriculture)—Mitterrand experienced moderation among the opposition in the region but a number of hostile CGT demonstrators who on occasion shouted out "Mitterrand treachery!" At Nîmes he told a crowd that he had come to the region "to better understand" the problems of the area and "to listen to others" in a spirit of dialogue. Here and in other towns in Languedoc-Roussillon he attempted to appear as a conciliator. Granting interviews to the major daily newspapers in the region, Mitterrand told *Midi libre* that "we have accomplished in four years the essentials that were forecast for seven years." The president added that he regretted "not being able to realize certain promises. But [he] still had time." He then indicated several examples where he might be able to make future changes, noting "the right of immigrants who have been in France for five years to vote in municipal elections" and "reducing unemployment once and for all."[32] In Carcassonne, Mitterrand denounced the aggressive attitude of the Communist leaders and appealed to the French to unite "around the modernization of the country."[33] This visit revealed a trend that would later be substantiated in public opinion polls—the intensity of the opposition to Mitterrand and his government had started to wane. This may have been gratifying to Mitterrand, but the political battle in the capital between Fabius and Jospin was not.

Mitterrand finally decided that the quarrel between the two dauphins had to end. On June 26 at Dun-les-Places in the Nièvre the president attempted to settle the debate, which was receiving more press coverage daily and undercutting his efforts prior to legislative elections to forge a national consensus around modernization. Besides, how could a president insist on national unity if he was not able to maintain some semblance of unity within his own party? In his own department of the Nièvre, Mitterrand declared, ". . . The head of government must explain, propose, lead. He is the natural leader of the majority. But the Socialist party is the real political arm of the majority and it is responsible for leading the campaign. . . ." After this intervention by Mitterrand, both the Matignon and the rue de Solferino, PS headquarters, considered the debate closed.[34] Nevertheless, if one reads closely between the lines of Mitterrand's statement, it was clear that he had equivocated somewhat in his effort to resolve the rivalry between Fabius and Jospin. Thus, while the statement ended the dispute, it was not an unmitigated victory for the head of the Socialist party.

With this embarrassing and potentially dangerous quarrel behind him, Mitterrand flew to Milan for an EEC summit where he made a number of proposals to strengthen the Community and to enhance his statesmanship role at home. At Milan the French president told other representatives, "Europe must begin to speak with one voice." Although the Milan summit did produce some disagreements on European unity—due mainly to the negative positions of Britain, Denmark, and Greece—EEC nations subsequently agreed to launch discussions aimed at "coordination of their foreign policy and common security."[35] European leaders at Milan and subsequent meetings strongly backed a new proposal by Mitterrand: the Eureka project, a European research program for nonmilitary uses of space and an alternative to Reagan's Strategic Defense Initiative. Leaders of Europe's largest electronic firms called Mitterrand's Eureka program "an essential element in permitting Europe to rise to today's technological challenge."[36] Several weeks after the Milan meeting, Mitterrand underscored his commitment to Eureka by pledging a 1 billion franc French contribution to the project at a meeting of EEC representatives in Paris. As *Le Monde* noted, given French economic difficulties, this pledge represented a considerable sum.[37] Mitterrand's Eureka campaign convinced many in France and in Europe that the technological challenge of the United States and Japan could only be met by a European effort. Since beginning his political career in the 1940s, Mitterrand has been a proponent of a strong Europe. With the Eureka program, France's destiny appeared—or at least Mitterrand wanted to make it appear—to be tied to the fortunes of Europe as a whole. Thus the French crisis was seen as part of a larger international crisis that saw the United States and Japan as Europe's principal competitors, an image that reinforced the necessity of the president's modernization theme.

After the small triumph in Milan, Mitterrand returned to France where he hosted a historic visit on July 8–10 by King Juan Carlos of Spain, whose country was soon to become a new member of the EEC. During this visit, Mitterrand and Juan Carlos signed a cooperative agreement, marking the first time since Napoleon that the two rival nations had pledged to work together. According to the terms of the accord, France and Spain promised to combine efforts in areas that included politics, economics, and security matters. This agreement was hailed by newspapers of the Left, Center and Right in both countries as signaling the beginning of a "new era" between the two nations.[38]

According to a well-known and well-informed political scientist and political commentator in France, Maurice Duverger, Juan Carlos' visit provoked Mitterrand to make one of his strongest statements to date on cohabitation with the Right after the 1986 elections. When the king met with the mayor of Paris, an aspiring presidential candidate, Chirac told him that if the opposition won the coming legislative elections, it would renegotiate the conditions of Spain's entry into the EEC, officially scheduled for January 1, 1986. Reportedly, Juan Carlos informed Mitterrand of Chirac's bold statement—not the first or the last that he would make in his political career—and the Socialist president felt compelled to respond to the Gaullist challenge since the president has constitutional authority to negotiate, ratify, and guarantee treaties. On July 10 near Grenoble, Mitterrand told reporters at a luncheon meeting, "If cohabitation means living in the same republic, then I say yes; if it means political confusion, I say no! . . . If there should be a confiscation of foreign policy by whomever in case of a change of majority, that would be a coup d'état."[39] From this time, Mitterrand began to define and clarify his perception of the chief of state's constitutional prerogatives, utilizing a traditional reading of the Constitution to defend his position.

Mitterrand's concern about the Right's intentions sprang from two sources. One was the aggressiveness that Mitterrand attributed to the Right, especially the Gaullists led by the highly visible mayor of Paris. After all, in the past there had been several right-wing attempts to ruin his political career, and de Gaulle had staged what Mitterrand believed to be a "permanent coup d'état" against the Fourth Republic. Mitterrand's second concern was related to the Constitution itself which is somewhat contradictory on the powers of the president and the prime minister. For instance, while Article 5 states that the president is the guarantor of national independence and the integrity of the national territory, as well as of respect for community agreements and treaties, Article 15 says that he is head of the armed forces, and Article 52 gives him the power to negotiate and ratify treaties, Article 20 says that it is the prime minister who "determines and leads national policy." Yet, according to Mitterrand's reading of the Constitution, which accorded with that of de Gaulle himself, and with the historical experience of the Fifth Republic, it is the president who controls foreign and defense policy and guarantees treaties. Until cohabitation became a distinct possibility, it was assumed, in fact, that under the Constitution foreign and defense policy constituted a "reserved domain" of the president.[40] It was now clear to Mitterrand and many in France that the Right planned to contest the president's constitutional prerogatives as heretofore understood.

Besides the departure of Juan Carlos and the president's strong statement defending his view of his constitutional powers, July 10 proved to be another important date for Mitterrand and his government. In faraway New Zealand, French secret service agents sabotaged the *Rainbow Warrior*, a vessel belonging to the Greenpeace environmental group that was protesting French nuclear testing in the South Pacific. Not only did the saboteurs sink the ship in the port of Auckland, but one crew member was killed as well. At the time, Mitterrand and the French public did not realize that the Greenpeace affair, which became the prime topic of attention in the press in the following month, would be the second most dangerous passage, behind the period of public protest in June and July of 1984, for the president.

Before stories surrounding the French Watergate hit the press, Mitterrand celebrated Bastille Day by attempting to establish the ground rules for cohabitation. Besides the usual morning tour down the Champs-Elysées reviewing French troops and observing the military parade that followed, he made an address that defended his presidential powers in case cohabitation became a reality, and tried to strengthen public confidence in the prime minister. In his Bastille Day address Mitterrand reiterated that he would not play a ceremonial role in any cohabitation arrangement and reaffirmed his right to exercise control over the foreign and defense policies of France by referring to Articles 5, 15, and 52 of the Constitution. He stated that "it is enough to hold to the text of the Constitution," but not to claim any "reserved domain," an attempt by Mitterrand to demonstrate that he would uphold the letter of the Constitution—at least his reading of it—but would not claim rights and prerogatives that were not legitimately his. In addition, in an effort to bolster Fabius after the unsuccessful duel with Jospin over the leadership of the 1986 legislative campaign,

Mitterrand expressed the hope that "Laurent Fabius will be able to govern France for a long time, for he is a remarkable prime minister."[41]

In late July two issues weighed heavy on Mitterrand. One was the Greenpeace affair, which had not yet surfaced as a major public issue in France but threatened to do so. After hosting an official visit by Prime Minister Yasuhiro Nakasone of Japan on July 13–16, the president and his trusted friend Roland Dumas, minister of external relations, made a secret trip to Switzerland on July 23. At Auvernier they met with the president of the Swiss Confederation, Kurt Fürgler, and the head of the Swiss Department of Foreign Affairs, Pierre Aubert. Supposedly, the purpose of the meeting was to obtain more information on the nationality of the two suspects, a couple, being held in New Zealand in connection with the sabotaging of the Greenpeace vessel, who had claimed Swiss nationality. However, it was soon revealed that the couple were actually Captain Dominique Prieur and Commander Alain Mafart of the secretive French General Directorate for External Security. As the details of the Greenpeace affair slowly began to emerge, many in France were reading a new book that had just appeared by Pascal Krop and Roger Faligot, titled *La Piscine* (The pool),[42] the code name for the French intelligence operation. For the remainder of July the scandal remained dormant.

Events in South Africa also concerned Mitterrand at this time. With violence escalating and Pretoria as intransigent as ever, on July 24 the French government recalled its ambassador and officially presented a far-reaching antiapartheid resolution to the Security Council of the United Nations. The French resolution called on the nations of the world to stop investment in South Africa and to refrain from supplying it with computer equipment that the police and the army could use to continue racial oppression. One American newspaper stated at the time that the French resolution against apartheid was "a decision by the Socialist government, facing elections, to adopt a genuine leftist stance on at least one issue. It is a diplomatic event just the same."[43] Following a UN debate on the French proposal, the Security Council adopted a modified resolution condemning apartheid and asking for voluntary sanctions against the South African government. With its resolution, the Mitterrand government had not only forced the United Nations to send a clear message to Pretoria, but had also launched a diplomatic initiative that received wide support from the French Left and was warmly applauded by elements of center and center-right opinion in France.[44]

While the stand on South Africa helped Mitterrand at home, insurrection on the French island of Guadeloupe and stinging press revelations about the Greenpeace affair caused great concern in France. Somewhat like New Caledonia, an independence movement was surfacing in Guadeloupe and, between July 24 and 26, violent demonstrations occurred at Pointe-à-Pitre. What began to cause Mitterrand great worry, however, were a number of accusations now surfacing in the Paris press that suggested that there was government involvement in the Greenpeace affair.[45] For the first time in a long while the French press, led largely by *Le Monde*, pursued investigative journalism to uncover tracks of the saboteurs in New Zealand. Consequently, with increasing press speculation on the affair, on August 7, almost a full month after the *Rainbow Warrior* was sunk, Mitterrand requested that his prime minister launch a "rigorous investigation" and bring the guilty to justice, "however high their status."[46] This request and Mitterrand's position on the affair made it seem as if he was shocked to learn that subordinates might have betrayed his government.

Consequently, on August 8 Fabius announced that Bernard Tricot, a former counselor of state and the general secretary of the Elysée under de Gaulle, would lead an investigation of the Greenpeace affair. Fabius also said that the conclusions of Tricot's report would be made public.[47] While the Paris press continued to charge high-level government involvement in the sinking of the *Rainbow Warrior*, Tricot was busy preparing what amounted to a whitewash of the affair.

Unwittingly, Mitterrand himself helped to generate opposition attacks over the Greenpeace affair when he reacted to an August 8 decision of the Constitutional Council that struck down part of the government's electoral law for New Caledonia. The council rendered a decision that stated in effect that equal representation was unduly compromised in favor of "other considerations of general interest." In several bold moves to prevent delays, Mitterrand requested that the nullified article of the government's law for New Caledonia be deliberated once again by the National Assembly, and he convened a special session to deal with the issue. In late August the Assembly reached a compromise on the contested article and the Constitutional Council approved the revision. However, Mitterrand's call for a special summer session meant that when the Greenpeace affair exploded in the press in August, opposition leaders were ready to pounce on it.[48]

For Mitterrand, the affair became a matter of grave concern on August 13 and 14 when several papers and newsweeklies—*USD, Evénement du jeudi, France soir,* and *L'Express*—reported that the bombing of the Greenpeace vessel had been decided on by the direction of the DGSE with the approval of the minister of defense, or even the military cabinet of the president. At this point the affair became a genuine Watergate for Mitterrand that directly threatened his presidency. Adding to the suspicion of high-level government involvement was the Tricot report, published on August 26 by the Matignon, which cleared the government and the DGSE of all responsibility.[49] While the truth was probably hidden from Tricot as he pursued his quick investigation and while he was probably free of any culpability in any cover-up operation, his report produced disbelief and stimulated more questions about the involvement of the Socialist government.

In some quarters, especially on the left, there was speculation that Mitterrand's enemies may have set this affair in motion—after all, he had been the target of two bizarre right-wing plots in the 1950s to destroy his political career. To some this argument seemed plausible since Mitterrand had appointed Pierre Marion, former chief of Air France, more or less to clean house within the DGSE. Marion proceeded to remove a number of right-wingers or right-wing sympathizers within the organization. After eighteen months of housecleaning, Marion was replaced by Admiral Pierre Lacoste. Some wondered if this affair was an effort by disgruntled DGSE agents, possibly in collusion with the Right, to destabilize the Socialist government and even topple Mitterrand.

Speculation at the time suggested that the tracks led to the government, namely to Defense Minister Charles Hernu, Prime Minister Fabius, high-level military advisers, and even the Elysée. Charles Pasqua, leader of the Gaullist opposition in the Assembly, called for the immediate resignation of Hernu and Fabius. Suspicion was still rampant in France in late August after Tricot filed his "rigorous investigation" into the incident.

Even though the Tricot report whitewashed government involvement, the charges and countercharges and the suspicion unleashed by the affair motivated the prime minister on August 27, one day following publication of the Tricot report, to request that the defense minister begin an investigation of the DGSE and to recommend remedial action. Earlier in August the newsweekly *Le Point* reported that Hernu had asked a staff member to send out an order that the *Rainbow Warrior* be watched and that the environmentalist vessel be kept away from the island of Mururoa, the French nuclear test area. Fearing the political damage that this affair could do to the Socialist government, *L'Unité* called for "the truth, the whole truth, and nothing but the truth, and quickly."[50]

On September 12 Mitterrand himself visited the French nuclear test center in the South Pacific to reaffirm, as he stated, France's determination to proceed with "experiments useful for its defense."[51] Several weeks earlier the president had issued an order to the military "to forbid, by force if necessary" foreign intrusion into the Mururoa test zone. His visit to the center as well as the directive to the military, a directive that was made public, were significant for several reasons.[52] First, it showed the determination of the Socialist president to continue nuclear testing to strengthen the nation's strike force and to serve as a warning to the Greenpeace organization. Second, Mitterrand's actions in an indirect way suggested that national security was involved in the Greenpeace affair, perhaps in the hope that the intensity of the affair could be reduced by such appeals.

The affair, however, would not fade from public attention. On September 17 *Le Monde* revealed that the sabotage of the *Rainbow Warrior* had been committed "by a third team of French agents" under orders to blow up the vessel. On September 20 Defense Minister Hernu resigned, stating in his letter of resignation, "Concerning the investigation that I have personally led without any complacency and with a total determination, I have known since last night . . . that key personnel in my ministry have hidden the truth from me. . . ."[53] In his letter of resignation Hernu recommended that the head of the DGSE, Admiral Pierre Lacoste, be relieved of his functions. Following this high-level resignation, Fabius stated in a press conference on September 22 that DGSE agents "had acted under orders; this truth had been hidden from Bernard Tricot."[54] Then, Fabius proceeded to place the blame for the scandal squarely on Hernu, declaring, "The truth is cruel. The responsibility . . . lies on a political authority, that is to say on a minister [Hernu]."[55] The prime minister was careful, however, to limit the responsibility to the defense minister by stating, "I had never been informed."[56] He also explained to the nation that it had taken so long to ascertain responsibility for the sabotage operation because "the truth was hidden from the president, M. Tricot, and myself."[57]

This conclusion to the affair, although the full truth may never be known, spared the military full responsibility. General Jean Saulnier, the chief military adviser to Mitterrand, had supposedly authorized the funds necessary for the Greenpeace operation. On August 1 Mitterrand nominated Saulnier to be his military chief of staff. However, the head of the DGSE, Lacoste, was dismissed and General René Imbot, army chief of staff and one-time head of the Foreign Legion, was appointed the director of the security agency. Furthermore, Hernu's replacement at the Ministry of Defense, Paul Quilès, promised in his first official statement that he would not permit the affair to stain the honor of the military. Although some military officials, including Mitterrand's personal adviser for military affairs, were not truthful when Tricot sought information for his seventeen-day investigation, the line of defense drawn by Fabius in his late September declarations on the affair seemed to limit the damage to the minister of defense, sparing further embarrassment to other areas of government and to the military. The Socialist party, eager to terminate the affair in order to minimize the political damage, told its supporters in the pages of *L'Unité* that "the prime minister has clearly singled out those responsible for the bombing of the *Rainbow Warrior*, Admiral Lacoste and Charles Hernu." For *L'Unité* this was the end of the affair.[58]

Did Mitterrand know about the Greenpeace operation before it was carried out and/or did he try to cover it up once the secret mission became public knowledge? Since his military adviser approved funds for the mission, telling Tricot that it was simply an "information mission," there is a possibility that the president knew of the general plan in advance, but there is no conclusive evidence that he had prior knowledge of the specifics of the operation. Mitterrand was able to maintain what American political observers call "plausible deniability," a defense that several recent presidents in the United States have used to safeguard their positions facing domestic and foreign policy scandals. Did Mitterrand participate in a cover-up? Between the sinking of the *Rainbow Warrior* on July 10 and his August 7 request that the prime minister launch an investigation, did any official communiqués pass between the president's office and other government offices regarding the affair? Since Mitterrand was informed by the minister of interior on July 17 that the two captured suspects were

French agents, why did he wait another three weeks before launching an official investigation? This, of course, was Mitterrand's greatest mistake, for the delay suggested that a cover-up operation was under way, a belief that persists even today in France.[59]

On the very night that Hernu submitted his resignation, Mitterrand sent his old friend and confidant a revealing letter, in which the president wrote, "I want to express my sorrow, my regrets and my gratitude." The letter ended with the words, "I am, as always, your friend."[60] Within a few weeks the affair quickly faded from public attention. Several months later Hernu was elected once again to the National Assembly. The French Watergate was much shorter and much less costly than the one that occurred across the Atlantic, despite the fact that the president had bungled badly. Had French investigative journalism and political culture resembled that of the United States, perhaps both Mitterrand and Fabius would have been forced to resign. As it was, Hernu's resignation, whether he was fully responsible or not for the Greenpeace affair, prevented disenchantment in the military and brought an end to a sordid affair that seriously threatened the Mitterrand presidency before the 1986 election.

In late September French attention shifted once again to its distant Pacific territory. On September 29 voting in regional elections gave control of three out of four regions to pro-independence parties, while the most heavily populated and most prosperous region, Nouméa, went to the conservative anti-independence party. Although the anti-independence group won 60.84 percent and gained a majority of seats in the Territorial Congress, a consultative body, the pro-independence party won control of the territory's Executive Council, composed of the presidents of the four regions of the island. The council was to assist the High Commissioner from Paris during the preelection period. This situation revealed to Mitterrand the deep division on the island and the difficulty that the islanders would have in reaching a consensus.

In another situation, however, Mitterrand saw an opportunity to play the role of an international arbiter. On October 2–5 Gorbachev made an official visit to France, the Russian leader's first visit to a Western nation since taking office. Since Gorbachev was relatively young, fifty-four years of age, and since his personal style was quite different from that of previous Soviet leaders, this visit captured the attention of many in and outside of France. While the French president and the new Soviet chief discussed commercial relations and France's $800 million deficit with the Soviet Union as well as human rights and the Soviet occupation of Afghanistan, the key issue was disarmament. In these discussions on nuclear arms, Mitterrand simply restated his own Gaullist position on the French *force de frappe*.

Mitterrand won support at home when he flatly refused the Soviet proposal for separate arms talks with Gorbachev. In an October 4 press conference with the Soviet head of state, Mitterrand stated, "France has no space capacity. We seek to remain above the threshold of sufficiency, credibility, effectiveness, not to engage in an arms race. So our possibilities of making any changes are restricted. . . ." Regarding Gorbachev's proposal for a 50 percent reduction in intercontinental weapons in exchange for cancellation of the Star Wars program in the United States, the French president declared that he had already told the United States and other allies that France "would not take part in the wider variety of space weaponry." Mitterrand added, "It is up to the United States and the Soviet Union to discuss it. They have the means to do so at their disposal."[61] By taking a firm stand on arms with the new Soviet leader, Mitterrand prevented his guest from promoting discord among members of the Atlantic Alliance.

His Gaullist but Atlanticist stance toward the Soviet Union won him praise from the French press, with the exception of the Communist newspaper *L'Humanité*. The conservative *Le Figaro* simply echoed Mitterrand's position, "France's position, firmly established since the time of General de Gaulle, is the following: The French deterrent force is not a subject of international discussion."[62] Mitterrand, of course, knew that by assuming a Gaullist posture and by demonstrating support for the Atlantic Alliance he could win support at home and solidify a domestic consensus, at least on defense and foreign policy issues. He also knew that expressions of anticommunism, however subtle, could win him and his party support in France.

Mitterrand continued to demonstrate his pro-Atlantic views as well as his anticommunism when he and the West German Chancellor Kohl visited West Berlin less than three weeks after Gorbachev's trip to France. The president took advantage of the visit to Berlin to reaffirm the French commitment to the city's security and survival, telling elected officials in West Berlin that his visit was "a sign of friendship, solid, lasting, and vigilant." Besides reviewing the troops stationed in Berlin, Mitterrand visited the Wall and laid a wreath at a monument commemorating East Germans who had been killed trying to escape to the West.[63]

To aid the construction of a domestic consensus on foreign and domestic policy matters in the preelection period, Mitterrand traveled to Brittany on October 7–8, his twelfth official trip to the provinces since becoming president. With this visit, as with recent tours of the provinces, he encountered a number of CGT demonstrators. He visited the various departments of the region, and gave press interviews, notably with the regional newspaper *Ouest-France*. Besides modernization, Mitterrand discussed the Greenpeace affair, cohabitation, and national defense. In his public remarks, Mitterrand on several occasions stressed what he called "the France that wins" as well as the need to modernize, stating, "It is our capacity to develop and to adopt that which will make the greatness of France."[64] Regarding the Greenpeace incident, he tried to assure reporters that the matter was now closed. On the question of cohabitation he suggested that he would observe the Constitution to the letter in any power-sharing arrangement with the Right, declaring, "Those who talk about cohabitation should consult the Constitution and not myself. It is the Constitution that answers questions. I believe what you call cohabitation is an internal problem of the opposition."[65] At Brest he raised the problem of national defense. According to Mitterrand, "France . . . must demonstrate its intransigence . . . in order to forbid others from encroaching on its just and rightful sovereignty."[66] While in Brittany, Mitterrand took time to visit the site at Guimaec where earlier in his life, as "Captain Morland" of the Resistance, he had landed in 1944 after returning from a secret mission to London. This visit provided the president with the opportunity to remind the electorate of his strong Resistance record and his contribution to the liberation of France.

Several interesting developments occurred in Brittany. On one occasion the regional press asked him to define "Mitterrandism." He replied by simply saying, "I don't know." This elusive answer allowed him to be ambiguous and not to tie himself to a set of policies or a particular approach to government. Concerning the PS and its internal rivalries, he revealed his rhetorical skill when he stated, "The different tendencies are my friends, and with them I made the Socialist party." He also took the opportunity to give his views of Socialist personalities, declaring, "Rocard is a man of worth who has his own personal view of the state of France; Jospin has an elevated conception, an ideal conception of Socialism and possesses great inner strength; Mauroy is solid and very committed to his convictions."[67] With the PS congress only a few days away, Mitterrand had to do his best to encourage party unity as the elections neared.

"Be united. Your diversity contributes to your richness; your debates can be your vitality." This was the message that Mitterrand sent to the delegates at the Socialist party congress in Toulouse on October 11–13, a congress that marked an important evolution in the PS. It came just five months before the legislative elections, and the president wanted the PS to display unity. Not only were the elections nearing, but public opinion polls showed that the Socialists had suffered a considerable drop in popularity. For instance, from 1973 to 1980 an average of 57 percent of the electorate had a positive opinion of the PS, far ahead of other parties. In June 1981 the percentage of positive opinions jumped to 79 percent. However, beginning in 1983 with the introduction of austerity the PS saw a drop in its ratings, and since 1984 more voters had a negative opinion of the PS than positive.

TABLE 8

The Popularity of the Socialist Party Since 1973

	Positive Opinion (percentage)	Negative Opinion (percentage)	Without Opinion (percentage)	Difference (percentage)
1973	55	25	20	+30
1974	64	22	14	+42
1975	61	24	15	+37
1976	58	24	18	+34
1977	58	28	14	+30
1978	55	33	12	+22
1979	54	33	13	+21
1980	53	34	13	+19
1981	64	26	10	+38
1982	60	30	10	+30
1983	50	39	11	+11
1984	44	45	11	-1
1985	42	48	10	-6

Source: *Figaro*/SOFRES poll, *Le Monde*, October 11, 1985.

In July 1986, the month of the Fabius-Jospin duel over the leadership of the legislative campaign, only 38 percent of the French had a positive view of the Socialist party (see table 8). Since Mitterrand was hammering away at the need for national unity, especially around the nationalization campaign, he greatly desired that his own party project a unified image in the approaching elections.

Adhering to the president's message and the election imperative, the Toulouse congress produced what Minister of Finance Delors called "a little Bad-Godesberg,"[68] a reference to a 1959 meeting where the German Social Democratic party officially jettisoned Marxism and made peace with capitalism. Jospin and Rocard were able to agree on a motion that saved the PS the embarrassment of a deeply divided congress. The various currents within the PS agreed essentially to go into the opposition and not become a minority force in a political coalition with the Right after the 1986 legislative elections—a stance that satisfied those in the party who wanted to keep the PS on the left. On the other hand, another article of the combined motion committed the party to continue its austerity policy, thereby satisfying the Rocardians, who represented about 28.5 percent of the delegates at Toulouse and who had called for economic realism.[69] Given the approaching elections, all tendencies within the Socialist party had a vested interest in seeking unity, but Rocard had more than 1986 on his mind. The former minister of agriculture, with less than one-third of the vote at Toulouse, knew that if he wanted to be president he had to reach some accommodation with party chief Jospin. After the compromise at Toulouse, Rocard declared, "There are no longer two socialisms."[70]

Prime Minister Fabius tended to agree with this view and believed that Delors's assessment of the party's meeting at Toulouse was correct. Fabius later stated, "The Toulouse congress was a Bad-Godesberg without doubt. . . . But you can say that the Toulouse congress was, under our government, a moment when the Socialists united in order to demonstrate that basically they had to . . . [confront] a modern society."[71] As *L'Unité* told its readers, from the Epinay congress in 1971 where Mitterrand took control of the party to the Toulouse congress, the Socialist party had been transformed "from a culture of opposition to a culture of government."[72] Many in France on the non-Communist Left had hoped that once the weight of the PCF was lifted from the electorate there would be a more creative and dynamic vision of socialism, a pre-Marxian view of socialism. Toulouse, however, showed that socialism in France had taken a different turn. Social democracy now reigned in Mitterrand's party.

The show of unity at Toulouse was matched by an electoral accord on the right. Five days after the PS congress the RPR and the UDF announced that they intended to present joint lists for the legislative elections in forty-five of the ninety-six departments, while presenting separate lists in forty departments and leaving others in eleven departments undecided. The opposition decided upon this electoral strategy as a response to the new proportional representation voting system. While the Socialist party fashioned a new image of itself, the opposition attempted to project some semblance of unity as the 1986 elections approached.

At this time, however, Mitterrand desired to reinvigorate his own image as a chief executive who cared about the Third World and who opposed U.S. policy in Latin America. Following the PS congress, Mitterrand made an official visit to Brazil and Colombia. During this eight-day respite from Paris, the French president attempted to strengthen important commercial relations with both nations. Mitterrand also restated France's support for the Contadora process to solve the "Nicaraguan problem," demonstrating once again that he opposed Reagan's military solution for the region. This was a position that resonated well with voters at home, since Mitterrand demonstrated his strong commitment, as de Gaulle had done earlier, to an independent foreign policy that showed that France was still an important actor on the world stage.

In other ways, Reagan also helped Mitterrand at home as the fall season brought some good news on the economic front. During the autumn the dollar began to drop, due, in part, to Reagan's intervention in the exchange market because of domestic pressure in the United States. Consequently, the dollar fell from about 10 francs to 7.55 francs, a loss of roughly 15 percent. Since roughly 40 percent of French imports are dollar-denominated, the plunging greenback eased inflation pressure in France and provided Mitterrand with more room to maneuver. Since the rate of inflation in France during the months of August and September was 0.1 percent, the weakening dollar helped to keep the price of goods and services low prior to the March 1986 election. Whereas inflation ran at 6.7 percent in 1984, a 5 percent rate, or less, seemed likely for 1985. With this positive economic trend, the Greenpeace affair all but forgotten, and the Socialists officially united and with a new image since the Toulouse congress, the coming election began to look less bleak for Mitterrand—that is, until the prime minister faced Chirac in a nationally televised debate.

Fabius's decision to debate the powerful and aggressive mayor of Paris, often referred to as *le bulldozer* because of his boundless energy and drive, was as much personal as it was political. He thought that it would help the party in the election campaign, and also wanted to repair any damage to his reputation within the party and with the president as a result of the July quarrel with PS chief Jospin. Fabius had also angered Mitterrand with his September press conference on the Greenpeace affair where he placed the blame squarely on the shoulders of the minister of defense, the president's close and valued friend. Before the debate with Chirac, it appeared that Fabius was on his way to a comeback with party members because of a rousing speech that he gave at the Toulouse congress. However, Chirac helped to end this comeback and to undermine Fabius's rising popularity with the electorate.

In their debate, which was watched by an estimated 48 percent of French households, Fabius and Chirac changed their personalities, with Fabius assuming an aggressive debating posture, and Chirac appearing almost a model of moderation.[73] Fabius ruled out any coalition with the PCF as long as it continued its hostility to the Socialist government, while Chirac promised not to govern with the extreme National Front. Responding to Chirac's call for a broad denationalization plan, Fabius said that such action would only depress French financial markets and aid foreign corporations. Chirac, however, hammered away at the need for less government intervention, lower taxes, reductions in government spending, and more flexible employment policies.

When Chirac criticized the terms of Spain and Portugal's recent entry into the EEC, mainly noting the impact on French farmers and fishermen, Fabius criticized the way in which previous right-wing governments had dealt with Greece's entry as well as Britain's contribution to the EEC. Regarding foreign policy, Fabius attempted to promote the four axes of the government's policies: "independence vis-à-vis the two superpowers, development and human rights, Europe as the future of France, nuclear deterrence and national independence." Chirac countered by telling the national television audience that foreign policy could only be conducted by a country that was economically sound and that was not in debt—this was not France according to Chirac. Concerning the delicate question of immigration, both Chirac and Fabius played to voters worried about this issue. For instance, when Chirac recommended closing the borders and taking action to oust illegal immigrants, the prime minister tried to defend his government's policies, noting that twelve thousand illegal immigrants had already been sent home in 1985.[74] What won the debate for Chirac, however, was the overly aggressive debating tactics employed by Fabius. The prime minister himself lost this debate. *L'Année politique* called Fabius's performance "mediocre."[75] One SOFRES–Europe 1 poll found that 44 percent of those who watched the debate thought that Chirac had won, while only 24 percent felt that Fabius was the victor, with 28 percent judging the debate a draw, and 4 percent expressing no opinion on the clash.[76] From this point onward young Fabius saw his public popularity wane.

In early November, Mitterrand continued to place a firm foundation under his Eureka program. On November 5–6 in Hannover, the foreign ministers and research ministers from eighteen European nations met to agree on a charter project and to agree on ten specific programs in the area of computer information, communications, robotics, lasers, and biotechnology. Discussions on the Eureka project also played a central role in the forty-sixth annual Franco-German summit in Bonn on November 7–8 where Mitterrand and Kohl announced that they would recommend Strasbourg as the permanent headquarters for Eureka, good news for a depressed area of eastern France.[77] The French president received broad support in Europe for Eureka, an accomplishment that was not lost on the electorate.

On November 20, Mitterrand took action that began a new campaign of political polemics. He announced that he was awarding a license for a fifth television channel to a French-Italian consortium comprised of French industrialist Jérôme Seydoux and Christophe Ribaud (the son of a close friend of the president) and the Italian entrepreneur Silvio Berlusconi. Mitterrand made his decision without consulting the High Authority governing audiovisual communications. Although Socialist supporters said that the decision would help to place radio and television squarely in the public sector, the opposition charged, and perhaps rightly so, that Mitterrand's decision was a political one, because the Seydoux-Berlusconi group was known to be sympathetic to the Socialists, and did in fact provide the Socialists with their own channel after the 1986 legislative elections. Others, such as Chirac, charged that the president's decision meant more U.S. programming for French television since Berlusconi had a reputation for relying on U.S. material. Responding to this charge, Berlusconi stated in a press conference that his group would not produce "spaghetti–Coca-Cola television, but spaghetti-Beaujolais."[78] Some even argued that awarding France's first private television channel to a Franco-Italian group threatened the nation's movie industry, since more movies would undoubtedly be aired on television.[79] Mitterrand's rather startling announcement generated protest from journalists, producers, and even from the High Authority for audiovisual matters itself. For the president, the intensity of the reaction was somewhat unexpected.

At the outset of the debate over the Seydoux-Berlusconi award, Mitterrand gave his fourth news conference, the first since April 1984, on November 21. While this conference covered international affairs and defense policy, Mitterrand used the occasion to defend the actions of his government and appealed to the electorate to support the Socialists in the coming elections. He expressed his belief that a recent meeting in Geneva between Reagan and Gorbachev had opened a positive dialogue between the two superpowers. He also noted the disparity between the atomic weaponry of the United States and the Soviet Union and that of other nations, and stated that France must maintain its own security by the strategy that it had followed to date. With regard to the tense Middle East, he told the press that he favored a policy of direct contact with the nations of the area, but that direct contacts had not always been successful. Consequently, he said that an international conference, or forum, or intervention by the permanent members of the Security Council might be appropriate.[80]

Above all, however, Mitterrand's fourth press conference focused on his government's policy at home. He told the press that it was "in the interest of France to continue the policy pursued since 1981." Aiming his remarks at the approaching legislative elections, Mitterrand declared that voters should "form a bloc" to defend the social gains made by his government. The president, moreover, vigorously defended his government's program, mentioning specifically decentralization, the Auroux laws, the attempt to end press monopolies, and the nationalization program. Defending the nationalizations, Mitterrand declared that denationalization "would be to misappropriate the national patrimony. . . ." He also stressed the government's success on the economic front, citing the significant drop in inflation, the stability of the franc, the equilibrium in the balance of payments in 1985, and the stability of unemployment.[81]

Since the announcement of the award to the Seydoux-Berlusconi group had already unleashed great controversy, much of the press conference focused on this issue. Here, Mitterrand defended his decision by saying that he had chosen a French and European solution that would offer protection against an overabundance of foreign programming. French programs on the new channel, he noted, would have to account for 30 percent of all programming within three years and 50 percent within five years. Realizing that the French public favored the liberalization of radio and television, a trend that stood in stark contrast to the presidencies of de Gaulle, Pompidou, and Giscard, Mitterrand did not fail to point out that his government had extended freedom to these sectors of the media. The president promised an additional channel within a year and a half.[82] Thus, his fourth press conference set the stage for the final months of the 1986 legislative campaign, a campaign that Mitterrand himself led.

Following this press conference, Mitterrand devoted considerable time to foreign affairs and foreign visitors arriving in Paris, not all of whom would receive a warm Gallic welcome. On November 25–26 the president of Senegal, Abdon Diouf, visited Paris, followed on November 27–29 by King Hassan of Morocco. Then, on December 2, Mitterrand and other chiefs of state met in Luxembourg to conclude an accord revising Common Market institutions, revisions that Mitterrand had actively sought. The representatives in Luxembourg agreed to adopt a majority voting system in the future in certain areas, to extend the powers of the European Parliament, to develop cooperation in the domains of technology and the environment, and to abolish all customs barriers within the Community before the end of 1992.[83] While the Luxembourg summit won Mitterrand favorable press coverage in France, when he returned to Paris a foreign visitor from the East caused Mitterrand public embarrassment and created a serious rift between the president and his prime minister.

Without informing Fabius in advance, Mitterrand invited Polish leader Wojciech Jaruzelski to the Elysée on December 4, marking the first time a Western leader had agreed to host the man who had the dubious distinction of trying to crush the Solidarity union movement in Poland. The Polish leader was greeted in Paris with street demonstrations by labor organizations and the Solidarity Committee in the

An artistic rendering of the *coup de Jarnac*, an unorthodox, but legal, blow delivered to his opponent in 1547 by the seventh Baron of Jarnac in the birthplace of François Mitterrand. The *coup de Jarnac* is a phrase still used by the French to describe unorthodox but legal maneuvers to defeat one's opponents, a strategy made famous by Mitterrand (Courtesy of the author).

A rising young political star, Mitterrand (1948) as secretary of state for information, one of eleven ministerial appointments that he will hold under the Fourth Republic (1946–58) (Courtesy of the French Embassy Press and Information Service).

Mitterrand (1956) as
minister of justice in the
government of Guy Mollet
under the Fourth Republic
(Courtesy of the French
Embassy Press and Infor-
mation Service).

At Communist party headquarters in Paris (December 1966), Mitterrand announcing the
electoral accord between the Federation of the Democratic and Socialist Left and the
PCF. With Mitterrand *(left)* are Waldeck Rochet, Communist *(center)*, and Guy Mollet,
Socialist *(right)* (Courtesy of the French Embassy Press and Information Service).

The newly elected President Mitterrand chats with people on the street near his apartment in the Latin Quarter of Paris, May 12, 1981 (Courtesy Wide World Photos).

The changing of the guard of the Elysée Palace on the morning of May 21, 1981. Outgoing President Valéry Giscard d'Estaing waits on the steps of the Elysée Palace to receive the newly elected socialist president, François Mitterrand, who will on this day officially begin his presidency (Courtesy Wide World Photos).

President Mitterrand
gestures while addressing
supporters at Rennes on
April 9, 1988, during his
first public campaign
appearance in the 1988
presidential contest (Courtesy Wide World Photos).

President Mitterrand and Gaullist Prime Minister Jacques Chirac for the last time
together on May 8, 1988, as they celebrate the World War II armistice in Paris. That
same day, French voters went to the polls to vote in the second round of the presidential
elections in which Mitterrand and Chirac were opposed (Courtesy Wide World Photos).

President Mitterrand and Prime Minister Michel Rocard *(left)* walk to the presidential stand at the Place de la Concorde on Bastille Day, July 14, 1989, to view the parade marking the Bicentennial of the French Revolution of 1789 (Courtesy Wide World Photos).

Enjoying a laugh with West German Chancellor Helmut Kohl at a joint press conference concluding the fifty-third French-West German summit in Paris on April 20, 1989 (Courtesy Wide World Photos).

Mitterrand expresses his support for former Soviet President Mikhail Gorbachev at a joint press conference at the Chateau of Rambouillet, southwest of Paris, in October 1990 (Courtesy Wide World Photos).

The president poses on the steps of the Elysée Palace with his newly appointed prime minister, Edith Cresson—the first woman to be appointed premier in the history of France—during the presentation of the new government to the press on May 17, 1991 (Courtesy Wide World Photos).

French capital. *Bateau-mouche* (tourist boat) operators even refused to give the Polish general a ride on the Seine. While Jaruzelski told Mitterrand that "this meeting is very important to me,"[84] the protest in Paris forced the Elysée to play down the occasion by having the visitor enter the palace through a side door and telling the press that the general was in Paris on a "technical stopover" on his way to North Africa.[85]

Mitterrand's decision to receive the Polish leader was motivated by his desire for a timely foreign policy triumph. In a later attempt to justify the meeting, Mitterrand suggested that he was applying a tough realpolitik to the Polish situation and that a dialogue with General Jaruzelski was necessary to promote a reconciliation between East and West and enhance the possibility of transcending the Yalta system. While this rationalization might in fact be the long-term factor that motivated Mitterrand, given the approaching legislative elections there was a significant short-term factor that motivated Mitterrand to agree to see the Polish leader. Although all of the details were never made clear, there was discussion in the press at the time that Jaruzelski's visit might assist the movement of Soviet Jews to Israel.[86] Mitterrand himself reinforced this explanation when he reportedly told an aide, "Let them bay, they will soon see that I was right."[87] Since the legislative elections were slightly more than three months away, Mitterrand, being the sophisticated politician that he is, would not have gambled on the Jaruzelski visit without seeing some short-term gain for himself and his party before the elections. Yet these gains never materialized and the reaction to the general's visit stung Mitterrand. Time proved that the president had indeed made a tactical error.

One of the strongest reactions to Mitterrand's guest came not from labor organizations or the operators of *bateaux-mouches*, but from the president's own prime minister. On December 4 Fabius told the National Assembly that he was "troubled" by Jaruzelski's visit, the first time in the history of the Fifth Republic that a prime minister had openly disagreed with a president. Fabius's remarks, besides greatly irritating Mitterrand, also intensified criticism of the prime minister within the Socialist party since the party took a quiet but supportive stance on the general's visit. Chevènement, among others, publicly criticized the prime minister, saying, "A minister keeps his mouth shut—a prime minister even more so."[88] Several days later at a PS leadership banquet at Château-Chinon, Chevènement and Minister of the Economy Pierre Bérégovoy took advantage of the occasion to criticize Fabius. The prime minister found himself isolated among the party leaders, who were worried about the repercussions on the legislative elections of his remarks.[89]

While the opposition quickly tried to exploit the situation by stating that Fabius should resign, Mitterrand had to work quickly to restore the party unity that had been achieved at Toulouse. To accomplish this, Mitterrand reportedly refused Fabius's offer to resign.[90] Fabius himself, however, has said, "This was not an affair to resign over, though I did tell M. Mitterrand what I thought of the visit."[91] Nevertheless, on December 6, while visiting Martinique in the West Indies, Mitterrand tried to put an end to rumors in the Paris press that Fabius would soon resign. Keenly aware of the need for party unity, he told reporters that the "government must continue the work that it has so well begun." Mitterrand also said that Fabius was "a good prime minister. There is complete harmony between him and me."[92]

While the president tried to create an image of unity between himself and Fabius, another Young Turk in the party gave an interview to *Newsweek* magazine that many French Socialists regarded as defeatist. Rocard stated in a mid-December issue of *Newsweek* that he did not think the Socialist party could win in 1986. Party head Jospin and other Socialist leaders deplored Rocard's inopportune remark. Rocard's defeatism, Fabius's falling popularity, and Jospin's mediocre ability to rally voters meant that in the final runup to the elections the sixty-nine-year-old president had to carry the burden of leading the campaign, despite earlier statements that he did not plan to be actively involved.

Meanwhile, Mitterrand had to confront new terrorist bombings in the capital. On December 7, bombs exploded at two of the largest department stores in Paris, Printemps and Galeries Lafayette, and left thirty-five injured. Similar attacks multiplied in the future and became a new and significant issue in French politics.

After hosting a Franco-African summit in Paris on December 11–13, Mitterrand appeared on December 15 in an hour-and-fifteen-minute televised interview produced by *son et lumière* specialist Mourousi, which provided the president an opportunity to begin the last phase of the legislative campaign, one day after the PS adopted its platform for the coming elections. Mitterrand told his audience in this interview that he was "jointly responsible for the work that had been accomplished during the past four and a half years. . . . [If] the

French have a complaint, it is to me that they must address it."[93] The president reminded his viewers of his government's social reforms, as well as the recent fall in the inflation rate and unemployment. He also mentioned his opposition to Reagan's Star Wars program. "Listen," he said, "do as you like in three months [in the elections], but at least guard what you have won."[94] While stressing that he would respect the vote of the majority in 1986, the president told his audience that he hoped that voters would elect the same majority that they had in 1981.[95]

Several days after this televised appearance, the government announced a novel agreement that it had signed with an American firm that would generate new jobs, aid investment opportunities, and boost French tourism. The Socialists agreed to permit the development of a "Euro-Disneyland" outside Paris in Marne-La-Vallée, a gigantic amusement park that the Spanish government had also sought. Few would have imagined in 1981 that Mitterrand's Socialist government, which had criticized what Minister of Culture Lang once referred to as "American cultural imperialism," would permit an American amusement park in France, especially so near Paris and in an area where the PCF once had a stronghold. While some criticized this arrangement, the Socialists hoped that the economic benefits of a Euro-Disneyland in France would be applauded by a large majority of the electorate.

Also prior to the end of 1985, the Mitterrand government adopted legislation limiting the number of electoral offices that any citizen could hold. On December 20 both the National Assembly and the Senate approved a law scheduled to go into effect in 1987 restricting individuals to two elected offices. France had had a long history of politicians, Mitterrand included, holding numerous elected offices at the same time. The new law represented an effort to open politics to more people and to prevent a right-wing monopoly of elected offices.

Following the announcement of the Euro-Disneyland agreement and the restrictions placed on the number of elected offices that an individual could hold, Mitterrand flew to Egypt where he spent Christmas as the private guest of President Mubarak. The Egyptian president later made an official visit to Paris early in the New Year.

Following his return from the Middle East, Mitterrand gave his New Year's Eve address that appeared to be more of a campaign speech than a New Year's greeting. Telling citizens "not to let go of the handrail," Mitterrand confirmed that he would play an active role in the campaign and that he would remain as president regardless of the outcome of the 1986 elections. As in past campaign speeches, he cited the social reforms of his government and the recent economic upturn in an effort to win support for his party.[96] Thus, as the New Year began, Mitterrand, who had stated a year earlier that he would not be actively involved in the legislative campaign, was now leading the effort to mobilize Socialist voters.

In many ways the hopes of Socialist party leaders concerning the upcoming legislative elections were expressed in an end-of-the-year issue of *L'Unité*. The cover depicted Mitterrand, Fabius, and Jospin in a sleigh driven by a single reindeer; the caption read, "We Always Believe in Santa Claus."[97]

In the middle of January 1986 the Socialists received a boost when *Le Monde* and other newspapers reported that in December 1985 the number of unemployed had fallen by 33,000, bringing the total down to 2,322,000. Parisian newspapers also revealed that for 1985 as a whole unemployment had dropped by 3.5 percent.[98] This, of course, was encouraging news to Mitterrand and the Socialists who could now claim on the eve of the elections some real progress on the most stubborn economic problem in France. Inflation for 1985, the French also learned, was relatively low, 4.7 percent, while the foreign trade deficit was about 24 billion francs, approximately the same level as in 1984. The economic situation seemed to be improving, but Mitterrand wondered if these positive gains would be reflected in the March 1986 vote.

On January 17, one day after the RPR and the UDF published a "platform to govern together" and pledged to end the state-directed economy but respect existing social programs, Mitterrand took to the campaign stump again by delivering a speech to several thousand supporters on Fabius's home turf at Grand-Quevilly, an industrial area outside of Rouen where the president's young protégé was first elected mayor and then deputy in the late 1970s. Just a few weeks earlier the PS executive committee had adopted a campaign platform that stressed three priorities: to develop solidarity, to extend liberties, and to give the nation the means collectively to master its future. In his speech, Mitterrand listed Socialist accomplishments since 1981, but he also attacked the recent RPR and UDF platform by referring to it as "the program of the rich against the poor." The president asked his audience to give his government "some time" to complete its program and for the electorate not "to cut the legs" of "a team that wins."

Regarding cohabitation, Mitterrand declared, "According to the results [of the 1986 elections], my role could vary . . . [but] my obligations, and my rights will be the same in all cases."[99] What Mitterrand attempted to do in this and other campaign speeches was to encourage voters to cast their ballots in the upcoming elections for the president. Commentators noted that Mitterrand's increased involvement in the campaign coincided with a strong increase in his popularity, up seven points since November (43 percent in November and 50 percent in January 1986—the first time since 1982 that the president's popularity had reached the 50 percent mark).[100] Like other heads of state of the Fifth Republic, Mitterrand wanted to utilize his popularity with voters and convince them to vote for him in 1986. Thus, the campaign slogan of the PS became: "Vote Mitterrand."

As Mitterrand had done so often in the past, on the eve of the 1986 elections he published a book to aid his cause. This new work, which appeared on January 30, was on a subject where there was a strong consensus in France—foreign policy and national defense. Earlier in the summer his friend Dumas had published an article in *Le Monde* titled "Consensus," which argued that French foreign policy was constant regardless of who was in power. Dumas attempted to use this issue to rally support for the Socialists. By publicizing an area where there was bipartisan agreement among the electorate, the president hoped to strengthen voter support. Mitterrand entitled his new book *Réflexions sur la politique extérieure de la France* (Reflections on the foreign policy of France), a work that comprised the president's most important public speeches on the subject. The new publication also included a 140-page preface, in which Mitterrand noted that French foreign policy was based on several important principles: national independence, balance between the two major power blocs, the construction of Europe, the right of self-determination, and the development of poor nations.[101] One day after the book appeared, *Le Monde* published excerpts and told its readers that it was a "defense and illustration of his policy, which will, without doubt, find a large echo in the current political debate."[102] Once again, Mitterrand used the power of the pen to promote his political cause.

Meanwhile, the divisions on the right were deepening. On February 2 former Prime Minister Barre, the most popular political figure in France at the time, announced that he would not participate in an opposition summit organized by Giscard at Clermont-Ferrand. According to Barre, he did not want to be associated with political figures ready to govern with Mitterrand. While Socialist mistakes with the economy were hurting the PS with the electorate, divisions on the right, due largely to the presidential ambitions of leading rightists, were hampering the opposition.

One factor that prompted a measure of national unity in France during the campaign and the postcampaign period was a series of terrorist attacks on French soil. On February 3 and 4 three bombings occurred that shocked citizens in the capital; one bomb exploded at a shopping center, another at a bookstore, and a third at a sporting-goods store. Another bomb at the Eiffel Tower was defused. All together, nineteen people were injured in these attacks, prompting the government to increase security in the metro, in train stations, and in airports. After the attacks a Middle Eastern terrorist group claimed responsibility for the bombings and demanded the release of three prisoners held in French jails, including Georges Ibrahim Abdullah who supposedly headed a Lebanese terrorist faction in Europe. These attacks, obviously, were designed to embarrass Mitterrand and the Socialists during the campaign. Yet these bombings were only a foretaste of what would follow the elections.

Mitterrand made his second direct intervention in the 1986 campaign since the first of the year by addressing a crowd of 20,000 people in former prime minister Mauroy's territory in Lille. To give added force to this appearance in an area that had been hard hit by unemployment, especially as a result of the Socialist modernization program, the president brought with him several ministers, including the young and popular minister of culture, Jack Lang, as well as Danielle Mitterrand. Also accompanying Mitterrand were a number of writers and entertainers, such as Régine Deforges, Françoise Sagan, and Michel Colucci. At this time a new Socialist party poster appeared that resembled the highly successful one employed in 1981. The 1986 poster, too, was red, white, and blue, depicting a church in a small village, and read, "For a Progressive Majority with Mitterrand."[103]

As in his campaign speech in mid-January at Grand-Quevilly, Mitterrand stressed the reforms over the last five years and defended his government, declaring: "We have wanted to build an open society, more open each day. [Since coming to power] we have called for justice against social inequalities. . . . [The French] have the right to prefer the majority of their choice. As for me, I prefer a progressive majority." As a result of Mitterrand's intervention in the campaign, Marchais of the PCF accused the Socialists of wanting to "transform the elections into a veritable plebiscite on the record of the president of the republic."[104]

One week after the Lille rally, Mitterrand continued his campaign rhetoric on television. The president told this audience, "The French are free to vote for whom they like, but it will truly be a pity if they lose their social gains." Emphasizing his determination not to remain inert after the elections, he stated, "I would prefer to renounce my functions rather than to renounce my prerogatives."[105]

Besides campaigning and dealing with terrorist attacks on French soil, Mitterrand had to respond to a serious development in Chad on the eve of the elections. With renewed Libyan aggression in Chad, especially an attack on the capital, N'Djamena, Mitterrand made a decision to use French planes to bomb a Libyan airbase in the north of Chad. He also launched Operation Sparrowhawk, which entailed sending about a thousand troops, together with aircraft and equipment, to the area. According to some political commentators, Qaddafi probably wanted to take advantage of the preelection period in France, but he miscalculated. Mitterrand's strong response to renewed Libyan aggression won him support from both the United States and Britain and was seen by French political observers as a political gain for Mitterrand.[106]

On the same day that the Libyan airbase was bombed, Mitterrand announced the appointment of the Socialist minister of justice, Robert Badinter, as president of the Constitutional Council, so as to strengthen Socialist representation in this important body. Since the purpose of the nine-member council was to review legislation to ensure its conformity with the Constitution, this appointment ensured the Socialists more leverage in the postelection period when the Right would surely dominate. While the opposition in general criticized this appointment, Chirac, realizing that he could possibly be the next prime minister, chose to be silent.

Just prior to the election, Mitterrand told the electorate once again that he did not intend to become a passive observer if the Right emerged victorious. On March 2, two weeks before the elections, he told a television interviewer that he would refuse to be "a ceremonial president" after March 1986. At the same time he stated that he would choose a new prime minister who reflected the outcome of the upcoming elections. On this issue Mitterrand declared, "The president names whomever he wants, but his choice must be in conformity with the will of the people."[107]

At this politically decisive moment, a delicate problem arose for the Socialists, the sojourn in France of the former Haitian dictator Jean-Claude Duvalier. Following the overthrow of Duvalier, the government had permitted him temporary exile in France until a more permanent home could be found. Yet his stay in France continued longer than expected because of the difficulty in locating a country that would accept him. Meanwhile, the government came under increasing criticism for allowing Duvalier to be in France. Fabius attempted to assure the electorate that the Socialists, too, wanted the deposed dictator to leave. Several days before the legislative elections the prime minister declared in a radio address from Rouen, "There is no reason for Duvalier to remain in France. . . . We do not want this dictator to remain on our country's soil."[108]

While Mitterrand attempted to project the image of an active president on both the domestic and international scenes, events in the Middle East demonstrated once again the president's helplessness in the troubled area. On March 4 four additional French hostages were taken in Beirut. To a large degree, these abductions, similar to the others that had occurred earlier, were linked to the president's policy in the battle-scarred area, a policy that saw France lending its support to Iraq by selling that nation millions of francs' worth of military supplies in the war against Iran. After the elections a new majority and a new prime minister would begin to change to some extent the tilt of French policy in the Middle East.

On the eve of the elections the Socialist party hoped to get 30 percent of the vote. While many in France wondered if the president would have to submit to the will of a right-wing government or resign, Mitterrand himself told his Socialist confreres, "Give me 30 percent and I will look after the rest."[109] The president knew that this share of the vote would provide him adequate support in the Assembly to engage in an active cohabitation with the Right. The prospects for the Socialists seemed hopeful prior to the March 1986 elections due to the economic upturn, including a fall in unemployment, the president's own rejuvenated popularity and his involvement in the campaign, and discord on the right. However, the campaign itself focused less on the major issues that occupied the minds of a large majority of the French—unemployment, the economic crisis, and training for young people—than it did on cohabitation.[110] Mitterrand used this constitutional issue and his rising popularity with the electorate to generate support for the PS. Although the Socialist party would lose the elections, its strong showing was partially a result of Mitterrand's decision to enter the campaign and transform the elections into a vote of confidence in himself.[111]

8

THE 1986 LEGISLATIVE
ELECTIONS AND COHABITATION

Victory in Defeat

One king, two crowns. Two mouths, one voice.
—French official on the relationship between Mitterrand
and Chirac

The March 1986 legislative elections began a new and uncharted period in the history of contemporary France, that of cohabitation.[1] As a result of the 1986 elections, Mitterrand appointed a right-wing prime minister, Chirac, and attempted to coexist with a new conservative majority under a constitution that was contradictory concerning presidential prerogatives. Because of the ambiguity of the Constitution and the presidential ambitions of the new Gaullist prime minister, not to mention the strong desire of the president to triumph over his adversaries, cohabitation became for Mitterrand an exercise in preserving political power. While power-sharing developed into a new and sophisticated political combat between the president and the Right, both Mitterrand and the prime minister had an important stake, at least initially, in maintaining the appearance of a peaceful cohabitation because of certain political imperatives. On the one hand, public opinion polls showed that a majority of the electorate desired to see power-sharing work in France; on the other hand, both Mitterrand

and Chirac needed time to improve their political popularity if they or their parties wanted to emerge victorious in the 1988 presidential elections. This rather bizarre political situation prompted the political editor of *Le Monde* to describe cohabitation as a *mariage blanc*, a marriage of opposing political forces that existed only in appearance. Yet power-sharing proved to be more complex than many initially realized. There was not one single cohabitation, but three: Elysée-Matignon, Matignon-Assembly, and RPR-UDF.[2] In reality, cohabitation brought a new form of guerrilla warfare to the French political system. Unknowingly, the French electorate had redefined the rules of political combat with their vote of March 1986.

At the outset of cohabitation several significant questions concerned the political class in France and the public in general. One question concerned the Constitution: would it accommodate cohabitation? The founder of the republic, de Gaulle, had not envisioned a power-sharing arrangement when the Constitution was drawn up and such an arrangement had never been attempted in the twenty-eight-year history of the republic. Another question concerned Mitterrand personally. What role would he play as president? Would he simply be a ceremonial president, a figurehead? Would he try to play the role of an impartial judge or umpire guarding the national interest? Or would he use his presidency to combat the program of the newly elected right-wing government? Decades earlier the republican Léon Gambetta had said, "When the voters make their voice heard, it will be necessary to submit or to resign."[3] Mitterrand himself stated during the campaign that he would not remain inert after the 1986 elections. No one really knew how Mitterrand would respond to this new political challenge. In time, the president would reveal his method of combat.

One of the fascinating aspects of the 1986 legislative elections is that although the Socialists lost the elections, due mainly to mistakes with the economy during Year I and their inability to reduce unemployment, Mitterrand emerged as the victorious combatant in the new power-sharing arrangement. Following the elections, Mitterrand heightened his presidential image and increased his popularity with the electorate as a right-wing prime minister and conservative government confronted a myriad of serious problems facing France. After a year of cohabitation, polls clearly revealed that Mitterrand was the leading candidate in the 1988 presidential race. His remarkable recovery with the electorate motivated the newsweekly *Le Nouvel Observateur* to describe Mitterrand as "the superstar president."[4] One of the keys to understanding Mitterrand's political career, as Fabius has noted, is to realize that he has an uncanny ability to rebound from defeats and to transform what appear to be setbacks into victories. Thus, the "unofficial victor" in the 1986 legislative elections was François Mitterrand.

While the March 1986 elections ended the Socialist experiment with government, the Socialists remained the leading party on the left as the Communists continued their drastic decline at the polls (see table 9). Although 21.5 percent of the voters abstained in 1986, leftist parties won a total of 44 percent of the vote, their lowest total since the 1960s. However, the Socialist party captured approximately 32 percent, the largest percentage won by any political party in 1986 and only five percentage points less than the PS score in 1981. This surprising performance was related, as mentioned earlier, to Mitterrand's active role in the campaign and to an economic upturn in France, including the decline in the strength of the dollar and a significant drop in the price of oil.

TABLE 9

The 1986 Legislative Election Results in Metropolitan France

	Votes	Percentage	Seats
Extreme Left Groups	427,743	1.53	
Communist Party	2,740,972	9.78	35
Socialist Party	8,702,137	31.04	206
Union of the Left	56,044	.20	2
Left Radicals	107,754	.38	2
Other Leftist Groups	287,177	1.03	5
Ecologists	340,138	1.21	
Regionalists	28,045	.10	
RPR	3,142,373	11.21	76
UDF	2,330,072	8.31	53
UDF-RPR Union	6,017,207	21.46	147
Other Rightist Groups	1,094,336	3.90	14
National Front	2,705,336	9.65	35
Other Extreme Rightist Groups	57,334	.20	

SOURCE: Dominique Frémy, *Quid des Présidents*, p. 583.

The election demonstrated that the Socialist party was firmly implanted throughout France, garnering less than 20 percent in only two departments. Moreover, while remaining strong in their traditional bastions in the southwest, the Socialists increased their strength in the west—winning more than 35 percent of the vote in Finistère and Loire-Atlantique—as well as in certain other departments in the south and Massif Central, such as Cantal and Aveyron. Regarding its appeal to various social groups, the PS received 46 percent of the votes of salaried public-sector employees, 31 percent of salaried private-sector employees, 32 percent of the liberal professions and upper-level management, 38 percent of middle-level management, 34 percent of workers, 29 percent of the retired, and 40 percent of the youth vote (see table 10). This exceptionally strong performance meant that the PS emerged with a majority of votes for the left in all but three departments: Allier, Cher, and Haute-Vienne. In sixty-seven departments, the PS won more than 70 percent of the Left's vote, and 80 percent in thirty-six departments.[5] Mitterrand and PS leaders had without doubt won a hegemonic position for the PS on the left.

This outcome, of course, was due to a large degree to the continued decline of the Communist party. With only 9.7 percent of the vote, the PCF slipped even further from its 11.2 percent score in the 1984 European Parliament elections when it was still participating in the Mitterrand government. Postelection analysis of the 1986 election results showed that the PCF won less than 10 percent of the vote in fifty-seven departments, while surpassing 20 percent in only three departments. Communist losses were especially heavy among the young and the working class, receiving only 6 percent of the vote among the former, and only one out of five votes from the latter (in 1978 50 percent of French workers voted for the PCF).[6]

While the 1986 elections saw the further decline of the PCF, the new proportional representation voting system that the Socialists introduced as a damage-control measure and which saved roughly thirty PS seats in the National Assembly also aided the political fortunes of the extreme National Front. Le Pen's FN won 9.8 percent of the vote, approximately the same score as the once-powerful PCF. Geographically, the FN did best in four principal regions, all having a large percentage of immigrants: Provence-Alpes–Côte d'Azur, Languedoc-Roussillon, Nord–Pas-de-Calais, and Alsace.[7]

Although the Socialists, compared to the Communists, did better than expected in the 1986 elections, the electorate voted Mitter-

TABLE 10

How the Electorate Voted in the March 16, 1986, Legislative Elections
(percentages)

	PCF	PS	RPR/UDF	FN	Other
Total	10	32	42	10	6
By sex					
Men	12	30	40	12	6
Women	7	34	45	7	7
By age					
Under 25	6	40	38	9	7
25–34	12	41	30	8	9
35–49	10	33	40	9	8
50–64	9	25	49	12	5
Over 65	10	23	53	9	5
By profession					
Farmers	7	21	54	11	7
Shopkeepers/Artisans	5	14	61	14	6
Liberal professions/ Upper-level Management	4	32	49	9	6
Middle-level Management	9	38	36	10	7
White-collar	12	44	33	7	4
Workers	20	34	29	11	6
Service personnel	15	31	40	6	8
No profession	11	29	45	9	6
By status					
Unemployed	13	33	33	14	7
Salaried private-sector	11	31	39	12	7
Salaried public-sector	12	46	28	7	7
Self-employed	6	21	53	13	7
Students	4	41	43	5	7
Housewives	6	26	52	8	8

SOURCE: *Libération*, March 18, 1986.

rand's party out of office because it had failed on three aspects of the economy. First, Mitterrand and the Socialists had all but promised that a decline in unemployment in 1981 would result from Socialist economic policies, especially the nationalization plan. Mitterrand, Mauroy and others had blamed unemployment on the failure of the Right, an argument that Socialist leaders used after assuming power until they began to shift the blame to the worldwide economic crisis. Nevertheless, the Socialists did not produce less unemployment, but generated more. Second, the Socialists told the electorate that a reflationary policy would provide a strong stimulus to France's ailing economy. Instead, reflation led to state borrowing at home and abroad, with France becoming a major debtor nation. Third, the Socialists had promised a "change of society" if elected. That change never really occurred, in spite of the long list of Socialist reforms.

Even before 1986 there were clear indications that these failures were losing the PS voters. The Socialists lost support in the legislative by-elections at the end of 1981, in the cantonal elections of 1982, in the municipal elections of 1983, in the European Parliament elections of 1984, and in the cantonal elections of 1985.[8] Mitterrand was very delighted to see his party, while losing, receive almost 32 percent of the vote in March of 1986. Regardless, the outcome of the 1986 elections and public opinion polls suggested that the electorate was less divided than the political class itself, with the far left and far right parties each receiving only 10 percent of the vote.

When the French went to the polls on March 16, they also elected representatives to twenty-two assemblies, the first time that they had directly elected such representative bodies. While Mitterrand's Socialist party fared relatively well in the National Assembly elections, the Right gained control of most of France's regions. In fact, the PS won control of only two regions, the industrial Nord–Pas-de-Calais and the much poorer Limousin in the center of France. However, as many commentators noted, the presence of the extreme FN complicated the Right's control of twenty regions. In five regions, for instance, the Right relied on support from Le Pen's party to win the regional assembly presidency. The right-wing surge in these elections represented one of the strongest advances by the Right since 1958.[9] The Socialists did not originally envision that their decentralization plan would enhance the power of the Right and the extreme Right. Nonetheless, with 206 PS deputies and 9 other deputies that the Socialists could depend on in the 577-seat National Assembly, Mitterrand found himself well-prepared to engage the French Fifth Republic in its first experiment with power-sharing between the Left and the Right.

Following the elections, Mitterrand's immediate concern was whom to choose from the right-wing majority as prime minister. A veritable political chess game confronted the president. If he chose a Socialist, or a Left Radical, or even a moderate Gaullist like Chaban-Delmas with whom he had a relatively good relationship, the majority in the National Assembly might refuse to support the prime minister. On the other hand, he as president had the power to dissolve the National Assembly if the majority failed to support his prime minister or if problems emerged between a new prime minister and himself. Thus a grave constitutional crisis was quite possible, and even likely, at the outset of cohabitation. How would the savvy Socialist president respond to the verdict of the 1986 legislative elections?

On March 17 Mitterrand spoke on radio and television, congratulating the new majority on its election victory, but warning that cohabitation could only succeed with "scrupulous respect . . . [for] our institutions, and common will to place national interest above everything else."[10] One day later, Mitterrand invited Chirac to the Elysée for a preliminary discussion on the formation of a new government that lasted more than two hours. The two long-time political foes discussed their views of cohabitation. At one point in the conversation Mitterrand requested that Chirac, if he became prime minister, appoint ministers of defense and external relations that he as president could work with harmoniously, a request that Chirac honored. Mitterrand was determined, as he made clear in many campaign speeches, to maintain control over the foreign and defense policies of France. In this tête-à-tête Chirac, for his part, supposedly informed the president that he wanted to introduce some parts of the Right's program by decree, a parliamentary method that Mitterrand would later challenge. With some general understanding on how cohabitation might proceed, on March 20 Mitterrand, against the better judgment of some of his advisers,[11] appointed Chirac his new prime minister.

Why did he choose his old Gaullist adversary? One reason is that Chirac represented the new majority and the president had promised to respect the will of the majority in appointing a new prime minister. The rather speedy appointment of Chirac suggested that the president would in fact observe the Constitution to the letter and save France from a constitutional crisis. Another reason, and probably the

most important, is because Mitterrand realized that the prime ministership was fraught with difficult challenges, such as the problems of
unemployment and terrorism, and that Chirac's popularity with the
voters would in time fall as he confronted the realities of power. The
president also knew that Chirac's feisty, aggressive, and often impulsive manner would cause problems for the prime minister. Furthermore, while Chirac was struggling with the day-to-day problems of
France, Mitterrand realized that he could remain above much of the
political fray and play the role of an arbiter among the right-wing
majority, the opposition, and the national interest. In brief, he believed that he could win the cohabitation battle and once and for all
defeat de Gaulle's ambitious, aggressive, and opportunistic political
heir.

Chirac was known for his ambition and driving energy. He was
educated at the Sciences Po and ENA. As a young man, he spent one
summer attending the Harvard Business School and even worked as a
dishwasher and counterman at a Howard Johnson's. He did his military service in Algeria. During the 1960s and '70s he held a number of
governmental posts and ministerial assignments, including prime minister (1974–76) under Giscard. In 1981 he challenged both Giscard
and Mitterrand for the presidency.

At the first postelection Council of Ministers' meeting on
March 26, a rather chilly affair, Mitterrand confronted his new political opponents. In this meeting, Chirac presented the Right's program,
including its plan to denationalize sixty-five French industries. Mitterrand told the cabinet members that he would accept only a limited
number of reforms carried out by decree because parliament should
have the right to debate such significant changes. He also informed
them that he would not sign decrees or support legislation that reduced the social entitlements of the French people. Mitterrand, of
course, could not completely reject Chirac's intention to reform France
by decree because the Socialists had themselves put measures into
effect by decree, notably in 1983 when they had abruptly changed
their economic course. Thus the first meeting between Mitterrand and
the Chirac cabinet set the stage for the drama of cohabitation.

The president's second stage-setting effort came on April 8
when he sent a message to the new Assembly, a message that was read
to the deputies by their new president, the Gaullist Chaban-Delmas,
and to the Senate by Alain Poher. In this statement, Mitterrand
explained his conception of cohabitation in detail. As in his first

Council of Ministers meeting, the president insisted that the legislature "should retain its full rights" and that recourse to Article 49-3 of the Constitution—which allows the government to pass legislation without a vote in the National Assembly if a motion of censure is not adopted—should not occur too often. Mitterrand also reiterated that reform by decree "will not be used to repeal social measures," especially those enacted by the Left between 1981 and 1986. He also emphasized "there will be no economic improvement without social justice and this justice cannot, must not, exclude any of those who contribute through their work and their creative capacities to the development and grandeur of our country." He reminded the Assembly and the public that the Right now had to take action on unemployment: "To complete the economic recovery that has already made important progress over the past years will require still more effort and tenacity. No one can consider this effort complete so long as unemployment remains the worst of our social ills."[12] Mitterrand let it be known that the new conservative government's policies, especially in the realm of economics, were not his own.

With regard to cohabitation per se, the president's statement stressed that the Constitution was the best way to chart a path for the power-sharing arrangement in France, emphasizing, "The Constitution, nothing but the Constitution, the entire Constitution." The president affirmed his responsibility to "ensure the continuity of the state and the regular functioning of the institutions." Mitterrand reminded his audience that his role as president included "national independence, territorial integrity, and respect for treaties," and "the obligation to guarantee the independence of justice and the protection of rights and liberties." On the other hand, the prime minister and the government are "to determine and conduct the nation's policies." In his message, Mitterrand underscored as well France's need to continue the construction of a strong Europe, and "the right of peoples to self-determination, the development of poor countries, and peace."[13] This address to both the National Assembly and the Senate allowed Mitterrand to remind the government and the public of his own political vision and at the same time to put Chirac and his colleagues on notice that he did not intend to play the role simply of a ceremonial president.

The following day Prime Minister Chirac formally presented his government's program to the National Assembly. The program of the new conservative government called for an antiterrorist campaign, a revision of EEC agricultural policies, a new land-based mobile defense component, improved relations with Iran, a heavy dose of economic liberalism—including denationalizations—a repeal of the wealth tax imposed by the Socialists, stricter immigration policies (including visa requirements for all non-EEC citizens), a noncommutable thirty-year prison term to replace the death penalty abolished by the Socialists, and wider police powers.[14]

To a significant degree, Chirac, who had in the past supported the idea of a state-directed economy, introduced a program that had a definite Reagan-like ring to it. Ironically, the revival of economic liberalism in France was, in part, a response to Mitterrand's first years in power. It was also fostered by Mitterrand's modernization rhetoric and his recognition of business beginning in 1982 and 1983. Thus, Mitterrand himself was partially responsible for Chirac's "Adam Smith liberalism."

Another aspect of Chirac's program, the tough law-and-order campaign, originated not on the left but on the extreme right. The Gaullist prime minister's crackdown on illegal immigration with random police checks, new visa requirements, and swift administrative procedures to deal with illegal aliens was partially a response to Le Pen's cry for a hard line toward France's large immigrant population. Moreover, Chirac knew that Le Pen was taking votes away from his own party and that the FN's 9.8 percent share of the vote in the legislative elections weakened the power and the unity of the new majority. The growing strength of the extreme Right greatly influenced the legislative agenda of Chirac's right-wing government.

Cohabitation, or what Mitterrand preferred to call "coexistence," as it unfolded after the appointment of a Gaullist prime minister, became a political drama in three acts.[15] Act One took up the first fifteen weeks, when power-sharing worked relatively smoothly as the president and the prime minister consciously attempted to project an image of a harmonious "odd couple," in order to cater to French public opinion and to enhance their own political popularity and that of their parties. Acts Two and Three began simultaneously in mid-July 1986. Act Two featured a president who attempted to reassert his prerogatives in order to defend his interpretation of the Constitution, while Act Three starred a president who began openly to challenge the Right's program. Thus in Act Two the president was on the defensive, and in Act Three he took the offensive. This fascinating drama was given additional stage time by the wave of terrorism that struck France in early September and created the need for national unity, at least in appearance. Yet as the 1988 presidential election approached, more friction developed between the Socialist president and the Gaullist prime minister as the power struggle intensified.

Act One, the "harmonious" phase of the power-sharing arrangement, lasted until Bastille Day. Up to that time, Mitterrand gave public speeches only on June 14 and 15, which stressed his responsibility to "watch over freedoms" and the need for political leaders to prefer "unity to division."[16] His public silence in Act One projected an image of a unifier and a guardian of national interests, suggesting to the public that he would assume the role of a judge or umpire and, on one occasion, would not rule out his resignation if there was excessive conflict between the Elysée and the Matignon.[17]

Behind the scenes Mitterrand slowly chipped away at Chirac's legislative program. For instance, after the prime minister announced a 6 percent devaluation of the franc against the mark on April 6, Pierre Joxe, head of the Socialist party group in the National Assembly, denounced the devaluation by stating that "the decisions of the government are not those of the president."[18] In meetings of the Council of Ministers and out of full public view, Mitterrand himself hammered away at Chirac's program. During the fifteen-week period comprising Act One, the president told the ministers that he had to ensure that the new security measures were not adverse to individual liberties (April 23 and May 28); that he opposed lifting required administrative procedures that businesses had to follow before laying off workers (April 30); that he had "deep concern" about a new law concerning New Caledonia (May 21); that he had "extreme reservations" about redefining the conditions under which foreigners could enter, stay, and be expelled from France (June 11); that he also had "extreme reservations" about selling off one or more of the three state-owned television channels (June 11). In addition to criticizing the government's program in the Council of Ministers, Mitterrand told young military officers at St.-Cyr that he opposed French entry into Reagan's SDI program, a program that Chirac favored, because the U.S.–controlled venture would limit France's freedom of action.[19] Concerning the initial phase of cohabitation, former President Giscard said that in his opinion power-sharing was proceeding "relatively well" but that he deplored the "almost weekly harassment" practiced by Mitterrand toward the government.[20] Subtly, the Socialist president was preparing a public attack, or what might be termed a series of *coups de Jarnac*, against the right-wing majority.

In late May it was not Mitterrand but Chirac's new government that was creating problems for the Right. On May 20 Chirac proposed that the National Assembly act on the government's desire to scrap the proportional representation voting system that had aided the Socialists and the National Front in the March 1986 elections. To pass this measure, the prime minister relied on Article 49-3 of the Constitution which denied debate and a direct vote on the issue and assured that the measure would become law—assuming that the president signed the reform and the Constitutional Council upheld it—if the opposition failed to win a no-confidence vote. Just a few days earlier, Chirac had used Article 49-3 to promulgate decrees on social and economic issues, including the denationalization of state-owned industries and banks. When the Socialists demanded a no-confidence vote in response to the proposed reform of proportional representation, Chirac won the vote by 289 to 284. However, the Communists and the National Front joined the Socialists in opposing the change in the voting system. Parliamentary politics had momentarily forged a strange alliance of interests.[21]

On the international scene, Mitterrand continued to try to strengthen his image as an international spokesman. On July 3–4 he visited the United States to participate with Reagan in the grandiose Independence Day celebration in New York harbor. There the French president gave a brief television address focusing on Franco-American friendship over the centuries. These events were closely covered by the French press and television. Like Reagan, Mitterrand sought to exploit the importance of symbols in the world of politics and would later sponsor his own extraordinary bicentennial celebration designed to strengthen his political consensus in France.

This voyage to the United States was quickly followed by a four-day official visit to the Soviet Union beginning on July 7. In his talks with Gorbachev and in a speech delivered on the evening of July 7 at the Kremlin, the French president focused on disarmament and human rights, two topics of great interest in France. On disarmament, he stressed the need for a balance of power, although France could not reduce its nuclear arsenal as long as the Soviet Union and the United States had not achieved "significant results in this area." Concerning human rights, the French leader said that it was a "moral duty" for all governments to respect such liberties.[22] Mitterrand's public comments in Moscow were meant for domestic consumption in France as much as for Soviet leaders.

On international issues in general, Mitterrand projected an image of harmony with his Gaullist prime minister. For instance, following the U.S. raid on Libya in mid-April—a raid that Mitterrand had supposedly encouraged Reagan to execute even though the French government denied the United States the right to fly over its airspace—the French Foreign Office issued a statement supported by the president and the prime minister that said in effect that France deplored "the intolerable escalation of terrorism" which fosters "reprisal actions that start a new cycle of violence."[23] This joint statement on Libya irked Giscard who declared that he "approved American action in Libya" and criticized Mitterrand and Chirac's decision not to permit U.S. aircraft to utilize French airspace.[24]

Mitterrand even attempted to project an image of unity with the Gaullist prime minister after Chirac invited himself to attend the May 4–6 summit of the seven industrialized Western nations meeting in Tokyo, a conspicuous attempt by Chirac to demonstrate that Mitterrand did not have exclusive control over foreign policy. As one political observer noted at the time, neither the Japanese nor Mitterrand could say no to Chirac's bold move since the prime minister controlled the travel budget for the French government.[25] Although both the president and the prime minister attended the Tokyo summit, each flew in separate planes to and from Japan. This method of travel would be used at future summits that the French "odd couple" attended in tandem, such as the June 26–27 meeting of the European Council at The Hague and the mid-November Franco-African summit in Togo. While many considered Chirac's presence in Tokyo a major test for cohabitation, in fact it posed few problems, other than an added expense for French taxpayers. Mitterrand tried to put the best face on the tandem travel arrangement by declaring, "There is only one voice for France."[26] Here, too, the president was trying to project a public image of a unifier and reconciler.

The curtain fell on Act One, and Acts Two and Three commenced, when Mitterrand simultaneously attempted to defend his presidential prerogative and publicly attacked the right-wing government's program. In a well-timed televised statement on July 14, Mitterrand announced that he would not sign into law a decree by the prime minister to denationalize sixty-five state-owned industries. He told French citizens that such privatization would threaten "national interests" and that the legislature should be permitted to debate such measures.[27] Although Chirac countered by bringing the denationalization bill to the National Assembly for debate and for a vote, and Mitterrand signed the legislation within three weeks after his initial refusal, the Socialist president had effectively reminded Chirac and his government of his constitutional right to review legislation and to block decrees. This action by Mitterrand also slowed down Chirac's legislative schedule and enhanced the possibility that some within the new majority would in time begin to criticize the slow pace of reform under the prime minister.

The Bastille Day attack came at a time when the president's popularity was rising and Chirac's was declining slightly. One July SOFRES poll showed Mitterrand with a 59 percent approval rating, while Chirac had a 47 percent rating, a slip of three points in one month. This poll also showed that 72 percent of the public believed that unemployment should be the government's highest priority.[28] At the same time, the public was not overly enthusiastic about the prime minister's denationalization plan. According to Jérôme Jaffré, an authority on French public opinion, only 42 percent of the public supported denationalization, with 29 percent opposed; furthermore, 39 percent opposed the denationalization of banks, while only 33 percent supported such privatization. Whereas there had been a relatively large groundswell of public support for the Socialist program in 1981, it was clear to Mitterrand that Chirac's agenda did not elicit the same level of public enthusiasm.[29] Not only did Mitterrand's Bastille Day declaration conform with general trends in public opinion, but he wrapped his message to Chirac's government in the red, white, and blue of the French flag as he delivered his speech from his Elysée office before a large tricolor and posed as the true guardian of constitutional authority and French national interests. On this occasion, symbolism once again became an important weapon that Mitterrand wielded against his opponents. After a wave of bombings in Paris in early September that necessitated governmental unity, Mitterrand would renew his defense of presidential prerogatives and his open criticism of Chirac's government.

During the first two weeks of September, as tens of thousands of Parisians returned from their summer vacations, terrorist bombs rocked the capital, leaving nine dead and 162 injured. At the time, it seemed as if Paris was becoming the Beirut of the West. Many of these bombings were attributed to a group calling itself the Committee for Solidarity with Arab Prisoners, believed to be comprised of the relatives and friends of the Lebanese Georges Ibrahim Abdallah, who was in a French prison and awaiting trial for his alleged complicity in the murder of an Israeli diplomat and an American military attaché in Paris. During the second week of September, terrorist bombings in Paris came to an abrupt halt, leading *Le Monde* to speculate that the Chirac government had concluded a "phantom agreement" with Syria whereby this key Middle Eastern power broker would attempt to use its influence in the area to prevent attacks in France in exchange possibly for arms, flexibility on the Abdallah case, and a change in French policy in the Middle East.[30] Nonetheless, Chirac insisted in a television statement that he would "cede nothing in the face of blackmail."[31] Besides making the security arrangements difficult for a papal visit in the Lyon area in early October, politically the September bombings had significant repercussions in France.

The frequency of the September bombings prompted both Mitterrand and Chirac to present an image of unity and national cohesion. Mitterrand even announced that given the serious situation in France he was postponing his decision on Chirac's plan to redraw the electoral districts of France because he needed time to study the proposal carefully and the prime concern now was terrorism. Consequently, during the month of September the public duel between the Socialist president and the Gaullist prime minister was temporarily suspended, giving added life to the cohabitation arrangement. Also, Mitterrand tactfully decided to let Chirac take major responsibility for the French response to the terrorist threat. The issue of terrorism was fraught with dangers and booby-traps, a situation that Mitterrand preferred to let Chirac tackle. While the political rewards would be great for any prime minister who effectively dealt with terrorism, the penalties for failure were enormously high.

Chirac's eagerness to succeed as prime minister and his strong presidential ambitions led him to attempt a major change in France's Middle East policy, namely an effort to reestablish a dialogue with Iran as well as other Arab states in the region. Although Chirac's leadership in this domain ran counter to Mitterrand's view that the president alone determines foreign policy, the chief of state was content to let his political opponent deal with a most delicate and dangerous situation. Chirac launched a change in policy in the Middle

East soon after taking office but pursued it more vigorously as a result of the September bombings in Paris.

The conservative government's Middle Eastern policy seemed to run counter to Socialist policy in the troubled region between 1981 and 1986. When Mitterrand assumed office in 1981 his government quickly gave the impression that it would side with Iraq in the Persian Gulf war by selling the Iraqis billions of francs worth of military equipment. Furthermore, within months of taking office, Mitterrand granted asylum to the former president of Iran, Bani Sadr, and agreed in principle with the Iraqi vice-president that France would rebuild a nuclear reactor at Osirak near Tabriz that had been destroyed by Israeli jets.[32] Chirac, however, was intent on playing both the Iranian and the Iraqi card simultaneously. After Chirac told the Assembly on April 9 that his government desired a dialogue with Iran, the new right-wing government encouraged Massoud Radjavi, an Iranian opposition leader living in France since 1981, to leave the country "voluntarily" on June 11 and to take up residence in Iraq, a nation at war with Iran and which owed France a considerable sum of money for military equipment. Chirac knew that the departure of Radjavi was one of the conditions necessary to normalize relations with Khomeini's government. Several weeks after Radjavi left France, two French hostages in Lebanon, Georges Hansen and Philippe Rochot, were freed because of "certain indications" that France was changing its Middle Eastern policy. When Chirac went to the airport at Orly on June 21 to welcome the hostages home, he made a public speech in which he thanked "the Syrian, Algerian governments, and, of course, Iran."[33] The initial success motivated Chirac to accelerate his policy tilt in the Middle East, although this acceleration later caused the prime minister some embarrassment both at home and abroad.

In the midst of the fall terrorist wave in France, Chirac's government passed a law replacing jurors with judges in cases dealing with terrorism. Several months later the right-wing government made this law retroactive, against Socialist protest, when the terrorist group *Action Directe* (Direct Action) threatened jurors in a case involving one of their members, Régis Schleicher.

In addition to combating terrorism in France, Chirac and the Council of Ministers agreed on a budget for 1987. The proposed budget limited the total increases in expenditures to 1.8 percent, helping to bring the budget deficit down to 129 billion francs from 145 billion francs in 1986. Priority in the new budget was given to defense, the economy, and security. This budget also projected a 3 percent decrease in taxes on revenues and slight increases for family allowances.

September also witnessed a right-wing victory in the traditionally conservative Senate. On September 28 one-third of the 319-seat Senate was reelected. The RPR won an additional 18 seats and the UDF 1 seat, both the PS and the MRG lost 2 seats, and the PCF gave up 9. Thus, the Right heavily dominated the Senate, with the Socialists having a total of 64 senators, the MRG 9, and the Communists 15; the Gaullist RPR found itself with 77 senators and the UDF with 154.[34] Time revealed, however, that the senatorial elections were not a true reflection of the changing public view of Mitterrand and the Socialist party.

Following the September wave of terrorist attacks, the presentation of the 1987 budget, and the senatorial elections, Mitterrand relaunched his active defense of his presidential prerogatives and his criticism of Chirac's conservative government. Early in the fall the president finally rendered his decision on new electoral districts drawn up by the right-wing government, a plan that would probably have had little impact on the outcome of the national elections but seemed to favor the Right on the local level. Mitterrand, knowing that public opinion did not feel attached to the redistricting plan and that he had little to lose, rendered a negative decision. Chirac countered by submitting the same legislation to the National Assembly, invoking Article 49-3 of the Constitution. The opposition petitioned to send the legislation to the Constitutional Council in an effort to block it. Yet the council decided that the redistricting plan did not violate the Constitution and that it could become law. Appeals to the Constitutional Council would be one of the tactics employed by the president and the Socialist opposition, as the right had done to them between 1981 and 1986, to prevent or slow down the enactment of Chirac's legislative agenda.

In October Mitterrand began to defend and to reassert his prerogatives in defense matters. On October 13, before a group of parachutists at the Caylus military base in Périgord, the president reiterated that he was commander in chief of the military and that he alone had responsibility for the entire nuclear strike force, strategic and tactical. The president also announced that he would remain vigilant on Chirac's plan for the military budget for 1987–91, which would soon be examined by the Council of Ministers. (On the question of defense and foreign policy, Mitterrand and the Socialists were buoyed in October when division on the right allowed former external affairs minister Dumas to be elected head of the National Assembly's powerful Foreign Affairs Committee by a 35–31 vote margin. With the president's friend Dumas in charge of this important committee, the Socialists could exercise greater leverage on defense and foreign policy matters.)

In the same speech at Caylus the president made a statement that strengthened his political position vis-à-vis Chirac, but which drew considerable media attention and began a wave of speculation about Mitterrand's candidacy in 1988. He declared:

> I am not a candidate; I am President of the Republic. Each time that I think about this subject [the 1988 elections] everything leads me to think that I will not be a candidate . . . I am not so ambitious to want to install myself indefinitely.
>
> Therefore all of my thoughts lead me to say that I do not intend to run. Will there be elements that intervene to make me say it is a mistake? I cannot think so. How much time is there for that? In principle seventeen months.[35]

This statement shocked many because in the spring PS leaders, among them Jospin, Fabius, and Bérégovoy, had announced, on the anniversary of Mitterrand's election as president, that he was their candidate for 1988. They also announced that they favored a five-year presidential term, an old campaign promise and a reform that might make a second term for Mitterrand more palatable to voters.[36] The Caylus declaration was intended by Mitterrand to suggest that he was acting as president of the republic and not as a presidential candidate in his conduct toward Chirac's government. Such a declaration, as he knew, enhanced his presidential authority with the public, warned Chirac that as president he would not be afraid to end cohabitation by dissolving the Assembly if his prerogatives were not respected, and strengthened his own popularity as guardian/arbiter of the republic—thereby enhancing his own candidacy if he decided to run for a second term in 1988.[37] By declaring his noncandidacy, at least for the moment, Mitterrand bolstered his political position in the bizarre and often comical affair known as cohabitation.

After this important speech and tactical maneuver, Mitterrand launched another barrage of criticism at the Chirac government. On

November 4, for instance, in the Socialist-controlled municipality of Montpellier, a university town in the south, he challenged four aspects of the Right's program. He questioned the appropriateness of calling for a pause in decentralization, weakening the ability of the state to respond to the nation's needs by cutting key programs in the budget, failing to provide adequate funding for research, and reducing social services (including Chirac's plan to introduce private hospitals). This barrage of criticism, following his earlier announcement that he might not be a candidate in the 1988 elections, allowed him to project the image of a true defender of public rights. Mitterrand had been cheered to see a crowd of people near the city hall carrying placards reading, "With François Mitterrand for a France That Wins."[38] From now on he began to speak out in a forceful manner on various aspects of Chirac's program.

During the first few weeks of November, he publicly stated his opposition to Chirac's plan to delay the modernization of the French nuclear submarine fleet in order to upgrade mobile tactical nuclear weapons. Mitterrand repeatedly told the press that the submarine-launched nuclear missiles were the heart of French deterrence and that as president he would not allow Chirac's 474-billion-franc military budget for 1987–91 to lead to the submarine fleet being downplayed. He was especially concerned that development of the multiple-war-head M-5 missile continue so as to provide France with more striking power. Throughout this debate on the military budget, the president reminded Chirac and the public that he was responsible for defense and that he would use his constitutional power in order to guarantee that France had a modern nuclear submarine fleet. To many it appeared that the Socialist president was echoing de Gaulle and, ironically, confronting Chirac with the Gaullist Constitution of the Fifth Republic. Mitterrand knew that in any public clash with the prime minister, it would be to the president's advantage to go into battle as the defender of the Constitution. Facing a possible showdown on this serious issue, Chirac and his government quickly revised the text of the military budget and gave priority to the nuclear submarine fleet. When the appropriations bill came before the Council of Ministers on November 5, Mitterrand stated that he found it "serious," "reasonable," and "coherent."[39] The president had won an important skirmish.

Several days later the public discovered an interview with Mitterrand in the pages of the popular newsweekly *Le Point*, his first full statement on cohabitation since the formation of the Chirac government. In this interview the president attempted to make clear the division of powers that he would accept under the power-sharing arrangement. Restating an old Gaullist idea articulated by Chaban-Delmas in the late 1950s, Mitterrand made a distinction between two domains: (1) foreign policy and defense, and (2) economic and social policy as well as public security. Concerning the first, he reaffirmed his preeminence and said that the prime minister is "sworn to carry out the foreign policy of France, continued or initiated . . . by the president in office." In the second domain "it is parliament and, if necessary, the people, that have the last word." As for the struggle against terrorism, he stated that this effort should be led by the prime minister but may require the "intervention" of the president "if decisions involve the foreign policy of France."[40]

This presidential statement on institutional powers appeared in the midst of a national and international debate on Chirac's handling of a foreign policy issue on the Middle East. On November 10, the same day that Mitterrand's exclusive interview appeared in *Le Point*, the *Washington Times* published the text of an explosive interview with the prime minister. The *Washington Times*, a conservative newspaper directed by Armand de Borchgrave, published the full text of Chirac's remarks after the prime minister had publicly denied suggesting in an interview with the *Washington Times* that Chancellor Kohl and German Foreign Minister Genscher had alleged that the Israeli secret service probably played a part in an April 17 attempted bombing attack against an El Al airplane at Heathrow Airport. Chirac had intimated in the interview that this bombing plot was an effort to embarrass Syria. Reports of this interview and the appearance of the full text shocked many in France and abroad.

Chirac's effort to render support to Syria came at a time when the government was conducting delicate negotiations with Middle Eastern states for the release of French hostages. Consequently, in early November, for instance, Chirac balked when the British government said it had conclusive proof that Syria was involved in the terrorist attempt against the El Al plane. Moreover, at the same time the press was reporting that Chirac's government had promised to supply Damascus with sophisticated weaponry. One month earlier, the French press reported that the Chirac government had agreed to repay a debt to Iran of more than $1 billion that dated back to the era of the shah. While Chirac's statements in the *Washington Times* appeared irresponsible, they were ostensibly tied to a plan to reorient French foreign policy in the Middle East and to liberate the remaining hostages. For Chirac, the release of the French hostages would enhance his own presidential ambitions, would demonstrate that he could direct foreign policy with competence, and would embarrass Mitterrand who, like Presidents Jimmy Carter and Ronald Reagan, had been frustrated in efforts to free hostages. Thus, Mitterrand's *Le Point* interview represented a timely effort to readjust the balance of power under cohabitation which had shifted to the Matignon.

When the published text of Chirac's interview with the *Washington Times* appeared on November 10, political observers wondered how Chirac's government would respond to a call for sanctions against Syria at a London meeting of EEC foreign ministers. At this significant meeting representatives from eleven of the twelve EEC nations agreed to limited sanctions against Syria; Greece was the only country opposed to this decision. Under the terms of the agreement, EEC states pledged not to authorize new arms sales to Syria, to suspend certain high-level visits to and from Syria, to review the activities of Syrian embassies and consulates, and to reexamine and reinforce security measures on Syrian airlines.[41] For Chirac the London meeting was a victory, because he could agree to the limited sanctions imposed. Shortly after this meeting the official radio station in Iran stated that Mitterrand's interview in *Le Point* demonstrated "serious differences between the president and the French prime minister on foreign affairs . . . [notably on] the question of the confidence that French diplomacy can or cannot accord to the progressive states of the region." Radio Teheran added, "M. Chirac seeks to preserve the long-term interest of France in this region in breaking with the erroneous policy of the Socialists . . . and in giving priority to the modification of French diplomacy in the Middle East." According to Radio Teheran, Mitterrand's policy for the region had been "marked by French support for Iraq, the intervention in Lebanon, and the trip of M. Mitterrand to Israel. . . ."[42] Two days after the London meeting of foreign ministers, two more French hostages were released in Lebanon. Seemingly, Syria, Lebanon, and Iran had rewarded Chirac for playing a different deck of cards in the Middle East. The question in France, however, was whether the electorate would reward the prime minister or whether they would see his Middle Eastern gambit as a compromise with terrorism. Commenting to the press on the tragic assassination of Renault head Georges Besse by Direct Action one week after the London meeting, Mitterrand subtly suggested that Chirac had compromised in the Middle East. According to the president, France must be united against terrorism "without defaulting, without compromise."[43]

While Mitterrand refrained from directly criticizing Chirac's handling of the Middle East, one of the president's closest allies, Pierre Bérégovoy, challenged the prime minister openly in the National Assembly. In a calm tone, Bérégovoy asked Chirac:

> What have you negotiated? What have you given up? Have you agreed to give Syria what we [Socialists] have refused to give to date? Have you renounced a policy of equilibrium in the Middle East that assures the integrity and independence of Lebanon, the right of Israel to live with secure and recognized borders, and the right of the Palestinians to have their own state?[44]

Chirac diplomatically refused to provide concrete answers to these questions.

While the situation in the Middle East and the hostage problem were sensitive subjects and Mitterrand criticized Chirac indirectly, he openly opposed the prime minister's position on various domestic issues and his intrusion into African affairs. On his way to the Franco-African summit in Togo, where just two months earlier he had parachuted in military personnel following a commando attack on the capital city, Mitterrand launched a broadside attack on the right-wing government. He stated in a radio interview that he opposed a new nationality code approved by the Council of Ministers, that he opposed Chirac's recent expulsion of more than a hundred Malians from France, and that he opposed official contacts between Chirac's government and the Angolan UNITA chief Jonas Savimbi.[45] The proposed nationality code, part of a series of reforms (e.g., jailing drug addicts and introducing private prisons) sponsored by Justice Minister Albin Chalandon, was an attempt to restrict French citizenship. Up to this point, the French government had granted citizenship at age eighteen to anyone born on French soil to non-French parents who had lived in France for five years. The new law proposed that instead of automatically granting citizenship at the age of eighteen, prospective citizens had to prove that they were "integrated" into French society and could speak an "appropriate level" of French. Mitterrand said that this new measure was inspired "by a philosophy that he did not share" and that he "deplored."[46] Earlier Mitterrand's minister of culture had supported what he called a "multicultural society"; the Right, however, demanded that foreigners be absorbed into a French melting-pot.[47] When Interior Minister Pasqua hired a charter aircraft and used swift administrative procedure to send home more than 100 Malians who had allegedly violated French law, including immigration laws, Mitterrand declared that he opposed this collective expulsion, intimating that the rights of these people might have been violated.[48] Chirac's controversial measures, according to some observers, were simply an effort to appeal to extreme right-wing voters attracted to Le Pen's racist and anti-immigrant party.

On the eve of the Franco-African summit, Mitterrand also denounced a recent meeting between UNITA's Savimbi, who had received support from South Africa, and Minister of Culture Léotard. The president called this meeting "regrettable." He was greatly concerned about the aims of the Chirac government in Africa and the image that the prime minister was creating. Not only had Léotard met with Savimbi, but Chirac had permitted South African leader P. W. Botha to dedicate a war memorial in France to South Africans killed in World War I; Botha's visit coincided with the Franco-African summit in Togo. Also, Chirac, who had a large international staff at the Matignon, had earlier appointed the seventy-three-year-old Jacques Foccart as his personal adviser for Africa, a man who had served de Gaulle in the same capacity and who had a reputation for subversion in Africa. Some wondered who was actually in charge of African policy—was it the Ministry of Cooperation headed by Michel Aurrillac, or was it Mitterrand's own specialist Guy Penne, or was it Foccart? Thus, Mitterrand used the opening of the Togo summit as an opportunity to criticize various aspects of Chirac's policies, including the prime minister's unannounced agenda for Africa.[49] In an effort to strengthen the impression that the Elysée was in charge of African policy, Mitterrand stated at the Togo summit that France would provide additional military aid to Chad in the face of Libyan aggression in the north. The president, however, ruled out any future military intervention in Chad.[50]

Following the Togo summit, Chirac's handling of New Caledonia provided Mitterrand with another opportunity to criticize the prime minister. In late November the separatist leader Jean-Marie Tjibaou came to Paris for a scheduled meeting with Chirac. A few days earlier, separatists on the island allegedly killed a youth, prompting Chirac to break off the meeting. Mitterrand, however, met with Tjibaou, letting it be known that he did not necessarily agree with the Right's policy with regard to the island. Months earlier the president had said that he had "very strong reservations" about Chirac's reform of the statute for the island giving more weight to settlers of European origin; Mitterrand also said that the government's plan could, in his view, stimulate anew "tensions between the various groups" in New Caledonia.[51]

After returning from the Togo summit, Mitterrand continued to hammer away at another Chalandon reform, a plan to create a private prison system to cope with overcrowding in French jails. Mitterrand criticized the plan, which penologists had also failed to support, in a Council of Ministers meeting in late November. To argue his case that private enterprise should not make profits from the incarceration of individuals, Mitterrand quoted Alexis de Tocqueville who in 1836 wrote the following in *Notes on the Penitentiary System:* "If the business of government is to assure the security of society . . . , the business of the entrepreneur is to make money."[52] The proposed reform and Mitterrand's reaction to it sparked a large-scale public debate in France on private prisons, a debate in which some of Barre's supporters sided with the president.[53]

One of the most significant presidential attacks on the Chirac government, however, involved an area where Mitterrand had had his own share of difficulty in the past: university reform and student protest. In November the government presented a reform of higher education to the National Assembly, a measure known as the Devaquet law after the minister in charge of higher education. Three key aspects of the proposed law troubled French students, on both the university and the high-school level: the proposed law gave each university authority to set its own admission standards, allowed the name of the student's university campus to be printed on the diploma, and raised the yearly tuition fee from 400 to 800 francs. Minister of Education René Monory, Alain Devaquet, and Chirac argued that the law was not geared to tighten the selection process of universities, but to allow universities to "orient" students to economic realities; selection standards, they said, could thereby be used to direct students into fields where there might be a greater opportunity of employment. The Devaquet law and the defense of it by the Chirac government proved that the prime minister had a great ability to mobilize students. He was aided, however, by the president of the republic.

As the students began to mobilize for a show of strength, Mitterrand gave a speech on November 22 in Auxerre in Burgundy where he appeared to fully sanction the rising student protest against the Devaquet law. In Auxerre, Mitterrand gave an address celebrating the one hundredth anniversary of the death of Paul Bert, a scientist, politician, and promoter of a secular system of education under the Third Republic. On this occasion the president declared that "the highest priority for the entire government [is to be] conscious of its responsibilities toward the French people, of providing a free, high-quality education for all, permitting access to a career, [and] to higher education. . . ." He added that France would have "a strong and prosperous republic only with the existence of social justice, a powerful national defense, and a quality system of education available to all."[54] Some within the Chirac government accused the president of throwing "oil on the fire" with his remarks.

On November 23, 200,000 people demonstrated in Paris in response to a call by the National Federation of Education (*Fédération d'Education Nationale*—FEN) and the PS for a show of support "for the future of youth" and opposition to the government's proposed reform measure. Up until this time, this demonstration represented the largest street demonstration against the new right-wing government since it assumed power. Yet student demonstrations quickly and dramatically increased in size. Following this protest, the National Union of French Students (*Union Nationale des Etudiants de France*—UNEF-ID), a student organization with Socialist leanings, called for a strike on Monday November 24, the mobilization of high-school students, and preparations for a massive demonstration on November 27, the day when the National Assembly planned to consider the Devaquet law. The aim of the November 27 demonstration, according to student leaders, was to have the law withdrawn, "pure and simple."[55]

On November 27 the largest student demonstrations since the revolt of 1968 took place, with 200,000 university and high-school students demonstrating in Paris before the National Assembly where the Devaquet law was being considered, and another 400,000 demonstrating in towns throughout the provinces. Furthermore, more than fifty of France's nearly seventy universities went on strike against the Chirac government.[56]

While this particular phase of the student revolt was not politicized like the upheaval of 1968, some of the slogans appearing in the November 27 demonstration suggested that many students were keenly aware of the political situation. For instance, some placards read, "Evacuate Devaquet, not the Immigrants," "Coca Cola, IBM, Tapie (a young, popular and successful French entrepreneur), No Thanks," and "The University Is Not for Sale." Another placard read, "Don't Touch My University" (a takeoff on the "Don't Touch My Pal" campaign of SOS-Racism in the early 1980s that aimed to fight increasing racist incidents and to protect the rights of immigrants).[57] One former leader of the 1968 French student revolt, Danny Cohn-Bendit, watched the massive demonstration in Paris from the sidewalk with glee.[58] Rather ironically, the very evening of the nationwide November 27 demonstration, the fourth part of Cohn-Bendit's television series on 1968, entitled "The Revolution That We Loved So Much," was broadcast; part four of the series was called "Democracy."

Chirac, for his part, appeared on television November 30 and maladroitly tried to calm emotions by telling the nation that his government had failed to explain fully the Devaquet law. He flatly refused to withdraw the measure from discussion in the National Assembly. With enormous false confidence, the prime minister stated, "I am totally serene."[59] Following this television appearance student leaders, such as Isabelle Thomas of UNEF-ID, charged that the prime minister was taking them for "imbeciles" and pledged to continue the protest.[60]

For Mitterrand and the Socialists the rapidly developing student protest movement was sweet revenge for the massive demonstration of June 1984 against their efforts to exercise greater control over private schools. Yet, as some noted in France, while in 1984 the cry was for "freedom of choice," in 1986 it was for "equality."[61] In the past student protest and the way in which Mitterrand responded to it had hurt his political fortunes. With the student revolt of 1986, students seemed to be on his side or, more correctly, he was on their side as he continued his guerrilla warfare against Chirac under the guise of cohabitation. Following the November 27 demonstration, the student coordinating committee called for another national demonstration on December 4, a demonstration that the police met with repression.

The December 4 student demonstration quickly ended Chirac's serenity. This protest, supported by FEN as well as the CGT, saw between 500,000 and 1 million students and their supporters demonstrate in Paris alone, with another 400,000 marching in the streets in the provinces. In the capital demonstrators stretched from the place de la Bastille to the Hôtel des Invalides, almost five miles of humanity protesting the Devaquet law. The march ended with tens of thousands of students on the Esplanade des Invalides near the National Assembly waiting to hear a rock concert. However, the concert was canceled following a meeting between student leaders and the minister of education, which otherwise yielded little. Monory had agreed earlier to meet with students following the demonstration to discuss the contested law. However, the minister of education was in no mood to compromise and the students, hopeful of some flexibility on the part of government, had to carry the bad news back to thousands of fellow-students at Invalides. Subsequently, student-police clashes erupted, terminating only when the police forcefully cleared the Invalides area, gravely injuring three people.

On December 5 Monory announced that he was taking charge of the dossier for university reform and that the contested sections of the law would be "temporarily" retired. Prior to this announcement spontaneous demonstrations involving thousands of students erupted in the Latin Quarter protesting police violence. Protestors proceeded to occupy the Sorbonne. During the night of December 5 the police beat to death a nonprotesting French student of Algerian descent, Malik Oussekine, on a small side street in the Latin Quarter.

The announcement of Malik's death ignited demonstrations of sympathy on December 6 by university and high school students. These demonstrations erupted into clashes with the police and left the Chirac government with a serious crisis. While students and police clashed in the heart of Paris, Devaquet submitted his resignation. The deterioration of the situation in Paris motivated Chirac to return home early from a European summit in London that he was attending in tandem with Mitterrand. During the same weekend Chirac participated in the tenth anniversary celebration of the Gaullist RPR and appeared to moderate his political rhetoric even though his minister of interior took a hard law-and-order stand in a speech to party representatives and insisted that Gaullists had to be prepared to "defend the republic." On the same evening as the RPR gathering, Mitterrand arranged a meeting with the prime minister and told Chirac that "national cohesion must come before everything else."[62] With mounting tension in the streets and pressure from the president to compromise, Chirac was forced to pursue a different tactic.

On December 8, which student leaders and their supporters had announced as a day of mourning, Chirac announced that his government was totally withdrawing the plan to reform the university.

Nevertheless, university and high-school students continued to demonstrate in protest at the death of Malik Oussekine. The students had won a major victory. Many students pledged that they would not take pressure off the Chirac regime, and student leaders announced a nationwide strike for December 10 to focus attention on the death of Oussekine and police repression. A number of organizations, such as FEN, the CGT, and the Communist party, supported the December 10 demonstrations.

One day prior to the December 10 protest, Chirac and Mitterrand took action to make the best of a difficult situation. Chirac announced before the National Assembly that the extraordinary session in January to consider the controversial nationality code and the private prison plan would not be held. This announcement meant that Chirac planned a "pause" in his government's reform program in order to try to regain public confidence. Mitterrand, on the other hand, said that Chirac's government was pursuing the correct course of action in announcing such a "pause." The president announced in a radio broadcast that he supported the students, declaring that he was "in phase" with them. Mitterrand also reaffirmed his role as a "judge/arbiter," and stated that he must intervene each time there was "danger." He clearly wanted the nation to know that he had played a principal role in averting further protest and violence. Concerning the prime minister, the president said that Chirac "had many qualities," but that he "wished that these qualities would be applied at the right place and at the right moment."[63]

L'Unité summed up the outcome of the student revolt in an article titled "Chiracism in Retreat." According to this article, "In just several days the political climate has completely changed. Winners: the university students, high school students, and their allies. Losers: Jacques Chirac and his supporters. . . . The president of the republic appeared as the only recourse."[64] Many Socialists delighted in Chirac's misfortune.

This extraordinary and unexpected student revolt led some in France to ask if French universities could even be reformed. Many wondered how much Chirac's errors and lack of finesse in handling the student protest would hurt his ambition to be president of the republic one day. Many speculated that Chirac might not have the statesmanlike qualities to be head of state, speculation that several foreign newspapers echoed.[65] Chirac had stumbled badly and had given Mitterrand another major victory in the battle over cohabitation.

The student revolt of November and December 1986 was the result of a number of significant factors. In part, it was obviously a reaction to the Devaquet law which students deemed too competitive and contrary to the egalitarian tradition of French education. In addition, young people knew that unemployment was extremely high in France. With one out of three youths out of work, France had the highest unemployment rate among youth of any Western nation.[66] The protest by students was also a reaction to the exclusiveness of the Right's legislative program, expressed not only in the Devaquet law, but also in the nationality code, the private hospital and prison reform, and the new visa requirements. Moreover, related to the exclusionary nature of the Chirac government was the element of racism. The death of Malik crystallized for many, young and old, the problem of racism, a problem that organizations like SOS-Racism had kept before the public. SOS-Racism had already sensitized many to the problems of racism with a huge rally in Paris in the summer of 1985 and with its "Don't Touch My Pal" campaign. Oussekine's death only revealed the depths of the problem to many, including the president. When Mitterrand visited the Oussekine family on December 8, he was accompanied by Elie Wiesel, who had just won the Nobel Prize for Peace. On his visit, Mitterrand promised to do all that he could to fulfill a request made by the brothers and sisters of Malik who asked him "to help immigrants to live in France in dignity."[67] Police repression, as so often happens in student revolts, was another element that mobilized the young to protest the Devaquet law and the Chirac government in general. The fear of police repression was clearly reflected in some of the student graffiti in Paris, one of which declared, "We Are Not in Chile!" Finally, Chirac's lack of willingness to compromise and to open a true dialogue with students greatly contributed to the December crisis. For the moment, Chirac had lost the youth vote.

Politically, the student revolt aided the fortunes of the president who gained new young allies in the battle over cohabitation and the march to the 1988 presidential elections. The youth of France were of special interest to Mitterrand and other politicians because of their heretofore relatively low voter turnout record, with only two-thirds voting in recent elections. After nine months of cohabitation the president had not completely equalized the power-sharing arrangement with Chirac, but Mitterrand was now clearly on the offensive and was beginning to win the war over cohabitation. As Chirac suggested in a television appearance on November 30, power-sharing was much easier in theory than in practice.

Capitalizing on the moment, notably the difficulties of the conservative Chirac government with the massive student revolt and an emerging strike of serious proportions in the public sector, in his New Year's Eve address Mitterrand announced that he had three wishes for the coming year. He hoped that the nation would realize that it was inextricably tied to Europe; "France," he said, "is our country, and Europe is our future." The president hoped, too, that France would continue to practice democracy and to give it real meaning, reminding his fellow citizens that he himself had avoided a constitutional crisis at the outset of cohabitation and had assured the continuity of the state. Finally, he wished that France would succeed in meeting the challenges posed by democracy, referring specifically to cohabitation and telling his audience that "democracy is by nature debate, a confrontation of ideas and interests."[68] It was clear that the president wanted to exalt a spirit of tolerance and dialogue and reinforce his image as a unifying force above the political fray.[69] As in his five previous New Year's Eve addresses, Mitterrand never mentioned the word "socialism."

As 1986 ended, characterized as a "feverish year" by the director of *Le Monde*,[70] it was not students who worried the Chirac government but public-sector workers, a situation that Mitterrand quickly capitalized on. Following the student revolt, French National Railroad (SNCF) workers began striking in mid-December, protesting, in part, an effort by the Chirac government to hold wage increases to 3 percent or less. During 1986 inflation in France was slightly more than 2 percent and the growth in the GDP was 2 percent—Chirac's government was determined to maintain anti-inflationary pressure as France faced a wave of strike activity at the end of 1986. The strike by railroad workers became the longest French rail strike since 1945. In time electrical workers as well as bus and metro workers in Paris joined the strike. The CGT sought, with little success, to extend the strike to the entire 4.5 million workers in the public sector.

On January 1, 1987, Mitterrand met with striking SNCF workers in the south of France at Brégançon in the Var, suggesting that he sided with the strikers. Of course, the majority quickly denounced this meeting. Mitterrand naturally desired to convey the image of a president seeking to keep a dialogue open between the government and striking workers. By the middle of January strikes in the public sector had subsided and Chirac was able to maintain his anti-inflationary policy.[71] Following his government's setback during the student revolt, Chirac could ill afford another major retreat.

The strike activity by SNCF, electrical workers, and others reflected, nevertheless, persisting discontent with Chirac's government. One SOFRES poll conducted in early January showed that 51 percent disapproved of the actions of the right-wing government, while 39 percent approved. At the same time, a BVA–*Paris Match* poll revealed that 56 percent of the public had a favorable view of the president, but only 39 percent rated Chirac positively.

Polls were also beginning to show a growing skepticism about cohabitation.[72] At the beginning of 1987 more thought that cohabitation was negative for France (47 percent) than positive (36 percent), although a few months later power-sharing increased in popularity.[73] Concerning the public's view of the functioning of cohabitation, as table 11 shows, confidence in power-sharing dropped significantly after the December 1986 student revolt and the December 1986–January 1987 public-sector strike. As Chirac's popularity slipped in the wake of the student revolt and the public-sector strike, both Mitterrand and Barre, a resolute opponent of cohabitation, saw their ratings improve. Mitterrand's decision to meet with striking workers

TABLE 11

Cohabitation and Public Opinion

	Percentage believing cohabitation functions well or rather well	Percentage believing cohabitation functions negatively or rather negatively
April 1986	50	22
June 1986	65	25
July 1986	66	24
October 1986	71	23
December 1986	66	26
February 1987	45	45
June 1987	58	32

SOURCE: Sondage SOFRES/*Le Point*, June 8, 1987, p. 63.

on the first day of the New Year was clearly an effort to take advantage of his mounting popularity and the sinking fortunes of Chirac. However, as friction mounted between the president and his prime minister, Barre witnessed an increase in popularity. As a result of this phenomenon, Mitterrand and Chirac eventually learned the art of what might be called "controlled friction" to minimize Barre's gains in the public opinion polls.

Later in the month of January the Constitutional Council handed Mitterrand and the Socialists a small victory when it ruled that the government's legislation to ease employment regulations was "irregular." Following this decision Mitterrand stated that the council had an important role to play in "checking the constitutionality of legislation." Barre, too, approved the council's actions, while the Gaullist Chaban-Delmas said that the council had gone too far.[74]

During January, Mitterrand tried to maintain his visibility as an international statesman. Following an official visit by King Hussein of Jordan, he flew to London where he addressed the Royal Institute for International Affairs and stressed the importance of developing Europe. In this speech, widely covered by the French press, he presented a step-by-step approach to a more united Europe, believing that Europe should begin to cooperate more effectively in labor laws, communication, technology, scientific research, and the prevention of terrorism. The president even envisioned the possibility of establishing a European defense community. In his speech he insisted on the necessity of a "political will" in order "to construct a true Community."[75]

While Mitterrand attempted to promote European unity, several thorny problems with the United States caused concern for the president, the prime minister, and Europeans in general. One problem was the falling value of the dollar, which had dropped below six francs on the currency exchange market. France, other West European nations, and Japan wanted Washington to intervene because the sliding dollar was seen as a convenient way for the Reagan administration to reduce its huge $169.8 billion deficit. Washington officials, however, were reluctant to stop the plunging greenback. The second problem with the United States concerned its export of agricultural products to Europe. After several weeks of heated debate and threats by the United States and European nations, the EEC and the United States reached an accord on the level of American trading within the European Community.

The economic situation on the home front gave the right-wing majority some confidence following the stormy weeks of student protest and the strike in the public sector. A poll published in the magazine *La Vie Française* showed that the business community viewed 1985 as a year of convalescence, while it saw 1986 and 1987 as a period marking the return of a healthy economy.[76] Moreover, the denationalization effort seemed to be winning public acceptance, especially from investors. Besides putting the diversified and profitable state-owned St. Gobain company on the auction block in December 1986, Chirac's government announced that it would sell off the Paribas bank, the television station TF 1, and the Havas news agency early in 1987, as well as four other banks. Economic indicators also showed that while unemployment had increased 5.5 percent in 1986 and was now at 10.7 percent, inflation for 1986 was a mere 2.1 percent—the lowest rate since 1964.[77] Mitterrand and the Socialists, therefore, attempted to criticize the government's record on employment and entitlements and to exploit divisions within the majority.

In the midst of growing contention between the Elysée and the Matignon and the increasing popularity of Mitterrand and Barre, Chirac gave a press conference on January 29 in the opulent setting of the Foreign Ministry in order to regain confidence with the electorate. Flanked by cabinet members, the Gaullist prime minister announced a list of social measures that his government would pursue: aid to small businesses, training for workers, worker participation in state-owned industries, flexible work hours, jobs for the handicapped, and hospital reform. With parliament returning from a recess in April, and with most of the major reforms already introduced, this press conference was an effort by Chirac to convince the electorate that he and his government would not remain idle in the months preceding the 1988 presidential election. He also wished to convince voters that his government was not simply one that favored the rich and the powerful.[78] Immediately following this press conference, Chirac had to contend with another public-sector strike. During the first week of February primary-school teachers, among the lowest paid of all public-sector workers, walked off their jobs. Fortunately for Chirac's government, the strike was short-lived.

For the Socialist party, unity became the watchword before an early April party congress at Lille. In February Jospin, Mauroy, and their supporters reached an agreement on a common motion at the upcoming congress, a fusion of the various tendencies within the party. Rocard helped to facilitate PS unity when he announced in early February that he would not run for president without the nomination of the Socialist party. Some within the PS had worried that Rocard would enter the first round of the presidential contest even if Mitterrand declared himself a candidate. While the PS strove for unity at this time, the majority seemed disunited.

On February 11 Giscard announced on television that he would not be a candidate for the presidency in 1988, much to the relief of Chirac. But Giscard also said that he favored reducing the presidential mandate to five years, one of the Socialists' propositions in 1981 and an idea that the French public favors (39 percent favored the change before the 1988 elections, 25 percent after the elections, and only 26 percent were opposed to a five-year term).[79] In a way, this announcement seemed to be a guerrilla warfare tactic aimed at both Chirac and Barre. Giscard, it will be recalled, had accused Chirac of "premeditated treason" in 1981 when the mayor of Paris refused to instruct his voters to mark their ballots for the incumbent in the second round of the presidential contest with Mitterrand. On February 13 at Toulouse the Gaullist prime minister stated flatly that his government would not propose such a reform that could divide the majority. Barre came out against the reform as well, suggesting that it did not correspond to de Gaulle's intentions for the Fifth Republic.[80]

Mitterrand himself attempted to strike a blow at the unity of the majority in mid-February when he announced his opposition to a plan adopted by the Council of Ministers for a future election in New Caledonia. The president stated that "reducing the debate to a simple electoral confrontation would be a serious historic error." Minister of Overseas Departments and Territories Bernard Pons charged that the president was "favoring extremism."[81] The explosive issue of New Caledonia had become a political football for the majority and the opposition.

While Mitterrand maintained his counterattacking strategy against the opposition in 1987, one key development allowed the majority to criticize the president and the Socialists on an issue that was extremely important to the nation: terrorism. On February 21, four principal members of the terrorist group Direct Action were arrested on a farm in Vitry-aux-Loges just outside of Paris. After this arrest members of the majority criticized Mitterrand and the PS for granting amnesty to a large number of prison inmates in 1981, including several members of Direct Action. Mitterrand tried to counter this criticism by referring to it as "extreme levity or an extreme indignity."[82]

The give-and-take between the majority and the Socialists continued when the National Commission on Communications and Freedom, a body that Chirac had created after the 1986 elections to serve as the supervisory board for the media, announced that it was reassigning the ownership of the fifth and sixth television channels. It said that Channel 5 would be awarded to the companies of Hersant and Berlusconi and that Channel 6 would be controlled by Metropole TV, a Luxembourg group. Mitterrand's earlier attempt to keep right-wing interests like Hersant from ownership of Channel 5 had failed. Hersant had also foiled Mitterrand's efforts to emasculate his power and visibility in France by standing as a Gaullist candidate in the 1986 legislative elections and winning a seat in the National Assembly.

To win support for the Socialists in the postelection period, Mitterrand continued to attack the Right's domestic policies and to use foreign policy issues to bolster his popularity. Following his decision in early February to strengthen the French contingent in Chad from fourteen hundred to twenty-two hundred men in order to forestall an expected Libyan offensive south of the sixteenth parallel, Mitterrand announced several weeks later that a recent proposal by Gorbachev for separate USSR–U.S. negotiations on Euromissiles "conforms to the interest of France and of peace"; the Soviet leader would also propose that short-range missiles in Europe be dismantled within a fixed period of time and that negotiation on this subject not be tied to negotiations on intermediate-range weapons. In his remarks Mitterrand was careful to stress, however, that French missiles would not be included in this count and that Europeans must be united in arms reduction. France, in other words, would continue its Gaullist stance on its nuclear strike force while the United States, the USSR, and possibly other European nations would, if they so desired, reduce short- and intermediate-range weapons. Mitterrand attempted to reinforce his view of French defense policy and disarmament questions in a press interview on March 10 in which he stressed the "consistency and the continuity" of French policy. Although Chirac echoed the president's position, another foreign policy issue revealed division and competition between Mitterrand and the Gaullist prime minister.

Both the president and the prime minister visited Spain on March 11–12 in an effort to further the recent dialogue with that country on a variety of issues. However, public discord erupted between the president and Chirac over the authorship of the new Franco-Spanish rapprochement. As will be recalled, Mitterrand supported Spain's entry into the EEC, while Chirac had contested the terms by which France's neighbor would enter the Community, reportedly, even to King Juan Carlos himself. Mitterrand seemed determined not to permit his political opponent to take credit for the improved relationship with Spain.[83]

When the French leaders returned home, Chirac found growing public opposition to his government's proposed revision of the nationality code. Approximately thirty thousand people demonstrated in Paris on March 15 against the Right's effort to limit the awarding of French nationality. Facing increasing opposition on this reform and at the same time hoping to win over Le Pen supporters, Chirac appointed a sixteen-member commission to study changing the requirements for citizenship. This commission comprised lawyers, historians, sociologists, philosophers, members of various religions, and people with foreign backgrounds. Chirac charged this commission with the task of recommending whether or not children of foreign parents in France should automatically be awarded French citizenship at the age of eighteen as stipulated by the existing code.[84] Given the divisiveness of this issue and the upcoming presidential elections, the prime minister seemed willing to settle for some symbolic reform of the nationality code to satisfy the right wing of his party and to weaken the appeal of Le Pen.

Mitterrand and the Socialists were also pleased to find that Chirac had additional problems after returning from the Franco-Spanish summit, namely serious disunity within the conservative government. When Interior Minister Pasqua announced a plan to censor certain pornographic publications "presenting a danger to youth," Minister of Culture Léotard, secretary general of the Republican party (PR), publicly declared that he was "opposed to all censorship."[85] Léotard continued to speak out on issues during the spring and summer of 1987 and to suggest that he, too, would be a presidential candidate in 1988. At one point, the minister of culture said that he was "neither a Chiracian nor a Barreist."[86] Léotard even gave an interview to *Le Point* and chided Chirac for not speaking out against the more conservative old guard in the RPR. The pugnacious minister of culture announced that his party would not support Chirac in the first round of the 1988 presidential election.[87] Léotard's outspoken manner eventually forced Chirac to demand that the minister of culture choose between his government responsibilities and his political campaigning. Following this directive from the prime minister, Léotard announced early in the summer at a ten-year anniversary celebration of his own Republican party that he intended to remain in government. He declared, "I am a minister and I will remain one; I have my freedom of speech and I will guard it."[88] Mitterrand referred to this crisis of the majority as a problem of cohabitation between the parties of the Right. The president utilized irony and humor in commenting on this affair while he was in Zurich inaugurating an International Festival on French Romanticism. In Zurich he told reporters, "It is rare that a minister cannot be a politician."[89]

While Chirac began to experience serious internal problems within the majority, Mitterrand hammered hard at the need to build a strong Europe and to improve the economic situation in France. On March 25, the thirtieth anniversary of the Treaty of Rome which established the Common Market, both the president and the prime minister participated in ceremonies at the Arc de Triomphe. At 8 P.M. that evening the president announced in a television appearance that he desired "a Europe endowed with a central political power" which decides "the means of its security." Shortly thereafter, Mitterrand met with Chancellor Kohl at Château Chambord where the two leaders discussed the security and defense of Europe. Polls showed that 88 percent of the French favored a common European defense, while 74 percent felt that France should aid West Germany if it came under attack.[90] Mitterrand and Chancellor Kohl later agreed to create a small joint Franco-German military unit outside the NATO command.[91]

Following the meeting with Kohl, Mitterrand continued to criticize the Right's economic record. Visiting Franche-Comté on the Swiss border, amid a warm welcome, he stressed the importance of solving the unemployment problem and defending the heavily indebted social security system. As the presidential election neared, it became clear that the economy would receive a great deal of attention from politicians.

Chirac at this time attempted to defend his economic policies and planned to announce his candidacy for the 1988 elections. In a television appearance late in March, the prime minister predicted that "France will in five years be the strongest economic power in Europe." While he pledged to continue his current economic program, he did not predict a major upturn in the economy in the near future. He also told his television audience that funds from the denationalization program would go toward improving autoroutes, the supermodern high-speed train known as the *train à grande vitesse* (TGV), research, and state-owned industries. By the end of the spring roughly one-fourth of the denationalization program would be complete, amounting to 34.5 billion francs for the state's coffers.[92] Although Chirac did not officially announce his candidacy for the presidency until early 1987, his television appearance prepared the ground for his presidential campaign.

Mitterrand, of course, realized that Chirac would have several major problems in the future elections. One problem was that Barre, running as an independent backed by the Union for French Democracy, was now much stronger in the polls than Chirac. (However, by the spring of 1988 polls would show Chirac pulling ahead of Barre due to several factors: the prime minister's tenacity and dynamic image, Barre's lackluster campaign, and Barre's lack of a solid party base.) Another problem was the division within the majority, especially the loud and dissenting voice of Léotard. Also problematic for Chirac was the appeal of Le Pen's National Front which would undoubtedly take votes away from the Gaullist RPR. Although Chirac's government scrapped the proportional representation voting system that had aided Le Pen's extremist party, polls predicted that the FN would capture 10 percent of the vote in the first round of the 1988 elections. Unfortunately for Chirac, two out of five Gaullists favored Le Pen's stance on issues.[93] The economy, too, was problematic. While inflation had dropped to 2.1 percent, the right-wing government had failed to reduce the unemployment rate. Chirac knew also that a major obstacle to his campaign would be Mitterrand himself, who had profited from cohabitation and who was the leading presidential candidate despite his continued declarations suggesting that he would not run in 1988.

As Chirac prepared to prime the electorate for his candidacy in the presidential race, many thought that the PS congress at Lille on April 3–5 would produce a Socialist candidate. Instead, Mitterrand and the leadership of the Socialist party decided for political reasons not to nominate a candidate at this time. Consequently, former prime minister Mauroy recommended to the congress that the best-placed alternative candidate—Rocard—be the party's nominee if Mitterrand decided not to run. The Socialist congress subsequently decided to call Mitterrand the "natural candidate" and Rocard the "potential candidate." For Mitterrand the advantages of this approach were obvious. If he remained a noncandidate until after the first of the year he could stay above the day-to-day political fray of the campaign and continue to enhance his presidential image, thereby minimizing the expected fall in popularity once he officially entered the campaign. Also, by remaining a noncandidate he would deprive the majority of a specific target at which to aim their attacks.

At the close of the Lille congress, party chief Jospin rejected the idea that the PS would pursue an alliance with the Center instead of seeking to attract Communist voters. Jospin wanted to give the impression that the Socialists would remain anchored on the left. Nevertheless, the PS had evolved since taking office in 1981 and had become a social democratic party like many other Socialist parties in Western Europe. This evolution was clearly seen at the Toulouse congress in 1985, in the removal of Jean Poperen, the rather orthodox overseer of electoral strategy, just prior to the Lille congress, and in the party's acceptance of Rocard as their candidate if Mitterrand decided not to run for the presidency in 1988.[94] The Lille meeting suggested to political observers that a reelected Socialist president might seek an alliance with the Center. Political speculation concerning the future strategy of Mitterrand and the PS heightened after Lille.

Shortly after the Lille congress, Chirac faced a vote of no confidence in the Assembly. This vote came at a time when the CNCL had just awarded 50 percent of TF 1, one of the most popular and successful state-owned television channels in France, to Francis Bouygues, the head of a huge construction firm who was known in some quarters as the "King of Cement," instead of to a group led by the Hachette publishing company. The controversial sale of TF 1 generated significant criticism of the Chirac government. In the midst of this controversy, on April 7 the prime minister won a slim vote of confidence in the Assembly, 294 to 282, with 211 PS, 35 PCF, and 32 FN deputies voting against Chirac.

While the PS cast a no-confidence vote on domestic policies, it voted in favor of the government's military budget for 1987–91. The Socialists, who could have abstained, felt comfortable with the military allocations of Chirac's government and realized that there was little real difference in principle between the defense policies of the Right and the Socialists. The PCF, however, voted against the measure and flatly refused to associate itself with the consensus on defense. PCF leaders now seemed to be engineering another zigzag in policy.

On the same day that the PS voted in favor of Chirac's military

budget, the Soviet leader Gorbachev made an important announcement on disarmament. While in Czechoslovakia he stated that he was
willing to negotiate with the United States on the reduction of short-
range nuclear weapons without waiting for an agreement on intermediate-range weapons. Mitterrand was well aware of the possibilities
and dangers of such a proposal, namely that it could give the advantage to the conventional forces of the Warsaw Pact nations and perhaps
denuclearize Europe. Thus, the French president let it be known at
the 750th anniversary celebration of Berlin that he favored disarmament proposals but that reductions must be "balanced." He also made
it clear that French weapons would not be included in any arms
reduction agreement between the United States and the Soviet
Union.[95]

Shortly after Gorbachev's proposal, Mitterrand had an opportunity to respond to another international issue of great importance,
the situation in the Middle East. On April 27–30 Itzhak Shamir,
prime minister of Israel, visited Paris. In this meeting with his Israeli
guest, Mitterrand reaffirmed his belief that an international peace
conference was needed to solve the dangerous Middle East problem.
Although Shamir opposed such a plan, Mitterrand knew that others in
Israel, like the Labor party foreign minister Shimon Peres, favored
it.[96] This proposed solution strengthened Mitterrand's image in
France as an international statesman.

Other international issues also caught the attention of the
French public in early May. On May 16 the National Assembly voted
in favor of the government's proposed referendum for New Caledonia.
Yet several days later the Socialists demanded that the law be reviewed
by the Constitutional Council. Shortly thereafter, separatists on the
South Pacific island called for a boycott of the proposed referendum.
This issue was like a time bomb waiting to explode. Fortunately for
Mitterrand and the Socialists, it was the Right's turn to try to bring
peace and order to the territory.

Domestic events were also highly important for Mitterrand and
the Socialists in the early summer months. During this period the
complicated embezzlement scandal known as the Carrefour affair
received considerable attention. The Ministry of Cooperation had
contracted with the association *Carrefour du Développement* to provide
facilities and services for the Franco-African summit in Bujumbura in
1984, and substantial funds turned out to be missing from the expenditures in connection with the event. Yves Chalier, chief of staff to

Christian Nucci, Socialist minister of cooperation, was implicated and fled to Brazil. Later, Chalier claimed that the funds had been taken with Nucci's knowledge and used in the minister's election campaign. It was also learned that Minister of Interior Pasqua, a Gaullist, had authorized a false passport so that Chalier could escape. According to some accounts, Pasqua had done so in order later to embarrass Nucci and his party, and hurt the Socialists at the polls. In June, PS deputies in the National Assembly unsuccessfully attempted to have Pasqua himself called before the high court hearing testimony in the affair, an effort that nevertheless caused the Chirac government some embarrassment. With both the Left and the Right implicated in the affair, neither side had much to gain by pursuing it.

Another issue of overriding importance began to capture the headlines in France and around the world. On June 11 Klaus Barbie, a former SS officer during World War II who was known as the "Butcher of Lyon," went on trial for crimes committed between 1942 and 1944. For several weeks the Barbie trials dominated the front pages of many newspapers as France confronted its past.

Another domestic development of importance at this time was the announcement by the Communist party that André Lajoinie, leader of the PCF group in the National Assembly, would be the party's presidential candidate in 1988. Earlier, Marchais had declared that he would not run again for the presidency. Under Marchais's tutelage the PCF had suffered a serious decline in France. One SOFRES poll published in Le Monde predicted that Lajoinie would receive a mere 4 percent of the vote in the first round of the 1988 presidential elections. This same poll revealed that 61 percent of PCF members would vote for Mitterrand in the second round, even if the party hierarchy instructed them to do otherwise.[97] Not only were the polls predicting a disastrous performance by the PCF in future elections, but infighting between the old guard and reformers, led by Pierre Juquin, rocked the party. More than 50 percent of PCF members favored reforming the party.[98] Later, the reform-minded Juquin announced, without the sanction of the PCF hierarchy, that he would be a presidential candidate in the 1988 elections. Mitterrand and the Socialists had assisted the demise of the PCF, but the Communists themselves had shown amazing capacity over the years to self-destruct.[99]

While the PCF unveiled a new presidential candidate, Chirac visited the Soviet Union in mid-May in an attempt to project an image of himself as an international statesman. Chirac expected a cool reception in Moscow because France had just expelled several Soviet diplomats who allegedly tried to steal secrets relating to the Ariane rocket. Nevertheless, the prime minister met with Gorbachev and discussed the French position on disarmament, had breakfast with fifteen dissidents, and gave a speech on Soviet television. Gorbachev's policy of *glasnost* even tolerated a Gaullist on Soviet airways.

As Chirac tried to cultivate a presidential image by visiting the Soviet Union, Mitterrand was doing the same by making an official visit to Canada, the first by a French president in twenty years. This visit came after the president attended the forty-ninth Franco-German summit in Paris where disarmament was the key issue; in the weeks that followed, French and German leaders would make an important announcement concerning the coordination of their military policies. During his visit to Canada Mitterrand toured various parts of the nation. He told the Canadian parliament that "France and Canada are in unison." He also emphasized during his stay that Québec is an integral part of Canada but that France would maintain a "direct and privileged" relationship with the French-speaking province.[100] While Mitterrand chose his words carefully with respect to Québec, his presence—but not necessarily his words—reminded some of de Gaulle's visit to Canada in the 1960s.

With the presidential election less than a year away, Chirac began to plead for unity within the majority. At the RPR congress at Porte de Versailles in Paris in late May, Chirac, who had been re-elected, called for unity and for a rejection of the extreme Right. Several days afterward, Chirac and Barre met at the mayor's office in Paris and agreed upon "a code of good conduct" in the presidential campaign. Both worried that divisions on the right would produce another Socialist victory, especially given Mitterrand's newfound popularity with the electorate. Furthermore, polls now showed that while 62 percent of the electorate wanted cohabitation to continue until the 1988 presidential elections, only 24 percent wished to see power-sharing beyond this point.[101]

As the Right attempted to reduce the chances of fratricide, Mitterrand prepared for an early June Venice summit of the industrialized nations of the Western world where he claimed a small but significant victory. Accompanied by Chirac, he stressed the need for continued growth, exchange-rate stability, resistance to protectionism, and a renewed emphasis on the Third World. Western representatives at the summit agreed to coordinate their economies further and to support Mitterrand's suggestion that wealthy nations aim to contribute 0.7 percent of their GNP to poor nations, one of the 110 Propositions of 1981. He later told the press that France "greatly contributed" to this discussion.[102] Mitterrand also proposed the establishment of an international ethics committee to oversee the way in which nations deal with AIDS.[103]

At the Venice summit, the Western leader also discussed a dangerous situation in the Persian Gulf that had special import for the French government and Chirac's efforts to improve relations with Iran. On May 17 an American ship, the U.S.S. *Stark*, had been attacked by Iraqi planes, leaving seventeen crew members dead. The Reagan administration was playing a more prominent role in the Gulf by reflagging Kuwait's oil tankers and providing an American naval flotilla to protect oil supplies being shipped from Kuwait, a nation that aided the Iraqis in their long and bloody war with Iran. Later France and Britain, who had been concerned about the heightened U.S. presence in the Gulf, reversed their policy and sent minesweepers and other vessels to aid the U.S. effort to keep the Gulf open, with France sending its ships to the Gulf of Oman and the Gulf of Aden.

The French government decided to send ships to the area in order to put additional pressure on Iran and to build support for its own confrontation with that troublesome nation. Several weeks following the *Stark* incident, an Iranian gunboat attacked a French container-ship in the Gulf. Shortly thereafter, a French citizen was murdered in the course of a highjack attempt at the Geneva airport. These incidents were ostensibly related to an ongoing two-week war of nerves between France and Iran. French officials in Paris had security forces surround the Iranian embassy in an effort to apprehend an Iranian official suspected of involvement in the September 1986 bombing attacks. The man in question was Wahid Gordji, an Iranian translator without diplomatic immunity according to French authorities. The Iranian government retaliated by not permitting officials in the French embassy in Teheran to leave their office-building and threatening to try the French ambassador on a number of charges. On July 17, France broke diplomatic relations with Iran.

During this dangerous confrontation between Paris and Teheran, some French officials began to attribute responsibility for the September 1986 bombing attacks not to the clan of Georges Ibrahim Abdallah as originally suspected, but to a pro-Iranian terrorist network with close ties to the Iranian embassy in Paris. Chirac's efforts to improve Franco-Iranian relations, like those of Reagan, seemed to have failed miserably. According to José Garçon, a journalist for the newspaper *Libération*, the fatal flaw in Chirac's Iran gamble was obvious:

> The gamble of rebuilding relations with Teheran without changing the special relationship with Baghdad is an illusion. The French government, however, has maintained close ties to Iraq because the nation owes France $4 billion for arms shipments and because France and Iraq have, in the words of Chirac, a common objective, "to prevent the spread of religious fundamentalism in the area."[104]

The press would soon force the prime minister to become very defensive about his Middle Eastern policies.

In late July and early August, Chirac's Iranian initiative caused him tremendous public embarrassment. On July 23 the Iranian daily *Ettelaat Hojatolislam* published an interview with Hashemi Rafsanjani, the speaker of the Iranian parliament, who charged that Chirac had requested that Iranian officials postpone releasing French hostages in Lebanon until after his right-wing government assumed power because he wanted to normalize relations with Iran. In France, *Libération* proceeded to run a front-page story on Rafsanjani's devastating charges; other newspapers quickly followed suit. This story forced the prime minister to make a television appearance and present what he called "the most categorical and formal denial to such insinuations," challenging "anyone to provide a shadow of proof, because it is absurd." Chirac also criticized Socialist leaders, such as the president's friend Dumas, for suggesting that Rafsanjani's revelation might be true. The prime minister even threatened to reopen the Greenpeace affair if the Socialists attempted to exploit the situation, saying, "I am not inclined, when it comes to question about the dignity of France, to raise problems . . . but I demand to be respected."[105] Chirac's difficulties in dealing with a "risk-taker nation" like Iran, like the maladroit efforts of the Reagan administration, tarnished the image of his government.

Moreover, in the same week that these startling revelations surfaced, the satirical newspaper *Le Canard Enchaîné* suggested that Chirac was playing both the Iranian and the Iraqi cards in the Middle East. This newspaper reported that Chirac had definitely committed France to rebuild the nuclear reactor at Osirak, destroyed by Israeli jets in June of 1981. The prime minister's spokesman, Jean-Jacques de Peretti, quickly called the story "grotesque and ridiculous."[106] Trying to protect the billions of francs that Iraq owed France for military weapons and demonstrating a change in policy toward Iran in order to assist the liberation of French hostages represented a contradictory and dangerous policy. To a large degree, the approaching presidential election and the prime minister's sagging fortunes in the polls motivated Chirac to gamble in the Middle East.

The summer months also saw attention focused on two other foreign policy issues—Franco-German cooperation in defense matters and the situation in Chad. Former prime minister Fabius made a statement to the press in mid-June that seemed to underscore and at the same time extend Mitterrand's call for something resembling a European security system. On June 15 Fabius responded to a suggestion by former chancellor Helmut Schmidt and a similar suggestion by Chancellor Kohl that France and Germany integrate part of their conventional forces. Fabius declared: "I think that he [Schmidt] is right. . . . It is necessary for France to consider the protection of Germany as part of the vital interests of France. It is now necessary to envision that we extend our nuclear umbrella to include Germany."[107] More than a year earlier the PS had made a similar suggestion to guarantee Germany's security, an idea that public opinion in France favored. Many realized that if Mitterrand and the government officially decided to protect Germany with France's nuclear umbrella, this would be an important step in creating a European defense system in the heart of Europe and would represent a move away from de Gaulle's limited vision of the *force de frappe*. Mitterrand and the Socialists appeared willing to "Europeanize" the general's defense policy. In fact, later in the year the president stressed in the pages of *Le Nouvel Observateur* the need to develop a European defense effort,[108] an idea that he would return to when radical transformations occurred in Eastern Europe in the future. Mitterrand also accepted Kohl's call for an experimental joint Franco-German unit of conventional forces outside of the NATO command. For Kohl, this joint effort represented one way of shoring up German conventional forces against any possible Soviet attack and possibly enticing France back into some limited participation in the NATO alliance; for Mitterrand, it represented a step toward building a strong French-German axis in a more autonomous Europe.

During the first part of August, Mitterrand and Chirac backed away from Chadian leader Hissène Habré's attempt to retake the "Aouzou Strip" separating Chad from Libya. The strip, a thin band of desert that is supposedly rich in phosphates and uranium, had been under the control of Colonel Qaddafi since 1973. When Habré visited Paris in July, he spoke of his intention to retake the region. French troops and planes stationed in Chad were there, however, to keep Qaddafi from crossing the sixteenth parallel, well to the south of the Aouzou Strip, and from entering the southern half of Chad. Habré's military campaign near the Libyan border was motivated mainly by the defection of Goukouni Oueddei, representing the Muslim forces in the north of Chad and once allied with Libya, to the side of Habré's supporters who embrace animist religions for the most part. Chad's newfound unity strengthened Habré's resolve to humiliate Qaddafi. Confronted with the new Chadian campaign north of the sixteenth parallel, Mitterrand said in an August 10 radio interview that while France supports Chad's struggle for "the reconquest of its independence and unity," Habré's campaign in the Aouzou Strip "engages only himself and the forces of his country." Mitterrand said that he had consulted Prime Minister Chirac and that they agreed that the 1,100 French soldiers in Chad, together with the fighter-bombers, transport planes, and anti-aircraft defenses, would not be employed to aid Habré's offensive. As Mitterrand put it, "As for the French military forces in Chad, which I discussed with the prime minister on Sunday, it will continue to respect the decisions already made by responsible French authorities, and nothing more." He added that the dispute over the Aouzou Strip should be resolved through international arbitration.[109] Both Mitterrand and Chirac knew the possible perils involved in confronting Qaddafi on the eve of the French presidential elections. The stakes were high for both men.

In late August it was not Chad but New Caledonia that drew the attention of the president and the prime minister. During the last week of August, Mitterrand criticized Chirac's government for the beating of a number of separatists in New Caledonia engaged in a peaceful demonstration on the eve of an early September referendum for the French overseas territory. The president referred to the beating, shown on French television, as "images of brutality" and stated, "Nothing is worse than a chain reaction of violence." Several weeks later, with separatists demanding a boycott of the election, the residents of the Pacific archipelago voted to retain their status as a French territory.[110]

During the first week of September Mitterrand attended a summit of forty-one French-speaking nations in Quebec, which he played a key role in sponsoring when the nascent group had met in Paris for an initial conference eighteen months earlier. Mitterrand hoped that this organization, representing a total population of 300 million, would eventually evolve into something resembling the British Commonwealth. The purpose of the summit was to provide French-speaking countries, especially France, with a major forum for political and economic cooperation. Despite disagreement over human-rights abuses in some of the participating nations, the conference leaders adopted a series of resolutions on international issues and agreed to one hundred projects in agriculture, communications, cultural exchanges, education, and scientific research. They also agreed to launch a series of athletic games among the participants, with the first competition scheduled for Morocco in 1989. The leaders from the forty-one nations scheduled their next meeting in Dakar, Senegal in March 1989.[111] For Mitterrand, this French-speaking group, known as *la francophonie*, was one way of demonstrating to the electorate at home and to the world at large that a well-organized French Commonwealth could play an important role on the world stage.

On the home front, Mitterrand and the Socialists intensified the presidential campaign, focusing on two issues. The first was the state of the economy. Although the business community had been rather optimistic about the future—at least until the mid-October stock market crash in the United States that sent the French stock market tumbling and undermined Chirac's plan to sell state-owned industries to private investors—a majority of the public had sensed for a long while that France was in a state of economic decline.[112] According to the OECD, the unemployment rate in France in the campaign period was approximately 11 percent and would rise to 12 percent in 1988. France's GNP was expected to grow by only 1.25 percent in 1987, while both Britain and Italy anticipated stronger growth. A $4.5 billion trade deficit was anticipated for 1987, about three times the deficit in 1986. Moreover, capital investment was still weak, adding to fears that the government was not doing enough to make France competitive.[113]

Mitterrand suggested at various times that the economy, especially unemployment, had not responded to the Right's measures. For instance, when the president visited Normandy he noted that

"France has the means to overcome the difficulties it is currently experiencing." He was suggesting, of course, that the Socialists had the answers to eradicate the nation's economic malaise. Countering Mitterrand's criticism and the attacks by other members of the opposition, Chirac appeared on a radio program and argued that since 1986 the destruction of industrial jobs had ended and that France ranked first in Europe in investment, due in large measure to the privatization of state-owned industry. He added, "Since 1986, we have seen significant improvement."[114] From the prime minister's point of view, the low inflation rate, a drop in the unit cost of labor, and an increase in company profits signaled a healthier economy. Before the meltdown of the American stock market, the problem for Chirac was how to convince the public that the economy was improving before the 1988 elections without resorting to reflationary measures. In the wake of the crash on Wall Street and its ripple effect around the world, it became more difficult for Chirac to defend his economic record, especially since much of his economic program was modeled on that of the Reagan administration. The intensification of the presidential campaign meant, of course, that the state of the economy would be hotly debated. In this regard, all of the major political candidates, Mitterrand, Rocard, Barre, and Chirac, used a single word to describe what it would take for France to transcend its economic problems: "effort."[115] This much the leading candidates had in common.

Mitterrand and the Socialists also attacked the majority on another issue: its collaboration with the extreme Right in and outside of France. In late spring a member of Chirac's own RPR, Minister of Foreign Trade Michel Noir, publicly criticized the prime minister's ambiguous relationship with the National Front. Noir even said that it would be better for the majority to lose the upcoming election than win in alliance with Le Pen's extremist party.[116] After trying to silence Noir, Chirac attacked the National Front and its racist views.

Yet the issue of collaboration with the extreme Right did not end here. Just prior to Bastille Day of 1987 a member of the majority, Hervé de Fontmichel of Giscard's party, formed an electoral alliance wih the National Front in order to win municipal elections in the southern town of Grasse. Shortly thereafter, a delegation of nine right-wing parliamentarians, representing the RPR, UDF, and FN, returned from a visit to South Africa and one member of the delegation, Jean Kiffer of the RPR, praised President P. W. Botha and announced that apartheid had been abolished.[117]

Reacting to these developments, on Bastille Day Mitterrand projected an image of a president who was a friend of the oppressed and who desired to protect France from a dangerous right-wing threat. After riding down the Champs-Elysées in a military jeep at the commencement of the Bastille Day parade and being applauded by the crowd, unlike 1982 and 1983 when he heard numerous shouts of "Resign Mitterrand," he mounted the reviewing stand at the place de la Concorde and stood side by side with President Habré of Chad, the only foreigner invited to the reviewing stand. In the traditional televised broadcast after the military parade, Mitterrand told the nation, "When I came to power Libya had integral control of Chad; today Chad is free."[118] He implied that under his leadership French assistance to Chad had saved the impoverished nation from Qaddafi's aggressive designs.

In this same Bastille Day statement the president attempted to link the majority with Le Pen's racist FN. Referring to the emergence of the National Front, Mitterrand warned that "political ideas threatening to the republic" were emerging. He even connected recent collaboration between the majority and the FN in Grasse with the startling statements of the parliamentary delegation that had just returned from South Africa, reminding the French that "any responsible citizen should be attentive to this development."[119] It was clear to many that Mitterrand was manning the political barricades in his confrontation with Chirac and the Right. With Chirac's favorable ratings in the polls in the early fall a mere 22 percent, compared to 52 percent the previous winter, the prime minister and others on the right began to attack Mitterrand as a political contender in the guise of an impartial arbiter.[120] Political sniping between the president and the Right was now carried out in full public view as political candidates and parties set their sights on the 1988 presidential elections.

Le Pen and Madame Le Pen, however, provided some comic relief for a nation engulfed in a presidential campaign. In the early summer Le Pen and his wife quarreled over a pending divorce. Rejecting his wife's demands for alimony, the right-wing leader suggested that she work as a maid if she needed money. In the third week of June, Madame Le Pen appeared in the centerfold of the French edition of *Playboy* magazine—partially dressed as a maid. In some circles, this issue was one of the principal topics of conversation for weeks. Helping to keep it alive, the satirical newspaper *Le Canard Enchaîné* published a photo of Le Pen on a beach in New Caledonia with his *derrière* fully exposed. Since the beach was not reserved for nudists, *Le Canard Enchaîné* charged that the FN leader was corrupting morals; it also reminded its readers that Madame Le Pen had recently posed in the nude as well. These incidents made Le Pen look foolish indeed to some voters.

Later, Le Pen made a major political blunder that many thought would cost him votes in the 1988 elections. Early in the fall he boldly stated in a radio interview that the Nazi gas chambers were "a minor point" in history. This shocking statement quickly drew condemnations from political and religious officials, such as the general secretary of the Gaullist RPR, Jacques Toubon, from former prime minister Fabius, and from Archbishop Lustiger of Paris. According to Fabius, this statement "unmasked" Le Pen. Fabius also declared that "some of my relatives were victims of this 'minor point.'"[121] Following Le Pen's statement, a poll revealed that 51 percent of the electorate believed that the National Front "has a place in French political life," compared to 42 percent who thought it did not. Furthermore the poll showed that only 23 percent of the respondents desired to see Le Pen become a candidate in 1988. The poll suggested that the National Front had become integrated into the political life of France, but that a significant portion of the electorate had reservations about Le Pen's running as a presidential candidate.[122]

Cohabitation, despite the rise of the FN, greatly aided the political fortunes of Mitterrand and the Socialist party. The president played skillfully to public opinion in the harmonious as well as the defensive and offensive stages of the power-sharing arrangement to restore his popularity and that of his party. On the sixth anniversary of Mitterrand's 1981 election to office, 58 percent of the respondents in one poll said that his election was "a good thing for France." His rating as a president of the Fifth Republic, according to the same poll, was second only to de Gaulle's, with 49 percent believing that de Gaulle was the best president, 20 percent choosing Mitterrand, 13 percent Pompidou, and 6 percent Giscard.[123] Polls showed in the summer and fall of 1987 and in the winter of 1988 that the seventy-one-year-old Mitterrand could win a presidential election. For instance, a poll published early in 1988 revealed that Mitterrand would defeat Barre (53 percent-47 percent) and Chirac (55 percent-45 percent). On the other hand, Mitterrand's rival within the PS, Rocard, could win against Chirac (52 percent-48 percent) but would lose to Barre (44 percent-56 percent).[124] The political warrior from Jarnac had bounced back once again and had truly found victory in defeat.

In reality, cohabitation was an essential element of the presidential campaign,[125] and at the same time represented a further democratization of the French political system. Mitterrand and the Socialists, as well as Chirac and the Gaullists, believed after the March 1986 elections that cohabitation was necessary in order to increase their popularity with voters as they looked ahead to the 1988 presidential contest. However, following the right-wing government's unpopular Devaquet law for higher education and the protest within the public sector, Chirac discovered that he needed cohabitation more than Mitterrand. The greater the friction between Chirac and Mitterrand, the greater the appeal of Barre, the prime minister's most serious challenger. Mitterrand, a master of ambiguity, used the power-sharing arrangement to create an image for himself as a unifier who would uphold the Constitution regardless of the majority in power, but he also utilized the novel experiment to launch a subtle form of political warfare against his foes on the right, especially the Gaullists. Nevertheless, this second experiment since 1981 with alternating governments further demonstrated the elasticity of de Gaulle's constitution and the ability of the French political system to function under either a left-wing or a right-wing government. Like the decision in 1962 to elect the president directly and the rebalancing of the forces of the Left and the Right in the 1970s, cohabitation represented an important stage in the democratic development of the nation.[126] Power-sharing reinforced the idea that alternative left- and right-wing governments were practical possibilities in France. In this regard, the French political system was no longer different from those of other Western democracies.

As one French newsweekly pointed out in the pre-1988 election period, the electorate was concerned with three questions: how will the nation be governed, who will govern, and what will be the program of the new government? The answers to these questions depended largely on the margin of victory in the 1988 presidential and legislative elections.[127]

9

THE 1988 PRESIDENTIAL AND LEGISLATIVE ELECTIONS

Mitterrand's Campaign Strategy

The center is everywhere and the circumference
nowhere.

—François Mitterrand

The presidential and legislative elections of 1988 were marked by paradoxes and realignments. Having ousted the Socialist party from power in 1986 and thus forcing Mitterrand to share power for two years with a right-wing government, the voters now reelected him by a wide margin (see table 12). Then, in the legislative elections, voters failed to give either the Left or the Right a clear majority in the National Assembly, necessitating that the president and his new prime minister, Socialist Michel Rocard, "invent" a majority in order to govern. The inability of any party or grouping to win a clear majority of votes in the National Assembly elections was also an unprecedented event in the annals of the Fifth Republic.[1] While the outcome of both the 1988 presidential and legislative elections is of great interest to students of contemporary France, it is important to examine Mitterrand's strategy before the elections. Not only will this help explain how he won—the first time in French history that a president had been reelected through universal suffrage—but also it

TABLE 12

Results of the 1988 Presidential Election

First Round

	Percentage of Vote	Number of Votes
François Mitterrand (PS)	34.09	10,367,220
Jacques Chirac (RPR)	19.94	6,063,514
Raymond Barre (UDF)	16.54	5,031,849
Jean-Marie Le Pen (FN)	14.39	4,375,894
André Lajoinie (PCF)	6.76	2,055,955
Antoine Waechter (Green)	3.78	1,149,642
Pierre Juquin (independent)	2.10	639,084
Arlette Laguiller (LO)[a]	1.99	606,017
Pierre Boussel (MPPT)[b]	.38	116,832

Second Round

François Mitterrand	54	16,704,279
Jacques Chirac	46	14,218,970

SOURCE: Compiled from data found in *Le Monde, Dossiers et documents: L'élection présidentielle, 24 avril/8 mai 1988* (Paris: Le Monde, 1988), pp. 28–29, 75.
[a] *Lutte Ouvrière* (Workers' Struggle).
[b] *Mouvement pour un parti des travailleurs* (Movement for a Workers' Party).

will illuminate the mind of a French leader that some view as the most accomplished political tactician in Europe.[2]

Before discussing Mitterrand's campaign strategy, however, it is necessary to briefly mention the record that Mitterrand ran on in the 1988 presidential contest. Despite mistakes made at the helm of the French state, especially in the realm of economic policy during the first year of the Socialist experiment, and his dangerously low popularity in the middle of his first term, Mitterrand had developed a rather strong record by 1988 and he knew that this record would be an advantage in the upcoming election. His decision to reverse the Socialist government's initial reflationary economic policy and pursue austerity increased unemployment but also reduced inflation to roughly 3 percent by the time of the presidential contest, and eased the balance-of-payments problem that had plagued France during the early 1980s. The general state of the economy was much healthier in 1988 than in 1981 or 1982. The Mitterrand government had also sponsored decentralization and had liberalized the state-dominated media. The Socialists had also made a number of social reforms, advanced the cause of women, and provided France with a new cultural policy that was applauded by many. Besides these accomplishments, Mitterrand had guided the nation through the uncharted waters of *alternance* twice, in 1981 and 1986, and had introduced France to its first experiment with cohabitation under the Fifth Republic. He also provided continuity in foreign and defense policy with his Gaullist-like approach to external affairs, providing his government with a national consensus in this domain of French policy. And much to the liking of the public, he advocated a more unified and mightier Europe and a strengthening of France's position within it. There were setbacks in his first term, but there were also accomplishments that many appreciated as the 1988 presidential campaign began.

He was convinced to run after polls showed that he was the only Socialist candidate who could win against either Barre or Chirac. His desire to prevent France falling into the grip of the Right once again—his entire career under the Fifth Republic had revolved around his opposition to the Gaullists—and his yearning for a greater measure of social justice drove him on. In many ways, his decision to run for the presidency an unprecedented fourth time revealed his determination to oppose the Right and govern France from the center. Mitterrand also believed that it was his destiny to lead a more just France that was different in its approach to social issues from the right-wing republic that he had replaced in 1981. Linked to his decision to run was his strong will to power, a desire to continue his political career beyond the two years of cohabitation with the Right. Another presidential victory would give further impetus to the construction of a centrist republic that would be different from de Gaulle's creation. Of course, Mitterrand is a political animal who has seldom backed away from a political fight, especially with the Right. In 1988 he was driven into battle with his right-wing opponents for one final major victory in his long political career that would make him the first president to be elected twice in direct elections. Mitterrand, a man with a keen sense of history, knew that victory in 1988 would secure for him a prominent place in the annals of France. His strong desire to do battle with his opponents and triumph over them was symbolic of his presidency and his long political career in general. Mitterrand officially became a candidate only one month prior to the election. Perhaps after the 1986 legislative elections Mitterrand did not truly know if he would run again, given his advanced age and his relatively low popularity rating. Nevertheless, his obligation as a Socialist president was to ensure the election of a Socialist candidate in 1988 and a Socialist victory in future legislative elections, despite the rhetoric that he was no longer a president of *le peuple de gauche* but rather of "all the French."[3]

To a large degree, Mitterrand's 1988 victory was closely related to a restructured and diversified image that emerged during cohabitation. The power-sharing arrangement between 1986 and 1988 provided him with a unique opportunity to modify significantly his public persona.[4] He acted as a president who was no longer a partisan but an umpire for the entire nation. When he began his term in office, it was clear to many in France that Mitterrand represented leftist voters. Yet the free-spending reflationary policy of Year I of the Socialist government resulted in a sharp increase in inflation, a serious balance-of-payments problem, and nagging unemployment, all of which helped to sap the popularity of the newly elected president. Consequently, even before the 1986 campaign, Mitterrand attempted to transform his image, by his turn to austerity in 1982 and 1983 and his recognition of the business community and the need to improve French competitiveness. However, the novelty of cohabitation offered him numerous additional opportunities to change his public persona.

Cohabitation allowed him to project the image of a president who had averted a serious constitutional crisis with the onset of power-sharing. Mitterrand's speedy appointment of Chirac as prime minister convinced many that their president would not provoke an institutional crisis by appointing a prime minister that the new conservative majority could not accept. In his April 8, 1986 message to parliament, Mitterrand, as previously mentioned, offered his view of cohabitation and said that he would follow the Constitution to the letter.[5] A leading political scientist, Jean-Luc Parodi, argues that from May through July 1986 alone, Mitterrand gained twenty points in the polls, especially from center and center-right voters who appreciated his effort to prevent a breakdown of government at the onset of cohabitation.[6]

The election of a conservative majority in 1986 also meant that the Socialist president and his party would no longer have to assume responsibility for the government's program. From March 1986 to May 1988, it would be the conservatives that had to deal with the often harsh realities of governing, including a nagging 11 percent unemployment rate, escalating terrorism, increasing student militancy, and a threatening public-sector strike. Power-sharing permitted Mitterrand to play a much loftier role than had heretofore been the case. While Chirac and the conservative majority governed, Mitterrand reigned, almost as an imaginary monarch.

Moreover, since cohabitation was popular with the French electorate, at least until the student revolt of late 1986 and early 1987 and the subsequent public-sector strike, Mitterrand knew that by appearing to support the new power-sharing arrangement, he could enhance his own popularity. At the same time cohabitation enabled Mitterrand to stress his role as a guarantor of continuity, unlike in 1981 when he had emphasized his role as the champion of reform. Yet cohabitation also allowed him to deploy his counterattacking abilities, one of his greatest assets, against Chirac's government.[7]

Thus, cohabitation enabled Mitterrand to rebuild his popularity with the electorate. He became the father of the nation, the impartial umpire, the architect of industrial modernization, the defender of continuity. His remarkable rebound in the polls vis-à-vis his principal challenger, Chirac, is clearly demonstrated in tables 13 and 14. Thus cohabitation became an essential part of the 1988 presidential campaign—in reality, cohabitation was presidential politics par excellence.[8] This is one of the reasons the 1988 presidential contest revolved more around the personalities and public images of Mitterrand and Chirac than substantial policy issues. In the world of politics, especially in the modern age of mass media, imagery is sometimes more important than substance.

Another major campaign strategy was designed to mobilize both Socialist and non-Socialist voters—which was essential if he was to win. Mitterrand used the ingenious method of not declaring his candidacy early in the race and actively encouraging other Socialists to run—especially his *frère-ennemi* within the PS, Rocard—as a way of mobilizing various factions of the party. Following Mitterrand's puzzling statement late in 1986 at Caylus suggesting that he might not seek a second term, the president met with his principal Socialist challenger and then told the press that Rocard was "the man of talent and conviction that France needs."[9] Rocard's candidacy appealed both to Socialists and to many centrists who viewed him as an economic realist beause of his earlier criticism of the reflationary policy pursued by his party in 1981. In addition to the *autogestionnaire* Rocard, the

TABLE 13

Mitterrand's Popularity Ratings, 1981–1988
(yearly average percentages)

1981	48
1982	47
1983	37
1984	32
1985	33
1986	51
1987	52
1988	56

SOURCE: Compiled from data found in *Le Figaro,*
L'élection présidentielle 1988: Resultats, analyses et com-
mentaires (Paris: Le Figaro, 1988), p. 35.

TABLE 14

The Popularity of Prime Minister Jacques
Chirac, 1986–1988
(percentages)

1986:	2nd quarter	54
	3rd quarter	47
	4th quarter	53
1987:	1st quarter	44
	2nd quarter	43
	3rd quarter	42
	4th quarter	42
1988:	1st quarter	46

SOURCE: Compiled from data found in *Le Figaro,*
L'élection présidentielle 1988, p. 36.

left-wing Socialist Jean-Pierre Chevènement announced his candidacy, while the loyal Mitterrandist and former prime minister, Laurent Fabius, suggested that he too was interested in the presidency. After Rocard actively launched his campaign for the presidency, Chevènement criticized the "liberal socialism" that "contaminates" the PS, referring mainly to Rocard and Fabius. Consequently, Mitterrand's ambiguous statements about his own candidacy enhanced the mobilization of voters by activating the various tendencies with the Socialist party.

This strategy gave Mitterrand numerous advantages. It meant that he could stay above the fray, continue to enhance his presidential image and make it difficult for the Right to attack him as a candidate. Ironically, Mitterrand knew that his noncandidacy would mobilize voters by activating the various tendencies with the PS, and allowing Rocard's campaign to attract both Socialist and non-Socialist voters.

One of Mitterrand's most crucial strategies for winning in 1988 was to pitch his campaign toward the center and to do battle there as he confronted his conservative challengers. He did this in several ways. One way was by advocating a program that was little different from that of his conservative opponents. In the second week of April, Mitterrand published a "Letter to all French Citizens" in *Le Monde* and a number of provincial dailies that announced his program for the future. What struck many observers was that Mitterrand's vision for the future, as well as that of the Socialist party, closely resembled the program of the Right. Only on two specific points did the position of Mitterrand and the PS on the issues differ to any significant degree from that of Chirac or Raymond Barre: a guaranteed minimum income and a fiscal policy that included a wealth tax. (A minimum income and a wealth tax were two points of Mitterrand's program that he hoped would appeal to PS voters and others on the left, especially disenchanted Communists.) Another way that he moved his campaign toward the center was by calling for an *ouverture,* an opening to the center. His most striking statement on *ouverture* came between the presidential and the legislative elections of 1988 when he declared: "It is not healthy that only one party governs. . . . It is necessary that other [parties] . . . take part in government."[10] Mitterrand realized that in the 1988 election approximately 80 percent of the voters were somewhere between the Center-Left and the Center-Right, with the extreme Left and Right anticipating approximately 20 percent of the vote. This is why Mitterrand chose the Center as his battleground.

According to many political analysts, Mitterrand was reelected because he won a large share of the centrist vote, while Chirac was unable to expand his traditional political base to include a large part of the middle class. Postelection polls revealed that in the second round of the election, 74 percent of the wage-earners from the public sector, 59 percent of the those from the private sector, and roughly 60 percent of the *classes moyennes salariées* voted for Mitterrand.[11] In the first round of the presidential contest alone, Mitterrand increased his centrist vote tally by 12 percent compared to 1981, while the right-wing candidates lost 15 percent of the centrist vote.[12] Clearly, Mitterrand's political rhetoric, style, and strategy were designed to win over crucial centrist voters.

Also as a campaign strategy, Mitterrand posed as an indispensable arbiter and unifier, conjuring up for many the image of de Gaulle himself. Not only did he remind the electorate that he had saved France from a serious constitutional crisis over cohabitation but that he, like de Gaulle, embodied the nation and was an impartial umpire guarding national interests. This rhetoric, not to mention his often Gaullist style, strengthened his image as a unifier, a theme that he stressed when he announced his candidacy. In his official statement of candidacy, he said that he was the only candidate who could preserve "civil peace," declaring, "I want France to be united. It will not be if it is taken over by intolerant views, by parties that want everything, by clans, by gangs."[13] This statement reminded many of de Gaulle who in earlier years warned the electorate against the "clans, combinations, clienteles, and passing whims of the regime of parties."[14] Unify and then mobilize the voters—this was an essential aspect of Mitterrand's campaign strategy.

By stressing his role as an arbiter and a national unifier, Mitterrand was able to exploit division within the Right, especially the issue of right-wing collaboration with the National Front. Gaullist collaboration with the extreme Right was one of the concerns of Barre's voters as the election approached. Mitterrand, of course, warned the electorate to be attentive to this development.[15]

In other ways, too, Mitterrand capitalized on his role as arbiter and unifier. For instance, during the wave of terrorism that struck France in September 1986 and its aftermath, an occurrence that gave added life to a peaceful cohabitation, Mitterrand and Chirac issued a number of statements suggesting that they had agreed on how to combat terrorism. But when it became clear that the Chirac government was attempting to reestablish a dialogue with Iran and strike deals with the Khomeini regime in order to free French hostages in the Middle East and reap the political benefits of such an accomplishment, Mitterrand let it be known on several occasions that he opposed compromising with terrorists. Mitterrand found many opportunities during the course of the presidential campaign to utilize his role as arbiter and national unifier in order to divide the Right. In the April 28, 1988 presidential debate between Mitterrand and Chirac, viewed by an estimated thirty million French citizens, the incumbent told this large national audience that "a RPR [Gaullist] state is a great danger."[16] In part, this was an effort to divide center and center-right voters from Chirac. How successful were Mitterrand's efforts to divide the opposition? Perhaps some indication is seen in the number of transfer votes in the second round of the election, where 14 percent of Barre's supporters and 26 percent of Le Pen's backers voted for Mitterrand. Division on the right and Mitterrand's exploitation of that division, ensured that the transfer votes in the second round favored the incumbent.

Another campaign strategy was to hammer away at the key issues on the minds of the voters, even though the official Socialist program was not much different from that of the conservatives. In April 1988, the top ten issues that concerned the electorate were unemployment (75 percent), education (65 percent), purchasing power (55 percent), social justice (54 percent), public safety (53 percent), individual freedoms (52 percent), economic growth (48 percent), freedom of information (42 percent), France's position in the world (41 percent), and immigration (33 percent). Postelection surveys revealed that Mitterrand was much more effective in addressing these concerns in his public addresses and appearances than either Barre or Chirac.[17] Moreover, on the eve of the presidential contest, 50 percent of the respondents to one poll said that Mitterrand would be the best defender of social justice, while only 30 percent gave Chirac such a rating. In the same poll, Mitterrand outscored Chirac on unifying the nation by 47 percent to 31 percent; on the proper functioning of the institutions of government by 43 percent to 32 percent; on assuring the education of French youth by 42 percent to 38 percent; and on protecting the purchasing power of consumers by 39 percent to 35 percent.[18] Between the two rounds, Mitterrand focused on three major themes: his role as a unifier, the proper functioning of government under his leadership, and his determination to defend social justice.[19] His eventual reelection would not be due to proposed social and economic reforms but to the fact that he won the battle of images with right-wing contenders. The struggle for credibility with the electorate in the presidential campaign involved reinforcing existing strong points of credibility, but also diversifying his image.[20] "Mitterrand I" had shrewdly prepared the political groundwork for the emergence of "Mitterrand II," the new president of France.

In order to strengthen his reelection bid, Mitterrand also tried once again to gain the support of the intelligentsia. On the eve of the presidential contest, he hosted an unusual conference of Nobel Prize laureates. The president's co-host was his friend Elie Wiesel, himself a Nobel laureate. Meeting in the Salle des Fêtes of the Elysée, seventy-six winners of prizes in literature, economics, science, and peace gathered to discuss the dangers and the hopes of humanity in the twenty-first century. Speaking before his distinguished guests, the president stated, "Politicians should be modest when faced with the man of knowledge." One American laureate at the conference said that most of Mitterrand's guests had "no idea" what they were doing at the presidential palace. Then, he added, "Obviously we are helping Mitterrand to win."[21]

These strategies, then, represented the basis of Mitterrand's campaign plan. In addition, a number of key mistakes by his chief opponent aided Mitterrand in the 1988 elections. One major question in the campaign was Mitterrand's age. However, this concern dissipated for many voters as they saw an impulsive and sometimes reckless Chirac attempt to maximize his election fortunes. At the end of 1987, amid protests by Mitterrand and the Socialists, the UN High Commissioner for Refugees, and by other nations—especially the United States and Great Britain—the Chirac government obtained the release of two hostages in the Middle East (Roger Auque and Jean-Louis Normandin) by permitting the suspected Iranian terrorist Wahid Gordji to return home, thereby ending a five-month standoff at Iran's embassy in Paris. Shortly thereafter, Chirac rounded up seventeen members of the People's Mujaheddin, an anti-Khomeini network operating in various countries, and summarily expelled them from France. According to some accounts, the conservative government also agreed to repay part of a $1 billion debt owed to Iran. As might be expected, Mitterrand quickly criticized Chirac's handling of the Iranian problem and demanded that the prime minister justify the expulsion of the Mujaheddin members. The former Socialist prime minister

Fabius called this incident "shameful" and contrary to France's tradition of providing a "shelter for political refugees who fight against fascism and terrorism."[22] But before Chirac officially announced his candidacy for the presidency early in 1988, he rescinded his expulsion order in an effort to mollify criticism in France and abroad.

Between the two rounds of the presidential contest Chirac took further rash actions that led many to question his leadership and judgment. For example, he struck a secret deal with the Iranian government in order to free three more French hostages in Lebanon. On the same day in New Caledonia, French soldiers stormed separatists who were holding twenty-three gendarmes hostage, killing a number of people. Then, Chirac brought home to France one of its secret agents who had sabotaged the *Rainbow Warrior;* this agent had been ordered earlier to serve a short "sentence" in the South Pacific for her activities. Some of Chirac's actions made Mitterrand's age and reflective qualities appear as a major advantage. Mitterrand's strategy and Chirac's mistakes helped to ensure victory for the incumbent.

The president's reelection revealed important changes among the electorate and French Socialists in general. The geography of French socialism was no longer that of the first half of the century. Between 1900 and the 1960s the heartland of socialism had lain south of an imaginary line running from La Rochelle to Geneva, in an older France little touched by industrial modernization. During the 1970s socialism began to extend its domain north of the La Rochelle–Geneva line; in 1981, out of 45 departments that gave Mitterrand a vote tally above his 28 percent average in the first round, 25 were north of the line. By 1988, out of the 49 departments providing Mitterrand a score superior to his 34 percent national average, 33 were located north of the old divide. While socialism still retains its strength in its traditional bastions, such as the southwest, the Nord, and Pas-de-Calais, it is much weaker in the southeast and along the Mediterranean where the National Front has made considerable inroads.[23] In general, since 1981 Mitterrand himself has made his greatest gains with voters in towns with populations up to 30,000 and has seen more modest gains in the larger towns and cities.[24] As one French political observer stated, "The electoral map of Mitterrandism is in 1988 a strange synthesis of Socialist, Radical, and Gaullist maps of the 1960s."[25]

The social composition of the Socialist electorate had changed as well. As noted above, Mitterrand won a significant share of the vote from the middle class, but he also won more of the female vote in 1988 than in 1981, demonstrating that women had moved leftward electorally and now represented the most progressive political force in France. On the one hand, substantially more women voted for Mitterrand (54 percent) than for Chirac (46 percent) in the second round. Compared to the 1981 presidential election, 4 to 5 percent more women marked their ballots for the Socialist candidate.[26] On the other hand, in 1988 women demonstrated a stronger resistance to the extreme Right than male voters. In the first round of the presidential contest, 17 percent of male voters cast their ballots for Le Pen and the National Front, while only 10 percent of women voters did likewise.[27] Since being given the vote by Charles de Gaulle in 1944, women have moved slowly toward the left electorally as an increasing number of them have entered the work force in an economy where unemployment affects women more than men (roughly 60 percent of the unemployed are women) and where women are often relegated to part-time positions (approximately 84 percent of the part-time positions are held by women).[28]

Mitterrand also made solid inroads among PCF voters. For instance, in nineteen departments where the PCF lost most of its voting strength from 1981 to 1988, the Socialist party had experienced a strong 5.5 percent increase, higher than the PS's average national increase over the same period (4.8 percent).[29] In the first round of the 1988 presidential elections, a stunning 42 percent of the working class voted for Mitterrand. Another party that cut into the voting strength of the PCF was the FN. In the 1988 presidential race, the National Front astonished many inside and outside of France by winning 14 percent of the vote.

TABLE 15

Percentage of First-Round Vote Won by the Major Parties, 1974–1988

	1974 *Presidential*	*1978* *Legislative*	*1981* *Presidential*	*1981* *Legislative*	*1986* *Legislative*	*1988* *Presidential*	*1988* *Legislative*
PS	43.3	24.7	25.8	37.5	32.7	34.1	37.5
PCF	—	20.5	15.3	16.1	9.8	6.8	11.3
Right	47.7	46.5	49.2	42.2	44.7	36.4	40.5
FN	0.8	0.2	—	0.4	9.7	14.4	9.6

Source: *The Economist*, June 11, 1988, p. 49.

The outcome of the 1988 presidential elections only underscored the "long march" of French socialism. As table 15 demonstrates, the PS has made impressive gains at the polls over the years. Even in the 1986 legislative election where voters ousted the PS as the majority party in the National Assembly, the Socialists won more than 32 percent of the vote, garnered less than 20 percent in only two departments, and were only 5 percent behind their historic 1981 vote tally. Two days after Mitterrand lost to Giscard in the 1974 presidential elections, he announced his future electoral strategy to Franz-Olivier Giesbert, a French journalist who is now the editor-in-chief of the newspaper *Le Figaro:* "My great project is to build a large hegemonic Socialist party which, in order to govern, will soon be supported by centrists and Communists."[30] The 1988 presidential elections demonstrated that he had achieved his goal.

These changes in voting patterns lead one to conclude that while Mitterrand had restructured and diversified his image, a new electoral socialism had emerged in France that was far more social democratic in its orientation than the socialism of 1981 that sought a rupture with capitalism. Furthermore, this new socialism was implanted throughout France and was supported by a new electorate.[31] Mitterrand's presidential campaign revealed a president with a new image. "Mitterrand I" was now replaced by "Mitterrand II." Mitterrand, the PS, and the electorate had undergone a fascinating metamorphosis.

Following his impressive victory in the second round of the presidential contest on May 8, Mitterrand dissolved the National Assembly and called for new elections. He asked his archrival in the PS, Rocard, to form a new government. Mitterrand knew that if he appointed one of his closest allies to head the Matignon, such as Bérégovoy, the impression would be that the Elysée was running the government.[32] There would be no such idea if Rocard was prime minister. Rocard would also strengthen the opening to the center because of his popularity with the public and his reputation as a right-wing Socialist. Moreover, this appointment would also be a way of using up Rocard's popularity, since prime ministers traditionally witness declines in their approval ratings as they confront the realities of power, as Chirac had painfully learned. On assuming the prime ministership, Rocard received some interesting advice from Chirac, an old acquaintance from his student days at the Institut d'Etudes Politiques with whom he had always maintained a friendly relationship.

Chirac told the new prime minister, "If I have one piece of advice to give you, it is to beware of François Mitterrand when he becomes friendly."[33] Was Mitterrand's selection of Rocard an attempt to prepare the way for a true dauphin in the post-Mitterrand years—perhaps someone like former prime minister Laurent Fabius, a loyal Mitterrandist?

Throughout their careers in the PS, Mitterrand and Rocard had had a poor relationship. Rocard had challenged Mitterrand for the presidency in 1981—an action that many Socialists had not forgotten or forgiven—and, with some "encouragement" from the president, mounted a campaign in 1988 as well. Besides their competition to control the Socialist party, both men were different in terms of background, temperament, and politics. Mitterrand, for instance, had come from a devout Catholic provincial family, while Rocard was raised as a Protestant in the Paris region. Mitterrand had studied political science and law but Rocard studied political science and attended the Ecole Nationale d'Administration where he developed an interest in finance. Mitterrand became known as something of an intellectual, whereas Rocard developed a reputation as a technocrat. The president, although reserved in his personal manner, knew how to take time out to smell the roses of life, enjoying browsing in bookstores or going for a walk in the woods. Rocard, a warm and outgoing man, had a reputation as a hard worker who always seemed to be in a hurry. Politically, Mitterrand believed that the state had an important role to play in improving the quality of life and ensuring social justice, while Rocard placed confidence in market forces and autonomous social processes.

Despite the differences and the fact that Mitterrand often found Rocard "incomprehensible," he knew that his rival could help the party win support from the center. When he appointed his new prime minister, however, Mitterrand also requested that three of his closest allies be returned to the key posts that they had held prior to 1986. Rocard agreed that Bérégovoy would be installed as minister of the economy, Dumas as minister of foreign affairs, and Joxe as minister of interior. When the government was announced, it comprised more than forty cabinet members, half of whom were non-Socialists. The new government represented an opening to the center, but also a restoration.[34]

Many in France, including the newly elected president and numerous pollsters, thought that the June 5 and 12 National Assembly elections would produce a large Socialist majority, especially since Mitterrand had won a landslide victory by French standards over Chirac in the presidential race. This was not the case for several reasons. First, Mitterrand had worried about winning too big a majority and had called for an opening to the center prior to the elections. On his annual pilgrimage to the Rock of Solutré near Macon in order to commune with nature and give reporters and photographers an opportunity to view the president amid "natural scenery," Mitterrand told the nation, as noted earlier, that it was necessary for other parties to take part in government.[35] In addition, the Socialists were hurt by an extremely high abstention rate in both rounds of the election. In round one, the abstention rate was 34.2 percent, the highest rate in French parliamentary history; in round two, abstentions were 28.9 percent, the highest percentage since 1945. Whether this was a product of apathy or protest, it weakened the vote tally for the Socialist party. Moreover, many pollsters simply erred with their projections for the National Assembly elections. The outcome held surprises for many, Socialists and non-Socialists.

While the legislative elections ousted Chirac's conservative majority, the elections suggested that voters desired a more balanced political system after giving a majority to the Left in 1981 and then to the Right in 1986. The results seemed to confirm the emergence of a centrist republic. Unlike in previous elections under the Fifth Republic, no single party or grouping won an absolute majority of seats. After round two, the PS and its allies had a total of 276 seats in the National Assembly, thirteen short of an absolute majority. The conservative UDF, the Gaullist RPR, and the rest of the Right captured 271 seats. The PCF, although it improved its performance by 5 percent more of the vote compared to the presidential contest, ended up with twenty-seven deputies, a decrease of eight from the old Assembly. The big loser was the National Front. The switch back from proportional representation to a majority voting system, enacted by the former conservative government, reduced FN strength in the National Assembly from 32 seats to only 1. These results meant that a minority cabinet would govern France, a situation that de Gaulle had hoped to avoid when he framed the Constitution of the Fifth Republic. While an absolute majority existed arithmetically with the PS obtaining 276 seats and the Communists 27, politically the old Union of the Left that brought Mitterrand to power in 1981 was no longer possible. Both Mitterrand and PCF chief Marchais rejected any suggestion to revitalize the old alliance, partly because of the disagreements between the two parties over economic policy, the scale of a new Socialist-sponsored wealth tax, the level of a new minimum wage, and defense expenditures. This meant, of course, that if the PS hoped to govern as a minority cabinet it would have to rely on Communist support on an ad hoc basis as well as on similar support from the Center. Because of the novelty of this situation and the initial reaction of the French stock market to the election outcome, Mitterrand gave a televised address only two days after the second round of the legislative elections and told the nation that "France is being and will be governed," reminding his fellow citizens that a number of other Western European nations functioned well with coalition governments.[36] Ironically, the electorate had imposed its own brand of *ouverture* on the president and his party.

The new political landscape in the aftermath of the 1988 elections only strengthened the president's importance and authority as the nation began what some political commentators called "cohabitation II." As Simone Veil, a well-known centrist, stated, "Since there is no majority, everything is in the hands of the president. This reinforces his powers."[37] However, some wondered what new image or images Mitterrand would sculpt for himself during his unprecedented second term and, more important, what would happen in France as the president tried to govern with a minority cabinet.

In the immediate postelection period, Mitterrand seemed content to reign while Rocard governed. The president knew that the prime minister's task was difficult as he tried to pursue simultaneously policies of national unity and austerity. As he had in the past, Mitterrand appeared to be waiting for the propitious moment to make an appearance on the center of the political stage to define the direction of his second term. When he would step onto center stage was anyone's guess. For the moment he simply reigned as Mitterrand II.

10

PROSPERITY, ROCARDISM, AND THE EUROPEAN CHALLENGE

The opening to the center is first of all the termination of the verbal civil war.

—Henri Emmanuelli

The most important event in Europe, perhaps for the world, since World War II is what is happening in Eastern Europe. . . . [The Europe of Yalta] is unraveling before our very eyes.

—François Mitterrand

Following Mitterrand's stunning victory over Chirac in the presidential contest, several major issues concerned him over the next two years. There was continued improvement in the economy, which brought the possibility of a wider opening to the center—as well as worries over Rocard's popularity. Due in part to the rosier economic climate, the newly appointed prime minister attained a popularity that rivaled and at times even surpassed that of the president. This situation forced Mitterrand and others to wonder if he had made a political mistake by selecting Rocard to lead the opening to the center. The year 1989 brought the bicentennial of the Revolution, which Mitterrand made into a projection of France's new centrism—an orientation that Rocard also seemed well suited to continue. Facing Rocard's popularity, Mitterrand had to find a way to reassert his own authority and become more than simply a ceremonial president. To do this, he would turn to another major issue in the field of foreign policy: how to respond to the breathtaking pace of change in Eastern

Europe and German reunification, while at the same time keeping EEC integration on track. The possibility that the upheaval in Eastern Europe would derail the economic and monetary union of the EEC, the question of the pace and nature of German reunification, the security of the frontiers surrounding Germany, especially that of Poland, the possibility of an enlarged and neutral Germany that might become an economic superpower within the EEC, and the future of the European security system greatly concerned him. Of course, he would also have to concern himself with the dangerous crisis in the Gulf. At the beginning of his second term, Mitterrand was comparatively inactive, but by the early months of 1990 he found himself actively involved in trying to preserve the unity of the Socialist party, especially his own faction, and to keep European integration on track as the Continent entered a new political era.

Following the second round of the June 1988 legislative elections, Mitterrand asked Rocard to form a government that reflected the desire to begin an opening to the center. Although Socialists were appointed to key ministries—Dumas (foreign affairs), Chevènement (defense), Jospin (education), Bérégovoy (finance), Joxe (interior), and Lang (culture)—twenty-four of the forty-eight ministers in the new government were non-Socialists who came from the splintered Center-Right or who had no party affiliation. From the Center-Right came Jean-Marie Rausch, the mayor of Metz and a Lorraine industrialist, the minister of foreign trade, and Jean-Pierre Soisson, the mayor of Auxerre, the minister of labor. Both Rausch and Soisson, supporters of Raymond Barre, had held the same posts under Chirac. The nonparty appointments included Léon Schwartzenberg, a noted cancer specialist, as minister of health, and Théo Braun, a fundraiser for centrist candidates and a pension specialist, as minister for the retired.

Besides successfully wooing a number of center-right politicians into the Rocard government, the Socialists gleefully witnessed serious divisions among the Center-Right in the National Assembly. Pierre Méhaignerie, for example, led a splinter group, the Union of the Center, that split off from the UDF. Méhaignerie attracted thirty-two deputies and nine allies to his new group, including Barre himself. Moreover, in the aftermath of the 1988 elections, Giscard's Union for French Democracy, besides seeing some of its members participate directly in the government and others support Méhaignerie's new center formation, found itself divided over the leadership of the Center-Right. Giscard proposed maintaining a coherent parliamentary group in order to lead what he called a "constructive opposition" to the Rocard government. On the other hand, supporters of Léotard, head of the Republican party and a rival of Giscard within the UDF, desired an alliance with Chirac's Gaullist RPR. Later, challenges within both the UDF and the RPR from a group of young "renovators," due in large measure to Giscard's defeat in 1981 and Chirac's poor performance against Mitterrand in the 1988 presidential elections, would threaten to splinter the opposition still further. Henri Emmanuelli, a Socialist deputy from the Landes region who is known for his gift for phraseology, suggested shortly after the formation of the Rocard government that "the Center is now going through a difficult period of puberty."[1]

Another victory of sorts for Mitterrand and the PS were the elections to parliamentary posts following the legislative contests. Laurent Fabius, supported by PCF votes in return for a promise to enable the Communists to have a larger say in the Assembly by lowering the minimum number of deputies needed to form a parliamentary group, defeated the Gaullist Chaban-Delmas in the election for the presidency of the National Assembly. For Fabius this new post at the Hôtel de Lassay, an eighteenth-century palace that serves as the office of the president of the National Assembly, represented a prestigious and safe position for a Mitterrandist who was one of the contending heirs to Mitterrand's throne. However, this election followed an earlier setback for both Fabius and Mitterrand only days after the president's reelection. Mitterrand had wanted Fabius to take over the reins of the Socialist party, but Henri Emmanuelli, the number-two man in the party, led a campaign to block the appointment. Jospin, who had served as first secretary since 1981 and who was the principal rival of Fabius, seemed resigned to accepting Mitterrand's wishes out of loyalty to the president. However, there was considerable concern among Socialist leaders that the PS should remain to the left of the president and that Fabius would use the party to advance his own presidential ambitions. Consequently, the PS hierarchy in a show of strength selected former prime minister Mauroy to lead the party.

In the early days of the new Rocard government, it looked as if the opening to the center would be fraught with problems because of statements made by two non-Socialist ministers. Within days of his appointment, Minister of Health Schwartzenberg created a furor when he said that he thought that all pregnant women and those undergoing surgery should be required to undergo AIDS testing and that the government should distribute drugs to addicts as part of a treatment program. For speaking out of turn and misrepresenting the government's policy, the minister of health was forced to submit his resignation only nine days after assuming office. One official in the Republican party used the incident to criticize the government, saying, "The resignation of Mr. Schwartzenberg illustrates the precariousness of the Rocard government, which doesn't have a majority and rests on uncertain political foundations."[2] Earlier in the week there was another embarrassing incident. Pierre Arpaillange, the minister of justice, stated publicly that the solitary confinement of convicted terrorists should end. At the time a number of Direct Action terrorists were being held in French prisons and the minister's statement was not well received in some quarters. After talks with Rocard, the two issued an amicable joint statement in which Arpaillange and the prime minister announced that terrorist prisoners convicted of violent crimes would be kept in solitary confinement.[3] The opening to the center was off to a shaky start.

In June 1988, both New Caledonia and the movement toward a unified Europe concerned Mitterrand and the government. On June 26 the government announced that an agreement had been reached by opposing forces in New Caledonia: the territory would remain under French authority for the next twelve months; a bill would be drawn up establishing the future organization of the territory which would be divided into three provinces; a referendum on self-determination would be held in 1998; and immediate economic aid would be provided by France. In the months that followed, the National Assembly would pass a bill consistent with this settlement, and Mitterrand would agree to hold a referendum on New Caledonia later in the year, the first referendum in France in sixteen years.

During the last week of June, Mitterrand attended a two-day European Community summit in Hannover. Here he focused on several worrisome issues regarding the planned European integration at the end of 1992. He warned other European leaders about lifting restrictions on the flow of capital between EEC nations before harmonizing the twelve's fiscal policies. If this was not done, he feared that money would flow to tax havens and the system might eventually collapse. Another issue concerned the plight of workers in the Europe of 1992. Mitterrand stressed the need for what he called a "social dimension," telling others that the single market must not "abandon workers on the side of the road."[4] At later summits he would advocate a Social Charter for the EEC in order to protect the rights of workers in the post-1992 Europe. Mitterrand knew that at home and abroad some on the left had criticized 1992 simply as a reform that would benefit wealthy capitalists. Moreover, in some countries there were groups such as the British Labour party that were skeptical of the future single market. By placing an emphasis on developing a Social Charter, Mitterrand knew he could generate more support for 1992, especially on the left. This also aided Mitterrand at home in his efforts to project the image of a president who was concerned about the plight of labor while supporting an idea that was intended to make the continent more competitive economically.

Following the presidential elections, however, Rocard and not Mitterrand was in the political limelight in France. Political observers had commented on this in the press and many wondered when the popular president would step onto center stage. The 1988 Bastille Day festivities provided him with an opportunity to joke about this matter. At his traditional garden party at the Elysée on July 14, he responded to questions regarding his low profile on the domestic scene by saying, "At this rate, I will have to run for a third term."[5] (He also used his traditional Bastille Day interview to appeal to Socialists and others on the left who were dissatisfied with the opening to the center, telling the nation that his role was to lead the forces of progress in a majority of the Left.[6]) At the outset of his second term he seemed satisfied not to play a major role in the day-to-day operation of the government, but to leave that to Rocard who appeared to be governing the nation in a manner different from that of previous prime ministers. Mitterrand now saw his own role, unlike during the 1981–86 period, as one in which he would set the general parameters of government policy and intervene only when necessary. On the question of nationalizations, for example, Mitterrand simply followed a *ni-ni* formula—neither nationalizations nor privatizations.[7] When Rocard wanted a lower wealth tax than that recommended by Finance Minister Bérégovoy and the prime minister eventually got his way, Mitterrand did not interfere. When Rocard removed his minister of health for speaking out of turn, the president also remained silent. The experience with cohabitation had shown Mitterrand how to remain above the political fray and still be effective. Early in his second term, however, there were several areas where Mitterrand did not abdicate his authority: foreign and defense policy as well as policy on control of the broadcasting media.

Although on the domestic front Mitterrand's profile was low, he kept a full schedule of appointments with international leaders and concerned himself with European and international issues. On Bastille Day, he took the opportunity to respond to Gorbachev's proposal for a European summit on conventional weapons, saying, "If we want to reduce tensions, we must balance the two sides." Yet Mitterrand, a cautious skeptic on Gorbachev's intentions for Europe, also said that any attempt to weaken the unity of the Atlantic Alliance was a "chimera." He then told the nation that Gorbachev would visit France later in the year.[8]

Bastille Day 1988 also held special significance for the French, because it marked the opening of a year-long celebration to commemorate the two-hundredth anniversary of the French Revolution of 1789. Unbeknownst to the world or to Mitterrand at the time, 1989, too, would mark a watershed in world history.

Then, from September 28–29, Mitterrand visited the United States. There he accepted an honorary doctorate from New York University, addressed the United Nations, and met with UN Secretary General Perez de Cuellar and President Reagan. When he met with the American president, Mitterrand agreed to Reagan's suggestion to host a future conference in Paris on eliminating chemical weapons. The two presidents discussed a range of East-West issues and regional conflicts. They also discussed the Conference on Security and Cooperation in Europe (CSCE), a thirty-five-nation group that was established in 1975 in Helsinki as a forum for confidence-building on security matters and human rights and includes all European states except Albania, plus the Soviet Union, the United States, and Canada.[9] (Mitterrand would later try to encourage the development of this organization after the fall of the Berlin Wall as a way to provide Europe with more autonomy in security matters.) While in Washington, he attended a ceremony at the Capitol launching American bicentennial celebrations for the French Revolution, and signed a resolution of both houses of Congress inviting Americans to celebrate the French Revolution. Commenting on the French bicentennial, Mitterrand noted the centuries of French-American cooperation, saying in a brief speech, "We were with you at the beginning of your history; you were with us to prevent the end of our history."[10] The bicentennial would be celebrated not only in France and the United States, but around the world.

The bicentennial celebration in France was of great symbolic importance to Mitterrand. One hundred years earlier, the 1889 centenary celebration had heralded the triumph of republicanism under the Third Republic. Mitterrand and his advisers envisioned the two hundredth anniversary as a celebration of human rights as embodied in the Declaration of Rights of Man and Citizen of 1789. Mitterrand knew that this was a noncontroversial way of celebrating a revolution that had both conservative and radical phases. Furthermore, this meant that the celebration in France would center on the year 1789, not 1793—the year of the Terror—or other controversial junctures of the Revolution. The president hoped the bicentennial would focus on what the French could agree on in their history. This, of course, permitted the extensive and lavish year-long celebration to be a consensus-building event that strengthened Mitterrand's opening to the Center at home and at the same time enhanced the nation's prestige abroad.[11]

The bicentennial committee charged with the responsibility of planning events for the celebration encountered some initial setbacks. Mitterrand's first two choices to head the committee, Michel Barion, head of the popular FNAC bookstore chain, and Edgar Faure, an old friend and veteran liberal politician, both died in quick succession. Mitterrand then appointed Jean-Noël Jeanneney to the position. Jeanneney was trained as a historian and had at one time headed Radio France. His father was a well-known Gaullist who had served as the general's minister of industry and minister of social affairs, a fact not lost on Mitterrand's Gaullist opposition and the Center-Right. The president was intent on using the bicentennial celebration to build a broad consensus on the past and the present.

Besides the planning for the upcoming bicentennial celebration, the fall of 1988 was taken up mainly with budget matters, regional council elections, and the opening of a new Assembly session. The 1988 budget proposal by Rocard, projecting a 2.6 percent growth rate and a 2.2 percent inflation rate, gave further indications that he wanted to pursue both austerity and solidarity, a policy that workers in the public sector would soon challenge as unfair and contradictory. On October 2, voters went to the polls to vote in regional council elections. The results pleased Mitterrand. The Socialists won 37.4 percent of the vote, giving leftist majorities control of one-third of all departments at the local level. What worried him and other observers was the high abstention rate, 47 percent. Political observers expressed concern that abstainers were becoming the largest party in France.

The day after the regional council elections, the Assembly opened its fall session with four main items on the agenda: the referendum on New Caledonia, a minimum-income bill financed by a wealth tax, the wealth tax itself, and a bill to establish a High Council for Audiovisual Affairs. Regarding the tax on wealth, the Socialists had had such a tax during the 1981–86 period, but the Chirac government had scrapped it. Now that the Socialists were back in power, albeit in a minority government, Mitterrand and his confreres wanted to restore the tax, in part to appease leftist voters; Rocard, however, advocated a relatively low tax to maintain the opening to the center. To strengthen its appeal as a government that was concerned about the less fortunate, if not at home then at least abroad, Bérégovoy announced that the government intended to increase aid to developing countries from 0.51 percent of the GNP in 1987 to 0.54 percent in 1989, with the goal of 0.7 percent as soon as possible. The bill to create a High Council for Audiovisual Affairs was a pet project of the president to ensure that the Right did not dominate the media.

October 1988 was also a month in which Mitterrand focused on international issues. From October 10–12, Soviet Foreign Minister Eduard Shevardnadze and a twenty-member delegation visited Paris. Mitterrand agreed to a Soviet proposal that three human-rights conferences would be held in Moscow in the near future, while the Soviets consented to the opening of a French cultural center in Moscow. It was also agreed that Mitterrand would visit the USSR on November 25 for the launching of Soyuz-TM-7, a Soviet spacecraft that was scheduled to carry a French astronaut into space, and that Gorbachev would visit France early in 1989.

October also found Mitterrand in discussions with leaders from the Middle East. From October 17 to 21, the Israeli president Chaim Herzog visited France, the first time that an Israeli head of state had come to France since the founding of the country in 1948. Mitterrand and the Israeli leader disagreed on how to begin the peace process in the Middle East, with the French president advocating an international peace conference. In late October, Mitterrand traveled to Ismailia, Egypt, for talks with Hosni Mubarak on the Palestinian question. Both leaders agreed on the necessity of convening an international peace conference on the Middle East. Mubarak supported

Mitterrand's suggestion of permitting the five permanent members of the UN Security Council to take charge of organizing such a conference.[12]

Shortly after the meetings with Israeli and Egyptian leaders, the French government had to react to new developments in the Middle East, namely the PLO's declaration that it was establishing an independent state of Palestine. Foreign Affairs Minister Dumas told the National Assembly that "French recognition of a Palestinian state poses no difficulties in principle . . . but it is contrary to French jurisprudence to recognize a state that does not have a defined territory." Dumas, reflecting Mitterrand's view, told the National Assembly that France would continue to work for an international conference on the troubled area.[13]

As this development unfolded in the Middle East, on November 6 the French went to the polls to vote in the referendum on New Caledonia. Prior to the referendum both the government and the UDF called for a "yes" vote, the RPR for abstaining, and the FN for a "no" vote. Although the referendum passed, the abstention rate, like voter turnout in other recent elections, was high, a record 62.96 percent.[14] This high abstention rate was attributed not only to the numerous trips that French voters had made recently to the voting booth but also to growing voter apathy due, in part, to the blurring of distinctions among the major parties as they adopted centrist positions in the new centrist republic.

The specific plan for New Caledonia that voters approved on November 6 meant that effective July 14, 1989, the territory would be divided into three provinces, each with an elected assembly with a six-year term, a legislative body, and executive power entrusted to a high commissioner appointed by the state. This plan would operate for a ten-year period and then a referendum on self-determination would be scheduled. Mitterrand and Rocard hoped that this solution would solve one of the thorniest problems that the Socialists had faced since coming to power in 1981, a problem that had the potential to divide France, to lead to more violence, and to be extremely difficult to manage because of the vast distance between Paris and New Caledonia.

Another region of the world of considerable interest to Mitterrand at this time was the United States. While Mitterrand was able to find common ground with Reagan—namely their distrust of the Soviet Union—and build an unexpectedly good working relationship on security matters, the election of George Bush meant that the French president would have to now confront a more liberal-minded Republican in the White House. Following Bush's election, Mitterrand sent a congratulatory message.

European affairs was the featured topic of the fifty-second French-German summit held in Bonn in early November. At the meeting, Chancellor Kohl, with whom Mitterrand had built a solid working relationship as they moved forward with European integration, briefed the French president on his recent visit to the Kremlin. Regarding French-German relations, both leaders agreed that their parliaments would be asked to ratify a plan for a joint defense council as well as a joint economic and finance council. The two leaders also discussed strengthening the European monetary system, cooperation in weapons construction, planning for the December European Council meeting in Greece, and objectives for the EEC in 1989. Another topic at the summit was broadcasting. They discussed the possibility of creating a future French-German television station featuring cultural programming. Mitterrand favored a French-German High Cultural Council composed of ten members from each of the two countries to oversee programming.[15] The French president had long been concerned about the quantity and the influence of American television programming in France and in Europe; he thought that the EC could utilize the media to build a European perspective as the Continent moved toward 1992. At this point, it looked as if Kohl, a man whom Mitterrand and others tended to underestimate, was in general agreement with the French president on European construction. Later, with the fall of the Berlin Wall, Mitterrand would question Kohl's commitment to a strong and secure Europe.

The idea of a more united Europe was celebrated in Paris on November 9 when a number of European leaders, including the presidents of West Germany, Greece, Portugal, and Cyprus, as well as six European heads of government, gathered in Paris to honor Jean Monnet on the hundredth anniversary of his birth. As Mitterrand had announced earlier, Monnet's ashes were transferred to the Pantheon. On this occasion, speakers praised Monnet for laying the foundations for the construction of Europe and stressed the need for greater economic, political, social, and cultural unity.[16] Monnet symbolized Mitterrand's vision of an integrated EEC and a stronger France in a reinvigorated Europe. Like the other symbols that Mitterrand had utilized during his presidency—such as visiting the Pantheon on the day of his inauguration, playing upon the image of de Gaulle and the Gaullist republic, manipulating images of a modernized France in a more competitive EEC, and constructing a number of huge architectural monuments in the capital—this was an important one that he hoped would underscore for the public his commitment to Europe.

The months of November and December 1988 brought good and bad news on the domestic scene. In early November, the government statistics office announced that the economy was stronger than expected. For example, in 1988, 150,000 jobs were created, the largest number since 1977; inflation would remain under 3 percent for the year; and the GNP had grown at a rate of 3.5 percent. Economic data later revealed that even the public sector was making a comeback, showing a $5 billion profit, against $3 billion losses earlier in the decade. The massive restructuring of industry under the Socialists was finally paying off. This improved economic situation was due, in part, to the fact that the Socialists had handed over a low-inflation economy to the conservatives in 1986, and Chirac in turn had removed credit and exchange controls, thereby spurring private investment (as, too, did Chirac's privatization plan). Even Usinor and Sacilor, the giant steel companies, showed a profit in 1988 of $750 million, while Renault's profits in 1988 reached $1.4 billion. At the time, GATT data showed France the world's fourth largest exporter in 1988, with a 5.9 percent share of the global market ($168 billion).[17]

Prosperity, however, whetted the appetite of labor for a more equitable distribution of France's new riches. Late in 1988, workers began seriously to challenge Rocard's policy of austerity and solidarity by demanding wage increases. Workers in the public sector mounted a strike that forced Rocard to react. When transport workers struck and crippled the capital, Rocard called out the army to help commuters get to work on time. The prime minister's position was that his government would negotiate with strikers on a case-by-case basis, but that pay raises should not jeopardize the newfound prosperity in France. In this regard, he proposed a series of catch-up pay raises, one immediately, and another in the following spring. This approach represented union-busting, Rocard style. While the prime minister was able to settle strikes in many sectors, others continued to strike, due partially to the pressure exerted on the GGT by the Communist party which criticized the government's austerity policy in an expanding economy. This serious wave of strike activity was produced not just by rising expectations, but because since 1983 the government had largely neglected the social consequences of its policies.[18] Eventually, Rocard negotiated what his government considered to be a noninflationary salary settlement.

In the midst of the strikes, Mitterrand met British Prime Minister Margaret Thatcher for a luncheon rendezvous at Mont-Saint-Michel. One development that concerned both Mitterrand and Thatcher was the attempt by Gorbachev to decouple Europe from NATO by appealing for what the Soviet leader called a "common European home." Mitterrand desired what he termed a "reconciled and independent Europe." He did not want to see Europe simply as a zone of influence shared by the United States and the USSR. What especially worried him were the neutralist tendencies in Europe, often encouraged by Gorbachev. Despite the progress on U.S.–Soviet disarmament talks, abandoning the security that NATO provided Europe would be premature and foolish.[19]

The Middle East was also on Mitterrand's mind as 1988 drew to a close. In mid-December, he praised the U.S. government's decision to enter into discussions with the PLO. From his perspective, this was a positive step since only a few weeks earlier Washington had decided not to grant a visa to PLO chief Yasser Arafat who planned to address the United Nations in New York, a decision that Mitterrand called "regrettable." When the U.S. government finally decided to talk with the PLO, this change in policy was received with general approval in France. Mitterrand himself commented on this turn of events by saying:

> I see the recent American decision as real progress in view of the courageous decision taken by PLO leader Yasser Arafat. . . . It is very important that the PLO has proclaimed a Palestinian state, has accepted U.N. resolutions 181, 242, and 338, has recognized Israel's right to exist, and has condemned terrorism. It has thus acquired the representative authority that some denied it but that France has recognized.[20]

Echoing the president's plan for peace in the Middle East, Foreign Minister Dumas once again called for a meeting of the five permanent members of the UN Security Council in order to prepare for an international conference on the region.[21] It seemed as if Washington was finally changing its attitude on how to achieve peace there. Now the task was to get movement in Israel. Mitterrand would later tell Prime Minister Yitzhak Shamir that Israel had to "take into account today's realities."[22]

On December 15–16, Mitterrand attended the fifteenth annual French-African summit held in Casablanca, Morocco, a meeting that brought together the leaders of thirty-seven nations. The African summit focused primarily on economic and financial issues and North-South relations. He called for solidarity between the two hemispheres, saying that "accumulating disparities and stagnation are the pernicious cause of an imbalance that, if it continues, will precipitate the world into unbounded disorder."[23] He also told the representatives in Casablanca that some French troops would be pulled out of Chad now that Libyan troops had been driven out.[24] He tried to assure African leaders that they would not be forgotten as Europe prepared the way for a single market. This summit, like other meetings with African leaders in the past, was important to Mitterrand because French influence in Africa helped France to maintain its rank on the world's stage, much like French involvement in the Middle East and in other Third World areas.

While Mitterrand received good press in francophone areas of the world at this time, at home the story was somewhat different. Before the year drew to a close, he found himself the object of ridicule in one of the leading newsweeklies. In late November, *Le Point* published an issue that portrayed him on the front cover as a reigning monarch, a Louis XIV. *Le Point* told its readers that "a monarchist spirit has invaded the second term," a reference to the president's aloofness and his seeming lack of involvement in the domestic issues of the time. In part, *Le Point* attributed Mitterrand's monarchist role to a vestige of cohabitation, a period where he had had to project the image of a president above the fray. The issue also contained a scathing interview with Thierry Pfister, a Socialist and a close adviser to former prime minister Mauroy. Earlier, Pfister had published a book critical of Mitterrand and his followers.[25] He now charged that the president's culture was leftist, but that his values were more republican than Socialist. Pfister mocked at what he saw as Mitterrand's desire to be immortalized: "'I am culture; I am art. I am the high monarch who frequents the artists of his time.' His two great construction projects— the pyramid at the Louvre and the arch at *La Défense*—say a great deal about his desire for immortality."[26] In the months ahead, the rising popularity of his prime minister would motivate Mitterrand not simply to visit the airports for flights out of France, but to become more engaged in the political life of the nation.

As the year ended, it was clear to many in France that 1988 stood in stark contrast to 1987, not just in terms of the domestic situation but also in terms of the international climate. Proof that the French economy had rebounded was seen in the creation of more jobs than those that had disappeared, coupled with the low inflation rate and strong economic growth. On the international scene, many of the regional conflicts ended in 1988, with the end of the eight-year Iran-Iraq war, the Soviet decision to leave Afghanistan, the cease-fire in Namibia, Cuba's decision to begin to remove troops from Angola, and the peace accord between Ethiopia and Somalia. More important for world peace, the United States and the Soviet Union made significant progress in controlling and reducing nuclear arms. On December 7, Gorbachev announced that his government would unilaterally reduce its military force by 10 percent. The new international climate was clearly reflected in the Olympic Games in Seoul where the United States, Soviet Union, China, and the two Germanies competed together for the first time in twelve years.[27]

While the world witnessed a deescalation of ideological struggles in 1988, French politics experienced a similar phenomenon. Eight years earlier when Mitterrand had first been elected, France was characterized by intense ideological polarization. Yet, by 1988, the situation had changed. For example, roughly 26 percent of the respondents in one poll now refused to classify themselves as either Left or Right. This development was related to the nation's experience with *alternance* and cohabitation, as well as with the rebirth of centrism in France, the decline of the PCF, and the growing positive attitude toward economic liberalism.[28]

The relaxation of the political struggle in France was also related to significant long-term sociological, economic, and demographic changes in France. One change which had influenced the nature of the political debate was the declining influence of the Church as the nation became more urban and more secular. A second important change was the deindustrialization of France, which tended to reduce social divisions as the service sector increased in size.[29] Closely linked to these two factors was a third change that affected political life, the changing demographics of the nation. For example, blue-collar workers now accounted for roughly 28 percent of the work force, compared to almost 39 percent in 1962, while farmers comprised slightly less than 6 percent, compared to 16 percent in 1962. Similarly, the number of artisans, merchants, and heads of businesses had declined to 8 percent from a level of 11 percent in 1962. On the other hand, the number of managers and those working in intermediate professions doubled, with white-collar workers now making up approximately 27 percent of the work force, a jump from a little more than 18 percent in 1962.[30] The increasingly skilled nature of the work force contributed to the formation of Mitterrand's new consensus politics and the emergence of a centrist republic.

The economy and other issues were the subject of Mitterrand's New Year's Eve message to the nation on the eve of 1989. Speaking from Strasbourg, the first time that he had presented his end-of-the-year wishes from the provinces, he focused on three main themes: the construction of Europe, the bicentennial, and the need to reduce excessive inequalities in France. He told the nation that he was delivering his address from Strasbourg for symbolic reasons. Strasbourg, he said, was the place where the Marseillaise was sung for the first time; it was the seat of the European Parliament and therefore the capital of Europe; and it was celebrating its two thousandth anniversary. In Strasbourg, said the president, one feels "at the same time French and European, European and French." As he reminded his audience, the nation had only four more years to prepare for the European single market, and only an integrated Europe could compete successfully with the United States and Japan. He also addressed the issue of the bicentennial, reminding French citizens that the first act of the summer of 1789 had been the proclamation of the rights of man and the sovereignty of the nation—"two principles that ever since have inspired all the battles for freedom and democracy." In France, he said, there was still much to do, such as defining a coherent and fair immigration policy and revising the restrictive law on the entry and residency of foreigners. While these first two themes helped Mitterrand to prepare the public for his desire to concentrate on European construction, and to utilize the bicentennial to emphasize human rights, the third theme, of reducing inequalities, permitted him to distance himself somewhat from Rocard's austerity and solidarity policy, especially as the nation witnessed growing strikes in the public sector. In closing, the president pointed out that 1988 had witnessed gains in global peace and disarmament and inspired hope that the future, notably 1989, would mark a new era.[31] No one truly realized what was in store for Europe and the world in the year ahead.

In January, an insider-trading scandal rocked France and its president. While a number of financial scandals had surfaced recently in the press, the most potentially damaging to Mitterrand was the Péchiney scandal. In November, the state-owned Péchiney concern bought Triangle, an American canning and packaging group, in a friendly takeover. Just before the takeover, several Frenchmen had purchased a large share of stock in Triangle, including Max Théret, who headed a French investment company and who had raised money for the Socialist party, and Roger-Patrice Pelat, a retired businessman. Both Théret and Pelat were old friends of Mitterrand, and Pelat was a member of the president's inner circle of friends; some even referred to Pelat as the "vice president."[32] The two first met in a German prisoner-of-war camp, and during Mitterrand's presidency, they were often seen strolling the streets of Paris together. According to one report, Pelat may have made as much as $365,000 in this stock market transaction.[33] Also indicted in the scandal was Alain Boubil, chief of staff for Finance Minister Bérégovoy, who between 1982 and 1988 had served as Mitterrand's adviser on industrial policy.

Realizing the potential damage that this scandal threatened for his presidency, Mitterrand took the offensive at the January 31 meeting of the Council of Ministers. Angry about the recent wave of scandals, especially Péchiney, and the way in which he believed the opposition was exploiting the situation, he let the ministers know that his counterattack would be to engage in battle on his own terrain—the political terrain. To do this, Mitterrand agreed to appear on television on February 12 for a two-hour interview/discussion. Before a national audience, Mitterrand tried to distance himself from the scandal, one that tainted him and brought into question the ability of the Socialists to manage state-run companies on the eve of important municipal elections scheduled for March.

In front of the television cameras, Mitterrand used an appeal to class and nationalism to counter the Péchiney scandal. Spending fifty minutes out of two hours on the scandal, he told his television audience that justice would be done, condemning those who seek "unearned easy money" from stock market activities. Denouncing the excesses of the free-market economy, what he termed "the gangsterism of the strongest" and "roving, predatory money," he announced that he would take action "to put in place a system that will prevent the ruin of the French economy and prevent it from being pillaged, particularly in the Europe of 1993." He also recognized the validity of many workers' demands, as if to distinguish himself from Rocard's earlier union-bashing. Regarding the upcoming municipal elections, Mitterrand expressed his hope for a union of popular forces and that the PS would not simply make a governing pact with the Center and reject all other political alliances.[34]

This timely appearance by a president who promised to guard France against greed and corruption and who seemed sympathetic to workers' demands for higher wages helped to prevent a further erosion in the public's confidence in himself and his party. But the televised counterattack did not help Mitterrand's old friend Pelat, who later died of a heart attack in the American Hospital in Neuilly.

When French voters went to the polls to vote in the municipal elections on March 12 and 19, Mitterrand had an opportunity to evaluate the success of his second term. The Socialist party and left coalitions won 27 cities and towns that they had lost to the Right in 1983. This meant that the PS now controlled 133 cities with populations over 20,000, more than any other party. The ecologists, too, made gains, especially in Alsace. The Greens' advances prompted Defense Minister Chevènement to say, "The young [today] are green just as CERES members were red in their day."[35] Organized as a political party in 1974 and representing a rising force in France (winning 10.9 percent of the vote in the 1989 European Parliament elections) and in Europe in general, they could not be overlooked. Mitterrand and Rocard had tried to woo the Greens earlier by naming Brice Lalonde, the Green presidential candidate in the 1981 presidential elections, as secretary of state for the environment. Toxic spills along the Rhine and in the North Sea had raised consciousness in France concerning environmental issues. With the Greens now capable of winning 10 percent in national elections, Mitterrand let it be known that he wanted to place environmental issues high on his agenda. Environmental concerns were now a new issue in French political life.

While the Greens gained in the municipal elections, the PCF continued its downward spiral. Chirac, however, won a landslide victory in Paris, and his former trade minister, Michel Noir, won handily in Lyon. Nevertheless, for the conservatives, the elections were a serious setback, which they blamed on their disunity. Both

Giscard and Chirac called for a joint center-right and Gaullist ticket for the June European elections. However, Méhaignerie, leader of the new center formation in the National Assembly, rejected this idea.

On the one hand, these election results and the further disunity on the right pleased Mitterrand, but on the other hand, the results worried him. While he was generally satisfied with the outcome, the elections underscored the increasing strength of Rocardism and Rocard's own popularity. The prime minister interpreted these elections as reinforcing his government. However, austerity and national unity, not to mention Rocard's brand of administrative socialism which stressed the reconciliation of economic reality with social need, were not Mitterrand's ideal. While the president did desire unity in order to enlarge his political consensus, he also realized that a Socialist government had a responsibility to promote social justice. Rocard's neoliberalism was not Mitterrand's vision for France in the 1990s. Mitterrand was also surprised to find Rocard's popularity growing with time, somewhat unusual for a prime minister. After the first year of Mitterrand's second term, Rocard had an approval rating of more than 60 percent, the same as that of the president,[36] and after fourteen months as prime minister, 62 percent of the public expressed confidence in Rocard, while at the same point in earlier premierships only 48 percent had expressed confidence in Mauroy, 45 percent in Fabius, and 44 percent in Chirac.[37]

Several factors explained the "Rocard phenomenon." Part of the prime minister's popularity was undoubtedly linked to the new-found prosperity and the divisions on the right. Rocard was also helped by his ability to find a solution for the crisis over New Caledonia, his efforts to conclude a settlement with striking public-sector workers and at the same time preserve his anti-inflationary policy, and his skill at piloting his way through the wave of scandals in late 1988 and 1989. In addition, Rocard's popularity was due to his "method": his emphasis on what he described as "work instead of talk," his willingness to explain issues in detail and to take small steps to reach his objectives, his promise to speak the truth, and his focus on the needs of the citizenry and on consensus. He is also a politician who believes, as he himself has said, that "compromise is a necessity and a principle of action." This method helped him to project an image of a prime minister who seemed to shun the national limelight and who was a realist.[38]

Regardless of the reasons for his amazing popularity levels,

Mitterrand felt placed in the shadows and thereby endangered. After the municipal elections, Mitterrand gave serious thought to how to foster a more progressive social and economic policy and how to get rid of Rocard. He even went so far as to tell Rocard on one occasion, "Mr. Prime Minister, during my entire political life, I have first and foremost watched for one thing: not to be boxed in. You should know that even while I am doing that, I open wide doors and windows."[39] In many ways, Rocard had become the new "foreign prince" in the Socialist party, an "outsider" as Mitterrand was with respect to the PS in the early 1970s but who helped to generate support for the party.

In order to move the Socialists beyond Rocardism, Mitterrand encouraged Rocard's Socialist rivals to criticize the prime minister's approach to government and his policies. He also encouraged his favorite dauphin, Fabius, to head the Socialist slate in the upcoming European Parliament elections. Although Fabius was initially hesitant, knowing full well that if his list did poorly it would set back his presidential ambitions, Mitterrand convinced him to take up the Socialist banner. Late in March, Mitterrand invited Fabius and his wife for dinner. He told his trusted protégé that the party had "to take maximum advantage of the disunity on the right." Then, he reportedly told Fabius, "The [results] of the municipal elections are good. . . . For better or worse, it is Rocard alone who, for the moment, is increasing in standing . . . if you head the European list, the ball can change courts."[40] Coming from the president, this convinced Fabius that he had to lead the European slate for the Socialists. His participation in the elections would win favor from the president, help to ensure Mitterrand's backing if he himself ran for the presidency, and test the political waters for a future presidential bid. After agreeing to run, Fabius and his camp said that a respectable score in the European elections would be around 25 percent, while Jospin, another aspiring dauphin, put the figure at 30 percent (Jospin himself had headed the PS list in 1984 in the midst of the *école libre* controversy and had won slightly less than 21 percent of the vote). Elysée officials more or less split the difference and claimed that 27 percent would be a healthy score.[41]

Besides convincing Fabius to head the PS list in the European elections, in March Mitterrand also hosted several foreign visitors, Mubarak of Egypt, Syria's Foreign Minister Al-Charek, and the president of Bangladesh, General Hussain Ershad. While talks with Mubarak focused on the prospects for peace in the Middle East, talks with Syria centered on ways to improve the relationship between the two countries and find a solution to problems in the Middle East, with France preferring prompt presidential elections in Lebanon and Syria demanding that political reforms be enacted simultaneously with elections. The inability to find a suitable peace process for the Middle East and continued conflict in the region continued to concern Mitterrand.

The resumption of intense fighting between Christian and Muslim forces in Lebanon prompted public outrage in France and forced Mitterrand to take action. As the fighting in Beirut intensified, six hundred French celebrities and political personalities attempted to call public attention to the blood-letting by requesting citizenship in the war-torn nation at the Lebanese embassy in Paris. In an April 2 front-page editorial in Le Monde, the opposition leader Léotard charged that Christians in Beirut were being killed while the French government followed a policy of appeasement.[42] Mitterrand and German Chancellor Kohl discussed the situation at their April 4 meeting in Guenzberg and made appeals to both Bush and Gorbachev to help end the fighting. In an effort to respond to the situation and give the impression at home that the government would not sit idly by as the slaughter continued, Foreign Minister Dumas demanded the withdrawal of non-Lebanese troops from Lebanon and then announced to the National Assembly and the nation that two French ships would be sent to the area to deliver food and medical supplies. Mitterrand also sent a special envoy, Bernard Kouchner, founder of an organization known as Doctors without Borders (MSF—Médecins sans Frontières) and secretary of state for humanitarian action in the Rocard government, to assist in the landing of humanitarian aid and the evacuation of the gravely wounded. Initially, Muslim forces criticized this French effort. When the UN Security Council decided to ask Secretary General Pérez de Cuellar to work with the Arab League to seek some solution to the fighting, Mitterand applauded the decision. He had lobbied the international community over the past several weeks for such a response.

Although tensions seemed to be relaxing between East and West, the Middle East and French policy there produced deep anxiety in some quarters in France. In this regard, protest erupted in the capital over a planned two-day visit by Yasser Arafat on May 2–3. Foreign Minister Dumas had earlier called the meeting with Arafat "a new step toward peace in the Middle East." He also said that the government would confirm the PLO's desire for both moderation and realism, as well as "the will for mutual recognition and peace" with Israel. Despite Dumas' positive view of the visit, Arafat's scheduled arrival in France created a storm of controversy among the nation's six to seven hundred thousand Jews, the largest Jewish population in Europe outside the Soviet Union. Contributing to the protest was a major public-relations gaffe on the part of government officials. Arafat's visit coincided with the day on which Israel and other Jewish communities commemorate the Holocaust, known in France by its Hebrew name, *Shoah*. Prominent French Jews sympathetic to Mitterrand's peace efforts in the Middle East made an appeal for calm. Pierre Mendès-France's widow went so far as to say, "It is a good thing that President Mitterrand hears what Yasser Arafat has to tell him." She reminded French Jews that her husband had stressed that one had to negotiate with one's enemy to seek peace. Simone Veil, a former minister of health and former president of the European Parliament who had been an inmate in Nazi prisoner-of-war camps and whose relatives died in concentration camps, said that she hoped the meeting between Mitterrand and Arafat would encourage the PLO to seek a peaceful solution in the region. Mitterrand himself tried to minimize the criticism by issuing a statement pledging, "Beyond the present circumstances, France will not forget the victims of the *Shoah* nor those of blind terrorism." He stressed that French foreign policy "is founded on the necessity of hearing all protagonists. To listen is not to agree, but to widen the field of information." The more than 3 million Arabs living in France remained relatively silent on Arafat's visit.[43]

When Mitterrand finally met with Arafat in early May for a ninety-minute conversation, the Palestinian leader distanced himself from terrorism and voiced support for Mitterrand's peace proposal for the Middle East. In referring to the Palestinian Charter, a twenty-five-year-old document that many associated with terrorism, Arafat said that it was *caduque*, a French word meaning "out of date" or "null and void." The PLO leader's willingness to participate in an international peace conference on the Middle East also gratified Mitterrand because this was a plan that the French head of state had long advocated and lobbied for on numerous occasions with world leaders.[44]

In May, as if to remove himself from the shadows of the Rocard government, Mitterrand began a diplomatic marathon. For instance, in late May he traveled to a summit in Ottawa, visited President George Bush in Maine (and received an honorary doctorate from Boston University[45]), attended a francophone summit in Dakar, and participated in a NATO summit in Brussels. The following month he traveled to Tunisia and Poland for official visits, and attended a meeting of the European Community in Madrid. These numerous voyages would be followed in July by plans to host Gorbachev in Paris, followed by the summit of the industrialized nations of the Western world and the simultaneous hosting of the bicentennial. This flurry of diplomatic activity held a number of advantages for Mitterrand. It gave him more visibility at home as France continued its flirtation with Rocardism. One French newsweekly at the time even noted that Mitterrand's international activity suggested that *"Tonton* [meaning "uncle" and referring to the president] was at the wheel."[46] This heightened level of activity also readied the PS for the upcoming European elections, Mitterrand's turn to assume the rotating presidency of the EC, the grand celebration of the bicentennial in July, and the Paris summit. One of Mitterrand's advisers said that the president felt compelled to increase his diplomatic activity because Gorbachev was so active on the international scene. This same adviser claimed that 1989 would be an exceptional year for diplomatic activity;[47] it would also prove to be an exceptional year for change in Eastern Europe.

Prior to the mid-June European Parliament elections, massive demonstrations for political democracy in China, followed by government repression, captured the attention of the world. When Chinese authorities unleashed the military on students in Tiananmen Square on June 4, Mitterrand, unlike Bush, responded quickly and firmly. He froze diplomatic activity and military relations with China and promised to extend visas for Chinese students. He also issued a strong statement of condemnation that declared, "A regime which, to survive, is reduced to shooting at young people, whom it has trained and who are rising up against it in the name of freedom, has no future."[48] Mitterrand called on China's leaders to engage in dialogue to solve their problems. Later when the Chinese government executed a number of young demonstrators for what it called "antirevolutionary crimes" Mitterrand spoke out again and pledged to be "the spokesman for all the anger and reprobation felt by the French people."[49] At a ceremony at Versailles honoring the two hundredth anniversary of the National Assembly, Mitterrand noted that the principles of the French Revolution were alive and well in a number of diverse countries, such as China, Poland, and the Soviet Union. He then declared, "Wherever people fight for freedom and justice, wherever hope survives, the message of the Revolution can be heard."[50] In the National Assembly, Foreign Minister Dumas, too, condemned the executions in China with strong language, telling the deputies that "the totalitarian machine is once again on the march, turning decisions of justice into the arbitrary decrees of assassination." The desire for liberty and democracy, said Dumas, cannot be stifled.[51] While the government crushed the democratic reform movement in China, the incredible courage of Chinese youth would later help inspire demands for change in Eastern Europe and the Soviet Union.

At this point, too, another significant event occurred, namely the death of Iran's Ayatollah Khomeini. Prior to the 1988 legislative elections, Mitterrand had fulfilled a commitment by the Chirac government and restored diplomatic relations with Iran after three French hostages had been released in May of the same year. In a press conference, Dumas asserted that "the death of Ayatollah Khomeini, who for ten years has embodied the Iranian Revolution, is a great event" and that he hoped that "Iran will find within itself, in peace and in the respect of rights, the means to take its due place in the international community."[52] Not long after Khomeini's death, representatives from the Foreign Ministry tried to begin discussions with Iran over financial disagreements. For France, the end of the Khomeini regime and the emergence of more moderate elements in Iran, not to mention the end of the Iran-Iraq war, represented a unique opportunity to change the tone and the direction of relations with a Middle East state that had often been linked in the 1980s to terrorism, and with the Arab world in general.

This new situation in the Middle East encouraged the French government to try to reassert its influence in the region. Months later, for instance, Mitterrand agreed to release three Libyan planes held in France and end sanctions against Qaddafi's government in order to obtain the release of the last French hostages. While Mitterrand and government officials tended to view this development as part of a larger policy to enhance the nation's influence in the Middle East, others, especially those abroad, viewed it as simply acquiescing to terrorist demands. What irked some observers was that Foreign Minister Dumas publicly thanked Colonel Qaddafi for helping with the release of the hostages, calling it a "noble and humanitarian gesture."[53] Despite the criticism, the government had shown that it could obtain the release of hostages, unlike the United States which approached the hostage problem in highly moralistic terms and not as an opportunity to establish a new relationship with the Arab world and to reassert its influence in the troubled region. Mitterrand knew that changes in the Middle East offered his government new opportunities.

Amid the repression of China and the change of leadership in Iran, French and European voters went to the polls on June 18 and voted in the European Parliament elections. Europeans would elect 518 representatives, with French voters sending 81 representatives to Strasbourg. In France, fifteen political groups competed in the elections. While abstentions ran high once again, at 51.1 percent, the elections produced several surprises. Fabius's PS list received a rather dismal 23.51 percent of the vote (twenty-two seats), as the UDF-RPR list headed by Giscard captured the largest number of votes, 28.87 percent (twenty-six seats). This performance elated Giscard, and to a lesser extent Chirac. Both were worried about youthful renovators within their parties, such as Michel Noir, Philippe de Villiers, Charles Millon, Bernard Bosson, Dominique Baudis, and others who had challenged the leadership of the old guard following the disappointing performance of Chirac in the presidential contest and the hung verdict in the legislative elections. The renovators had even threatened to run their own list in the European elections but eventually backed down. Nevertheless, centrists entered their own list, headed by Veil, and splintered the Right. While Veil's list received 8.42 percent of the vote, the ecologists captured 10.59 percent. The PCF slate won a mere 7.71 percent and the FN garnered 11.73 percent of the vote, giving this extremist party a third-place finish in the European Parliament elections. The mediocre results of the PS forced the Socialists to ponder their election strategy—should the party move more toward the left or should it try to enhance the opening to the center? Many socialists hoped that this question would be one of the central issues debated at the PS congress in Rennes in the following year in order to mobilize the party's supporters.

July 1989 proved to be one of the most important months for the Mitterrand presidency in terms of heightening the nation's image abroad and strengthening the political consensus at home. At the Madrid summit of EC leaders on July 1, Mitterrand assumed the presidency of the European Community.[54] Moreover, in Madrid, European leaders agreed on a process to facilitate an economic and monetary union. With the EC presidency now in Mitterrand's hands, the French leader would strongly urge his colleagues to move toward unity, one of his key goals for his second term, and to adopt a Social

Charter at their meeting later in December in Strasbourg. During his six-month presidency, Mitterrand would actively take steps to further the integration of Europe in anticipation of 1992.

A second factor that allowed Mitterrand to enhance his image abroad and at home in July was a visit by Gorbachev, who had become a fashionable guest as his popularity grew in the West (in France at the time, two out of three people had a positive view of him).[55] During the first week of July, Gorbachev carried his diplomatic offensive to Paris for ten hours of talks with Mitterrand and French officials. Aware of the importance that the French attached to the bicentennial, he attempted to link French and Russian history, especially the events of 1789 and 1917. Among other activities, he and his wife, Raisa, visited the Bastille and attended a state dinner at the Elysée where he declared, "The spirit of the French Revolution has always been present in the . . . life of our country."[56] During his stay, Gorbachev requested and obtained a meeting at the Sorbonne with French students and intellectuals, a meeting to counter, in part, the criticism by many French intellectuals of the Soviet Union in the aftermath of Solzhenitsyn's earlier revelations. Besides signing a total of twenty-two agreements for economic, scientific, and cultural cooperation, Mitterrand and Gorbachev called for an immediate cease-fire in Lebanon. In a joint press conference, Mitterrand declared that the visit had established an "outline for good and solid cooperation."[57] Gorbachev concluded his visit to France by addressing the European Council in Strasbourg, where he spoke of a "common European home," a theme that he had used earlier and one that he mentioned several times during his visit in order to encourage France and other European nations to distance themselves from the United States and NATO. This meeting with Gorbachev drew considerable international attention because it came just prior to the summit of the Western nations in Paris and the two hundredth anniversary of the French Revolution.

The third factor that permitted the French president to strengthen his nation's prestige abroad and his own image at home was the grand bicentennial celebration, a key symbol employed by Mitterrand in his second term, which also included a summit with Western leaders. The bicentennial functioned to underscore the country's role as an important although medium-size actor on the international scene, as well as to strengthen the political consensus in France. While many of the summers of Mitterrand's presidency had been hot ones due to various crises that had confronted the government, fortunately the summer of 1989 was relatively free of domestic crises and allowed a festive nation to focus on its bicentennial celebration.

The bicentennial was not just a French but a worldwide extravaganza. In France 7,500 events or exhibitions were planned for the bicentennial; abroad it was celebrated in 115 countries with a total of three thousand events or exhibitions.[58] The celebration cost the French government approximately 432 million francs,[59] but it produced record revenues for the tourist industry in France by attracting hundreds of thousand of visitors. Profits from tourism for 1989 were estimated at more than $5 billion. The festivities also provided Mitterrand with an opportunity to stress the unity of the nation, his key campaign theme in the 1988 presidential election.[60]

The 1989 celebration had not been planned without political opposition. The original celebration for the two hundredth anniversary of the Revolution, "Expo '89," which was discussed at the beginning of Mitterrand's first term, became the subject of a serious disagreement between the president and the mayor of Paris when Chirac realized the tremendous symbolic value of sponsoring such a festivity. Expo '89 entailed combining a world's fair for Paris with a celebration of the Revolution. Chirac proceeded to place obstacles in front of Mitterrand's plans to celebrate 1789 in such a fashion. Consequently, on July 5, 1983 the president announced that the event would not take place because the mayor of Paris would not cooperate.[61] Chirac won this particular battle over political symbols, at least for the moment.

With Expo '89 canceled, Mitterrand decided to link his *grand projet* construction scheme with the bicentennial celebration.[62] The new architectural monuments for Paris became an integral part of the two hundredth anniversary celebration. France has long prided itself on being the center of art and culture, an image that Mitterrand attempted to reinforce by sponsoring a number of *grands projets* for Paris in order to rekindle images of French greatness and movement toward the future. In his first press conference in September of 1981 and then again in March of 1982 the president announced a number of large construction projects for the capital. The projects included, as mentioned earlier, the completion of the Musée d'Orsay (begun under the presidency of Valéry Giscard d'Estaing), an Institut du Monde Arabe, a center for science and industry as well as a center for music in the northeastern sector of Paris at La Villette, enlarging the Louvre by recasting the Cour Napoléon and moving the Ministry of Finance to the quai de Bercy, erecting a grand Arche de la Défense, and building a new opera house at the place de la Bastille. The original estimated cost of these architectural projects was 15.7 billion francs;[63] yet the final cost would well exceed this figure. No other French president had even undertaken such an ambitious building program. Mitterrand revealed with these massive projects that he was a true *batisseur* (builder).

Why did he decide to mark his presidency with the *grands projets*? One reason is that they have tremendous symbolic value, reviving notions of French glory and greatness and bestowing political benefits on the president and his party. In the fall of 1981, Mitterrand told his Council of Ministers that he "could not have a great policy for France without great architecture."[64] Minister of Culture Lang wrote in *L'Architecture d'aujourd'hui* that "architecture is not the expression of a society, as is often said, but of those who lead it. . . ."[65] According to one French authority on Mitterrand's *grands projets*, the president consistently supported the undertaking and completion of the building program, even though his government had adopted an austerity program in 1982 and 1983. Furthermore, he insisted on an early completion for many of the projects,[66] obviously in an effort to inaugurate various sites according to a political timetable. The opera at the Bastille, for instance, was inaugurated before it was completely finished, that is, during the 1989 Bastille Day festivities and in the presence of the heads of state from the seven major industrialized nations of the Western world who were in Paris for their fifteenth economic summit. This inauguration was followed by a gala dinner at another *grand projet*, the Musée d'Orsay. Mitterrand used the unfinished Arche de la Défense—also inaugurated before its completion—as well as the new section of the Louvre for his meetings with the leaders of the Western world. The new arch even became the official symbol of the economic summit, known as the "Summit of the Arch." Of course, Mitterrand was not the first French president to use public architecture as a means of projecting political power and prestige. De Gaulle had had plans for Les Halles and Pompidou for Beaubourg. Nevertheless, Mitterrand's *grands projets* were unprecedented in their number and represent an unparalleled effort to change the architectural image of the capital. Opposition leader Raymond Barre even said on one occasion that the scale of the undertaking revealed a certain "Louis XIV complex."[67] The president, however, ignored his critics, and architecture become his second *domaine réservé*.[68]

Besides conforming to French notions of greatness and reaping the obvious political benefits from such an undertaking, there were several other reasons why Mitterrand launched these projects. The president is a man of culture and wants to leave a visible legacy of his term in office. What could be more visible than huge edifices adorning Paris? Moreover, after the Socialists' economic program stalled in Year I, a massive building program for the capital could be seen as something tangible left by the Socialist president and his party. While some criticism surfaced concerning the projects, notably over the pyramid at the entrance to the Louvre, generally they have been popular with the public. By promoting French culture with these new edifices, not to mention consistently devoting 1 percent of the national budget to the Ministry of Culture since coming to power in 1981, Mitterrand has won votes. Mitterrand also realized that expenditure for culture aids the promotion of tourism and increases revenues. In defending the cost of the building program, the Socialists argued that it would also raise the level of cultural awareness, and that the construction alone would employ roughly ten thousand people for five years.[69] The *grands projets* are important symbols for Mitterrand because they project the achievements of France in art and culture under a Socialist president.

The *grands projets* not only suggest a cultural and architectural rebirth in Mitterrand's France, but also underscore French advances in technology. Many of the projects use state-of-the-art technology, such as I. M. Pei's huge glass pyramid above the striking underground addition to the Louvre. (Technology will also be featured at the $400 million computerized national library that Mitterrand plans to construct in run-down eastern Paris.) To some, the *grands projets* represent an extension of French technological achievements following the Concorde supersonic aircraft, the Ariane rocket, and the TGV high-speed train. Not only do these projects help Mitterand to win support at home, but they also enhance France's reputation abroad. The government commission that coordinated the *grands projets*, for example, developed a traveling exhibition aimed at foreign audiences. Called *Grands Projets: Paris 1979–1989*, this exhibition was shown in Copenhagen, Seoul, Osaka, Tokyo, and New York before it returned to Paris in 1989. According to one expert in French art and architecture, "The *grands projets* . . . [were], of course, sent abroad to exemplify state policies, to promote French achievements, and to conjure up a vision of the Paris that they will soon engender."[70]

Moreover, the *grands projets* are atypical of public architecture in France and tend to reinforce the nation's futuristic aspirations as the twenty-first century nears. Not only do these architectural projects have a postmodern and high-tech aspect to them, but their atypical style, coupled with the fact that in half of the cases they were designed by foreign architects (including one Chinese-born American), suggest that France is opening itself to the the rest of the world. In France, public opinion was solidly behind Mitterrand's effort to construct a powerful and competitive EEC. Thus, the *grands projets* lend support to the Socialist president's political program for France at home and abroad. As one scholar notes, "The story of cultural policy and the politics surrounding it . . . [is] a microcosm of much of the Socialist experience."[71]

One of the amazing aspects of the bicentennial event was that Mitterrand and his staff found a means of celebrating the Revolution with relatively little dissent concerning their interpretation of 1789. When one celebrates the Revolution, does one celebrate the fall of the Bastille, the formation of the National Assembly, the proclamation of the republic, or the Declaration of Rights of Man and Citizen? How does the Terror, the Directory, or Napoleon fit into the celebration? What does one celebrate when one honors the Revolution?

To a significant degree, Mitterrand attempted to give the impression that "La Révolution est un bloc," a view expressed decades earlier by Georges Clemenceau. While on a state visit to Bulgaria prior to the bicentennial celebration, Mitterrand voiced Clemenceau's view of the Revolution. Moreover, several of Mitterrand's confreres—Règis Debray and Max Gallo, for example—urged the French to forget about the quarrels of the past and focus on the glories as France celebrated 1789. Not surprisingly, the Bicentennial Commission, the organization responsible for planning the 1989 festivities, published a catalog listing more than 130 official conferences to be held in 1989, but there was only one session on the Terror. The government desired to project the image of a united nation with a common heritage,[72] one that stressed the republican tradition of the Revolution and served the interests of the president.

This republican slant was seen in the great emphasis placed on human rights, as expressed to a large degree in the Declaration of Rights of Man and Citizen of 1789. In 1989, human rights became the most popular slogan in contemporary France. For the Left, it seemed that this phrase and the images associated with it had, to a degree, replaced socialism and communism as concepts symbolizing progress.[73] In an exclusive interview in *L'Express*, published on July 14, 1989 in five languages, Mitterrand reinforced his preferred republican interpretation of the Revolution by rejecting the idea that Robespierre and Napoleon should be included in the Pantheon: "Robespierre is a key figure in our history, and he has his own kind of greatness, but he was responsible for too many bloody events. Napoleon would not find a place in my personal Pantheon either, although for different reasons."[74] Moreover, on Bastille Day 1989 Mitterrand told reporters in his traditional television appearance that Carnot and Danton deserve a place in the Pantheon. The left-leaning newspaper *Libération* said that "this preference is not without political significance. Danton is a *montagnard*, a leftist [albeit a highly controversial figure for many on the left] but he struggled against the Terror. . . . Carnot [instrumental in raising an army to save France in 1792] contributed to the Thermidorian reaction that destroyed Robespierre and the Terror which tarnished his image." Mitterrand even remarked in this interview that the beheading of Louis XVI was a "tragic symbolic act," calling the king a "brave man" and noting that he would not have voted for the king's execution![75]

Mitterrand tried to project a republican image of the Revolution devoid of any real subversive dimension. Besides focusing on the year 1789 and human rights, the bicentennial celebration also stressed the slogan of the Revolution—liberty, equality, and fraternity. Yet equality in 1989 meant, if anything, political equality. Mitterrand's celebration also underscored the intellectual contributions of the nation's great philosophers, such as Rousseau, Voltaire, and Condorcet, as well as the impact of the Revolution abroad, as seen in the major exhibition at the Grand Palais called *"La Révolution Française et l'Europe."*[76] The republican image of the Revolution projected in 1989 reminded some of the image of the Revolution that emerged under the Third Republic, especially between 1889 and 1914.[77] In government circles in the France of 1989 there was a great nostalgia for the Third Republic, due in part to the president's desire to teach the nation a new republican alphabet reminiscent of a bygone era.

Mitterrand used the bicentennial in another interesting way. He scheduled the summit of the seven leading industrialized nations of the Western world to take place during the celebration, and also invited leaders from the world's poorest nations that included four presidents from Latin America, fifteen heads of state from Africa, and five leaders from Asia. This was a clear example of a president using domestic and international events to his advantage. By hosting the summit at this time, he was able to keep public attention focused on himself and his leadership of France as his nation celebrated its glorious history. This scheduling also suggested that Mitterrand was showing other Western leaders the power and glory of France and that the world leaders attending the summit were paying homage to the French Revolution and, of course, indirectly to the leadership of François Mitterrand.

Not only would Western leaders attending the economic summit view the morning Bastille Day parade down the Champs-Elysées, but they also sat by the president's side and watched a futuristic evening parade billed as a "grand opera-ballet" called *La Marseillaise*. The production was the work of advertising wiz Jean-Paul Goude, a former art director of the American magazine *Esquire* and creator of major television commercials in France, and featured six thousand participants representing various cultures from around the world. Capping the evening was a spectacular dual fireworks display at the Etoile and the place de la Concorde. The *Financial Times* of London called Mitterrand's show a "grandiose production," "extravagant," but a personal triumph for Mitterrand. This paper also said that "never had the participants of a summit been so completely dominated by its staging. President Mitterrand's show in honor of the bicentennial of the Revolution would have dazzled even King Louis XIV. . . ."[78]

In France, André Fontaine, director of *Le Monde*, called the Bastille Day celebration "the largest *fête* and the most successful that the capital has known for some time."[79] In assessing the political gains and losses as a result of the celebrations, *Le Monde* noted that it was Mitterrand's chief opponent, Chirac, who had lost the most; this paper told its readers: "The largest error in appreciation has perhaps been committed by M. Jacques Chirac, voluntarily absent from the most memorable July 14 celebrations seen since Liberation in the capital, of which he is the mayor."[80] For *Le Monde*, the national festivity was a double success for Mitterrand, producing a harmonious summit and silencing many of his critics.[81] When the president gave a reception at the Elysée to thank 350 people for planning and orchestrating the bicentennial and the summit, he told them that their work had "permitted France to be at the center of world attention."[82] The bicentennial had given Mitterrand an opportunity to use a powerful symbol in French history—the Revolution—to display and to strengthen the nation's republicanism and centrism and to underscore France's influential place in world affairs.

Energized by the success of bicentennial festivities, Mitterrand devoted himself in the fall to European Community affairs, international affairs in general, and an explosive domestic issue raised by three young schoolgirls of Arab descent. Shortly after the *rentrée*, Mitterrand, as president of the EC, met with several European leaders to discuss the continuation of the construction of Europe, especially the economic and monetary union, the Social Charter, audiovisual affairs, and environmental issues. At his third annual French-Spanish summit in Spain and at a meeting with Chancellor Kohl, he discussed details of European construction and the rising call for reform in Eastern Europe. Concerning this meeting, Hubert Védrine, an Elysée spokesman and a key presidential adviser on international relations, said that both the French president and the German chancellor attached "considerable importance" to changes in the East because they could modify the postwar balance of power in Europe.[83] The same day that Mitterrand met with Kohl, he addressed the European Parliament in Strasbourg and stressed that the EC should reach a decision by year's end in five major areas: economic and monetary union, social policies, broadcasting policies, environmental policies, and the Lomé IV agreement (negotiations for a cooperative agreement among the EEC and sixty-six nations in Africa, the Pacific and Caribbean). He also proposed a December meeting between the EEC and twenty-two Arab states to further the dialogue with leaders from the Middle East.[84] He told European leaders that the reform movement in the East had great historical significance: "The most important event in Europe, perhaps for the world, since World War II is what is happening in Eastern Europe. . . . [The Europe of Yalta] is unraveling before our very eyes."[85] Gorbachev, he said, played a positive role in East European developments and recommended to the representatives at Strasbourg that Europe should assist him. Nevertheless, Mitterrand began to worry that the unstable situation in Eastern Europe might derail plans for European integration and began to stress the need to accelerate the process.[86] A few months later, the fall of the Berlin Wall and the question of German reunification heightened these fears for Mitterrand who thought that the new situation would cause confusion within the EEC or would be given priority over European integration.

In France, as a strike at the large Peugeot automobile firm was making headlines, an affair involving three young schoolgirls in the

Paris suburb of Creil created a storm of national controversy that divided the government, the Socialist party, and the nation. When Leila and Fatima Achaboun, born in France of Moroccan parents, and Samira Saidini, of Tunisian origin, wore Islamic scarfs covering their heads to class, the principal expelled them, commencing what the French called the "affair of the Islamic scarfs". By the middle of October, the affair was front-page news and even the subject of debate in the National Assembly. As the affair gained momentum in the press, it became clear that this incident raised important questions about the meaning of secular education in France, the role of Islam in the nation, women's rights, French national identity, and the future contours of domestic politics.[87]

This affair not only heightened anti-Arab sentiment, but divided the PS and forced the government to reconsider its immigration policy. Henri Emmanuelli, number two in the Socialist party at the time, announced that he sided with the principal. Fabius, too, came out in favor of observing strict secularism in the schools. This was the same position taken by a number of right-wing politicians, including Charles Pasqua. However, Prime Minister Rocard and Education Minister Jospin called for more flexibility. Jospin eventually ruled that the three schoolgirls should not be barred from class and recommended that they, along with their parents, meet with school officials so that all concerned could come to better understand secular education in France. Later, this affair contributed to a victory by the National Front in a parliamentary by-election in Dreux in which an extremist FN candidate won a stunning 61 percent of the vote. In the wake of this affair and the FN victory in Dreux, some mayors refused to issue residence permits to Arabs and to enroll immigrant children in school; they also blocked construction of certain religious buildings. Strong anti-Arab sentiment would also contribute to a later wave of racist violence against Arabs residing in France. To counter concerns raised by the affair, the Rocard government announced that the economic situation would not permit France to accept new immigrants, now totaling between 3.5 and 4.5 million. Instead, the government announced that it would concentrate instead on integrating France's immigrant population. It also announced a crackdown to curb illegal immigration and would establish an interministerial committee (Budget, Education, Health, Justice, and Labor) to deal with immigrant issues relating to housing and education.[88] In the months ahead, the Socialist party would back a Communist-sponsored bill to curb extremists. This bill barred anyone found guilty of inciting racism from holding public office or government jobs. The bill passed by a margin of 307 votes to 265, with the Gaullist RPR and the UDF opposing it. These measures were part of what Rocard called his government's antiracism strategy. The immigrant issue was once again on the minds of many in France, including the government, and was at the heart of the domestic political debate.

Another subject which would soon dominate the headlines not just in France but around the world was the German question. On November 9, the Berlin Wall, the great symbol of a divided Europe and the Cold War, came tumbling down, a momentous event that caught Mitterrand and world leaders by surprise. Due to a steady stream of East Germans fleeing to the Federal Republic through the porous borders of nations surrounding the GDR, the pressure of a reform movement there as well as in Eastern Europe in general, and Gorbachev's refusal to back violent repression, the East German government finally began dismantling the Wall. Displaying a certain inertia after the Wall fell, Mitterrand found himself the subject of criticism for not responding quickly to the new situation in Europe. Former President Giscard charged that Mitterrand, president of the EC until the end of the year, was letting the United States and the Soviet Union, whose leaders were scheduled to meet soon at Malta for a superpower summit, make the first analysis of the changes in the East. Mitterrand reacted to this criticism by calling an impromptu summit, an informal dinner at the Elysée for European Community leaders. This hastily called meeting allowed him to demonstrate that France and the European Community desired to encourage and strengthen political democracy in the East, "to accelerate the decline of totalitarianism" as Mitterrand put it, and to ease fears that Eastern European events would dominate the EC meeting scheduled for Strasbourg on December 8–9. Mitterrand and his guests examined short-term emergency aid for Eastern Europe (France had earlier announced a $630 million aid package for Poland), ways to link the Eastern bloc to the EC, and the creation of a European Reconstruction and Development Bank (known by its French acronym, BERD) to provide Eastern Europe with low-interest loans.[89]

While Mitterrand and other Western leaders hailed the end of the Berlin Wall,[90] the vision of a reunified Germany greatly concerned him for a number of reasons. Following the collapse of the Wall, Chancellor Kohl gave the impression that Germany alone would control the pace of unification. Kohl, appearing more and more like a modern-day Bismarck, initially favored a speedy reunification process. Mitterrand, on the other hand, wanted first to push forward with European integration and then German reunification, with Europe having a voice in the timetable and process of the unification of the two Germanies. Furthermore, would a reunified Germany remain in NATO or would it seek neutral status? Mitterrand favored, at least for the near future, an enlarged Germany firmly anchored in the West and in the Atlantic Alliance. Related to the general security issues was the question of the borders of a reunited Germany, especially the Polish border. Kohl created suspicion in France and elsewhere when he refused to give firm guarantees on the question of the German-Polish border. Then there was the problem of European integration: would the new situation in the two Germanies and Eastern Europe slow down and possibly sidetrack the movement toward 1992? Kohl, in fact, had stunned Mitterrand by asking shortly after the fall of the Wall for a slower pace for the planned economic and monetary union of the European Community. After a series of behind-the-scenes conversations, Bonn announced that it would support a French-sponsored conference on the economic and monetary union.[91] Finally, the reunification of Germany would disrupt the postwar economic order and possibly create an economic superpower in the heart of Europe. This worried Mitterrand because he had anticipated that France and Germany would be equals in the Europe of 1992, and that European unity would enhance the power and prestige of France on the Continent and in the world at large. The unexpected events in the East had surprised Mitterrand, and in the weeks and months ahead he would be forced to exert his influence to anchor an enlarged Germany securely in an integrated EEC and to help shape the new Europe.

Presiding over the forty-second European Council meeting in Strasbourg on December 8–9, Mitterrand tried to obtain a new commitment on European economic and monetary integration. Two days prior to this meeting, Mitterrand met with Gorbachev in Kiev and endorsed the Soviet leader's view that nothing should be done in Germany without taking into account European equilibrium and that a thirty-five-nation meeting of the Conference on Security and Cooperation in Europe should be called late in 1990 to discuss the future of Europe. By playing his Soviet card, Mitterrand gained much needed leverage at Strasbourg and added weight to his recommendation that German unification had to slow down and that reinforcing the European Community was the first order of business.[92] Representatives at Strasbourg agreed to hold a special conference late in 1990 to facilitate European integration. They also approved the French-sponsored Charter of Social Rights, gratifying the French president. In the final statement at the Strasbourg meeting, the representatives endorsed German unification, but stressed that Germany should respect existing agreements and that the unification process should take place in the context of European integration and the East-West dialogue (a view that Mitterrand expressed when he visited East Germany a few weeks later). Reaffirming the unity of the European Community, the final statement at Strasbourg declared: "At this time of profound and radical change, the Community is and must remain a point of reference and influence. . . . It remains the cornerstone of a new European architecture and, in its will to openness, a mooring for a future European equilibrium."[93] At this time the EC also affirmed its support of the changes in progress in Eastern Europe, pledging to aid those nations that were adopting a democratic government.

Following this meeting in Strasbourg, Mitterrand met with President Bush, their sixth meeting in ten months, in the French West Indies. The two presidents expressed general agreement on the historical significance of the dramatic changes in Eastern Europe. They also discussed stronger cooperation between the EC and the United States, and NATO issues.[94] On the subject of the Atlantic Alliance, Mitterrand had earlier echoed the views of Bush and Gorbachev on the stabilizing role of the alliances by calling NATO and the Warsaw Pact "a framework it should be unwise to break out of at this time."[95]

In December, in an effort to strengthen his nation's global influence, Mitterrand tried to assure France's friends and allies that the republic's foreign policy would not exclude other areas of the world as a result of the new situation in Eastern Europe. At a European-Arab conference in Paris on December 21–22, foreign ministers from both sides overlooked their political differences in order to renew a dialogue that had stalled in the 1970s. This meeting produced a desire on both sides to resume economic, cultural, and technological cooperation. Mitterrand spoke at the closing session at the Elysée, stressing that the rapprochement of the two Europes would not come at the expense of relations with Arab and African nations, that it was not possible for Europe to choose between the East and the South.[96] Nevertheless, the falling dominoes of authoritarian regimes in Eastern Europe began to fill the headlines of French newspapers and capture the attention of the public and the government.

The popular challenge to the oppressive Ceaucescu regime encouraged the French government on December 26 to issue a communiqué expressing solidarity with and support for the Romanian people. Prior to the execution of Ceaucescu, Dumas recorded a message for Romanian television that called the events there "a historic Christmas for the Romanian people." The French government also sent the secretary of state for humanitarian action, Bernard Kouchner, and a team of thirty-six doctors, surgeons, and nurses to Bucharest. At France's initiative, the EEC sent a delegation to Romania to decide how European aid could best be utilized to assist the masses. These efforts in Romania would be followed by a visit by Foreign Minister Dumas and Agriculture Minister Henri Nallet in order to offer French aid in reconstructing the nation.[97]

As 1989—a truly remarkable year in European and world history—drew to a close, Mitterrand, like other Western leaders, struggled to stay ahead of the breathtaking changes in Eastern Europe. In his traditional New Year's Eve message to the nation, an address that coincided with the end of his six-month term as the president of the EC, he focused on the situation in Europe and advanced a vision for the continent that drew considerable attention around the world. In his televised address he linked the events in Eastern Europe with the great principles of the French Revolution that his own nation had just celebrated: liberty, equality, and fraternity. Now, two hundred years later the same dreams had "overturned the other Bastilles" where dictatorship reigned. Regarding the significance of these events, Mitterrand said that "the changes that have occurred during the last months in Eastern Europe are the most important events that we have seen since World War II and will be considered without doubt among the great events of history." However, these changes in the East, said the president, posed difficult new questions for the future: What would be the future of NATO and the Warsaw Pact? At what pace would disarmament proceed? What would be the form and conditions of German reunification? Would existing borders be respected? What type of cooperation would there be between Western and Eastern Europe? Would the reawakening of nationalism in Europe accompany these changes?

To avoid many of the problems that existed in the Europe of

1919 after World War I, Mitterrand proposed in his New Year's Eve message a two-stage process for Europe. First, as the EC had just agreed at Strasbourg, integration within the EEC must advance as planned. This according to the president, would provide Eastern European nations with a reference point, a stable union to look toward. The second stage, according to Mitterrand, remained to be invented. He proposed for the 1990s the creation of a European Confederation "that will unite all of the nations of our continent in a common and permanent organization for trade, peace, and security." This confederation would be open to all nations that adopted a pluralistic political system. Mitterrand himself favored utilizing the Helsinki process, the CSCE, for discussing the future of a new Europe, unlike the Bush administration which tended to favor an enlarged Atlantic Alliance (at Malta Bush had opposed Mitterrand's desire to call a meeting of the CSCE in 1990) or the Soviets who envisioned stronger ties between the EEC and Comecon. Mitterrand's call for a European Confederation reminded many of de Gaulle's earlier vision of a united Europe: "Europe, the mother of modern civilization, . . . [must] unite from the Atlantic to the Urals in harmony and in cooperation in order to develop its immense resources and to play, along with the United States, Europe's offspring, the role that awaits it."[98] This, of course, was not the first time that the Socialist chief of state had borrowed from de Gaulle on foreign policy matters. While most of Mitterrand's address centered on the future of Europe in the wake of the reform movement in the East, the remainder of his New Year's Eve statement focused on his hope that France would end racism, and would continue to play a leading role in the struggle against poverty, underdevelopment, and pollution.[99]

Thus, by the early part of the year, various European leaders had proposed three different conceptions of a new Europe. Gorbachev had called earlier for a "common European home"; Delors at the European Commission talked of a Europe of concentric circles (e.g., the EEC, the European Free Trade Association [EFTA], the Eastern bloc, and beyond);[100] and now Mitterrand was calling for a large European Confederation. While Gorbachev was interested in weakening NATO, Delors and Mitterrand were scrambling to find some way of ensuring the success of the plans for 1992 and preventing nationalistic aspirations and ethnic rivalries from creating chaos. Mitterrand's proposal for a European Confederation as well as Delors's idea for Europe inspired many on the Continent to continue to dream of a resurgent Europe that might one day recapture its central place on the world's stage.

Early in January, Minister of Defense Chevènement agreed to an interview in the pages of the newsweekly *Le Point*, an interview that reflected the developing views of many in government on a European Confederation, including those of the president. Regarding the changes in the East and the creation of a European Confederation, Chevènement stressed that in the Europe of the future Germany should not have access to nuclear weapons. When asked if EC integration was now impossible given the upheaval in the East, the defense minister said no, in part because Mitterrand's idea of a confederation permitted the construction of Europe from a truly European perspective. Moreover, a confederation would permit the EC to give a political, cultural, and human dimension to an enterprise in Eastern Europe that might otherwise represent the economic colonization of the eastern half of the continent. When asked how his own nation could play a more important role in a large Europe, Chevènement reminded his readers that apart from the USSR, France was the only continental nation with its own nuclear weapons, a fact that would allow it to play a stabilizing role in a new Europe. For the defense minister, there were two requirements for peace and stability: clear acceptance of the Oder-Neisse frontier between Germany and Poland and no nuclear weapons for Germany. Chevènement's statements helped to flesh out the view of a future Europe that was emerging among French government officials, along with France's role in a new Europe.[101]

Early in the new year, Mitterrand met with Chancellor Kohl at the president's private retreat in the Landes region near Bordeaux, the first time that Kohl had visited this rustic vacation home. Mitterrand was relieved to learn at this January 4 meeting that the German chancellor agreed with the need to reinforce the economic and political structure of the EC and supported the idea of creating a European Confederation open to the emerging democracies of Eastern Europe. Both leaders also pledged to act in concert on the rapid changes in the East.

On January 11, Japanese Prime Minister Kaifu visited Paris. While Eastern Europe was not on the agenda, a related subject was discussed—trade. Mitterrand told his visitor that Japanese markets were "impenetrable" for other nations and cited this problem as a potential source of conflict between France and Japan. How to compete with both Japan and the United States was a major worry for

Mitterrand as well as other European leaders. A few weeks earlier, Mitterrand had told a group of 150 European businessmen at the Elysée that "the European single market is perhaps the principal way, perhaps, the only way possible for our business to have a base broad as those of our American and Asian competitors. . . . We must build a coherent space, but not a fortress. . . . We are ready to accept competition without protectionism."[102]

Despite the trade problems with Japan, Eastern Europe continued to dominate the attention of the president and the public. Mitterrand visited Hungary on January 18–19 and met with interim President Matyas Szuros. Accompanying the French president were seven cabinet members and a delegation of bankers and industrialists. In their talks, Mitterrand and Szuros reached agreement on a number of political issues and economic arrangements. In a joint press conference the Hungarian leader said that his government would cooperate with efforts to construct a European Confederation. One economic agreement reached was a decision to grant Hungary a $350 million loan over the following three years.[103] It was obvious to Mitterrand that Hungary and other Eastern European countries needed a quick infusion of economic aid, and he wanted France and its Western European partners to provide a large portion of it rather than seeing Eastern Europe become solely dependent on American dollars and be transformed into a new sphere of influence for the United States.

To assist the emerging democracies of Eastern Europe, Mitterrand, as mentioned earlier, initiated the creation of the European Reconstruction and Development Bank. In January, thirty-six experts from Western and Eastern Europe met in Paris to prepare the foundations for this bank designed to assist Eastern Europe to convert to market economies. The plans for BERD called for the European Community to maintain at least a 51 percent controlling interest out of the total capital of $16 billion, but permitted other nations, such as the United States, Japan, and the Soviet Union, to invest in the institution. Presidential adviser Attali, who presided over the BERD meeting in Paris and who was later named president of BERD, promised that the bank would be fully operational by the end of the year.[104]

As Mitterrand and the government launched a major investment effort in Eastern Europe, French citizens learned that their own economy had continued to improve in 1989 and the economic projections for 1990 looked good indeed. New data on the French economy revealed at this time that the bicentennial year had been excellent for business. Investment, consumption, and exports were all strong in 1989, and the economy grew at a rate of 4.5 percent. In fact, over the previous three years industrial production had increased 16 percent, while between 1980 and 1986 it had remained relatively constant. To a large degree, this economic upturn was the result of increased consumer demand abroad, which had raised French exports by more than 9 percent for each of the past three years. In addition, purchases of industrial equipment were up by 6–7 percent in 1989. The weak point in the economy, in addition to an unemployment rate that hovered around the 10 percent mark, was a trade deficit of $7.7 billion in 1989, an increase of $4.3 billion over 1988.[105]

Besides learning about improvements in the economy, the French public got a preview of how its government intended to meet the challenge of 1992. During the first month of the new year, Air France concluded an agreement to enhance its competitiveness in a more integrated Europe. The state-owned airline purchased a 54.48 percent interest in UTA, a private carrier, at a cost of $666 million. Air France also announced that it would increase its interest in Air Inter, a domestic carrier, from 37 percent to 72 percent. A few months later another state-owned industry, Renault, revealed that it was merging part of its operation with Volvo of Sweden. One official from the Ministry of Industry noted at the time that the world economy was in the process of restructuring and that "the general crumbling of customs barriers and the construction of the single European market are prompting . . . firms to expand so that they can reach a bigger market and better face competition, especially from the Japanese. A large company today has no hope of survival unless it can grow beyond the 'critical size' that allows it to finance the enormous research costs needed to come up with new products."[106] The price for a more competitive Europe might likely be mergers and takeovers.

In February and March of 1990, political changes not just in Europe but also in East Asia, Latin America, and the Middle East concerned Mitterrand. While he made a five-day visit to Pakistan and Bangladesh in February, Minister of Foreign Affairs Dumas visited Vietnam in an effort to revitalize relations, promising to aid the Vietnamese with their modernization efforts. In Vietnam, however, Dumas noted the significant events in Eastern Europe and reminded Vietnamese government officials of their obligation to respect human rights.[107]

In February, too, crucial elections in Nicaragua and the continuation of the bloodbath in Lebanon demanded a response from the French president. Although he had been a critic of Reagan and Bush's Latin American policy, especially in Nicaragua, when the Sandinistas held elections on February 25 and the opposition candidate won, Mitterrand sent a message to both sides. He praised Daniel Ortega for putting Nicaragua "on the road to democracy." The French president told Violeta Chamorro, the victor, that he "remembered the role played by Pedro Joaquin Chamorro [Chamorro's husband who was editor of the newspaper *La Prensa* and who was assassinated in 1978] in overthrowing the Somoza dictatorship." Mitterrand also conveyed his hope that "the work of reconciliation and peace will continue."[108] In late February, Mitterrand found it necessary to respond to a request from the Middle East. The Lebanese Christian militia leader Samir Geagea had written to Mitterrand asking that France intervene to stop the massacre that was occurring as his forces battled the rival Christian forces of General Michel Aoun. On February 23, Mitterrand sent a letter to Geagea and requested that all sides "put an end to this murderous madness" and to observe a cease-fire that had gone into effect.[109] The battle between Christian forces in Lebanon complicated any solution to the country's serious problems.

Meanwhile, the upcoming elections in East Germany, the future of the Western Alliance, and European integration encouraged Mitterrand to assume a highly visible role in the international arena. One of Mitterrand's first major statements on German unification appeared in an interview in the *Daily Times*. This interview permitted the French president to reach the English-speaking world as well as France since he knew that his statement would be covered at home also. This interview suggested, too, that Mitterrand, like Prime Minister Thatcher, had concerns about various aspects of German unity, especially the pace and the method of reunification, and that the French and English position on the question might be closer than many expected. In the statement, Mitterrand acknowledged "that reunification is now becoming a fact and appears to be the wish of the German people. . . . It is up to the Germans to decide, and France does not intend to decide for them." However, he added:

> This unification will not take place in a political, legal or strategic vacuum. . . . Reunification must take place in a peaceful manner; that is, by taking into account international treaties and agreements and by respecting the security interests of other countries

in view of preserving the stability of the European continent. Extensive reflection is therefore needed concerning the political and strategic landscape that is changing before our eyes. . . . What will be the future, the organization of European security? What is in store for the alliances? What will be the status of a reunited Germany? What correlation will there be between these developments and the Vienna negotiations on conventional forces and disarmament in general? What will be the plans for the CSCE in this new configuration?[110]

Mitterrand was worried also that a neutral Germany would give the Soviet Union an advantage in Europe and weaken France's eastern flank. He did not want to see the end of NATO. There was too much uncertainty, he said, to "let ourselves be carried away by euphoria generated by the winds of liberty blowing in the East and to deprive ourselves of the means of ensuring our security."[111]

Shortly after this interview appeared, Foreign Minister Dumas wrote an article entitled "One Germany—If Europe Agrees" for the *New York Times*, another effort to encourage Western governments to begin to play a role in the pace and the form of German unification. Dumas argued that the German question was at the heart of building a new Europe. "German unification," he asserted, "can be achieved only if it is accepted by all European countries. For Germany's neighbors, and most of all for Poland, it must be absolutely clear that borders cannot be altered. . . . Everything revolves around a simple idea: German unity must be accompanied by a strengthening of European stability, and the opportunity lends itself to this."[112] The CSCE, Dumas said, was the way for Europe to discuss its future, and he noted that this was why France had earlier called for a CSCE summit before the end of the year. A European Confederation should be the political model for Europe, a model that would promote cooperation and unity. Referring to such a confederation, Dumas said, "it is within this framework that we, together, can build a future of peace and prosperity for Europe."[113]

In early March, Mitterrand continued to express his concern over Kohl's quick march toward unification and his casual attitude to related security matters. On March 9 he met for two hours with President Wojciech Jaruzelski and Prime Minister Tadeusz Mazowiecki of Poland, and suggested that, like his Polish guests, he was not satisfied with Bonn's pledge to respect the existing German-Polish border. One day prior to this meeting with Polish leaders, the

West and East German parliaments passed a common resolution saying that "the Polish people are assured that their right to live in secure borders will not be questioned by Germans through territorial claims either now or in the future." Nevertheless, Mitterrand agreed with Jaruzelski that this declaration of intent did not specify which borders would be respected. Mitterrand's Polish visitors called the German declaration "a quarter-step forward," and the French president himself issued a strong statement supporting the Polish claim: "I think this declaration should be still more precise. This is not just any frontier. This is the Oder-Neisse line. Any declaration that does not recognize this clearly is not sufficient."[114] While the two Germanies and the Allied powers agreed to a "two plus four" framework for discussions on reunification, giving the United States, the Soviet Union, France and Britain the right to approve the external aspects of an enlarged Germany, suspicion of Kohl grew in Western capitals in the first few months of the year.

Following the March 18 elections in East Germany, the first free elections since the end of the War, in which Kohl's conservative allies, known collectively as the "Alliance for Germany," won an overwhelming victory, the French government urged a speedy economic union of the two Germanies so that the issue of European integration would not be clouded. On March 20 Dumas gave radio interviews in which he called for the Western European nations to accelerate the pace toward economic and monetary unification. The French foreign minister requested that the planned December meeting of the EC, at which representatives were to pave the way for integration, be advanced. Dumas also made a speech in Berlin at this time that echoed his president by insisting that the Oder-Neisse frontier with Poland be guaranteed prior to German unification. While Mitterrand and the French government publicly endorsed German unification and while two out of three French citizens supported it,[115] behind the scenes Mitterrand and government officials were suspicious of Kohl's intentions concerning the Polish border and the calendar for European integration.

Mitterrand was convinced that what was needed was an acceleration of European integration in order to anchor a reunited Germany in the Western camp and to strengthen EC stability. Following the East German elections, Kohl announced that he hoped for economic union for the two Germanies by the summer of 1990 and that political unification would likely not occur until after the December 1990 elections in the Federal Republic, probably sometime in 1991; the former Social Democratic chancellor Willy Brandt supported a similar timetable. This did not exactly ease French worries over Chancellor Kohl's commitment to meet the EC rendezvous with 1992. What did relieve some of the anxiety, however, was Kohl's willingness to send a joint message with Mitterrand to European Council President Charles Haughey of Ireland on April 19. Mitterrand and Kohl recommended that the European Community achieve economic, monetary, and also political unity by January 1, 1993. Furthermore, they requested that this be discussed at the April 28 meeting of the European Council in Dublin. According to the message sent to Haughey, "Given the profound transformations in Europe, the establishment of the single market and the realization of economic and monetary unity, we judge it necessary to accelerate the political unity of the community."[116] When EC leaders met in Dublin, they agreed to attempt to achieve greater unity by studying ways to strengthen economic, monetary, and political integration. Nevertheless, there was a certain vagueness about what political union would mean, although many realized that it implied more power for the European Commission, the European Parliament, and the Council of Ministers, as well as a greater coordination of foreign and defense policies. Also noteworthy at the Dublin meeting was Kohl's statement that he favored membership of a reunited Germany in NATO, a position opposed by the Soviet Union unless it represented a transitional phase to a pan-European security system.[117] The instability in Eastern Europe motivated Mitterrand and other leaders of the EC to speed up the process of integration.

Complicating the question of European unity was the determination of one Baltic state, Lithuania, to secede from the Soviet Union. If the Western alliance backed Lithuania and a major international crisis developed over this issue, the situation could possibly set back the unity of the EEC and Mitterrand's plan for a European Confederation. Not surprisingly, when Mitterrand met President Bush in Florida in the early spring for four hours of talks, both agreed to put ties with Moscow ahead of Lithuanian independence. Mitterrand told the press that "priority must be given to a dialogue."[118] Like Bush, Mitterrand believed that his nation's relationship with the Soviet Union was more important than that with Lithuania. Both leaders agreed to work through diplomatic channels to encourage a dialogue between Vilnius and Moscow. History would have to judge this decision by French and American leaders to side with Gorbachev.

Also at the Key Largo meeting, Mitterrand and Bush stressed the importance of keeping NATO strong and U.S. forces in Europe. This was important to Mitterrand because the United States could balance a mighty Germany after reunification. The two leaders agreed that an enlarged Germany should be a full member of NATO; however, Mitterrand said that Germany's membership in the Atlantic Alliance "must take into consideration the Soviet Union's security interests." Furthermore, Mitterrand did not endorse Bush's view of NATO as the dominant security arrangement in Europe.[119] The French president wanted to discuss European security requirements with the CSCE and to construct a European pillar of defense.

Several days after meeting with Bush, Mitterrand encouraged Kohl to send a joint French-German letter to the Lithuanian government recommending that it slow down its drive to independence— a legitimate demand according to Mitterrand and Kohl—and negotiate with the Soviet Union. In this letter to Lithuanian President Vytautas Landsbergis, they stressed that independence "requires time and patience and should be sought through classic channels of dialogue." (At this time, Moscow began to cite the French accord with New Caledonia as a possible model for the independence movement in the Soviet Union.) While Moscow endorsed the Paris-Bonn appeal to Lithuania, the government of the Baltic state asked that France and Germany act as mediators in the conflict with the Soviet Union. French presidential spokesman Védrine ruled out French mediation but suggested that his government would host negotiations if the two nations so desired.[120]

In addition to worries about European integration and security matters, Mitterrand had another major problem—a conflict within his own faction of the Socialist party. On March 15–18, the PS met in Rennes, and for the first time in almost twenty years the party failed to agree on a policy statement and on the membership of its secretariat. This disunity at Rennes was prompted by a battle between two presidential aspirants, Fabius and Jospin, both of whom are in competition to be the true Socialist heir after Mitterrand completes his second mandate, assuming that he does not run for a third term. What was especially disturbing to the president was that the infighting at Rennes was prompted by two young Mitterrandists. Fabius had been able to obtain the backing of a number of Socialist notables prior to the congress, such as Bérégovoy, Lang, Quilès, Penne, Attali, and Poperen. He represented a modern brand of socialism that resembled social democracy. Moreover, he wished to open up the party and expand its membership, currently around 180,000 members and comprising a high proportion of teachers and few workers, and under-representative of women.[121] Fabius sees himself as representing the political tradition of Blum and Mendès-France; in this regard he is closer to Radicalism than to Jaurèsism.[122] In many ways, Fabius's socialism resembles Rocard's.

Jospin, minister of education and the former head of the PS, favored a slightly different brand of socialism that anchored the party slightly more on the left and that envisioned a central role for it in bringing about reform.[123] Jospin's supporters at Rennes included Mauroy, Delebarre, Nallet, Emmanuelli, and Chevènement (his ex-CERES faction was now baptized "Socialism and Republic").

Both Socialist leaders knew that if there was to be a duel for the title of dauphin the time was now. The opposition was seriously divided. Only one month earlier, for example, the RPF had been forced to meet to settle a serious challenge to Chirac posed by an alliance between Charles Pasqua, representing the conservative wing of the party, and Philippe Séguin, who represented the more liberal wing of the RPR. In the end, party leaders backed Chirac. In addition to the schisms within the opposition, legislative elections were three years away and the presidential elections were not scheduled until 1995. Mitterrand, however, was so concerned about the political fall-out from the possibility of serious infighting at Rennes that he made an appeal for unity and even sent a special mediator to prevent disaster. These measures proved unsuccessful, however, as a Jospin-Mauroy-Chevènement alliance, cautiously supported by Rocard, stymied Fabius in a rancorous congress. The rank and file in the PS, as well as the press, openly criticized the battle that erupted in Rennes.

Mitterrand himself, however, contributed to the disputes at Rennes. Just prior to the congress, Mitterrand had called Fabius to the Elysée, which suggested to many Socialists that the president had chosen his heir. Yet as with many of Mitterrand's political moves, a degree of ambiguity surrounded the meeting. He did not announce publicly that he had chosen the president of the National Assembly as his dauphin, but he created the impression that this was the case. Why would he favor Fabius? One reason was that he saw himself in the young Fabius, sometimes referred to as Mitterrand's "double" by observers in France. Mitterrand began his political career on the national level at a young age, much like Fabius. A second reason for favoring him was that he was a loyal and trusted member of the Mitterrand political family. Jospin was a Mitterrandist also, but the president had been much closer to Fabius. A third reason for wanting Fabius in the Elysée, and perhaps the most important reason, was that he believed that the head of the National Assembly would be able to continue the opening to the center and solidify the centrist republic that had emerged under Mitterrand's presidency.[124] However, the Socialist party, which had rejected his earlier effort to place Fabius at the head of the PS immediately after the 1988 elections, rebuffed the president once again.

Shortly after the Rennes congress, Mitterrand more or less imposed a compromise whereby the party papered over its differences and selected Mauroy as first secretary, and a Fabius supporter, Marcel Debarge, for the number two spot. But what would be the consequences of the Rennes meeting? Perhaps this is what Mitterrand had in mind when he suggested a few days after the congress that Rocard was now well placed to be his heir. Mitterrand told *Libération* that "there is no reason why Michel Rocard should not serve until the end of this legislature [1993]." He warned that if the 1993 elections were lost, then "the presidential elections will bring victory to a man of the Right." As a political veteran, Mitterrand knew that fear breeds unity. His statement in *Libération* created a common target for both Fabius and Jospin—Prime Minister Rocard.[125] Would the two young warriors at Rennes, who after the congress were able to place more of their followers in important positions in the secretariat, unite and try to find a way to shut out Rocard? Would Jospin be able to forgive Mitterrand for favoring Fabius at Rennes or would the minister of education ally with Rocard in the future and forge a new balance of power in the party that might threaten to put the Mitterrandists in the minority? Would Rocard, who attended the Rennes meeting but kept a low profile, emerge as the heir to the Elysée? While Rocard's future was uncertain because of the difficult problems he would undoubtedly face in the future as prime minister, Mitterrand's tactic was clear: play the PS against Rocard, a man who, as noted earlier, is popular with the public but not necessarily within the PS.

For Fabius and Jospin, however, there was another problem— the aspirations of Jacques Delors, the atypical Socialist who served as president of the European Commission. Delors, too, had attended the Rennes meeting but had deliberately remained out of the limelight. Given Mitterrand's skill at juggling the various tendencies with the Socialist party, it seemed highly likely that he would attempt to play Fabius and Jospin as well as Chevènement and Delors against Rocard. As if to mobilize the party and the nation less than one week after the Rennes fiasco, Mitterrand announced on television that he wanted the government to begin serious fiscal reform as a way of minimizing inequalities. He characterized such reforms as "easy to imagine, [but] difficult to realize."[126] Would this reform effort, as well as later efforts by Mitterrand to encourage Rocard to focus more on social reform, become the centerpiece of the government's future domestic policy? Would this new thrust help to bring some unity to the party? After Rennes it was clear that the Socialist party still needed Mitterrand if it was to avoid fratricidal wars. How he would play the various tendencies within the party was debatable; what was not debatable was that he would play them.

From the beginning of his second term through April 1990, diverse and serious issues confronted Mitterrand and the French government. While the Socialists and the nation welcomed the newfound prosperity, the Rocard government had to find ways to continue economic growth without stimulating demands by workers for inflationary wage increases. Fortunately, the Rocard government has experienced, to date, less social unrest than in the early and mid-1980's. Rather miraculously the government had been able to maintain its policy of austerity and national solidarity. On the other hand, the popularity of Rocard was somewhat of an embarrassment for Mitterrand and the Socialists in general. While Mitterrand and the PS were elected in 1981 on a program that called for a break with capitalism in France, by 1990 it was clear that it was socialism that had been transformed—the PS had become a social democratic party and Rocard had emerged as one of its shining new symbols. Moreover, the Rennes congress had revealed serious new divisions within the Socialist party as young Mitterrandists struggled to become the legitimate heir. Luckily for the PS, the Right too, was deeply divided, with a number of reformers within both the UDF and the RPR challenging the old guard. Would the president be able to manufacture a united PS and mobilize the electorate as the party anticipated elections in 1993 and 1995?

In the international arena, early in 1989 it still seemed as if

Europe would have its rendezvous with 1992, but the political unrest in Eastern Europe and the Soviet Union beginning late in 1989 worried many—especially Mitterrand—that European integration would be sidetracked; and if it did occur, a united Germany would likely emerge as an economic superpower in the heart of Europe and France might have to live in its shadow. Related to the new political architecture in Europe was the question of security. What type of security system would France and Europe adopt in the months and years ahead? What would happen to the Atlantic Alliance and the Warsaw Pact, especially in light of the fact that Gorbachev had rescinded his demand that a reunited Germany be neutral? Would the Continent one day witness the formation of a European security system, as Mitterrand had called for early in 1990, that would be linked to the Conference on Security and Cooperation in Europe? Would such an organization supersede NATO and the Warsaw Pact, or would it serve as a counterbalance to the existing alliance systems? And on the personal level, would Kohl eclipse Mitterrand as the leading statesman of Europe and spoil Mitterrand's effort to be the Continent's leading European in the 1990s?

At the beginning of the new decade, it was clear that political parties in France, including the Socialist party, were undergoing reformulation in a new centrist republic in the wake of the nation's experience with cohabitation and Mitterrand's opening to the center. However, it was not centrism that concerned Mitterrand so much, but the need to envision a new architecture for the continent following the crumbling of authoritarian regimes in the East and the waning of Soviet power and influence. A new Europe had to be envisioned to ensure that the integration of the EEC would succeed and that an enlarged Germany would not threaten the security of the Continent. Given Kohl's preoccupation with reunification and Thatcher's general opposition to a strengthened EEC, Mitterrand knew that history had thrust upon him a large burden and responsibility. In France and Europe uncharted waters lay ahead as Mitterrand confronted his greatest test as president of the republic, the European challenge.

CONCLUSION

I can remember once talking about the events of history as if one were talking about a galloping horse, a stampeding horse. Some of the riders who clamber aboard the stampeding horse of history manage to tame it. Others don't quite succeed that far, but without fully taming it, they do at least manage to make it take a different direction.

—François Mitterrand

Charles de Gaulle once said that he had "a certain idea of France." Mitterrand, too, has had an idea of France, but one more focused on realigning the Gaullist political system of the Fifth Republic than promoting French grandeur. While Mitterrand's idea of France has been less ambitious than de Gaulle's, in some ways the accomplishments are more noteworthy.

Over the past decades, Mitterrand has played an instrumental role in transforming the French political landscape. He has successfully constructed a hegemonic Socialist party that is capable of governing, marginalized the PCF, rebalanced the forces of the Left and the Right, and introduced France to *alternance* and to a centrist republic. The varied multiparty system of the Fourth Republic and early years of the Fifth Republic has now been replaced by a system comprising four principal parties: the PS, PCF, UDF, and RPR. This change to a quadripartite political arrangement has led to the withering away of the bipolar political system that once characterized the Fifth Republic. Politics have been deideologized and include a surprising degree of consensus. Part of the reason for these fundamental changes is that Mitterrand has been highly successful at weakening the Communists, splintering the Right and moving his own party to the center. His political career, especially his presidency, shows that he has forced the galloping horse of history, as he called it, to take a different turn.

From the beginning of the Fifth Republic, Mitterrand has desired a more centrist republic, one centered between the Gaullists on his right and the Communists on his left. From his perspective, the "unexpected revolution"[1] during his presidency was not so much that a consensual centrist republic emerged, but that it was accompanied by a strong dose of economic liberalism. Both the PS and the Right shed much of their faith in a state-directed economy, with the Socialists becoming more sensitive to market forces and the Right advocating a Reaganesque liberalism. Although unbridled capitalism was not Mitterrand's wish for France, the new centrist republic has been part of his political design for decades.[2]

What is it about Mitterrand, a man who has roamed the corridors of power in France for nearly half a century, that has made him such a consummate politician? One of the most obvious answers to this question is that those political characteristics that he acquired largely under the Fourth Republic and that made him so enigmatic before 1981 worked to his advantage once he assumed the presidency and seemed well suited to the changing political terrain of France.

His political pragmatism, for instance, has permitted him to adapt to changing political circumstances and to survive politically. His willingness to form an electoral alliance with the Communists in the early 1970s to enhance the possibility of defeating the Right, to modify his anticapitalist rhetoric and image after severe economic problems surfaced in 1982–83, to use cohabitation to his and his party's advantage, to launch an opening to the center on the eve of the 1988 elections, and then to work with a minority government headed by his long-time rival within the Socialist party are all indicative of his pragmatic political mind.

Another acquired characteristic is Mitterrand's ability to rebound after major electoral and personal setbacks, and turn adverse situations to his advantage. For example, once his Socialist government encountered economic difficulties in the early 1980s, he shifted to austerity, began a program of industrial modernization, and skillfully manipulated images of a modernized nation in a mighty Europe capable of successfully competing with the United States and Japan.

Then, he turned the defeat in the 1986 legislative elections into an eventual victory by coexisting with the Right and transforming his leftist image into one of a president of all the French. While Mitterrand's enigmatic personality has been largely the product of his political career under the Fourth Republic, his experience as president of the Fifth Republic reveals that the Fourth Republic trained him well in the art of political survival. His earlier career and his presidency show that he has an uncanny ability to adapt to and to fight his battles on various political terrains. In this regard, he is often at his best when counterattacking his political opponents, as cohabitation revealed to Chirac's conservative government and to all of France. He is a superb political tactician and "escape artist."

To adapt to different political terrains and battle his opponents he has often relied on ambiguity. In fact, in France he is often seen as the "prince of ambiguity." During his political career he has consciously refused to limit his options or to restrain his room for maneuver. For example, prior to the 1988 presidential elections he strongly suggested to the public that he might not be a candidate. During the early phase of his second mandate, to cite another example, he did not intervene in the affairs of the Rocard government (1988–91), but gave the public the impression on several occasions that he hoped to transcend Rocardism. Nevertheless, his penchant for ambiguity is a function of a political pragmatism that is aimed not merely at creating a centrist republic or maintaining personal power, but also at advancing a Republican socialism that centers around social justice and that is rooted almost as much in his religious upbringing as it is in his own political development. One must not forget that Mitterrand's social conscience was fashioned to a large degree by highly religious parents who were dedicated to helping the poor and the downtrodden. His need for ambiguity is closely related to his experience under the Fourth Republic where a quick succession of governments demanded flexibility on the part of a young and ambitious minister like Mitterrand. In some ways, he is a man of the Fourth Republic who has imposed its ways on the Fifth Republic.

Many of the personal qualities of Mitterrand the man have also aided him as president. His persistence, will to power, and patience have prolonged his political life. Prior to 1981, many in France doubted that Mitterrand, who had unsuccessfully run for the presidency against de Gaulle and Giscard, would ever become the occupant of the Elysée. Moreover, when his popularity fell to record lows in 1984 after his economic policies failed, few expected that Mitterrand would be reelected in 1988. Many in France did not believe that he would run for a second term after voters turned his Socialist party out of power in the 1986 legislative elections. This tenacity, or what some might prefer to call resolute stubbornness, and his will to remain at the center of power, have greatly aided his long career. Patience, too, has assisted his ambition. As noted earlier, he views time as an ally and has been willing to wait for the propitious moment to act, as with his "cooperation" with Chirac during the earlier months of cohabitation before he went on the offensive against the right-wing government. His political timing, partially a product of his vast experience and his patience, is usually superb.

Within the PS and under his presidency, Mitterrand has relied on two personal qualities that many of his friends and acquaintances say mark him as a man: friendship and loyalty. These are the two pillars of the Mitterrand approach to the PS and to his presidency.[3] In the party and in government, he expects both friendship and loyalty of his close colleagues and rewards these qualities in others, opening himself at times to charges of cronyism. An example of his reliance on friendship and loyalty is his relationship with Fabius. Since joining the PS, Fabius has been a trusted and loyal Mitterrandist. Mitterrand has rewarded Fabius in several ways, some of which have been rebuked by the PS: appointing him prime minister in 1984, attempting to place him at the head of the Socialist party following the 1988 elections, and subtly suggesting to the PS on the eve of the 1990 Rennes congress that Fabius was the chosen heir.

Related to this requirement for friendship and loyalty is Mitterrand's great networking ability in forging working relationships and alliances with a vast array of people. On one occasion he discussed the qualifications for the presidency, stressing three prerequisites: experience, intelligence, and a system of political networks. While he suggested that Rocard lacked the necessary alliances, especially within the PS,[4] Mitterrand throughout his political career has himself been a supreme networker, not just on the domestic level but on the international scene as well. The numerous and fleeting governments of the Fourth Republic demonstrated to Mitterrand early in his life that if he wanted a successful political career, he had to have friends and acquaintances in high positions. One should not forget that he even found an accommodation with the conservative Reagan in the 1980s, even though Washington was highly suspicious of Mitterrand when he was first elected because of his leftist program and because he appointed four Communists to ministerial positions. He has also been able to develop a sound working relationship with Chancellor Kohl of Germany, a Christian Democrat who is considerably to the right of Mitterrand politically.

Mitterrand is also capable of sincere and thoughtful actions. For instance, when Alain Savary died in 1988, his family let it be known that they did not want the president to attend the funeral. Savary had been an opponent of Mitterrand's within the PS and had had to resign as minister of education in 1984 when the president withdrew the Savary law to reform private schools due to widespread protests. Mitterrand, however, did attend Savary's last rites and sat respectfully near the body of his former minister during the service. The French journalist Giesbert uses this same example at the outset of his anecdotal account of the Mitterrand years to convey to the reader that despite what he sees as Mitterrand's Machiavellian character and his apparent coldness, the French leader is capable of showing respect for others. (Some might see this as rude and insensitive given the family's wishes.) For Giesbert, "This man . . . is never what one believes him to be. He is at once better and worse." As Giesbert also observes, death seems to erase bitterness for this political warrior, perhaps as a result of his religious upbringing and strong belief in the individual.

While many political commentators in France criticize Mitterrand's keen ability to maneuver, to rely often on ambiguity instead of a clear vision, and to wear various masks depending on circumstances, he is often praised for his eloquence, another personal quality that he has used to his advantage as the chief executive. To a large extent, this command of the language, both written and spoken, is a product of his varied abilities and interests. As a man of culture, as a trained lawyer, as a skillful writer, he has been able to speak for France at home and abroad with a degree of eloquence that is sorely lacking today in many Western nations. At home he is admired for this skill.

Mitterrand, too, is not simply an intelligent politician/statesman with a wealth of experience and networks, but one who possesses a certain political clairvoyance, who is able to read the mood of the public, and who learns from his mistakes. He revealed this clairvoyance in 1986 when he realized that a defeat could be transformed into a victory by changing his image, sensing that centrism could win votes given the growing faith in economic liberalism in France. He also revealed his understanding of complex political forces in 1988 when he asked Rocard to lead the opening to the center, a government that became extremely popular. He is also a man who often profits from his errors. For instance, after it was obvious that the reflationary policy of Year I was exacerbating economic problems, he admitted his misjudgments and turned to austerity as had other Western nations. Following a series of nationwide protests in 1984, he scrapped the reform of private schools, and used the occasion to reposition his government. Another example of learning from his mistakes is seen in Mitterrand's improved use of the media and political symbols. After losing to Giscard in 1974, in part because of his lackluster perform-ance in a televised debate, he has come to understand that politics today sometimes revolves almost as much around imagery as it does around policy. His willingness to utilize media experts such as Séguéla and Goude to advise him on the best use of the media and how to enhance his public relations effectiveness shows that he now under-stands the important role of media in political life. His elaborate bicentennial celebration revealed not just to world leaders attending the Paris summit in 1989 but to many others—including the opposi-tion at home—that he had become a master of sorts at media politics and the skillful use of political symbols.

Ironically, Mitterrand has been more successful as his nation's political system became more "Anglo-Saxonized," to borrow a phrase from one French observer. As politics in France became more con-sensual during his first term, his political fortunes increased and led to his reelection in 1988. This was due partially to his ability to win more centrist support by projecting a *Tonton* image after his rupture with the debilitated PCF in 1984, his adroit use of cohabitation to weaken Chirac's presidential hopes, and an improved economic situation. Mit-terrand knew that a centrist republic would create an identity crisis for the Right that would be to his benefit.

At the same time that Mitterrand has had a great impact on the political history of the Fifth Republic, this same Gaullist republic has had an impact on him. As president, he has been forced to reconcile himself and his party to the Constitution and the institutions of the republic, to a Gaullist foreign and defense policy, to a certain degree of compromise on secular education, to economic liberalism, and to linking France's future to the EEC. These significant reconciliations have made him a great progressive synthesizer[5] who has provided the

Fifth Republic with added legitimacy. The reform-minded idealist who was intoxicated with victory in 1981, like many in the Socialist party, is now more sober and realistic about the exercise of power and the possibility for change. Today he is aware that the leftist campaign of 1981 may not be repeated in France in the foreseeable future given the popularity of liberalism and the weakening of Marxism in Eastern Europe. He knows that the traditional Left, at least for the moment, is in "the dustbin of history." Realism has now become his watch word.

Mitterrand's first two terms in office have been quite different. While at the outset of his first term he had a plan for governing France, the Common Program and the 110 Propositions, the second term began with little more than a call for unity. In his first term, too, he focused primarily on difficult domestic economic and political problems, some of which were of his own making. His turn to austerity in 1982 and 1983 and the restructuring of industry, coupled with a fall in the value of the dollar and an increase in international demand for French products, greatly aided Mitterrand in escaping what looked like economic disaster in 1984. His recognition of the business community beginning in the early 1980s, after reflation failed to refuel the economy, and his new image, especially under cohabitation, helped him to subdue many of his political problems. The beginning of his second term, following a period of inertia, was taken up largely with international events, notably the integration of the EEC and the rise of a new Europe. This resolute European has now made European construction the focal point of his second term. If the economic upturn and his reelection are any indication, he was fairly successful in confronting the major problems of his first mandate. However, he has been criticized in France for being too "hexagonal"—that is, concerned only with events and trends within the "hexagon" formed by France's frontiers—between 1981 and 1988 and not providing the nation with a larger global vision.[6] One wonders if his second term will be as successful as the first given the internal quarrels within the Socialist party and the complex problems (and opportunities) facing European nations following the historic changes that were initiated on the continent in 1989.

As one views Mitterrand's presidency, however, there is a strong element of continuity running throughout his term in office. Unexpectedly, Mitterrand has maintained a Gaullist foreign and defense policy for France, despite his earlier criticism of the same policy.

In his first term, this was done, in part, to maintain a consensus in one area while he attempted reform in another. Without a bipartisan foreign and defense policy, the numerous reforms of the Socialist government might not have been possible, nor would his experiment with cohabitation. Even in his second term with the opening to the center, his foreign and defense policy have reminded many of de Gaulle, especially after the fall of the Berlin Wall when he called for a European Confederation and a Europe united from the Atlantic to the Urals. Mitterrand knows that the continuation of a Gaullist external policy strengthens his own consensus and the opening to the center. Thus his Gaullist approach to external affairs has been a realistic policy given the domestic political context and his need for a national consensus in this domain.

With regard to the United States, however, Mitterrand's Gaullist foreign policy struck a balance between de Gaulle's demand for national independence and friendship with the superpower across the Atlantic. While he opposed the U.S. government's Latin American policy and the Strategic Defense Initiative, for instance, he sided with American officials in the 1980s on the necessity for vigilance toward the Soviet Union. Prior to the outbreak of the brief 1991 war against Iraq, precipitated by Saddam Hussein's invasion of Kuwait, Mitterrand advocated a nonmilitary solution to the crisis in the Persian Gulf, including an international conference on the Middle East. However, when war commenced against Iraq in January of 1991, Mitterrand placed 10,000 troops and 100 French aircraft under U.S. command and played a significant role in evicting Iraqi troops from Kuwait. In the aftermath of the Gulf War, he supported George Bush in opposing Saddam Hussein, especially on the issue of the development of nuclear facilities in Iraq. French-American relations have never been so steady and confident in the postwar years as under the Mitterrand presidency.

Despite Mitterrand's Gaullist foreign policy, as well as his solid relationship with the U.S., beginning in 1989 and 1990 he gave clear indications that he desired to see greater cooperation among European nations in the area of foreign and defense policy. This was evident at the November 1990 Conference on Security and Cooperation in Europe where he and other representatives agreed to reduce drastically conventional arms on the Continent, approved German unification, and created new structures for the CSCE that would provide for the regular meeting of foreign ministers, a permanent secretariat in

Prague, a conflict resolution center in Vienna, and an election monitoring office in Warsaw. Mitterrand and other heads of state and government at this meeting signed a "Charter of Paris for a New Europe" that hailed the end of the "era of confrontation and division." Shortly after this CSCE summit, Mitterrand and German Chancellor Kohl signed a declaration on the development of a common European foreign and security policy, an idea that Mitterrand had advocated in order to enhance European autonomy, but also to increase the global influence of France as it works in unison with its European neighbors, and to firmly anchor a reunited Germany to the West. Mitterrand's desire for a common European security policy seems to indicate that he is now intent on altering the Gaullist external policy that has long characterized his nation. The new emphasis on Europe could also mean that one of the new divisions within the French body politic will center on political parties that are pro-EEC and those that emphasize *la patrie*, a factor that should further splinter the Right and aid Mitterrand to solidify the new centrist republic.

A political observer in France once commented that most presidents make a few strategic decisions during their terms and spend the remainder of their time repairing gaffes.[7] To a certain degree, this is true of Mitterrand himself. The Socialist president made his share of mistakes, three of the more important being his decision at the beginning of his presidency to pursue expensive neo-Keynesian economic measures without fully taking into account the economic situation in the Western world, his reading of the narrow 1981 election victory as a mandate for large-scale change, and possibly his appointment of Rocard as prime minister. The first two mistakes rudely revealed to the Socialists the difficulty of transforming Western capitalism. The most Mitterrand and his government could do was to try and give capitalism a slightly more human face. His appointment of Rocard was an effort to widen the opening to the center, use up his archrival's popularity, and prepare the way for the continued success of his own tendency within the Socialist party. In the aftermath of the Rennes meeting of the PS, where warring factions failed to reach agreement as two dauphins battled for the right to Mitterrand's throne, Fabius was weakened, a Jospin-Rocard alliance threatened to push the remaining Mitterrandists into a minority position, and Rocard became the strongest contender for the Elysée. Although the president replaced Rocard as prime minister on May 15, 1991, with the appointment of Edith Cresson to the premiership, Rocard is still the best-placed

Socialist as the nation begins to anticipate the 1995 presidential election. Sometimes politics resembles a theater of contradictions.

Nevertheless, despite making some mistakes, Mitterrand has made six key "reactive decisions" during his term that produced beneficial results. One, of course, was the decision to abandon reflation and pursue an austerity program, the most difficult and agonizing decision given Socialist mythology and campaign promises. This decision, however, was forced on Mitterrand by the realists in his government, such as Finance Minister Delors, and by the poor performance of the French economy after one year of Socialist reflation. Closely related to the adoption of austerity was a second decision, the emphasis placed on modernization. By stressing the need for France to modernize its industrial base, Mitterrand and the Socialists rationalized the increases in unemployment and blamed an ailing and uncompetitive economy on the Giscard presidency as they led the nation through the painful process of restructuring industry. Another reactive decision that paid off was Mitterrand's commitment to defend the deployment of almost six hundred new NATO missiles in Europe in late 1983. Although he sincerely worried about the buildup of Soviet military strength, he cleverly used the deployment issue by turning it into a crusade in order to take attention off French domestic problems. The most crucial decision of Mitterrand's first term was the withdrawal of the Savary law for private schools. As some noted at the time, this decision, coupled with his proposed referendum on public liberties, "redistributed the cards" in France, improved the psychological climate of the nation, and saved the Mitterrand presidency from disaster. This decision showed Mitterrand's political genius at its best, revealing his ability to maneuver and to turn a potentially damaging situation into one that worked to his advantage. Following the 1986 legislative elections came Mitterrand's decision to attempt cohabitation with a right-wing government. He knew, of course, that cohabitation would provide him with an opportunity to counterattack his opponents—one of his greatest strengths—and to create the image of an umpire above the political fray and the guardian of national interests, much as de Gaulle had done earlier. As president, Mitterrand was more successful in building support for himself and his party during cohabitation than during the 1981–86 period when he and the PS possessed an absolute majority in the National Assembly. The sixth reactive decision was to respond, albeit slowly at first, to the European challenge that emerged in 1989 and 1990. Mitterrand's initial effort to shape a new continent had a decidedly Gaullist ring to it. Nonetheless, he sought to ensure French security in the context of a more closely integrated and autonomous Europe, one that would hopefully see a strong French-German axis in order to increase his nation's power and influence both on the continent and in the international arena.

What does the future hold for Mitterrand for the remainder of his term? He will certainly have to pay close attention to the popularity of Rocard, who is now able to fully devote himself to preparing for the 1995 presidential campaign. When Rocard submitted his resignation as prime minister in mid-May of 1991, his stepping down was presented as a mutually agreed-upon divorce. However, Mitterrand reportedly requested his resignation. While Rocard's popularity remained relatively high during his tenure as prime minister, critics (including some Socialists) demanded that the government pay more attention to the need for social justice and further reform, especially as the economic situation improved. In this regard, late in the fall of 1990 the Rocard government confronted demonstrations by high school students for educational reform and protests by trade unions opposed to a government-sponsored social security tax reform. In the midst of these challenges, Rocard barely survived a no-confidence vote in the National Assembly as conservatives and Communists supported a censure motion to block the controversial social security tax proposal. Moreover, prior to his resignation, Rocard had difficulty piecing together majorities in the National Assembly. Although he is no longer prime minister, Rocard is popular with the electorate and, rather ironically, may well be the Socialist who eventually inherits Mitterrand's throne. However, Mitterrand can be expected to play the tendencies within the Socialist party to ensure that his own faction remains dominant. When Mauroy announced early in the summer of 1991 that he would give up the leadership of the PS, *Le Monde* suggested that Fabius was a likely candidate to head the Socialist party;[8] this, obviously, would place Mitterrand's protégé in a key post and position him for a presidential bid in 1995.

Mitterrand must prepare for the 1993 legislative elections as well. Of course, this is one of the main reasons he appointed Cresson to become France's first woman prime minister, an appointment that gives the government a new and more dynamic image. A loyal Mitterrandist since the 1960s, she served as minister of agriculture (1981–83), minister of foreign trade and tourism (1983–84), minister of industrial restructuring and foreign trade (1984–86), and minister of European affairs (1988–1990). Cresson brings to the premiership a more leftist orientation than Rocard, an orientation that suggests she will attempt to tackle social problems. She also is expected to demand that France strengthen its industrial competitiveness as the rendezvous with an integrated Europe approaches. In fact, she resigned her position as minister of European affairs under the Rocard government in October of 1990 because she felt that Rocard had failed to mobilize industry in order to increase French competitiveness. Known for her outspoken manner and sometimes called "the fighter," in her first public address as prime minister she roundly criticized Japan for its protectionism and then proposed to merge the finance, trade, and industry ministries into one powerful ministry similar to Japan's ministry of international trade and industry. Bérégovoy, Rocard's highly respected finance minister, was appointed to head this new superministry. With Cresson as prime minister, Mitterrand can be expected to now play more of a role in domestic affairs as he and the government seek to reduce unemployment (10 percent in October of 1991), rectify social inequalities, prepare France for the opening of the European borders in 1993, and strengthen the position of the Socialists as the legislative elections of 1993 and the presidential elections of 1995 approach. Despite the formation of the new government, Cresson's approval rating fell to 28 percent by September 1991.

Mitterrand must also pay attention to the rise of racism, fanned partially by the emergence of the FN (which he himself must take some responsibility for aiding electorally as he tried to divide his right-wing opponents with proportional representation) and the divisive affair of the Islamic scarfs. For example, in October 1990 the French were made painfully aware of the problem of racism and the alienation of immigrant youth in their country when a refurbished North African neighborhood near Lyon erupted in violence following a controversial accident involving a police car and a motorcycle. To a certain degree, Mitterrand and his new prime minister acknowledged that racism and integration are major problems when Cresson appointed a minister of social affairs and integration. SOS-Racisme has warned the government that the condition of immigrants in the suburbs, Paris, and elsewhere poses a potentially explosive problem that demands immediate attention. And, in a related context, Mitterrand will have to tackle the difficult problem of immigration as well as a new wave of anti-Semitism, dramatically called to the attention of the nation and the world with the May 1990 desecration of a Jewish cemetery in the small southern town of Carpentras.

Of course, Mitterrand must also devote much of his time and energy to the development of a new Europe, ensuring that German reunification and the instability in Eastern Europe, due to the recent breathtaking political changes (including the attempted coup in the Soviet Union in August 1991 by Communist party hardliners) as well as to national and ethnic rivalries, do not hinder European integration, and that the Continent finds a way to ensure peace and security. Most likely, he will continue to advocate a greater role for the Conference on Security and Cooperation in Europe in order to transcend the Yalta system and provide the Continent with more autonomy as a new Europe emerges. The November 1990 meeting of the CSCE in Paris was called by some Europeans a second Congress of Vienna. The CSCE is an important part of Mitterrand's plan for a new Europe. He will also likely continue to support an important role for NATO, but a modified role that permits the development of the CSCE and a possible European security system. At the outset of his second term, it seemed as if Mitterrand was content to assume a low profile as his popular prime minister governed the nation. Surprises at home and abroad ensured that Mitterrand would have an active second term as president of France.

Mitterrand may also hold something special for the future. To a large degree, his duel with de Gaulle involved a "battle over institutions," with Mitterrand defending the Fourth Republic with its weak president compared to the omnipotent presidency of the Fifth Republic.[9] While he vigorously opposed what he viewed as de Gaulle's coup d'état in 1958, he has had to reconcile himself, as already mentioned, to the institutional arrangements of the Fifth Republic (rather willingly and without too much difficulty during his presidency). Yet before he leaves office he may attempt to balance the key institutions of the republic. For example, he has suggested on several occasions that he favors reducing the seven-year presidential term to five years, a reform supported by the French public. This change, perhaps together with enhancement of the authority of the National Assembly by restricting the use of Article 49-3 of the Constitution, the transformation of the Constitutional Council into a supreme court open to the appeals of individual citizens—a reform that Mitterrand announced he favored on Bastille Day 1989—and other reforms could provide France with a strong system of checks and balances that would alter the presidential monarchy that de Gaulle created for himself in 1958. Mitterrand's willingness actively to sponsor some of these changes will depend on the political situation, of course. If he himself does not run again for the presidency, or if the Right gains new electoral strength, he may well attempt institutional reform that will make him the victor in his long battle over institutions with de Gaulle. If Mitterrand does attempt such reforms and they are successful, this would be his final *coup de Jarnac* before retiring to write his memoirs. It would be a fitting ending to the story of this political warrior.

What will be Mitterrand's historical legacy? Surely, he will be remembered for the numerous reforms of his Socialist government, but above all for modernizing, pacifying, and democratizing the political system of the Fifth Republic. Although his impact has been relatively slight on the economy, culture, ideology, and foreign policy, and he has not been able to create the type of society that he desires, French political life has changed in significant ways because of his presence. The realigned political system, the acceptance of *alternance*, the degree of consensus and pluralism of France's new centrist republic are attributable in large measure to Mitterrand. As a result of these changes, the French political system is much more like that of other Western democracies. Thus, Mitterrand will be viewed in the future as a "political revolutionary" of sorts. He will also be remembered as a consummate politician, what one writer has called a *homo politicus*. During the course of his long career he has emerged as the dominating figure on the left in twentieth-century France, and his significance far surpasses that of Jaurès, Blum, or Mendès-France.[10] He will be credited, too, for his determined efforts to establish the EEC as a powerful trading bloc and to advance European integration, his most pressing task during the early years of his second term.

In discussing his own legacy as president, Mitterrand once said rather sarcastically that he is missing something that de Gaulle and Clemenceau, the two towering political figures of twentieth-century France, both had in their careers: war.[11] While Mitterrand did play an important role in the Resistance, he was not a general with international visibility during the war, nor has he led his nation during a time of global conflict, except for the short war against Iraq in 1991, or an Algerian crisis. In talking about his own legacy, he often likes to avoid comparisons with de Gaulle, saying that the general represented one of the last great leaders of the nineteenth century.[12] Perhaps the Socialist president has found in the European challenge his rendezvous with history.[13] Mitterrand's response to this momentous challenge will likely determine his final place in the history of twentieth-century France.

Notes

PREFACE

1. Quoted in *The New York Times Magazine*, February 28, 1988, p. 32.

2. With regard to this important point, I must acknowledge the comments of Edward Berenson who served as chair and commentator of a panel titled "French Politics in the 1980s" at the Sixteenth Annual Conference of the Western Society for French History, November 2–5, 1988, University of California, Los Angeles.

3. The notion of a prince-president is discussed in Jacques Julliard, "La tentation du Prince-Président," *Pouvoirs* 41 (1987): 27–36.

4. Denis MacShane, *François Mitterrand: A Political Odyssey* (London: Quartet Books, 1982).

5. Catherine Nay, *Le noir et le rouge: ou l'histoire d'une ambition* (Paris: Grasset, 1984); see also Catherine Nay, *The Black and the Red: François Mitterrand, The Story of an Ambition*, trans. by Alan Sheridan (New York: Harcourt Brace Jovanovich, Publishers 1987). Several scholarly monographs have appeared in English on the Mitterrand presidency; for example, see Julius W. Friend, *Seven Years in France: François Mitterrand and the Unintended Revolution, 1981–1988* (Boulder: Westview Press, 1989); George Ross, Stanley Hoffmann, and Sylvie Malzacher (eds.), *The Mitterrand Experiment: Continuity and Change in Modern France* (Cambridge: Polity Press, 1987); and Sonia Masey, Michael Newman (eds.), *Mitterrand's France* (London: Croom Helm, 1987).

6. Quoted in Priscilla Parkhurst Ferguson, "Braudel's Empire in Paris," *Contemporary French Civilization* 12, no. 1 (Winter/Spring 1988): 74.

INTRODUCTION:
THE ENIGMA, THE MAN, AND HISTORY

1. This broadcast, entitled "Auto-Portrait," was produced by Pierre Jouve and Ali Magoudi who also published a book based on their study of Mitterrand: *Mitterrand: Portrait total* (Paris: Carrer, 1986).
2. Franz-Olivier Giesbert, *François Mitterand ou la tentation de l'histoire* (Paris: Seuil, 1977), p. 9. Also see Nay, *Le noir et le rouge;* Thierry Desjardins, *François Mitterrand: Un socialiste gaullien* (Paris: Hachette, 1978); Jean-Marie Borzeix, *Mitterrand lui-même* (Paris: Stock, 1973), p. 7; Jean-Marie Colombani, *Portrait du Président: Le monarque imaginaire* (Paris: Gallimard, 1985); Serge July, *Les Années Mitterrand: Histoire baroque d'une normalization inachevée* (Paris: Grasset, 1986); Catherine Nay, *Les sept Mitterrand: ou les métamorphoses d'une septennat* (Paris: Grasset, 1988); Jean Daniel, *Les Religions d'un Président: Regards sur les aventures du mitterrandisme* (Paris: Grasset, 1988); Franz-Olivier Giesbert, *Le Président* (Paris: Seuil, 1989). Giesbert's work, although it quickly became a best-seller in France, is an anecdotal and highly subjective critical account of the Mitterrand presidency.
3. Dorothy Pickles, *Problems of Contemporary French Politics* (London: Methuen, 1982), p. 144.
4. Dominique Frémy, *Quid des Présidents de la République . . . et des candidats* (Paris: Robert Laffont, 1987), p. 607.
5. Quoted in *Le Monde*, May 12, 1981.
6. François Mitterrand, *Ici et maintenant* (Paris: Fayard, 1980), p. 44.
7. Colombani, *Portrait*, pp. 197–98.
8. Quoted ibid., p. 168.
9. Ibid., p. 199.
10. *Le Monde*, September 29, 1982; see also Colombani, *Portrait*, p. 105.
11. July, *Les Années Mitterrand*, p. 182.
12. See Giesbert, *Mitterrand*, pp. 145–53, 186–98.
13. See Wayne Northcutt, "The Domestic Origins of Mitterrand's Foreign Policy, 1981–1985," *Contemporary French Civilization* 10, no. 2 (Spring/Summer 1986): 233–67; also Stephen E. Bornstein, "An End to French Exceptionalism? The Lessons of the Greenpeace Affair," *French Politics and Society* 5, no. 4 (September 1987): 3–16.
14. See Wayne Northcutt, "The Changing Domestic Policies and Views of the Mitterrand Government, 1981–1984: The Crisis of Contemporary French Socialism," *Contemporary French Civilization* 9, no. 2 (Spring/Summer 1985): 141–65.
15. French Embassy, Press and Information Service, *News from France* (May 19, 1987), pp. 6–7; see also IPSOS, BVA, and

Louis Harris polls reviewed ibid., November 20, 1987, p. 8.

16. Laurent Fabius, interview with the author, June 10, 1987, Paris.

17. François Mitterrand, *The Wheat and the Chaff* (translation of *La Paille et le grain* [Paris: Flammarion, 1975] and *L'Abeille et l'architecte* [Paris: Flammarion, 1978]), trans. Richard S. Woodward, Concilia Hayter, and Helen R. Lane (New York: Seaver Books, 1982), p. 167.

18. Danièle Molho, interview with the author, Paris, July 13, 1983.

19. Pickles, *Contemporary French Politics*, p. 144.

20. Ibid.

21. Nay, *The Black and the Red*, p. 301.

22. Molho, interview.

23. Frémy, *Quid des Présidents*, p. 605.

24. Quoted in Jouve and Magoudi, *Mitterrand*, p. 13.

25. Ibid., pp. 94, 98.

26. See Nay, *The Black and the Red;* also Daniel, *Les Religions d'un Président.*

27. Fabius, interview.

28. Quoted in Frémy, *Quid des Présidents*, p. 603.

29. Fabius, interview.

30. Giesbert claims that his tardiness is a product of his exaggerated sense of self-importance and protocol (see Giesbert, *Le Président*, pp. 352–54).

31. Nay, *The Black and the Red*, p. 371, n. 5.

32. Mitterrand, *The Wheat and the Chaff*, pp. 218–19.

33. Jouve and Magoudi, *Mitterrand*, p. 73.

34. Jacques Julliard, conversation with the author, Twentieth Annual Meeting of the Society for French Historical Studies, University of Virginia, Charlottesville, Virginia, April 6, 1984. Julliard noted that while Mitterrand is ill at ease with the Anglo-Saxon world and does not speak English, his chief competitor in the Socialist party, Michel Rocard, admires and is comfortable with Anglo-Saxon nations and their culture and speaks English relatively well.

35. Fabius, interview.

36. See Tony Judt, *Marxism and the French Left: Studies on Labor and Politics in France, 1830–1981* (Oxford: Clarendon Press, 1986), pp. 239ff.

37. See Thierry Pfister, *Dans les coulisses du pouvoir: La comédie de la cohabitation* (Paris: Albin Michel, 1986).

38. See *Le Monde, Dossiers et documents: Les élections législatives du 16 mars 1986*, pp. 2–40.

39. Wayne Northcutt, *The French Socialist and Communist Party under the Fifth Republic, 1958–1981: From Opposition to Power* (New York: Irvington, 1985), pp. 35–37.

40. *Le Nouvel Observateur*, May 4–10, 1981, p. 32.

41. *Le Monde, Dossiers et documents, Les élections législatives 1986*, pp. 30–33.

42. Pierre Mendès-France, *Gouverner, c'est choisir*, 3 vols. (Paris: Julliard, 1953–58).

43. See Jean-Marie Colombani and

Jean-Yves Lhomeau, *Le Mariage blanc: Mitterrand-Chirac* (Paris: Grasset, 1986).

44. Quoted in Claude Manceron and Bernard Pingaud, *François Mitterrand: L'homme, les idées, le programme* (Paris: Flammarion, 1981), p. 59.
45. *Le Monde*, July 2, 1981.
46. See July, *Les Années Mitterrand*, p. 13.
47. See Stanley Hoffmann,

"Gaullism by Any Other Name," *Foreign Policy*, no. 57 (Winter 1984–85): 38–57.
48. See Northcutt, "The Domestic Origins of Mitterrand's Foreign Policy."
49. Colombani, *Portrait*, p. 113.
50. Giesbert, *Le Président*, p. 11.
51. See Phillippe Bauchard, *La Guerre des deux roses: Du rêve à la réalité, 1981–1985* (Paris: Grasset, 1986), pp. 171–73.

CHAPTER I
THE EARLY YEARS

1. Frémy, *Quid des Présidents*, pp. 550–51.
2. Giesbert, *Mitterrand*, p. 16.
3. Quoted ibid., p. 17.
4. Ibid., p. 18.
5. Frémy, *Quid des Présidents*, p. 550.
6. Mitterrand, "Auto-portrait."
7. Colombani, *Portrait*, pp. 48–49.
8. Nay, *The Black and the Red*, p. 11.
9. See ibid., pp. 11–12.
10. François Mitterrand, *Ici et maintenant*, p. 16.
11. François Mitterrand, *Ma part de vérité* (Paris: Fayard, 1969), p. 16.
12. Giesbert, *Mitterrand*, p. 22.
13. Nay, *The Black and the Red*, p. 41.
14. Giesbert, *Mitterrand*, pp. 19–20.
15. Ibid., p. 21.
16. Mitterrand, *The Wheat and the Chaff*, pp. 218–19.
17. Giesbert, *Mitterrand*, p. 17.
18. Ibid.
19. Mitterrand, *Vérité*, p. 18.
20. Quoted in Nay, *The Black and the Red*, p. 16.
21. Giesbert, *Mitterrand*, p. 19.
22. Quoted in Frémy, *Quid des Présidents*, p. 552.
23. Julliard, conversation.
24. Giesbert, *Mitterrand*, p. 18; Nay, *The Black and the Red*, p. 6.
25. Giesbert, *Mitterrand*, p. 20.
26. Ibid., pp. 19–21.
27. Ibid., p. 19.
28. Molho, interview.
29. Mitterrand, *Vérité*, pp. 20–21. Gaston Doumergue, a member of the Radical Socialist party in the 1920s and 1930s, was a popular president in France between 1924 and 1931 who played the role of a judge or umpire between the various political parties. Mitterrand himself would attempt to project the same image under cohabitation following the March 1986 legislative elections, when he had to coexist with a right-wing government. Edouard

Daladier was a prominent member of the Radical party under the Third Republic.

30. Ibid., p. 21.
31. *Le Monde*, May 12, 1981.
32. Ibid.
33. Mitterrand, *Politique*, 2 vols. (Paris: Fayard, 1977–81), 1:4–5.
34. MacShane, *Mitterrand*, p. 28.
35. Mitterrand, *Vérité*, p. 21.

36. *Le Monde*, May 12, 1981.
37. Mitterrand, *Vérité*, p. 26.
38. Ibid., p. 25.
39. Ibid., p. 30.
40. Ibid., p. 27.
41. Quoted in Frémy, *Quid des Présidents*, p. 551.
42. MacShane, *Mitterrand*, pp. 35–36.
43. Mitterrand, *Vérité*, p. 23.

CHAPTER 2

THE FOURTH REPUBLIC

1. See Roland Cayrol, *François Mitterrand, 1945–1967* (Paris: Fondation Nationale des Sciences Politiques, 1967), pp. 9–14. For a brief but thorough review of Mitterrand's political career under the Fourth and Fifth Republics, see *Le Monde*, May 12, 1981.
2. Borzeix, *Mitterrand*, p. 8.
3. Mitterrand, *Vérité*, p. 35.
4. Quoted in MacShane, *Mitterrand*, p. 66.
5. Quoted in Giesbert, *Mitterrand*, p. 119.
6. Ibid., p. 172.
7. Ibid., p. 174.
8. Ibid., p. 90; see also Philip Williams, *Politics in Post-War France: Parties and the Constitution in the Fourth Republic* (London: Longmans, Green, 1958), pp. 142–46. For an understanding of Mitterrand's role in the UDSR, see *Les Cahiers de l'UDSR, Discours de René Pleven, 3e congrès national, juin 1949*, p. 2, Archives of the Fondation Nationale des Sciences Politiques, Paris, France

(hereafter cited as FNSP), Coll. 8, 1452–16.
9. Mitterrand, *The Wheat and the Chaff*, p. 167.
10. Manceron and Pingaud, *Mitterrand*, p. 67.
11. Mitterrand, *Vérité*, pp. 23–25; also consult Mitterrand, *Politique*, vol. 1, for a discussion of this important phase of his life.
12. Mitterrand, *Vérité*, p. 35.
13. *Les Cahiers de l'UDSR, Interventions de René Capitant, J. Lanet, François Mitterrand, 3e congrès national, 11 juin 1949*, pp. 41–42 (FNSP, Coll. 8, 1452–18).
14. Manceron and Pingaud, *Mitterrand*, p. 28.
15. Williams, *Politics in Post-War France*, pp. 143–46.
16. Philip Williams, *La vie politique sous la IV République* (Paris: Colin, 1971), p. 284.
17. See, for example, *Les Cahiers de l'UDSR, Interventions de Capitant, Lanet, Mitterrand*, 1949 (FNSP, Coll. 8, 1452–16).
18. See Mitterrand, *Politique*, vol. 1, pp. 341–46.

19. Quoted in Giesbert, *Mitterrand*, p. 97.
20. Charles Moulin, *Mitterrand intime* (Paris: Albin Michel, 1982), p. 81.
21. Mitterrand, *Présence française et abandon* (Paris: Plon, 1957), p. 182.
22. Quoted in Giesbert, *Mitterrand*, p. 107. Mitterrand claims that the Free French forces in London advised him to accept the *Francisque* to improve his cover as a member of the Resistance.
23. Quoted in Cayrol, *Mitterrand*, p. 23.
24. Quoted ibid.
25. Giesbert, *Mitterrand*, p. 102.
26. Mitterrand, *Vérité*, pp. 35–36.
27. Ibid., p. 35.
28. France, *Assemblée nationale, J.O., Débats parlementaires, 2e séance du 10 novembre 1954*, p. 6080.
29. Quoted in Paul Clay Sorum, *Intellectuals and Decolonization in France* (Chapel Hill: University of North Carolina Press, 1977), p. 189.
30. Quoted in Giesbert, *Mitterrand*, p. 117.
31. France, *J.O., Débats parlementaires, séance du 12 novembre 1954*, pp. 4967–68; also Mitterrand, *Politique*, vol. 1, pp. 113–15.
32. Giesbert, *Mitterrand*, p. 162.
33. Quoted ibid., p. 116.
34. See Mitterrand, *Aux frontières*, pp. 11–14.
35. France, *J.O., Débats parlementaires, séance du 6 janvier 1953*, p. 30.
36. Mitterrand, *Présence et abandon*, p. 11.
37. Quoted in Giesbert, *Mitterrand*, p. 150.
38. Mitterrand, *Vérité*, p. 45.
39. Mitterrand, *Politique*, 1: 91–93.
40. For a discussion of the affair and the firing of Baylot, see Moulin, *Mitterrand intime*, pp. 110–14; Borzeix, *Mitterrand*, pp. 75–80; Giesbert, *Mitterrand*, pp. 145–53.
41. Mitterrand, *Politique*, 1: 209.
42. See Cayrol, *Mitterrand*, pp. 43–45. For the position of the UDSR on Europe, consult *Les Cahiers de l'UDSR, Rapport sur l'unité européenne, 5e congrès national, 1951* (FNSP, Coll. 4, 278); also *Les Cahiers de l'UDSR, Motions, 4e congrès national, octobre 1950* (FNSP, Coll. 8, 1452–25), pp. 3, 12.
43. At a meeting of the foreign policy commission of the UDSR, Mitterrand revealed his foreign policy preferences when he declared, "The western Mediterranean and the African bloc before Europe and the Atlantic; Europe before Asia" (quoted in Cayrol, *Mitterrand*, p. 43).
44. Quoted in Cayrol, *Mitterrand*, p. 45.
45. *L'Express*, April 10, 1954, p. 7.
46. Ibid., April 17, 1954, p. 7.
47. Mitterrand, *The Wheat and the Chaff*, p. 9; see also Mitterrand, *Vérité*, pp. 25–27.
48. *Les Cahiers de l'UDSR, Interventions de Capitant, Lanet, Mitterrand, 1949* (FNSP, Coll. 8, 1452–18), p. 36.
49. Ibid., pp. 31–33.
50. See Mitterrand, *Politique*, 1: 311–29; and Mitterrand, *Le Coup d'état permanent* (Paris: Plon, 1964).

51. Quoted in Moulin, *Mitterrand intime*, p. 130.
52. See *Les Cahiers de l'UDSR, Interventions de Capitant, Lanet, Mitterrand, 1949* (FNSP, Coll. 8, 1452–18), p. 26.
53. Quoted in Cayrol, *Mitterrand*, p. 27.
54. Ibid.
55. Ibid.
56. Ibid., pp. 27–28.

57. See Mitterrand, *Vérité*, pp. 42–45.
58. MacShane, *Mitterrand*, p. 59.
59. The Republican Front included the UDSR, SFIO, and Mendès-France and his followers.
60. Mitterrand, *Politique*, 1: 370.
61. Ibid.
62. Quoted in Giesbert, *Mitterrand*, p. 179.
63. Quoted ibid., p. 180.

CHAPTER 3

THE GAULLIST FIFTH REPUBLIC

1. Nay and other political observers in France have stressed this point; see, for example, Nay, *The Black and the Red*, pp. 207–9.
2. This ironic situation was noted by Julliard, conversation with the author.
3. The establishment of the Fifth Republic revealed to Mitterrand's friends and enemies his stubbornness and his ability to respond to setbacks and challenges. Nay believes that if Mitterrand has succeeded, it is due to (1) his "almost abnormal stubbornness," and (2) his ability to rise up and meet challenges; Nay, *The Black and the Red*, p. 209.
4. Quoted in MacShane, *Mitterrand*, p. 77.
5. Nay, *The Black and the Red*, p. 217.
6. Quoted in MacShane, *Mitterrand*, p. 78.
7. Frémy, *Quid des Présidents*, p. 558.

8. See ibid.; Giesbert, *Mitterrand*, pp. 187–98.
9. Nay, *The Black and the Red*, pp. 235–43. This point was also stressed by Molho and Julliard in interview and conversation with the author.
10. Quoted in Nay, *The Black and the Red*, p. 234.
11. Quoted ibid., p. 235.
12. Mitterrand, *Vérité*, p. 68.
13. Molho claims that after the Algerian war, Mitterrand arrived on the left (Molho, interview).
14. Quoted in Nay, *The Black and the Red*, p. 242.
15. See Neil Nugent and David Rowe, *The Left in France* (London: Macmillan, 1982), pp. 52–53.
16. Ibid., p. 53.
17. Quoted in Nay, *The Black and the Red*, p. 247.
18. Quoted in MacShane, *Mitterrand*, p. 106.
19. Quoted in Frémy, *Quid des Présidents*, p. 558.
20. See Mitterrand, *Vérité*.
21. Quoted in MacShane, *Mitterrand*, p. 135.

22. Nay, *The Black and the Red*, p. 304.
23. See, for example, Mitterrand, *The Wheat and The Chaff*, pp. 77–79, 118–20, 173–74.
24. See Mitterrand, *Socialisme du possible*.
25. Colombani, *Portrait*, p. 82.
26. Mitterrand, *Vérité*, p. 90; see also Mitterrand, *Ici et maintenant*, pp. 43–72.
27. Colombani, *Portrait*, pp. 140–41.
28. This motivation was also stressed by Molho (interview).
29. See Yves Roucaute, *Le Parti socialiste* (Paris: Huisman, 1983).
30. Nugent and Rowe, *The Left in France*, pp. 57–58.
31. Quoted in MacShane, *Mitterrand*, pp. 163–64.
32. Colombani, *Portrait*, p. 55.
33. Quoted in Giesbert, *Le Président*, p. 45.
34. Nugent and Rowe, *The Left in France*, pp. 57, 86.
35. Northcutt, *The French Socialist and Communist Party*, p. 30.
36. Michel Winoch, "La gauche en France depuis 1968," in Jean Touchard, *La gauche en France depuis 1900* (Paris: Seuil, 1970), pp. 355–60.
37. In the late 1970s several Communist parties in Western Europe began to drop some of their Marxist-Leninist baggage and distance themselves from the Soviet Union. Détente between East and West facilitated this important change in the CPs of Italy, Spain, and France.
38. See *Le Monde*, April 13–15 and 25–28, 1978; also Northcutt, *The French Socialist and Communist Party*, chapter 4.
39. See *Le Monde, Dossiers et documents: Les élections de mars 1978*.
40. Molho, interview.
41. *Le Monde*, April 13, 1978.
42. See Northcutt, *The French Socialist and Communist Party*, chapter 2.
43. See Mitterrand, *Politique*, 2: 224–28; and Mitterrand, *Ici et maintenant*, pp. 9–14.
44. *Des femmes en mouvements*, June 5–12, 1981, p. 6.
45. Stanley Hoffmann, "France: The Big Change," *New York Review of Books*, June 25, 1981, p. 47.
46. See Mitterrand, *Politique*, 2: 305–24.
47. Parti socialiste, *Projet socialiste pour la France des années 80* (Paris: Club Socialiste du Livre, 1980), p. 78.
48. Ibid., p. 341.
49. Howard Machin and Vincent Wright, "Why Mitterrand Won: The French Presidential Elections of April–May 1981," *West European Politics* 5, no. 1 (January 1982): 15.
50. *L'Année politique, économique et sociale en France* (1981): 13.
51. Molho, interview.
52. Hoffmann, "France," p. 27.
53. *L'Année politique* (1981): 10.
54. See Wayne Northcutt and Jeffra Flaitz, "Women and Politics in Contemporary France: The Electoral Shift to the Left in the 1981 Presidential and Legislative Elections," *Contemporary French Civilization* 7, no. 2 (Winter 1983): 183–98; and Northcutt and Flaitz, "Women, Politics, and the French Socialist Government," *West European Politics* 8, no. 4 (1985): 50–70.

55. *Le Canard Enchaîné*, September 17, 1980.
56. *Le Monde*, October 5–14, 1980.
57. *Le Nouvel Observateur*, June 1–7, 1981, p. 56.
58. Hoffmann, "France," p. 49.
59. See Mitterrand, *Ici et maintenant*, p. 232.
60. *Le Monde*, July 2, 1981.
61. Molho, interview.
62. See Hoffmann, "France" for an excellent discussion of these issues.
63. *L'Année politique* (1981): 15.
64. Frémy, *Quid des Présidents*, p. 564.
65. Colombani, *Portrait*, p. 177.
66. Ibid., p. 564.
67. Ibid.

68. Many political observers, such as Molho, noted that Mitterrand improved his performance on television (Molho, interview).
69. Quoted in Frémy, *Quid des Présidents*, p. 569.
70. *Le Monde*, May 12, 1981. The day after his election victory Mitterrand visited the grave of his trusted friend and counsellor Georges Dayan who had died in 1979. Dayan had served with Mitterrand in the 25th Infantry Regiment in World War II; after the war he was elected to the National Assembly from Gard.

CHAPTER 4
DREAMS, ILLUSIONS, AND REFORMS

1. Pierre Mauroy, *A gauche* (Paris: Albin Michel, 1985), p. 50.
2. Bauchard, *La Guerre des roses*, p. 34.
3. Ibid.
4. *L'Année politique* (1981): 9.
5. Quoted in Frémy, *Quid des Présidents*, p. 569.
6. At one point in the inauguration day festivities at the Elysée, Mitterrand told Mendès-France: "If I am president, it is thanks to you."
7. *L'Unité*, May 23, 1981.
8. Quoted in *The Economist*, July 18, 1981, p. 52.
9. See ibid., October 17, 1981; February 13, 1981.
10. *Le Monde*, June 6–7, 1981.
11. Ibid., June 4–5, 1981.
12. Ibid., June 15, 1981.

13. Ibid., July 14, 1981.
14. Ibid., June 12, 1981.
15. *L'Unité*, June 27, 1981.
16. Ibid., July 4, 1981.
17. *Le Monde*, June 24–25, 1981.
18. Ibid., July 2, 1981.
19. Alfred Grosser, *Affaires extérieures: La politique de la France, 1944–1984* (Paris: Flammarion, 1985), pp. 288–313.
20. See Northcutt and Flaitz, "Women, Politics and the French Socialist Government," *West European Politics* (1985), pp. 50, 56–57.
21. Vincent Wright, ed., *Continuity and Change in France* (London: Allen & Unwin, 1984), pp. 55–56.
22. Ibid., pp. 68–69.
23. William Andrews, "The Power

of Paris," *French Politics and Society*, no. 4 (December 1983), pp. 21–22.

24. Wright, *Continuity and Change*, pp. 55–56.

25. Ibid., p. 52.

26. Howard Machin and Vincent Wright, eds., *Economic Policy Making Under the Mitterrand Presidency* (New York: St. Martin, 1985), p. 16.

27. Ibid.

28. Volkmar Lauber, "Socialist Economic Policy in the Eyes of Sympathizer-Critics," *French Politics and Society*, no. 8 (December 1984), p. 32.

29. Bauchard, *La Guerre des roses*, p. 27.

30. Quoted ibid., p. 10.

31. Colombani, *Portrait*, p. 40.

32. See Frémy, *Quid des Présidents*, p. 578.

33. *Le Monde*, September 23, 1986.

34. Denis MacShane, *French Lessons for Labour* (London: Fabian Society, 1986), p. 2.

35. *L'Unité*, September 19, 1981.

36. *Le Monde*, September 25–26, 1981.

37. Ibid., September 28–29, 1982.

38. Ibid., October 11–12, 1981.

39. Ibid.

40. *L'Année politique* (1981): 81.

41. Frémy, *Quid des Présidents*, pp. 576–77.

42. *Business Week*, October 5, 1981, pp. 54–55.

43. *Le Monde*, October 25–26, 1981.

44. Quoted in Machin and Wright, *Economic Policy*, p. 21.

45. *Le Monde*, October 25–26, 1981.

46. Ibid.

47. Ibid.

48. Ibid., December 1, 1981.

49. Ibid.

50. *L'Année politique* (1981): 85–86.

51. Ibid. (1982): 15.

52. *Le Monde*, January 2, 1982.

53. Ibid.

54. See Bauchard, *La Guerre des roses*, pp. 75–76.

55. Nay, *The Black and the Red*, p. 242. The nine council members are not screened and approved by an agency of the government, as is the case in the United States and other liberal democracies, nor are they required to have a legal background. Members of the Constitutional Council serve nine-year nonrenewable terms, and the membership is appointed by thirds every three years. Three members are appointed by the president, three by the president of the National Assembly, and three by the president of the Senate. The president of the Constitutional Council is appointed by the president of the republic. The council's president has a casting vote.

56. Quoted in John Keeler, "Toward a Government of Judges? The Constitutional Council as an Obstacle to Reform in Mitterrand's France," *French Politics and Society*, no. 11 (September 1985), p. 17.

57. Ibid., p. 22.

58. This information was supplied by Alec Stone who completed a doctoral dissertation at the University of Washington on the Constitutional Council under Mitterrand. Guy Carcassone, a French scholar, political commentator, and aide to Michel Rocard,

maintained that the heightened role of the Constitutional Council facilitated a greater knowledge of the Constitution and was a vital instrument in consensus-making (Guy Carcassone, "Le ménage à trois: gouvernement, parlement, conseil constitutionnel," paper presented at a conference on "A France of Pluralism and Consensus? Changing Balances in State and Society," Columbia University/New York University, New York, October 9–11, 1987).

59. *L'Année politique* (1984): 17.
60. Ibid. (1981), p. 16.
61. Frémy, *Quid des Presidents*, p. 547.
62. Minister of Culture Léotard would eventually strike a compromise with Balladur in which the minister of finance agreed to relinquish part of his sprawling office space over a period of time in order to permit an expansion of the Louvre. For a discussion of Mitterrand's cultural policy, see David Wachtel, *Cultural Policy and Socialist France* (Westport, Conn.: Greenwood Press, 1987).

63. *L'Année politique*, (1982): 35–36; also see *Le Monde, Dossiers et documents: Les élections législatives du 16 mars 1986*, p. 6.
64. *L'Unité*, April 2, 1982.
65. Quoted in *Business Week*, April 26, 1982, p. 49.
66. *Le Monde, Dossiers et documents: Les élections législatives, 1986*, p. 6.
67. Quoted in *L'Année politique* (1982): 49–50.
68. *Le Monde*, May 2–5, 1982; also *L'Année politique* (1982): 49–50.
69. *L'Année politique* (1982): 52.
70. Ibid., p. 54.
71. Ibid., p. 52.
72. *Le Monde, Dossiers et documents: Les élections législatives, 1986*, p. 6.
73. Quoted in Bauchard, *La Guerre des roses*, p. 86.
74. *L'Année politique* (1982): 57.
75. *Le Monde*, June 6–7, 1982.
76. *L'Année politique* (1982): 59.
77. On May 18 at the meeting of the Council of Ministers, Mitterrand said that the Falklands conflict represents "an alliance obligation" because "it is a test for Europe" (July, *Les Années Mitterrand*, p. 69).

CHAPTER 5

FROM THE PLAIN TO THE MOUNTAIN

1. See Stanley Hoffmann, *Mitterrand's First Year in Power*, Monographs on Europe, The Center for European Studies (Cambridge: Harvard University, 1982), pp. 19–24.
2. *Le Monde*, June 10, 1982.
3. Ibid.
4. Quoted in Bauchard, *La Guerre des roses*, p. 101.
5. Frémy, *Quid des Présidents*, p. 574.
6. See *Le Monde*, June 13–14,

1982; *L'Année politique* (1982): 59–62.

7. *Le Monde, Dossiers et documents: Les élections législatives, 1986*, p. 6.

8. *L'Année politique* (1982): 12.

9. Ibid., p. 13.

10. *Le Monde, Dossiers et documents: Les élections législatives, 1986*, p. 6.

11. Bauchard, *La Guerre des roses*, pp. 107–8.

12. Quoted ibid., p. 110.

13. *L'Année politique* (1982): 68–69.

14. See, for example, *L'Unité*, July 9, 1982.

15. See *Le Monde*, June 20–July 20, 1982.

16. Quoted in *L'Année politique* (1982): 68–69.

17. Ibid.

18. See Wayne Northcutt, "The Changing Domestic Policies and Views of the Mitterrand Government, 1981–1984," *Contemporary French Civilization* 9, no. 2 (Spring/Summer 1985): 151–52.

19. See *Le Monde*, August 11–19, 1982.

20. *L'Année politique* (1982): 71–73.

21. Ibid., p. 73.

22. *Le Monde*, September 13, 1986.

23. It is curious that Marion would reveal this information in the midst of the 1986 bombing attacks. Was he trying to embarrass Mitterrand and/or attempting to improve his own reputation as a man of action? His motives are not clearly known.

24. *L'Année politique* (1982): 78.

25. See ibid., p. 12.

26. See ibid., p. 82.

27. *L'Unité*, October 1, 1982.

28. *L'Année politique* (1982): 90.

29. Quoted in Colombani, *Portrait*, p. 70.

30. July, *Les Années Mitterrand*, p. 74.

31. *Le Monde*, November 18, 1982.

32. See Northcutt and Flaitz, "Women, Politics and the French Socialist Government," *West European Politics* (1985), p. 64.

33. See ibid.

34. Janice McCormick, "Apprenticeship for Governing: An Assessment of French Socialism in Power," in Machin and Wright, *Economic Policy Under the Mitterrand Presidency*, pp. 52–54.

35. *Le Monde*, November 26, 1982.

36. *L'Année politique* (1982): 97.

37. Quoted in Lewis Coser, "Mitterrand's First Two Years: An Advanced Welfare State in One Country," *Dissent* 30, no. 2 (Spring 1983), p. 166.

38. *Le Monde*, January 1–2, 1983.

39. This blunder led to an investigation, the resignation of Maurice Remy, president of Télédiffusion de France (TDF), and the firing of Jean Guillermin, director general of TDF.

40. *L'Année politique* (1983): 20–21.

41. See Jérôme Jaffré et. al., *SOFRES: Opinion publique, Enquêtes et commentaires 1984* (Paris: Gallimard, 1984), p. 36; and *Le Monde*, July 19, 1984.

42. *L'Année politique* (1982): 12.

43. *Le Monde*, October 14, 1983; also see *L'Année politique* (1983): 68.

44. See *L'Année politique* (1981): 15–16.

45. *Le Monde*, February 4, 1983.

46. *Ibid.*, February 17–18, 1983.

47. Quoted in *L'Année politique* (1983): 30–31.
48. See Diana Pinto, "Mitterrand, Lang, and the Intellectuals," *French Politics and Society*, (May 1983), pp. 10–12.
49. See Wayne Northcutt, "The Changing Domestic Policies and Views of the Mitterrand Government," *Contemporary French Civilization* 9 (1985), pp. 149–50.
50. *Le Monde, Dossiers et documents: Les élections législatives, 1986*, pp. 7–8.
51. *L'Année politique* (1983): 14.
52. Ibid., pp. 14–15.
53. Bauchard, *La Guerre des roses*, pp. 141–43.
54. July, *Les Années Mitterrand*, pp. 90–92; Bauchard, *La Guerre des roses*, pp. 141–51.
55. Bauchard, *La Guerre des roses*, p. 144. According to Nay, Fabius supported, at least initially, leaving the EMS (Nay, *The Black and the Red*, p. 343).
56. Fabius, interview.
57. *L'Année politique* (1983): 37; and Bauchard, *La Guerre des roses*, p. 15.
58. July, *Les Années Mitterrand*, p. 100.
59. *Le Monde*, March 25, 1983; also *L'Unité*, April 1, 1983.
60. See July, *Les Années Mitterrand*, p. 107.
61. *L'Unité*, June 21, 1983.
62. McCormick, "Apprenticeship for Governing," in Machin and Wright, *Economic Policy Under the Mitterrand Presidency*, pp. 55–56.
63. *L'Année politique* (1983): 11.
64. Ibid., pp. 10–11.
65. *Le Monde*, April 26, 1983.
66. *L'Année politique* (1983): 42.
67. Ibid.; also *Le Monde*, April 27, 1983.
68. *L'Année politique* (1983): 46.
69. *Le Monde, Dossiers et documents: L'histoire au jour de jour, 1974–1985*, p. 45.
70. Ibid., p. 43.
71. The Bretton Woods agreements of 1944 produced a system of fixed exchange rates that remained the foundation of the economic relationship among Western nations until 1971 when a floating system of exchange rates was introduced.
72. *Le Monde*, May 31, 1983.
73. *L'Humanité*, June 8, 1983.
74. *Le Monde, Dossiers et documents: Les élections législatives, 1986*, p. 8.
75. *Le Monde*, May 31, 1983.
76. Ibid., June 10, 1983.
77. Ibid.
78. Ibid.
79. *L'Année politique* (1983): 52.
80. Ibid.
81. *Le Monde, Dossiers et documents: Les élections législatives, 1986*, p. 8.
82. Ibid., p. 8.
83. Bauchard, *La Guerre des roses*, p. 164.
84. Ibid., p. 166.
85. July, *Les Années Mitterrand*, pp. 110–11.
86. Bauchard, *La Guerre des roses*, p. 165.
87. Quoted ibid., p. 165–66.
88. *Le Monde, Dossiers et documents: Les élections législatives, 1986*, p. 8.
89. *L'Année politique* (1983): 60.
90. Ibid.
91. *Le Monde*, September 17, 1983.
92. *Le Monde, Dossiers et documents: Les élections législatives, 1986*, pp. 8–9.

93. *Le Monde*, January 1, 1984.
94. Ibid., July 19, 1984.
95. Quoted in July, *Les Années Mitterrand*, p. 124.
96. Ibid., p. 122.
97. See *Le Monde*, November 4–6, 1983.
98. Ibid., November 18, 1983.
99. *L'Année politique* (1983): 75.
100. Ibid.
101. *Le Monde*, November 18, 1983.
102. *L'Année politique* (1983): 68.

103. *L'Unité*, December 16, 1983.
104. *L'Année politique* (1983): 79.
105. *Le Monde*, January 3, 1984.
106. On December 31, a bomb exploded at the Marseille train station killing five people. Terrorism abroad and at home began to occupy the minds of many in France as 1983 drew to a close.
107. *L'Année politique* (1984): 17.
108. *Le Monde*, January 3, 1984.

CHAPTER 6

RETREAT AND MODERNIZE

1. Fabius, interview.
2. These figures are compiled from information in Frémy, *Quid des Présidents*, pp. 601–2.
3. *L'Année politique* (1984): 16.
4. See, for instance, Colombani, *Portrait;* Bauchard, *La Guerre des roses;* and July, *Les Années Mitterrand.*
5. *Business Week*, March 5, 1984, p. 43.
6. Ibid., May 21, 1984, p. 51.
7. Ibid., June 11, 1984, p. 62.
8. *L'Année politique* (1984): 13.
9. Colombani, *Portrait du président*, p. 110.
10. *Le Monde, Dossiers et documents: Les élections législatives, 1986*, p. 9.
11. *Le Monde*, February 8–9, 1984.
12. Quoted in *Business Week*, March 12, 1984, p. 48.
13. Jérôme Jaffré, *SOFRES: Opinion publique, 1985* (Paris: Gallimard, 1985), p. 110; Jaffré, *SOFRES: Opinion publique, 1984* (Paris: Gallimard, 1984), pp. 14 and 63–73.
14. *Le Monde*, February 14, 1984.

15. Ibid.
16. See Mitterrand, *The Wheat and the Chaff*, pp. 119, 173–75; Bauchard, *La Guerre des roses*, p. 335.
17. Mitterrand, *Politique* 2: 322.
18. MacShane, *French Lessons for Labour*, p. 16.
19. *Le Monde*, July 14, 1984.
20. *Le Point* poll published in *The Economist*, March 10, 1984, p. 50.
21. Bauchard, *La Guerre des roses*, p. 191.
22. Ibid., p. 199.
23. *Le Monde, Dossiers et documents: Les élections législatives, 1986*, p. 9.
24. *L'Année politique* (1984): 9.
25. *Le Monde*, April 5–8, 1984.
26. *L'Unité*, April 6, 1984.
27. Ibid., April 20, 1984.
28. *Le Monde*, April 5–6, 1984; *L'Année politique* (1984): 37.
29. *Business Week*, April 23, 1984, p. 40.
30. *L'Année politique* (1984): 38.
31. *Libération*, May 10, 1984.
32. *L'Année politique* (1984): 12.

33. *Le Monde, Dossiers et documents: Les deuxièmes élections européennes (juin 1984)*, p. 69.
34. Ibid.
35. *Libération*, June 20, 1984.
36. Ibid.
37. *L'Année politique* (1984): 12.
38. Ibid. (1985): p. 17.
39. Ibid. For an excellent discussion of the Le Pen phenomenon, see Martin A. Schain, "The National Front in France and the Construction of Political Legitimacy," *West European Politics* 10, no. 2 (April 1987): 229–52.
40. *Le Nouvel Observateur*, June 22, 1984, pp. 22–25.
41. *Le Monde, Dossiers et documents: Les élections européennes* (1984), p. 69.
42. *L'Année politique* (1984): 12.
43. *Le Monde, Dossiers et documents: Les élections européennes (1984)*, p. 71.
44. Jaffré, "Les élections législatives, 1986," *Pouvoirs* 38 (1986): 145.
45. *The Economist*, March 31, 1984, pp. 45–46.
46. *L'Année politique* (1984): 11.
47. Quoted in Bauchard, *La Guerre des roses*, p. 251.
48. *Le Monde*, July 6–8, 1984.
49. See Jaffré, "Les élections législatives, 1986," *Pouvoirs* 38 (1986).
50. *L'Année politique* (1985): 10.
51. *Le Monde*, July 14, 1984.
52. This term was first employed by July, *Les Années Mitterrand*, p. 185.
53. Quoted in Bauchard, *La Guerre des roses*, p. 268.
54. *L'Année politique* (1984): 58.
55. Fabius, interview.
56. Jaffré, SOFRES: *Opinion publique, 1984*, p. 14.
57. *L'Année politique* (1985): 10.
58. Julliard, conversation with the author.
59. *Le Nouvel Observateur*, August 10–16, 1984, pp. 26–27.
60. *L'Unité*, August 31, 1984.
61. Jaffré, *SOFRES: Opinion publique, 1984*, pp. 145–46.
62. *Le Monde*, July 26, 1984.
63. See *L'Année politique* (1984): 12.
64. Fabius, interview; see also *L'Année politique* (1984): 12–14.
65. Fabius, interview.
66. *L'Année politique* (1984): 63.
67. *Le Monde*, July 3, 1983.
68. *The Economist*, October 13, 1984, p. 77.
69. Fabius maintains that the severe economic problems of the Socialist government occurred before his appointment as prime minister (Fabius, interview).
70. *L'Année politique* (1984): 17.
71. *L'Unité*, September 14 and 28, 1984.
72. *L'Année politique* (1984): 71–72.
73. *Le Monde, Dossiers et documents: Les élections législatives, 1986*, p. 10.
74. *Le Monde*, December 12–14, 1984.
75. *Le Monde, Dossiers et documents: Les élections législatives, 1986*, p. 11.
76. Ibid., p. 11.
77. Fabius, interview.
78. *L'Unité*, December 7, 1984 and January 4, 1985; also Fabius, interview.
79. *Le Monde, Dossiers et documents: Les élections législatives, 1986*, p. 11.
80. *Le Monde*, November 24, 1987.
81. *L'Année politique* (1984): 79.

82. Ibid., pp. 78–79.
83. Ibid., p. 79.
84. Ibid., p. 17.
85. *Le Monde,* December 18, 1984; see also *L'Année politique* (1984): 85.

86. *Le Monde, Dossiers et documents: Les élections législatives, 1986,* p. 10.
87. *Le Monde,* January 2, 1985.

CHAPTER 7

PREPARING FOR THE 1986 LEGISLATIVE ELECTIONS

1. *L'Année politique* (1985): 16.
2. Ibid.
3. Ibid., p. 17. One opposition senator had suggested repatriating a number of immigrants by giving them 120,000 francs and requiring a guarantee that they would not return. While the government said that it favored this proposal, it did not act on it, fearing the reaction in some political quarters. A *Figaro*-SOFRES poll conducted on December 10, 1985, showed that 71 percent wanted to see illegal immigrants returned to their own countries, while 67 percent desired to see the flow of new immigrant workers stop, but 90 percent found it normal that the immigrant population would heighten unemployment and increase social welfare costs (ibid.).
4. *Le Monde, Dossiers et documents: Les élections législatives, 1986,* p. 11.
5. *Le Monde,* January 26–27, 1985.
6. *Business Week,* January 14, 1985, p. 45.
7. See *The Economist,* January 26, 1985, pp. 44–45.
8. *Le Monde, Dossiers et documents: L'Histoire, 1974–1985,* pp. 216–17.
9. *L'Année politique* (1985): 23–24.
10. *The Economist,* January 26, 1985, p. 45.
11. *Le Monde,* January 20–22, 1985.
12. *Le Monde, Dossiers et documents: L'Histoire, 1974–1985,* p. 213; Bauchard, *La Guerre des roses,* p. 305.
13. *Le Monde,* February 4, 1985; see also French Embassy, *News from France,* February 15, 1985, p. 1.
14. Ibid.; see also *L'Unité,* February 8, 1985.
15. *L'Année politique* (1985): 27.
16. *Le Monde,* February 8–9, 1985.
17. *L'Année politique* (1984): 14–15.
18. Ibid., p. 12.
19. July, *Les Années Mitterrand,* p. 228.
20. *L'Unité,* April 12, 1985.
21. See July, *Les Années Mitterrand,* pp. 227–28.
22. *Le Monde, Dossiers et documents: Les élections législatives, 1986,* p. 12.
23. *Le Monde,* April 27–30, 1985; see also John T. S. Keeler and Alec Stone, "Judicial-Political Confrontation in Mitterrand's

France," in George Ross, Stanley Hoffmann, and Sylvia Malzacher, eds., *The Mitterrand Experiment: Continuity and Change in Modern France* (Cambridge, Mass.: Polity Press, 1987), pp. 173–74.

24. *Le Monde*, April 30–May 1, 1985; see also *The Economist*, May 11, 1985, p. 50.
25. *Le Monde*, May 7, 1985.
26. French Embassy, *News from France*, May 7, 1985, p. 2.
27. *Libération*, June 20, 1985.
28. *Le Monde*, May 26–27, 1985.
29. See Wayne Northcutt, "The Domestic Origins of Mitterrand's Foreign Policy, 1981–1985," *Contemporary French Civilization* 10, no. 2 (1986): 234–35.
30. *L'Unité* attempted to calm Socialist party members by saying that the Fabius-Jospin debate did not constitute a "war of chiefs," but a difference in understanding of the campaign (*L'Unité*, June 21, 1985).
31. Quoted in July, *Les Années Mitterrand*, p. 257.
32. *Le Monde*, June 25, 1985.
33. *Le Monde, Dossiers et documents: L'Histoire, 1974–1985*, p. 215.
34. *L'Année politique* (1985): 48–49.
35. *Le Monde*, July 24, 1985.
36. Ibid., June 27, 1985.
37. Ibid., July 18–19, 1985.
38. Ibid., July 11, 1985.
39. See ibid., July 12, 16, August 6, 1985.
40. See ibid., July 16, 1985.
41. *L'Année politique* (1985): 54–55.
42. Pascal Krop and Roger Faligot, *La Piscine: Les services secrets français, 1944–1984* (Paris: Seuil, 1985).

43. *Washington Post* editorial published in *The International Herald Tribune*, July 27–28, 1985.
44. *Le Monde*, July 26, 1985.
45. Ibid., July 10–August 8, 1985.
46. Ibid., August 8–9, 1985; *Dossiers et documents: L'Histoire, 1974–1985*, pp. 214–15.
47. *Le Monde*, August 9 and 10, 1985.
48. Keeler and Stone, "Judicial-Political Confrontation," in Ross et al., *The Mitterrand Experiment*, p. 174.
49. Ibid., August 27–28, 1985.
50. *L'Unité*, September 20, 1985.
51. *Le Monde, Dossiers et documents: L'Histoire, 1974–1985*, p. 215.
52. Ibid.
53. *Le Monde*, September 22, 1985.
54. *Le Monde, Dossiers et documents: L'Histoire, 1974–1985*, p. 215.
55. Ibid., p. 214.
56. Ibid.
57. French Embassy, *News from France*, September 30, 1985, p. 1.
58. *L'Unité*, September 27, 1985.
59. *Le Monde, Dossiers et documents: L'Histoire, 1974–1985*, pp. 214–15.
60. *Le Monde*, September 22, 1985.
61. French Embassy, *News from France*, October 15, 1985, p. 2.
62. Ibid.
63. Ibid., p. 3.
64. *Le Monde*, October 8, 1985.
65. Ibid.
66. Ibid., October 10, 1985.
67. *L'Année politique* (1985): 67–68.
68. Ibid., pp. 68–69.
69. See *Le Monde*, October 15, 1985.
70. Ibid.
71. Fabius, interview.
72. *L'Unité*, October 18, 1985.

73. Frémy, *Quid des Présidents*, pp. 580–81.
74. For a summary of the debate see French Embassy, *News from France*, special report included in issue of October 29, 1985.
75. *L'Année politique* (1985): 77.
76. Frémy, *Quid des Présidents*, p. 581.
77. French Embassy, *News from France*, November 18, 1985, p. 1.
78. *Le Monde*, November 23, 1985.
79. French Embassy, *News from France*, special report included in issue of December 2, 1985, p. 1.
80. *Le Monde*, November 22–23, 1985.
81. Ibid.
82. Ibid.
83. Serge-Allain Rozenblum, *1985: Les Evénements de l'année* (Paris: Collection de la Revue Politique et Parlementaire, 1986), p. 58.
84. *Le Monde*, December 5, 1986.
85. Ibid., December 5–6, 1985.
86. See July, *Les Années Mitterrand*, p. 264.
87. *The Economist*, December 7, 1985, p. 51.
88. *Le Monde*, December 6, 1985.
89. Ibid., December 8–9, 1985.
90. July, *Les Années Mitterrand*, p. 267.

91. Fabius, interview.
92. *Le Monde*, December 8–9, 1985.
93. Ibid., December 17, 1985.
94. Ibid.
95. Ibid.
96. Ibid., January 2, 1986.
97. *L'Unité*, December 20, 1985.
98. *Le Monde*, January 17, 1986.
99. Ibid., January 19–20, 1986.
100. Ibid.
101. Mitterrand, *Réflexions sur la politique extérieure de la France: Introduction à vingt-cinq discours (1981–1985)*, (Paris: Fayard, 1986), pp. 7–135.
102. *Le Monde*, January 31, 1986.
103. Ibid., February 7, 1986.
104. Ibid., February 9–10, 1986.
105. Frémy, *Quid des Presidents*, p. 582.
106. French Embassy, *News from France*, February 24, 1986, p. 1.
107. Ibid., March 7, 1986, p. 1.
108. Ibid., p. 2.
109. *The Economist*, March 22, 1986, p. 45.
110. French Embassy, *News from France*, March 7, 1986, p. 2.
111. Fabius reminded the electorate during the campaign that "good sense says not to jump into the unknown" (i.e., cohabitation). See Frémy, *Quid des Présidents*, p. 583.

CHAPTER 8

THE 1986 LEGISLATIVE ELECTIONS AND COHABITATION

1. According to Frémy, the word "cohabitation" was first used in print by Giscard in an article in *L'Express* in 1983 (Frémy, *Quid des Présidents*, p. 585). However, Giscard discussed power-sharing in the late 1970s as he himself faced the pos-

sibility of governing with a left-wing Assembly.

2. Stanley Hoffmann, "Cinquième bis ou Quatre et demie: Note sur le Début des Cohabitations," *French Politics and Society*, no. 14 (June 1986), p. 6.
3. *L'Année politique* (1986): 10.
4. See *Le Nouvel Observateur*, July 4–10, 1986, pp. 24–27.
5. Jaffré, "Les élections législatives, 1986," *Pouvoirs* 38 (1986): 149–50; *Libération*, March 18, 1986.
6. Ibid.
7. Jaffré, "Les élections législatives, 1986," *Pouvoirs* 38 (1986): 154–55.
8. *L'Année politique* (1985): 9–10.
9. Ibid., p. 11.
10. Colombani, *Le Mariage blanc*, p. 217.
11. See Pfister, *Le Comédie de la cohabitation*.
12. *Le Monde*, April 9–10, 1986.
13. Ibid.; see also French Embassy, *News from France*, March 10, 1986, p. 7.
14. *Le Monde*, April 10–11, 1986; see also French Embassy, *News from France*, March 10, 1986, p. 8.
15. This breakdown was suggested by Jean-Marie Colombani in *Le Monde*, October 30, 1986.
16. Colombani, *Le Mariage blanc*, p. 228.
17. *Le Monde*, May 20, 1986.
18. Colombani, *Le Mariage blanc*, p. 219.
19. Ibid., pp. 218–31.
20. Ibid., pp. 227–28.
21. *Le Monde*, May 20–24, 1986.
22. French Embassy, *News from France*, July 8, 1986, pp. 1, 9.
23. Colombani, *Le Mariage blanc*, p. 220.
24. Ibid.
25. *The Economist*, May 3, 1986, pp. 57–58.
26. Quoted in Colombani, *Le Mariage blanc*, p. 222.
27. *Le Monde*, July 15–16, 1986.
28. French Embassy, *News from France*, August 11, 1986, p. 6.
29. *Le Monde*, May 29, 1986.
30. See ibid., September 24 and October 30–31, 1986; Edouard Masurel, ed., *L'Année 1986 dans Le Monde: Les principaux événements en France et à l'étranger* (Paris: Gallimard/Le Monde, 1987), pp. 145–47.
31. Quoted in Frémy, *Quid des Présidents*, p. 590.
32. Ibid., p. 599.
33. Colombani, *Le Mariage blanc*, p. 228.
34. French Embassy, *News from France*, October 6, 1986, p. 1.
35. Ibid., October 15, 1986.
36. Colombani, *Le Mariage blanc*, p. 222.
37. *Le Monde*, October 15, 1986.
38. Ibid., November 6, 1986.
39. Ibid., November 7, 1986.
40. See *Le Point*, November 10, 1986, pp. 52–55; also *Le Monde*, November 11, 1986.
41. Ibid., November 12, 1986.
42. Ibid.
43. Ibid., November 19, 1986.
44. Ibid., November 14, 1986.
45. *Le Figaro*, November 13, 1986; see also *Le Monde*, November 15, 1986.
46. Ibid., November 14, 1986.
47. See *L'Année politique* (1986): 15.
48. *Le Figaro*, November 13, 1986.
49. Ibid.; *Le Monde*, November 14–16, 1986.
50. Ibid., November 14, 1986.
51. *Le Point*, November 24, 1986, p. 61.

52. *Le Monde*, November 20, 1986.
53. Ibid., November 20–21, 1986.
54. Ibid., November 25, 1986.
55. Ibid., November 22–25, December 10, 1986.
56. Ibid., November 29, 1986.
57. *Libération*, November 28, 1986.
58. Ibid.
59. *Le Monde*, December 10, 1986. At this time Justice Minister Chalandon launched an attack on cohabitation, stating on the tenth anniversary of the RPR: "Behind the appearance of an impartial arbiter [referring to Mitterrand] . . . is a determined opponent who undermines, by his public critiques, the efforts of the government" (*Libération*, December 1, 1986).
60. Ibid.
61. Ibid., November 29, 1986.
62. *Le Monde*, December 9–10, 1986.
63. Ibid., December 11, 1986.
64. *L'Unité*, December 12, 1986.
65. *Libération*, December 10, 1986; *Le Monde*, December 10, 1986.
66. Ibid.
67. Ibid.
68. Ibid., January 2, 1987.
69. Ibid.
70. See *L'Année politique* (1986): 371.
71. See *Le Monde*, December 19, 1986–January 17, 1987.
72. French Embassy, *News from France*, January 29, 1987, p. 5.
73. *Le Point*, June 8, 1987, p. 63.
74. French Embassy, *News from France*, January 29, 1987, p. 1.
75. See *Le Monde*, January 15–17; French Embassy, *News from France*, January 29, 1987, p. 2.
76. Ibid., February 13, 1987, pp. 6–8.
77. For a summary of *Le Nouvel Economiste*'s overview of the French economy during 1986, see French Embassy, *News from France*, January 7, 1987, p. 7.
78. *Le Monde*, January 30–31, 1987.
79. Ibid., February 11–12, 1987.
80. Ibid., February 14–15, 1987.
81. French Embassy, *News from France*, March 3, 1987, p. 3.
82. *Le Monde*, March 8–9, 1987.
83. Ibid., March 12–14 and April 12–13, 1987.
84. French Embassy, *News from France*, June 30, 1987, p. 3.
85. *Le Monde*, March 20–28, 1987; *The Economist*, March 26, 1987, pp. 53–54. In France a 1949 law gives the government the power to restrict publications "destined for children." Some claimed that Chirac's government used this 1949 law to impose a general censorship.
86. *Le Monde*, July 12–13, 1987.
87. *Le Point*, June 8, 1987, pp. 55–59.
88. *Le Monde*, June 9, 1987.
89. Ibid., June 5, 1987.
90. Louis Harris poll summarized in French Embassy, *News from France*, May 5, 1987, p. 6.
91. *Le Monde*, June 21–25 and 27, 1987.
92. French Embassy, *News from France*, June 30, 1987, p. 5.
93. *The Economist*, May 30, 1987, p. 46.
94. Ibid., April 11, 1987, pp. 44–45.
95. French Embassy, *News from France*, May 19, 1987, p. 1.
96. *Le Monde*, April 28–May 2 and May 10–11, 1987.
97. Ibid., June 13, 1987; see also *The Economist*, June 20, 1987, p. 56.

98. Ibid.
99. Observation of William Keylor, commentator on a panel on "Politics in Post-War France," Thirty-Third Annual Conference of the Society for French Historical Studies, Minneapolis, Minnesota, March 19–21, 1987.
100. French Embassy, *News from France*, June 2, 1987, p. 1.
101. *Le Point*, June 8, 1987, p. 63.
102. French Embassy, *News from France*, June 15, 1987, p. 1.
103. *Le Monde*, June 10–11, 1987.
104. Quoted in the *New York Times*, July 22, 1987.
105. Quoted ibid., August 3, 1987.
106. Ibid., August 6, 1987.
107. *Le Monde*, June 17, 1987.
108. *Le Nouvel Observateur*, December 18–24, 1987, pp. 22–26. Chirac told military officers and others on December 12, 1987: "Were West Germany to be a victim of . . . aggression, who can doubt that France's commitment would be immediate and wholehearted? There cannot be a Battle of Germany and a Battle of France" (French Embassy, *News from France*, December 23, 1987, p. 1). French military analyst Dominique Moïsi called the prime minister's statement a "Copernican Revolution in Gaullist thinking" (*New York Times*, December 21, 1987).
109. Ibid., August 11, 1987.
110. Ibid., August 27, 1987; see also French Embassy, *News from France*, September 29, 1987, p. 1.
111. *New York Times*, September 3 and 6, 1987.
112. *L'Année politique* (1986): 16.
113. *New York Times*, July 29, 1987; see also *Le Monde*, March 1986–October 1987.
114. French Embassy, *News from France*, June 30, 1987, p. 1.
115. *L'Année politique* (1986): 15.
116. See *Le Point*, May 25, 1987, pp. 24–27; June 8, 1987, pp. 28–29.
117. *New York Times*, July 15, 1987.
118. *Le Monde*, July 16, 1987; *New York Times*, July 15, 1987.
119. Ibid.
120. Ibid.
121. Ibid., September 16, 1987; also *Le Monde*, September 15–18, 1987.
122. *Le Point*, October 19, 1987, pp. 26–27.
123. French Embassy, *News from France*, May 19, 1987, pp. 6–7.
124. Ibid., June 2, 1987, p. 6; see also *New York Times*, January 3, 1988.
125. This view of cohabitation was stressed by Nicholas Wahl at a conference on "A France of Pluralism and Consensus? Changing Balances in State and Society," Columbia University/New York University, October 9–11, 1987.
126. Olivier Duhamel, "La Cohabitation, étape du développement démocratique," paper presented at 1987 conference on "A France of Pluralism and Consensus?"
127. See *Le Point*, July 20, 1987, p. 19.

CHAPTER 9

THE 1988 PRESIDENTIAL AND LEGISLATIVE ELECTIONS

1. See *Le Monde, Dossiers et documents: Les élections législatives, 5 juin/12 juin* 1988 (Paris: Le Monde, 1988), p. 2.
2. See *Le Nouvel Economiste*, May 13, 1988, p. 15.
3. Just prior to the presidential elections, Catherine Nay, a Gaullist political journalist and unrestrained critic of the president, published *Les sept Mitterrand: ou les métamorphoses d'un septennat*. She charged that there was not one Mitterrand between 1981 and 1988, but that the president wore a number of different masks, some of them simultaneously. For instance, after his 1981 election, he was "François-Léon Blum"; from the 1983 municipal elections to the 1986 legislative elections he was "François-Ronald Reagan"; under cohabitation, François the Umpire; and on various occasions, François-Charles de Gaulle. Nay's book quickly became a bestseller.
4. See *Le Figaro, L'élection présidentielle 1988: Résultats, analyses, et commentaires* (Paris: Le Figaro, 1988), pp. 34–36.
5. *Le Monde*, April 9–10, 1986; see also French Embassy, *News from France*, March 10, 1986, p. 7.
6. *Le Figaro, L'élection présidentielle 1988*, p. 34.
7. See July, *Les Années Mitterrand;* Bauchard, *La Guerre des deux roses;* Colombani, *Portrait du Président.*

8. Wahl, contribution at a conference on "A France of Pluralism and Consensus? Changing Balances in State and Society," Columbia University/New York University, October 9–11, 1987.
9. *Le Monde*, November 8, 1986.
10. Ibid., May 24, 1988.
11. *Le Monde, Dossiers et documents: L'élection présidentielle, 24 avril/8 mai 1988*, p. 82.
12. Ibid., p. 48.
13. *Le Monde*, March 24, 1988.
14. Ibid.
15. *New York Times*, July 15, 1987.
16. *Le Monde, Dossiers et Documents: L'élection présidentielle, 1988*, pp. 64–65.
17. Ibid., pp. 23–27.
18. Ibid., p. 83.
19. Ibid., pp. 82–83.
20. Ibid., p. 25.
21. Quoted in *New York Times*, January 19, 1988.
22. Ibid., December 13, 1987.
23. *Le Figaro, L'élection présidentielle 1988*, p. 13.
24. Ibid., p. 37.
25. Ibid., p. 13.
26. *Le Monde, Dossiers et documents: L'élection présidentielle, 1988*, pp. 46–47, 82–83.
27. See ibid., pp. 46–47.
28. See Northcutt and Flaitz, "Women and Politics in Contemporary France," *Contemporary French Civilization* (Winter 1983): 183–98; and "Women, Politics and the French Socialist Government," *West European Politics* (1985): 50–70.

29. *Le Figaro, L'élection présidentielle 1988*, p. 13.
30. Quoted in Giesbert, *Le Président*, p. 381–82.
31. See *Le Figaro, L'élection présidentielle 1988*, pp. 12–13.
32. Giesbert, *Le Président*, p. 326.
33. Quoted ibid., p. 340.
34. See ibid., pp. 322–31.

35. *Le Monde*, May 24, 1988.
36. French Embassy, *News from France*, June 14, 1988, p. 1.
37. Reactions to the outcome of the 1988 legislative elections are noted in various Parisian dailies; see, for example, *Le Monde*, June 14, 1988.

CHAPTER 10

PROSPERITY, ROCARDISM, AND THE EUROPEAN CHALLENGE

1. *Le Point*, August 1, 1988, p. 21.
2. Quoted in *New York Times*, July 10, 1988.
3. Ibid.
4. French Embassy, *News from France*, July 1, 1988, p. 1.
5. *Le Monde*, July 16, 1988; see also *The Economist*, July 23, 1988, p. 46.
6. Ibid. He also announced to the nation that a new national library, "the largest and the most beautiful in the world," would be constructed in Paris.
7. See *Le Point*, November 6, 1989, pp. 36–37.
8. *Le Monde*, July 16, 1988.
9. Ibid., October 1, 1988; also French Embassy, *News from France*, September 19, 1988, p. 1, October 6, 1988, p. 1.
10. Quoted ibid., October 6, 1988, p. 1.
11. See Wayne Northcutt, "François Mitterrand and the Political Use of Symbols: The Construction of a Centrist Republic," *French Historical Studies* 17, no. 1 (Spring 1991): 141–58.

12. French Embassy, *News from France*, October 28, 1988, p. 2.
13. Ibid., November 16, 1988, p. 1.
14. See *Le Monde*, November 8, 1988.
15. Ibid., p. 2.
16. *Le Monde*, November 10–11, 1988.
17. See, for example, French Embassy, *News from France*, March 23, 1989, p. 8.
18. See *Le Point*, December 12, 1988, pp. 24–25.
19. Ibid., November 28, 1988, p. 34.
20. Quoted in French Embassy, *News from France*, December 21, 1988, p. 1; see also *Le Monde*, December 16, 1988.
21. French Embassy, *News from France*, December 21, 1988, p. 1.
22. Ibid., February 22, 1989, p. 1.
23. Ibid., December 21, 1988, p. 2.
24. *New York Times*, December 18, 1988; *Le Monde*, December 16–19, 1988.
25. See Thierry Pfister, *Lettre*

ouverte à la génération Mitterrand (Paris: Albin Michel, 1988).

26. Quoted in *Le Point*, November 21, 1988, pp. 32–33.

27. *L'Année politique* (1988): 9–12.

28. *Le Point*, December 19, 1988, pp. 28–29. In France at this time, 59 percent viewed liberalism as positive, 45 percent thought profit was positive, and one-third of the Socialists judged privatization favorably (ibid., November 27, 1989, p. 46).

29. See ibid., June 12, 1989, pp. 44–46.

30. French Embassy, *News from France*, April 7, 1989, p. 4.

31. *Le Monde*, January 3 and 4, 1989. Mitterrand's statements on improving the laws for immigrants were in part a reference to the restrictive Pasqua law of September 1986.

32. See *Le Point*, January 9, 1989, pp. 24–27.

33. *New York Times*, February 17, 1989; see also Giesbert, *Le Président*, pp. 345–48.

34. *Le Monde*, February 14, 1989.

35. Quoted in *Le Point*, April 3, 1989, p. 51.

36. French Embassy, *News from France*, May 16, 1989, p. 1.

37. *Le Point*, October 16, 1989, pp. 48–49.

38. Ibid., July 4, 1988, pp. 27–28; Giesbert, *Le Président*, pp. 340–42.

39. Quoted in *Le Point*, November 6, 1989, p. 36.

40. Quoted ibid., April 10, 1989, p. 47.

41. Ibid., April 10, 1989, pp. 47, and May 1, 1989, p. 47.

42. *Le Monde*, April 2–3, 1989.

43. See *New York Times*, April 30, 1989; *Le Monde*, April 30–May 5, 1989.

44. See ibid.

45. In the United States, some French scholars found it difficult to understand why Mitterrand accepted an award from an institution headed by the conservative John Silber, and why Silber agreed to such an award. Reportedly, Elie Wiesel, an acquaintance of both men, acted as an intermediary and convinced them that the award was appropriate.

46. *Le Point*, May 29, 1989, p. 46.

47. Ibid.

48. French Embassy, *News from France*, June 14, 1989, p. 1.

49. Ibid., July 6, 1989, p. 2.

50. Ibid., p. 11.

51. Ibid., p. 2.

52. Ibid., June 14, 1989, p. 1.

53. *New York Times*, April 11, 1990.

54. Technically, he became head of the Council of the European Community. The council comprises European heads of state and government who meet several times a year to discuss EC and foreign-policy issues.

55. *New York Times*, July 5, 1989.

56. Ibid.; see also *Le Monde*, July 4–8, 1989.

57. French Embassy, *News from France*, July 6, 1989, p. 1.

58. Ibid., January 12, 1990, p. 6.

59. According to Prime Minister Rocard, 325 million francs were budgeted for the Bicentennial Commission, 89 million francs for the one hundreth anniversary of the Eiffel Tower, and 16–18 million francs for security, pri-

marily for the summit (*Le Monde*, July 14–15, 1989).

60. See François Mitterrand, *Lettre à tous les français* (a fifty-four-page 1988 campaign statement published by the PS and distributed in France).

61. *Le Monde*, July 7, 1983.

62. François Chaslin, *Les Paris de Mitterrand: Histoire des grands projets architecturaux* (Paris: Gallimard-Folio, 1985), p. 26.

63. Ibid., p. 237.

64. Ibid., p. 21.

65. Ibid., p. 19.

66. Ibid., pp. 236, 252.

67. Ibid., p. 242.

68. Ibid., p. 12.

69. Ibid., p. 241.

70. Hélène Lipstadt, "*Les Grands Projets:* 'Paris 1979–1989' in New York, 1988," *French Politics and Society* 6, no. 4 (October 1988): 46.

71. David Wachtel, *Cultural Policy and Socialist France* (Westport, Conn.: Greenwood Press, 1987), p. xi.

72. See Martha Zuber, "La Fête du Bicentenaire," *French Politics and Society* 7 (1989): 37.

73. François Furet, Jacques Julliard, and Pierre Rosanvallon, *La République du centre: La fin de l'exception française* (Paris: Calmann-Lévy, 1988), pp. 59–60.

74. Quoted in *L'Express*, July 14, 1989 (supplement, "Liberté"), p. 8.

75. *Libération*, July 15–16, 1989. Weeks earlier a well-publicized poll, which Mitterrand was undoubtedly aware of, showed that a majority of respondents were opposed to the execution of the king.

76. See, Diana Pinto, "Autour du Bicentenaire de la Révolution Française," *French Politics and Society* 7, no. 3 (Summer 1989): 137–41.

77. This was the image of the Revolution according to an exhibition entitled "Images de la Révolution 1789–1989" at the Musée d'Histoire Contemporaine in the Invalides from June 1 to August 31, 1989. Consult Michel Vovelle, ed., *Les Images de la Révolution française* (Paris: Publications de la Sorbonne, 1988).

78. *Le Monde*, July 18, 1989.

79. Ibid., July 19, 1989.

80. Ibid., July 18, 1989.

81. Ibid., July 19, 1989.

82. Ibid., July 21, 1989.

83. Ibid., October 26, 1989.

84. Earlier in the fall, he had asked that the conflicting parties in Lebanon observe a cease fire proposed by the Arab League and supported by the UN general secretary and the United States.

85. See *Le Monde*, October 26, 1989; and French Embassy, *News from France*, October 30, 1989, p. 1. Earlier in the month he told a 320-member visiting delegation of Soviets that "even armed frontiers hold back neither men nor ideas." He also stressed that he favored more exchanges between Eastern and Western Europe. In 1987, 350 French citizens had been hosted by Gorbachev (ibid., October 16, 1989, p. 2).

86. In addition to these concerns, Mitterrand tried to counter the perception in some quarters, especially in the U.S., that the

single market of 1993 would exclude outsiders. Industry Minister Roger Fauroux told businessmen in Washington on September 18, 1989 that there would be no "Fortress Europe." See French Embassy, *News from France*, September 20, 1989, p. 3.

87. David Beriss, "Scarves, Schools, and Segregation: The Foulard Affair," *French Politics and Society* 8, no. 1 (Winter 1990): 1.

88. French Embassy, *News from France*, December 13, 1989, pp. 9–10. See also *Le Monde*, October 21–28, 1989.

89. Ibid., November 21, 1989.

90. The only major political figure in France to praise the old regimes in Eastern Europe after the fall of the Berlin Wall was the communist Marchais. He said that the overall balance sheet of the East was "positive" (ibid., November 14, 1989; see also ibid., November 12–13, 1989).

91. *New York Times*, December 8, 1989.

92. See ibid.

93. Quoted in French Embassy, *News from France*, December 13, 1989, p. 1.

94. Ibid., December 29, 1989, pp. 1–2.

95. Ibid., December 13, 1989, p. 1.

96. *Le Monde*, December 23, 1989; see also French Embassy, *News from France*, December 29, 1989, p. 2.

97. Ibid.; also January 12, 1990, p. 1.

98. Quoted in Giesbert, *Le Président*, p. 377.

99. *Le Monde*, January 2, 1990.

100. Delors called for massive aid for Eastern Europe, German reunification, full membership for East Germany in the EEC, and associate membership for other East European nations.

101. *Le Point*, January 8, 1990, pp. 31–32.

102. French Embassy, *News from France*, December 13, 1989, p. 4.

103. Ibid., February 1, 1990, p. 1.

104. To assist the emerging democracies in the East, the Sophia–Antipolis Foundation, the French version of Silicon Valley located near Nice, sponsored a $13 million program in conjunction with regional universities in order to train Eastern Europeans desiring to launch small businesses (ibid., February 27, 1990, p. 4).

105. Ibid., February 1, 1990, p. 5.

106. Ibid., p. 9.

107. French Embassy, *News from France*, February 27, 1990, p. 1.

108. Ibid.

109. Ibid., p. 2.

110. Ibid., February 27, 1990, p. 10.

111. Ibid.

112. *New York Times*, March 13, 1990.

113. Ibid.

114. Ibid., March 9–10, 1990.

115. Ibid., March 7, 1990.

116. French Embassy, *News from France*, April 24, 1990, p. 1.

117. See *New York Times*, April 29 and May 3, 1990.

118. Ibid., April 20, 1990.

119. See French Embassy, *News from France*, April 24, 1990, p.

1; and *New York Times*, May 4, 1990.

120. See ibid., April 27 and May 3, 1990.

121. Julius W. Friend, "The PS Faces the 1990's," *French Politics and Society* 8, no. 1 (Winter 1990): 18; also "Report from Rennes," ibid., no. 2 (Spring 1990): 1–3.

122. *Le Point*, January 15, 1990, pp. 40–41.

123. Ibid.

124. Ibid., March 18, 1990, pp. 32–33.

125. *New York Times*, March 25, 1990. In a SOFRES–*Le Point* poll of members of the National Assembly, 63 percent of all deputies said that if a presidential election were held within the next two years, Rocard would be the best Socialist candidate; 75 percent of PS deputies cited Rocard (*Le Point*, April 23, 1990, pp. 36–37).

126. Ibid., April 2, 1990, pp. 30–31.

CONCLUSION

1. See Friend, *Seven Years in France*.

2. Giesbert says of Mitterrand, "He does not show the way. He follows it" (Giesbert, *Le Président*, p. 11). This, however, is an overdrawn generalization that does not completely reflect Mitterrand's political career. For instance, he has consistently tried to build a strong Center by weakening the PCF and the Right.

3. See *Le Point*, November 21, 1988, pp. 36–37.

4. Ibid., April 30, 1990, p. 28.

5. See ibid., May 14, 1990, pp. 44–47.

6. Giesbert, *Le Président*, p. 12.

7. July, *Les Années Mitterrand*, pp. 12–13.

8. *Le Monde*, May 18, 1991.

9. See *Le Point*, May 14, 1990, pp. 44–47.

10. The author agrees with Giesbert on Mitterrand's place in the history of the French Left (see Giesbert, *Le Président*, pp. 380, 383).

11. Ibid., p. 380.

12. *L'Express*, September 11, 1987, p. 15.

13. This view is also shared in France; see, for example, *Le Point*, December 4, 1989, p. 43.

Select Bibliography

BOOKS, DOCUMENTS, AND INTERVIEWS

Adams, Williams, and Christian Stoffaec, eds. *French Industrial Policy*. Washington, D.C.: Brookings Institution, 1986.

Ambler, John. *The French Socialist Experiment*. Philadelphia: Institute for the Study of Human Issues, 1985.

Ardagh, John. *France in the 1980's*. Harmondsworth: Penguin Books, 1982.

Avril, Pierre, and Gérard Vincent. *La IVᵉ République: Histoire et société*. Paris: MA Editions, 1988.

Bacot, Paul. *Les Dirigeants du Parti socialiste: histoire et sociologie*. Paris: Presses universitaires de Lyon, 1979.

Balassa, Bela A. *The First Year of the Socialist Government in France*. Washington, D.C.: American Enterprise Institute, 1982.

Bauchard, Philippe. *La Guerre des deux roses: Du rêve à réalité, 1981–1985*. Paris: Grasset, 1986.

Beaud, Michel. *Le Mirage de la croissance*. Vol. 1. *Le Politique économique de la gauche (mai 1981–décembre 1982)*. Paris: Syros, 1983.

Bell, David S., ed. *Contemporary French Political Parties*. New York: St. Martin's Press, 1982.

———, and Byron Criddle. *The French Socialist Party: Resurgence and Victory*. Oxford: Oxford University Press, 1984.

Borella, François. *Les Partis politiques dans la France d'aujourd'hui*. Paris: Seuil, 1973.

Borzeix, Jean-Marie. *Mitterrand lui-même*. Paris: Stock, 1973.

Bourdon, Roger, et al. *Le PCF, Etapes et problèms*. Paris: Editions Sociales, 1981.

Brown, Bernard. *Socialism of a Different Kind: Reshaping of the French Left*. Westport, Conn.: Greenwood Press, 1982.

Buci-Glucksmann, Christine, ed. *La Gauche, le pouvoir, le socialisme*. Paris: PUF, 1983.

Cayrol, Roland. *François Mitterrand, 1945–1967*. Paris: Fondation Nationale des Sciences Politiques, 1967.

Cerny, Philip. *The Politics of Grandeur: The Ideological Aspect of de Gaulle's Foreign Policy*. New York: Cambridge University Press, 1980.

———, and Martin A. Schain. *Socialism, the State and Public Policy in France*. New York: Methuen, 1985.

Chapsal, Jacques. *La Vie politique sous la Vᵉ République*. Paris: PUF, 1984.

Chaslin, François. *Les Paris de François Mitterrand: Histoire des grands projets architecturaux*. Paris: Gallimard, 1985.

Claude, Henri. *Mitterrand: ou l'atlantisme masqué*. Paris: Messidor, 1986.

Clément, Claude. *L'Affaire des fuites: objectif Mitterrand*. Paris: Orban, 1980.

Clerc, Christine. *Chronique d'un septennat*. Paris: Stock, 1988.

Clerc, Denis, Alain Lipietz, and Joel Sartre-Buisson. *La crise*. Paris: Syros, 1983.

Codding, George Arthur. *Ideology and Politics: The Socialist Party of France*. Boulder, Colo.: Westview Press, 1979.

Cohen, Stephen, and Peter A. Gourevitch. *France in the Troubled World Economy*. Woburn, Mass.: Butterworths, 1982.

Colliard, Sylvie. *La Campagne présidentielle de François Mitterrand en 1974*. Paris: PUF, 1979.

Colombani, Jean-Marie. *Portrait du Président: Le monarque imaginaire*. Paris: Gallimard, 1985.

————, and Jean-Yves Lhomeau. *Le Mariage Blanc: Mitterrand-Chirac*. Paris: Grasset, 1986.

Commission of the European Communities, Directorate-General for Employment, Industrial Relations and Social Affairs. *Social Europe* (1/90). Luxembourg: Office for Official Publications of the European Communities, 1990.

Conte, Arthur. *Les Premiers ministres de la Ve République*. Paris: Le Pré Aux Clercs, 1986.

Cotta, Michèle. *Les Miroirs de Jupiter*. Paris: Fayard, 1986.

Cotteret, Jean-Marie, and Girard Mermet. *La Bataille des images*. Paris: Larousse, 1986.

Criddle, Byron. *Socialists and European Integration: A Study of the French Socialist Party*. London: Routledge & Kegan Paul, 1969.

Daniel, Jean. *Les Religions d'un président: Regards sur les adventures du mitterrandisme*. Paris: Grasset, 1988.

Debray, Régis. *La Puissance et les rêves*. Paris: Gallimard, 1984.

————. *Les Empires contre l'Europe*. Paris: Gallimard, 1985.

De Closets, François. *Toujours plus*. Paris: Grasset, 1982.

De Gaulle, Charles. *Mémoires de Guerre*. 3 vols. Paris: Plon, 1954–59.

————. *Discours et messages*. 5 vols. Paris: Plon, 1970–71.

————. *Mémoires d'espoir*. 2 vols. Paris: Plon, 1970–71.

————. *Lettres, notes, carnets*. 12 vols. Paris: Plon, 1980–88.

Delion, André, and Michel Durupty. *Les Nationalisations*. Paris: Economica, 1982.

Denis, Stéphane. *La Leçon d'automne: Jeux et enjeux de François Mitterrand*. Paris: Albin Michel, 1983.

Derogy, Jacques. *Enquête sur un Carrefour dangereux*. Paris: Fayard, 1987.

Desjardins, Thierry. *François Mitterrand: Un socialiste gaullien*. Paris: Hachette, 1978.

Doumic, Jean-François, and Hélène Lacharmoise. *Le Guide du pouvoir*. Paris: Editions Jean-François Doumic, 1989.

Duhamel, Alain. *Le Ve Président*. Paris: Gallimard, 1987.

Duhamel, Olivier, Elisabeth Dupoirier, and Jérôme Jaffré, eds. *SOFRES: Opinion publique, Enquêtes et commentaires, 1984*. Paris: Gallimard, 1984.

————. *SOFRES: Opinion publique 1985*. Paris: Gallimard, 1985.

————. *SOFRES: Opinion publique 1986*. Paris: Gallimard, 1986.

————. *SOFRES: L'Etat de l'opinion: Clés pour 1987*. Paris: Seuil, 1987.

————. *SOFRES: L'Etat de l'opinion: Clés pour 1988*. Paris: Seuil, 1988.

————. *SOFRES: L'Etat de l'opinion: Clés pour 1989*. Paris: Seuil, 1989.

Duhamel, Olivier, and Jérôme Jaffré. *Le nouveau président*. Paris: Seuil, 1987.

Dunilac, Julien. *François Mitterrand sous la loupe*. Paris: Slatkine, 1981.

Du Roy, Albert, and Robert Schneider. *Le Roman de la rose*. Paris: Seuil, 1982.

Duverger, Maurice. *Bréviaire de la cohabitation.* Paris: PUF, 1986.

Ehrman, Henry. *Organized Business in France.* Westport, Conn.: Greenwood Press, 1981.

———. *Politics in France.* 4th ed., Boston: Little, Brown, 1983.

Elleinstein, Jean. *Le P.C.* Paris: Grasset, 1976.

Estier, Claude. *Mitterrand président: Journal d'une victoire.* Paris: Stock, 1981.

Fabius, Laurent. *Le Coeur du futur.* Paris: Calmann-Lévy, 1985.

———. Interview with the author, Paris, France, June 10, 1987.

Le Figaro. *L'Election présidentielle 1988: Résultats, analyses, et commentaires.* Paris: Le Figaro, 1988.

Flaitz, Jeffra. *The Ideology of English: French Perceptions of English as a World Language.* Berlin: Mouton, 1988.

Fonteneau, Alain, and Pierre Alain Muet. *La Gauche face à la crise.* Paris: Fondation Nationale des Sciences Politiques, 1985.

France. *Assemblée nationale, J.O. Débats parlementaires, 1946–1989.* Paris: Imprimerie Nationale, 1946–1990.

Frears, J. R. *Political Parties and Elections in the French Fifth Republic.* London: C. Hurst, 1977.

Fredet, Jean-Gabriel. *Les Patrons face à la gauche.* Paris: Ramsay, 1982.

Frémy, Dominique. *Quid des Présidents de la République . . . et des candidats.* Paris: Robert Laffont, 1987.

French Embassy, Press and Information Service. *News from France.* Washington, D.C.: 1985–1991.

Friend, Julius W. *Seven Years in France: François Mitterrand and the Unintended Revolution, 1981–1988.* Boulder, Colo.: Westview Press, 1989.

Furet, François, Jacques Julliard, and Pierre Rosanvallon. *La République du centre: La fin de l'exception française.* Paris: Calmann-Levy, 1988.

Giesbert, Franz-Olivier. *François Mitterrand ou la tentation de l'histoire.* Paris: Seuil, 1977.

———. *Jacques Chirac.* Paris: Seuil, 1987.

———. *Le Président.* Paris: Seuil, 1990.

Giscard d'Estaing, Valéry. *Démocratie française.* Paris: Fayard, 1976.

Grjebine, André. *L'état d'urgence.* Paris: Flammarion, 1983.

Grosser, Alfred. *Affaires extérieures: La politique de la France, 1944–1984.* Paris: Flammarion, 1984.

Guastoni, Mario, ed. *Gauche: Premier bilan.* Paris: Revue Politique et Parlementaire, 1985.

Guidoni, Pierre. *Histoire du nouveau Parti socialiste.* Paris: Tema, 1973.

Halimi, Gisèle, et al. *Quel président pour les femmes? Réponses de François Mitterrand.* Paris: Gallimard, 1981.

Hall, Peter A. *Governing the Economy: The Politics of State Intervention in Britain and France.* New York: Oxford University Press, 1986.

Hamon, Hervé, and Patrick Rotman. *La Deuxième Gauche, Histoire intellectuelle et politique de le CFDT.* Paris: Ramsay, 1982.

Hernu, Charles. *Défendre la paix.* Paris: J. C. Lattès, 1985.

Hinkler, François. *Le Parti Communiste au carrefour: essai sur quinze ans de son histoire.* Paris: Albin Michel, 1981.

Hoffmann, Stanley. *Mitterrand's First Year in Power.* Monograph in Europe Series of the Center for European Studies. Cambridge: Harvard University Press, 1982.

———, and William G. Andrews, eds. *The Fifth Republic at Twenty.* Albany: State University of New York Press, 1981.

Hurtig, Christiane. *De la SFIO au nouveau Parti socialiste.* Paris: Colin, 1970.

Jenson, Jane and George Ross. *The View from Inside: A French Communist Cell in Crisis.* Berkeley and Los Angeles: University of California Press, 1984.

Johnson, R. W. *The Long March of the French Left.* New York: St Martin's Press, 1981.

Jouve, Pierre, and Ali Magoudi. *Mitterrand: Portrait total.* Paris: Carrère, 1986.

———. "Auto-Portrait." (French television documentary on the life and political career of François Mitterrand, aired on TF 1 on January 21, 1987).

Joxe, Pierre. *Parti socialiste.* Paris: Epi, 1973.

Judt, Tony. *Le Marxisme et la gauche française, 1830–1981.* Paris: Hachette, 1986.

Julliard, Jacques. *Le IVᵉ République.* Paris: Calmann-Lévy, 1968.

———. *Le Génie de la liberté.* Paris: Seuil, 1990.

July, Serge. *Les Années Mitterrand: Histoire baroque d'une normalisation inachevée.* Paris: Grasset, 1986.

———. *La drôle d'année.* Paris: Grasset, 1987.

———. *Le Salon des artistes.* Paris: Grasset, 1989.

Kédros, André. *Les Socialistes au pouvoir: Europe 1981–1985.* Paris: Plon, 1986.

Keeler, John. *The Politics of Neocorporatism in France: Farmers, the State and Agricultural Policy-making in the Fifth Republic.* New York: Oxford University Press, 1986.

Kesselman, Mark, ed. *The French Workers Movement: Economic Crisis and Political Change, 1968–1982.* London and New York: Allen and Unwin, 1984.

Krop, Pascal, and Roger Faligot. *La Piscine: les service secrets française, 1944–1984.* Paris: Seuil, 1985.

Labbé, Dominique. *François Mitterrand: Essai sur le discours.* Paris: La Pensée Sauvage, 1983.

Lacorne, Denis. *Les Notables rouges: La construction municipale de l'Union de la gauche.* Paris: Fondation Nationale des Sciences Politiques, 1980.

Lacoste, Yves. *Géopolitique des régions francais.* 3 vols., Paris: Fayard, 1986.

Lacouture, Jean. *Pierre Mendès-France.* Translated by George Holoch. New York: Holmes & Meier, 1984 (originally published as *Pierre Mendès-France.* Paris: Seuil, 1981).

———. *De Gaulle.* 3 vols., Paris: Seuil, 1986.

Lancelot, Alain and Marie-Thérèse. *Annuaire de la France politique: mai 1981–mai 1983.* Paris: Fondation Nationale des Sciences Politiques, 1984.

Lauber, Volkmar. *The Political Economy of France: From Pompidou to Mitterrand.* New York: Praeger, 1983.

Laude, David. *François Mitterrand.* Paris: Edipa, 1974.

Lavau, Georges. *A quoi sert le Parti communiste français?* Paris: Fayard, 1981.

Lebacqz, Albert. *Journal politique de l'année 1982: Les socialistes face à la crise.* Paris: France-Empire, 1983.

Lecomte, Claude. *Au secours: L'alternance est là.* Paris: Messidor, 1986.

Lellouche, Pierre. *L'Avenir de la guerre.* Paris: Mazarine, 1985.

Loschak, Danièle. *La Convention des institutions républicaines: François Mitterrand et le socialisme.* Paris: PUF, 1971.

Machin, Howard, and Vincent Wright, eds. *Economic Policy and Policy-making under the Mitterrand Presidency, 1981–1984*. London: Frances Pinter, 1985.

MacShane, Denis. *François Mitterrand: A Political Odyssey*. London: Quartet Books, 1982.

———. *French Lessons for Labour*. London: Fabian Society, 1986.

Makarian, Christian, and Danièl Reyt. *Un inconnu nommé Chevènement*. Paris: La Table Ronde, 1986.

Manceron, Claude, and Bernard Pingaud. *François Mitterrand: L'homme, les idées, le programme*. Paris: Flammarion, 1981.

Manin, Bernard, ed. *La France en politique 1988*. Paris: Esprit Fayard Seuil, 1988.

Martin, Roger. *Patron de droit divin*. Paris: Gallimard, 1984.

Massenet, Michel, ed. *La France socialiste: un premier bilan*. Paris: Hachette, Collection Pluriel, 1983.

Masurel, Edouard. *L'Année 1986 dans Le Monde: Les principaux événements en France et à l'étranger*. Paris: Gallimard, 1987.

Mauroy, Pierre. *Héritiers de l'Avenir*. Paris: Stock, 1977.

———. *C'est ici le chemin*. Paris: Flammarion, 1982.

———. *A gauche*. Paris: Albin Michel, 1985.

Mazey, Sonia, and Michael Newman, eds. *Mitterrand's France*. London: Croom Helm, 1987.

McCarthy, Patrick, ed. *The French Socialists in Power, 1981–1986*. Westport, Conn.: Greenwood Press, 1987.

Melitz, Jacques, ed. *The French Economy: Theory and Policy*. Boulder, Colo.: Westview Press, 1985.

Mendès-France, Pierre. *Gouverner, c'est choisir*. 3 vols., Paris: Julliard, 1953–58.

———. *Oeuvres complètes*. 5 vols., Paris: Gallimard, 1984–89.

Milesi, Gabriel. *Jacques Delors*. Paris: Belfond, 1985.

Minc, Alain. *La Grande illusion*. Paris: Grasset, 1988.

Ministère des relations extérieures. Direction générale des Relations Culturelles, Scientifiques et Techniques. *Le Projet culturel extérieur de la France*. Paris: Documentation Française, n.d.

Mitterrand, François. *Aux frontières de l'Union française* [At the frontiers of the French union]. Paris: Julliard, 1953.

———. *Présence française et abandon* [French presence and withdrawal]. Paris: Plon, 1957.

———. *La Chine au défi* [China under challenge]. Paris: Julliard, 1963.

———. *Le Coup d'état permanent* [The permanent coup d'état]. Paris: Plon, 1964.

———. *Ma part de vérité* [My part of the truth]. Paris: Fayard, 1969.

———. *Un Socialisme du possible* [Socialism of the possible]. Paris: Seuil, 1970.

———. *La Rose au poing* [The rose in the fist]. Paris: Flammarion, 1973.

———. *La Paille et la grain* [The wheat and the chaff]. Paris: Flammarion, 1975.

———. *Politique* [Politics]. 2 vols., Paris: Fayard, 1977–81.

———. *L'Abeille et l'architecte* [The bee and the architect]. Paris: Flammarion, 1978.

———. *Ici et maintenant* [Here and now]. Paris: Fayard, 1980.

———. *The Wheat and the Chaff*. Translated by R. S. Woodward, C. Hayter, and H. R. Lane. New York: Seaver Books, 1982.

———. *Réflexions sur la politique extérieure de la France: Introduction à vingt-cinq discours*

(1981–85) [Reflections on the foreign policy of France: Introduction to twenty-five speeches (1981–85). Paris: Fayard, 1986.

———. *Lettre à tous les Français*. [Letter to the French]. Paris: Parti socialiste, 1988.

Molho, Danièle. Interview with the author, Paris, France, July 13, 1983.

Mollet, Guy. *Bilan et perspectives socialistes*. Paris: Plon, 1958.

Le Monde. Dossiers et documents: Les élections législatives de mars 1978. Paris: Le Monde, 1978.

———. *Dossiers et documents: L'élection présidentielle, 26 avril/10 mai 1981*. Paris: Le Monde, 1981.

———. *Dossiers et documents: Les élections législatives de juin 1981*. Paris: Le Monde, 1981.

———. *Dossiers et documents: Les élections municipales de mars 1983*. Paris: Le Monde, 1983.

———. *Dossiers et documents: Les deuxièmes élections européennes (juin 1984)*. Paris: Le Monde, 1984.

———. *Dossiers et documents: Bilan économique et sociale 1985*. Paris: Le Monde, 1986.

———. *Dossiers et documents: Les élections législatives de mars 1986*. Paris: Le Monde, 1986.

———. *Dossiers et documents: L'histoire au jour de jour. Tome IV: Une aussi longue crise (1974–1985)*. Paris: Le Monde, 1986.

———. *Dossiers et documents: Bilan économique et social 1986*. Paris: Le Monde, 1987.

———. *Dossiers et documents: Bilan du septennat: L'alternance dans l'alternance (1981–1988)*. Paris: Le Monde, 1988.

———. *Dossiers et documents: L'élection présidentielle, 24 avril/8 mai 1988*. Paris: Le Monde, 1988.

———. *Dossiers et documents: Les élections législatives, 5 juin/12 juin 1988*. Paris: Le Monde 1988.

Mossuz-Lavau, Janine, and Mariette Sineau. *Enquête sur les femmes et la politique en France*. Paris: PUF, 1983.

Moulin, Charles. *Mitterrand intime*. Paris: Albin Michel, 1982.

Nay, Catherine. *Le noir et le rouge, ou l'histoire d'une ambition*. Paris: Grasset, 1984.

———. *The Black and the Red: The Story of an Ambition*. Translated by Alan Sheridan. New York: Harcourt Brace Jovanovich, 1987.

———. *Les sept Mitterrand, ou les métamorphoses d'un septennat*. Paris: Grasset, 1988.

Newman, Michael. *Socialism and European Unity: The Dilemma of the Left in Britain and France*. London: Junction Books, 1983.

Noland, Haron. *The Founding of the French Socialist Party, 1893–1905*. Cambridge: Harvard University Press, 1956.

Nora, Pierre, ed. *La CFDT en Questions*. Paris: Gallimard, 1984.

Northcutt, Wayne. *The French Socialist and Communist Party Under the Fifth Republic, 1958–1981: From Opposition to Power*. New York: Irvington Publishers, 1985.

Nugent, Neil, and David Lowe. *The Left in France*. London: Macmillan, 1982.

Parti socialiste. *Programme de gouvernement du Parti socialiste*. Paris: Flammarion, 1972.

———. *L'État des Francais ou les promesses non tenues, 1974–1981*. Paris: Club Socialiste du Livre, 1981.

———. *Projet socialiste pour la France des années 80*. Paris: Club Socialiste du Livre, 1981.

————. *La France et le Changement: Rencontres des actions du changement, Paris 20–23 janvier 1983*. Paris: Club Socialiste du Livre, 1983.

Peyrefitte, Alain. *Quand la rose se fanera: du malentendu à l'espoir*. Paris: Plon, 1983.

Pfister, Thierry. *Dans les coulisses du pouvoir: La comédie de la cohabitation*. Paris: Albin Michel, 1986.

————. *La Vie quotidienne à Matignon au temps de l'Union de la gauche*. Paris: Folio: 1986.

————. *Lettre ouverte à la génération Mitterrand*. Paris: Albin Michel, 1988.

Picar, Michel. *Danielle Mitterrand: Portrait*. Paris: Ramsay, 1982.

Pickles, Dorothy. *Problems of Contemporary French Politics*. London: Methuen, 1982.

Quermonne, Jean-Louis. *Le Gouvernement de la France sous la Ve République*. Paris: Dalloz, 1983.

Rebérioux, Madeleine. *Les Femmes en France dans une société d'inégalités: Rapport au ministre des Droits de la femme*. Paris: Documentation Française, 1982.

Rey, Françoise, Jean-Pierre Mithois, and Denis Poncet. *Mitterrand II: les secrets d'une campagne 22 février–8 mai 1988*. Paris: Belfond/Acropole, 1988.

Robrieux, Philippe. *Histoire intérieure du parti communiste, 1920–1982*. 3 vols., Paris: Fayard, 1980–82.

Rocard, Michel. *Parler vrai: textes politiques*. Paris: Seuil, 1979.

————. *Plan intérimaire: Stratégie pour deux ans 1982/1983*. Paris: Flammarion, 1982.

————. *A l'épreuve des faits: Textes politiques, 1979–1985*. Paris: Seuil, 1986.

————. *Réponses pour demain*. Paris: Syros, 1988.

Rocard, Michèle. *Au four et au moulin*. Paris: Albin Michel, 1987.

Rosanvallon, Pierre. *Misère de l'économie*. Paris: Seuil, 1983.

Ross, George. *Workers and Communists in France: From Popular Front to Eurocommunism*. Berkeley and Los Angeles: University of California Press, 1982.

————, Stanley Hoffmann, and Sylvia Malzacher. eds. *The Mitterrand Experiment: Continuity and Change in Modern France*. Cambridge: Polity Press, 1987.

Roucaute, Yves. *Le Parti socialiste*. Paris: Huisman, 1983.

Roudy, Yvette. *La Femme en marge*. Paris: Flammarion, 1982.

Roussel, Eric. *Georges Pompidou*. Paris: JC Lattès, 1984.

Rozenblum, Serge-Allain. *1985: Les Evénements de l'année*. Paris: Collection de la Revue Politique et Parlementaire, 1986.

Salomon, André. *PS, la mise à nu*. Paris: Laffont, 1980.

Schifres, Michel, and Michel Sarazin. *L'Elysée de Mitterrand: Secrets de la maison du prince*. Paris: Alain Moreau, 1985.

Schneider, Robert. *Michel Rocard*. Paris: Stock, 1987.

Schwartz, Laurent. *Ou va l'Université: Rapport du Comité national d'éducation*. Paris: Gallimard, 1987.

Simmons, Harvey. *French Socialists in Search of a Role, 1956–1967*. Ithaca: Cornell University Press, 1970.

Simonnot, Philippe. *Le grand bluff économique des socialistes*. Paris: JC Lattès, 1982.

Singer, Daniel. *Is Socialism Doomed? The Meaning of Mitterrand*. New York: Oxford University Press, 1988.

Sorum, Paul Clay. *Intellectuals and Decolonization in France*. Chapel Hill: University of North Carolina Press, 1977.

Stockholm International Peace Research Institute. *World Armaments and Disarmaments: SIPRI Yearbook, 1983–1988*. London: Taylor & Francis, 1983–1989.

Suffert, Georges. *De Defferre à Mitterrand, la campagne présidentielle.* Paris: Seuil, 1966.

Szafran, Maurice. *Les Familles du président.* Paris: Grasset, 1982.

Tiersky, Ronald. *French Communism, 1920–1972.* New York: Columbia University Press, 1974.

Touchard, Jean. *La Gauche en France depuis 1900.* Paris: Seuil, 1977.

Union démocratique et socialiste de la Résistance. *Les Cahiers de l'UDSR.* Archives of the Fondation Nationale des Sciences Politiques, Paris, France.

Verdier, Robert. *PS/PC: Une lutte pour l'entente.* Paris: Seghers, 1976.

Wachtel, David. *Cultural Policy and Socialist France.* Westport, Conn.: Greenwood Press, 1987.

Wall, Irwin. *French Communism in the Era of Stalin.* Westport, Conn.: Greenwood Press, 1983.

Willard, Claude. *Socialisme et communisme français.* Paris: Armand Colin, 1978.

Williams, Philip. *Politics in Post-War France: Parties and the Constitution in the Fourth Republic.* 2nd ed., London: Longmans, Green, 1958.

———. *La vie politique sous la IVᵉ République.* Paris: Colin, 1971.

Williams, Stuart. *Socialism in France: From Jaurès to Mitterrand.* New York: St. Martin's Press, 1983.

Wright, Vincent, ed. *Continuity and Change in France.* London: George Allen & Unwin, 1984.

ARTICLES AND SCHOLARLY PAPERS

Andrews, William. "The Power of Paris." *French Politics and Society,* no. 4 (December 1983): 21–22.

Berger, Susanne. "French Politics and Society at a Turning Point." *French Politics and Society,* no. 15 (November 1986): 3–8.

Carcassone, Guy. "Le ménage à trois: Gouvernement, parlement, conseil constitutionnel." Paper presented at a conference on "A France of Pluralism and Consensus? Changing Balances in State and Society," Columbia University/New York University, October 9–11, 1987.

Coser, Lewis. "Mitterrand's First Two Years: An Advanced Welfare State in One Country." *Dissent* (Spring 1983), pp. 165–69.

Duhamel, Olivier. "La Cohabitation, étape du développement démocratique," paper presented at a conference on "A France of Pluralism and Consensus? Changing Balances in State and Society," Columbia University/New York University, October 9–11, 1987.

Hoffmann, Stanley. "Cinquième bis ou Quatre et demie: Note sur le Début des Cohabitations." *French Politics and Society,* no. 14 (June 1986), pp. 3–7.

———. "France: The Big Change?" *New York Review of Books,* June 25, 1981, pp. 47–53.

———. "Gaullism by Any Other Name." *Foreign Policy,* no. 57 (Winter 1984–1985), pp. 38–57.

Jaffré, Jérôme. "Les élections législatives du 16 mars 1986: La défaite de la gauche et les progrès du parti socialiste." *Pouvoirs,* no. 38 (1986), pp. 145–57.

Keeler, John. "Toward a Government of Judges? The Constitutional Council as an Obstacle to Reform in Mitterrand's France." *French Politics and Society*, no. 11 (September 1985), pp. 12–24.

Machin, Howard, and Vincent Wright. "Why Mitterrand Won: The French Presidential Elections of April–May 1981." *West European Politics* 5, no. 1 (January 1982): 5–35.

McCormick, Janice. "Apprenticeship for Governing: An Assessment of French Socialism in Power." In Howard Machin and Vincent Wright, eds., *Economic Policy and Policy-making Under the Mitterrand Presidency, 1981–1984*, pp. 44–63.

Northcutt, Wayne. "The Changing Domestic Policies and Views of the Mitterrand Government, 1981–1984: The Crisis of Contemporary French Socialism." *Contemporary French Civilization* 9, no. 2 (Spring–Summer 1985): 141–65.

———. "The Domestic Origins of Mitterrand's Foreign Policy, 1981–1985." *Contemporary French Civilization* 10, no. 2 (Spring–Summer 1986): 233–67.

———. "François Mitterrand and the Political Use of Symbols: The Construction of a Centrist Republic." *French Historical Studies* 17, no. 1 (Spring 1991): 141–58.

———. "The Metamorphosis of François Mitterrand and the French Electorate: The 1988 Presidential and Legislative Elections." *Contemporary French Civilization* 13, no. 1 (Winter–Spring 1989): 19–31.

———. "The 1986 French Legislative Elections: Who Really Won?" *Australian Journal of Politics and History* 33, no. 2 (1987): 90–99.

———. "The 1988 French Presidential Election: François Mitterrand's Campaign Strategy." *Proceedings of the Western Society for French History* 16 (1989): 291–301.

Northcutt, Wayne, and Jeffra Flaitz. "Women and Politics in Contemporary France: The Electoral Shift to the Left in the 1981 Presidential and Legislative Elections." *Contemporary French Civilization* 7, no. 2 (Winter 1983): 183–98.

———. "Women, Politics, and the French Socialist Government." *West European Politics* 8, no. 4 (1985): 50–70.

Pinto, Diana. "De l'Anti-Américanisme à l'Américanophilie: L'Itinéraire de l'Intelligentsia." *French Politics and Society*, no. 9 (March 1985), pp. 18–26.

———. "Mitterrand, Lang, and the Intellectuals," *French Politics and Society* (May 1983), pp. 10–12.

Schain, Martin A. "The National Front in France and the Construction of Political Legitimacy." *West European Politics* 10, no. 2 (April 1987): 229–52.

NEWSPAPERS AND PERIODICALS

L'Année politique, économique et sociale en France
Business Week
Le Canard Enchaîné
Contemporary French Civilization
Défense Nationale
The Economist
L'Enjeu
Esprit

European Economy (publication of the Commission of the European Communities, Directorate General for Economic and Financial Affairs)
L'Express
Des Femmes en mouvement
Le Figaro
French Politics and Society
L'Humanité
International Herald Tribune
Interventions
Libération
Le Matin
Le Monde
New York Times
Le Nouvel Economiste
Le Nouvel Observateur
Le Nouvelle Revue Socialiste
Le Point
Politique étrangère
Pouvoirs
Proceedings of the Annual Meeting of the Western Society for French History
Revue Politique et Parlementaire
Telos
Les Temps Modernes
Tocqueville Review
L'Unité

Index

A *t* following a page number indicates a table.

387